The English Morality Play

The English Morality Play

Origins, History and Influence
of a Dramatic Tradition

Robert Potter

University of California, Santa Barbara

Routledge & Kegan Paul
London and Boston

First published in 1975
by Routledge & Kegan Paul Ltd
Broadway House, 68–74 Carter Lane,
London EC4V 5EL and
9 Park Street, Boston, Mass. 02108, USA
Set in Monotype Baskerville
and printed in Great Britain by
Willmer Brothers Limited, Birkenhead
Copyright Robert Potter 1975

ISBN 0 7100 8033 6

Contents

Contents

Preface

A book begins as an unsatisfied idea. This one, once the idea for
a paper which suggested a thesis (which detoured into an unexpected
theatrical revival) and expanded into a dissertation on its way to
becoming the present book-length study, poses a series of questions
about a special kind of medieval and Renaissance play and attempts
in some measure to answer these questions.

A book ends as an unsatisfied idea. I hope the book will help to
indicate to its readers that the kind of play which we describe and
usually dismiss as a 'morality play' had an art and a purpose and a
history and an influence of its own, worthy of more attention and
understanding. In several dimensions of the study, including the
anthropological background, the morality's influence on mature
Elizabethan drama, and the analogous drama of the Continent,
I think this book offers as many suggestions for new departures as it
does comprehensive or rigid conclusions. I hope it will encourage
more thinking and writing about the early drama, and more productions of early plays. It has often been demonstrated that these
plays deserve (and will please) a modern audience. To perceive
them we need only suspend our disbelief, and they will show us
what we least expect to find, which is ourselves.

I had wanted to dispense with the usual list of acknowledgments,
in order to let the book speak for itself. Two personal considerations
make me doubt the wisdom of doing so:

(1) There is a man that I know who once performed the miracle of
convincing an eminent Hollywood non-actress that she could act.
So thoroughly did he accomplish this miracle that even the lady's
colleagues in the Academy of Motion Picture Arts and Sciences,
who knew better, were convinced that she could act. They gave her
an Oscar. And I watched her myself (it was in the early days of
television) climb up on the stage, take the statuette in her claws, and
make a short speech. Too short. She didn't mention the miracle-
worker.

vii

(2) On another occasion, the author of a book left me out of his prefatory acknowledgments list. It was a fine book, and I was proud of my work in the editing of it.

Therefore, with all due respect, I am naming the names of some of my many creditors – including the name of the man who left me out of his acknowledgments. It appears below, with the rest.

Sears Jayne, who introduced me to the study of the early drama, and the idea of scholarship;

Albert B. Friedman, who advised and directed me in writing the dissertation from which this book derives;

French Fogle, Martin L. Wine, George Wickes, J. Michael Miller, Marjorie Nicolson, Marshall Waingrow, and several others with whom I worked at Claremont Graduate School;

John Barton, whose masterful BBC series 'The First Stage' introduced me and so many others to the early drama in performance;

The staff of the Huntington Library, where I worked on early histories of the theater;

The staff of the Theater Collection of the New York Public Library, where I spent a hot summer (in the old quarters on Fifth Avenue) on modern productions of *Everyman* and other early plays. Also the staffs of the British Museum Newspaper Library in Colindale and the Enthoven Collection at the Victoria and Albert Museum;

A number of people at Bristol University where I spent a Fulbright year: Bertram Joseph, Glynne Wickham, Oscar Brockett, and also Marion Jones, who made the fortuitous mistake of letting a novice director (me) stage the revival of Bale's *King John* for the 1964 Bristol Shakespeare Festival. Also the cast of that production, together with whom I learned much at first hand about morality plays in performance: David Male (King John), Martin Hoyle (Sedition), David Shawyer (Clergy), Richard Howard (Civil Order), John Harper (Nobility), Jack Jarzavek (Cardinal Pandulphus), John Rudlin (Pope Innocent III), and Jane Lapotaire (England);

The members of the Medieval Drama Seminar of the Modern Language Association, and the Institute for Renaissance and Medieval Studies, Ohio State University, where portions of this study were first presented;

Several colleagues at the University of California, Santa Barbara, and elsewhere who have dealt with the manuscript and otherwise encouraged me in this project at one stage or other, in particular John R. Elliott Jr, Homer Swander, David McPherson, Colin Franklin, R. A. Foakes, Martin Stevens, and Richard Helgerson;

Sally Alabaster Potter, who doubled in the role of Good Angel and Lady Lechery;

Thomas B. Markus, a collaborator in several theatrical ventures;

My four children, to whom the book is dedicated.

Any study of a medieval art form which begins with pre-history and ends with twentieth-century political theater obviously makes transit through many areas of highly specialized scholarship. I have tried to do justice to these multiple contexts; no doubt I have only partially succeeded. I have tried not to lose sight of the precise subject – a dramatic tradition which attempts to objectify theatrically the human predicament. That, in its full dimensions, is the subject of this book.

R.A.P.

A*

London, 1901

The newspapers of London in the summer of 1901 – in that impregnable capital of world commerce and empire which was Yeats', Shaw's, Henry Irving's and Henry James' London – were concerned with casualty lists from the Boer War and announcements of charity drives in the name of the late Queen Victoria, who had died early in the year. Theatrical notices carried the names of Herbert Beerbohm Tree, Ellen Terry, Sarah Bernhardt, Mrs Patrick Campbell. It was an unlikely moment for the rebirth of the medieval drama, as for theatrical experiment in general. Though still occasionally denounced from the pulpit as a place of wickedness and deceit, the London theater purveyed the most harmless trifles available; its audience was safely protected from politics and religious controversy by the censors of the Lord Chamberlain's office, and from experiment by the sagacity of commercial managements. The tiny but vociferous opposition to this state of affairs was mainly promoting the cause of Modern drama (that is, Ibsen), insisting that the real accents and problems of the modern world be somehow intruded into the dream world of the theater. There were, however, a very few radical antiquarians bent on redeeming the theater by means of the classics. And the foremost of these was William Poel, founder of the Elizabethan Stage Society.

Poel's idea, pursued with inadequate resources in a succession of impromptu halls and theaters, was to present the plays of Shakespeare and his contemporaries under an approximation of Elizabethan conditions. Poel had no fear of difficult plays or obscure period pieces, and his early productions included the first modern stage performance of Marlowe's *Dr Faustus* and Milton's *Samson Agonistes*. For these courageous undertakings Poel earned a modest reputation and audience of devotees who kept the Elizabethan Stage Society functioning despite persistent financial difficulties. In 1901, after Poel's mother had died unexpectedly, the scholar A. W. Ward, Poel's friend and adviser, suggested that he might find consolation in reading a medieval play about death called *Everyman*. Poel read the play and determined at once to produce it.

Although a skeptic and a free thinker himself, Poel was always the stickler for authenticity; he decided that this religious play should be presented in religious circumstances. The authorities of the Church of England, as it happened, did not share his view. Poel's offer to stage *Everyman* in the cloisters of Westminster Abbey was summarily rejected by Dean and Chapter, and a similar initiative to utilize Canterbury Cathedral proved unsuccessful. At last Poel managed to find a disestablished location in London, and it was there, in the authentically medieval setting of the Master's Courtyard of the Charterhouse (a former monastery turned pensioners' home), that *Everyman* was presented on Saturday afternoon, 13 July 1901.

Poel's production was, to say the least, experimental. It was not merely the first production of *Everyman*, or any other morality play, in modern times; it was, so far as can be determined, the first modern performance of a medieval play.[1] There was little fanfare, however. Those in the audience who had never heard of moralities may even have approached the play with an open mind, unaware of what a morality play might be. But those who knew their dramatic history must have come with grim resolution, anticipating the worst. Moralities were tediously didactic medieval dramatic allegories in which the characters were not Real People, but Abstractions.

In Poel's performance the 'lifeless abstractions' of the medieval text turned out to be what they must always, invisibly, have been – not walking categories, but realized figures, parts in a play. It is clear that many were agreeably surprised. The critic of *The Times*, who found himself complaining that Fellowship had a North Country accent, pronounced the experiment a remarkable success: 'Brush away from a morality the dust, set it in the cool quadrangle of the Charterhouse on a hot July afternoon, quicken it with human speech and action, and the veriest Philistine will find it hard to cavil.'[2]

The reviews were enthusiastic, numerous, and unanimously glowing. Taken together they give evidence of a performance that challenged virtually every shibboleth of the Victorian stage. It was, to begin with, an *outdoor* performance, as the *Daily News* critic noted:[3]

> many conditions which would have destroyed the illusion of
> the theatre ... the stone courtyard, with the spectators
> crowding the windows as well as the ground area, the
> open sky, with the sparrows flitting around over the stage,
> the entrance of the characters on a level with and almost
> through the ranks of the audience – all these were things

which would have been quite outside the frame of a dramatic
picture, but gave added dignity to this moral abstraction
in dramatic form.

The set was complex and decidedly unusual: 'one of the most
impressive religious services that one has ever known . . . there were
two "stages" – one must be pardoned the unwilling use of so soiled
a word.'[4] Against the great hall the main multi-leveled set had been
erected. It had for its upper level 'a battlement representing heaven'[5]
and on its lower level an interior with simple medieval properties
including a chair. There was, in addition, a separate stage some
40 ft away, 'a little chapel or loggia to which part of the action
. . . was transferred.'[6]

Indeed Poel had staged the play with intuitive regard for medieval
conventions of Mansion and Place staging, with a series of specific
localities and a flexible neutral stage area, 'the platform was earth,
as were also the courtyard and the little raised chapel or shrine that
stood in the angle some 40 feet away.'[7]

A performance of this sort was a decided oddity in the age of
the proscenium arch and the 'fourth wall' theory, with its unchallenged assumption that actors and audiences must be kept in their
respective places, to create the magical illusion. To all this, *Everyman*
offered a paradoxical simplicity, and many, including the critic of
the *St James's Gazette*, were deeply impressed:[8]

> the whole thing was so moving, so human, so real . . . . Even then,
> in the open air in a courtyard and enclosed with antiquated
> buildings with no distinction of lighting to differentiate
> betwixt performers and auditors, and with such characters
> as Adonai (the Supreme Being), and Death bodily
> introduced upon the Stage, the essential human vitality of
> the whole thing was what most strongly appeared.

The presence onstage of a character representing God was in 1901
not merely a violation of theatrical conventions, but an actual
violation of the law.[9] That it was done in Poel's production without
provoking an incident is probably a tribute to tasteful staging, a
private theater audience, and simple good luck; later, in other
circumstances, objections would be raised. But on this occasion
God the Father did appear, both in *Everyman*, and in the Abraham
and Isaac play from the Chester cycle which Poel's company
performed as an afterpiece.

Behind this issue of Divinity on stage is a profound artistic point.
In an illusionistic theater such as the Victorians', an actor is
pretending to be someone, to an audience that pretends that he *is*

3

that someone; in a presentational theater such as the medieval drama (or the epic theater of Bertolt Brecht), the actor makes no such pretense. He presents a character – God Almighty if necessary – to an audience whose attention is directed toward a higher, and invisible, hypothetical truth which the visible actors present.

Everyman is a play about the moment of death and thus, from the medieval perspective, a play about the shape and meaning of life. The structure is inevitable, and the final movement of the play brings Everyman to his grave. In Poel's production this was accomplished by a move out of the main acting area, onto the courtyard proper, thus invading the psychological territory of the audience in a way which would be effective today, and must have been quite shocking to a 1901 London audience.

The success of the production prompted a second performance the following week-end, and the *Athenaeum* printed a lengthy and perceptive review, recommending the experience:[10]

> There are many points from which the entertainment may be regarded, and from all it is significant. The first thing that strikes one is that the primitive drama, which seems so dull and didactic, may well have passioned our forefathers – is, indeed, capable of passioning us; the second that this particular piece, played no better and no worse than it was on this occasion, is capable, when its merits are known, of attracting all London and becoming the 'sensation' of the season . . . those who care to witness an entertainment unique in its kind are counselled to take an opportunity that most probably will not recur.

The recurrence, however, came quickly enough. An additional performance was presented the following week 'for the benefit of the Queen Victoria Memorial Fund.' Two weeks later, and for the same charity, *Everyman* was performed in the Quadrangle of University College, Oxford. In the autumn a special performance was given at the Royal Pavilion in Brighton. By the following season *Everyman* was being staged commercially in London, at St George's Hall and the Imperial Theatre.

The Poel production of *Everyman* went on to tour the provinces and America, and to become an international success. Modern audiences throughout the world were introduced to the morality play, previously known only to scholars, and the influence spread quickly to twentieth-century playwrights as diverse as von Hofmannsthal, Yeats, and Shaw – each of whom found something of immediate use in this ancient dramatic idea.[11]

Since its revival in 1901, *Everyman* has emerged as a classic – a familiar stage play and an almost inevitable anthology piece. The Poel revival was decisive in a literary as well as a theatrical sense. In the years prior to 1901 *Everyman* had appeared in modern anthologies only twice.[12] By contrast, in the short period 1901-14 at least seventeen separate new editions of the play were published (of which four are acting editions) and there were five additional reprints in anthologies. In the years since World War I there have been more than twenty further editions (about two-thirds of them acting versions).[13] *Everyman* has been performed in parish halls and theaters, by the Birmingham Repertory Company and the Old Vic, in King's College Chapel, Cambridge, at Canterbury Cathedral and at Westminster Abbey. It has been presented in innumerable university and school productions in Britain and America and elsewhere in the world, in ancient and modern dress, in a musical adaptation in 1904, as an opera in 1915, as a cantata in 1939, in pantomime on BBC television in 1938, and as a film in 1957.[14] It is *the* morality play in so far as the twentieth century is concerned.

The success of *Everyman* has created a logical and problematical result – the conception of a large tradition in the terms of one specific play. Much has been written about *Everyman*, but very little about the nature of the dramatic form to which it belongs, and of which it is the most indelible, if not necessarily typical, example. This book begins as an attempt to provide an historical context for *Everyman* and the other moralities as a particularly characteristic kind of medieval play. The aim is to reconstruct the morality play as a dramatic tradition, beginning with conjectured origins in ritual and the medieval idea of the forgiveness of sins. We will not be dealing with a rigid, formal genre of literature, susceptible of easy definition, but rather with a popular and developing drama of ideas – which changed as visibly as the world did, intellectually and historically, under the pressure of the Renaissance and the Reformation. We will be examining the ways in which a variety of post-medieval playwrights, including Skelton, Bale, Sackville and Norton, Marlowe, Jonson, Shakespeare, Lope de Vega and Calderón, made use of this dramatic tradition. The focus will be on the drama of England, where the tradition proved most strong and significant, though one chapter will survey texts and performances elsewhere in Europe. Finally the study will consider how, at length, the morality play came to be misunderstood by scholars and critics in the eighteenth and nineteenth century, and how it was rediscovered and transformed in twentieth-century theater.

Chapter I

The idea of
a morality play

The great majority of surviving English medieval plays are dramatizations of historical events. The medieval drama took its beginning
in a symbolic re-enactment of the Resurrection – the axial historical
event of Christianity. An elaboration of this dramatic idea, working
backward in history to the Creation and forward to Doomsday,
produced the characteristic textual architecture of English medieval
drama: cycles of scriptural plays, for popular performance at the
feast of Corpus Christi, in which all human history could be com-
prehended. From a distance of centuries we are beginning to
perceive these cycles as very considerable works of art.[1]

Parallel to this historical corpus is a smaller and less clearly
perceived body of plays, a form of drama known to us as the morality
play. Like the cycles, these plays are Christian, anonymous, and
'popular,' written in English to be performed for the general
population. But where the cycles take their form in fulfilling the
totality of human history and defining its crucial rhythms, the
morality play takes its shape from a different figure and pattern – the
life of the individual human being.

1 The unity of medieval drama

The medieval morality plays, which flourished in England at the
same time as the Corpus Christi cycles, took many theatrical guises,
from the cosmic pageantry and spectacle of *The Castle of Perseverance*
(1405–25) and *Wisdom* (1450–1500) to the barnyard scurrilities of
Mankind (1465–70), from the topical satire of *Hickscorner* (1513) to the
universality of *Everyman* (1495). But they seem to have been a single
and very specific kind of play about the human predicament.

A concept – what it means to be human – is represented on the
stage by a central dramatic figure or series of figures. Subsidiary

6

characters, defined by their function, stand at the service of the plot, which is ritualized, dialectical, and inevitable: man exists, therefore he falls, nevertheless he is saved. This pattern, repeated in every morality play, should enable us not only to understand the form, but also to fix its place in the unity of medieval religious drama.

Literary historians, generally passing through to other destinations, have made a habit of dividing the English medieval drama into three distinct and unconnected groups of vernacular plays: 'mystery' plays (based on Scripture), 'miracle' plays (based on the lives of the saints), and 'morality' plays (based on the struggle between vices and virtues). There are many things wrong with this tripartite division. The terminology, for one thing, is arbitrary and unhistorical, since those who wrote, performed, and witnessed the plays observed no such distinctions, the term 'miracle' having been loosely used in the fifteenth century to describe scriptural and saints' plays alike, and the terms 'mystery' and 'morality' being late borrowings from French literary criticism.[2] Moreover, the division embodies a serious misunderstanding of the nature of the morality play.

Seeking literary sources for the quaint abstract names of morality-play characters, critics have traced the allegory of the plays to the *Psychomachia*, a fourth-century Roman epic poem in which personified virtues and vices battle over the soul of man. This identification rests on the somewhat tenuous connection between the epic and the battle of virtues and vices in the morality play *The Castle of Perseverance*. But the *Psychomachia* is a distant, and at best an indirect source. The immediate origins of the morality play, which we will be exploring in this chapter, are in the tradition of sermons and penitential literature advocating repentance and preaching the forgiveness of sins.[3] The imprecise identification of the morality play with the *Psychomachia* has led some critics to describe the action of the dramas in terms of an epic battle between virtues and vices. But it is the figure of mankind who stands at the center of these plays, and the shape of his life which unfolds to determine the pattern of events.

The persistence of the morality play as a theatrical concept may be seen in the plots of two widely-separated plays in the tradition. In John Skelton's *Magnificence* (1515) a 'noble prince of might' lives in prosperity, counseled by virtuous advisers, until a group of unwholesome visitors arrive. They gain positions of influence under false pretenses, and inform the prince of his virginal inexperience. Soon the virtuous advisers have been discharged, and the prince is led through extravagance into adversity and poverty. Abandoned by his counselors, the prince is at the point of despair when the virtuous advisers reappear and lead him to a wise repentance, through which he is restored to 'joy and royalty.'[4]

7

The Castle of Perseverance (1405–25), a play of about a hundred years earlier, stages very much the same series of actions. Its hero, *Humanum Genus*, begins in childish innocence, but is seduced into sin by his bad angel, and tempters such as World and Flesh. From this condition he is rescued by a good angel and agents of repentance (Confession and Penance), and brought to the safety of a castle called Perseverance. Later, in his old age, he is lured away from the castle and into sin once more, in which condition death comes upon him. He is saved from damnation by repentance, and the intervention of Mercy invoking the grace of God.[5]

The pattern in these dramas is not one of combat, but rather a sequence of innocence/fall/redemption. If we grasp this idea of the morality play, it is now possible to see the medieval religious drama as a totality, in which the morality play performs the same ceremony in the microcosm of the individual human life as that of the Corpus Christi cycle in the macrocosm of historical time.

What we *call* the medieval religious plays is relatively unimportant; what should be emphasized is their fundamental unity of purpose. Directed to an audience of believers, all the plays celebrate the permanent truth of Christianity as a theology, a theory of history, and an explanation of the human condition; all present theatrically the evidence to sustain such a world view, through the interaction of the familiar and the unknown, the material and the spiritual, the past, present, and future; all visualize theatrically the significance of human life *sub specie aeternitatis*.

The Corpus Christi play and the morality play may be seen as two manifestations of the same dramatic purpose. For both, life and history are a process. Both present man as a divine, fallen, redeemed creature, and do so in such a way as to suggest to the members of the audience that they are participants in the process, with significant choices to make. The Corpus Christi play allows the audience to participate vicariously in sacred events as spectators of the Fall, Flood, Incarnation, Crucifixion, and Last Judgment. The morality play epitomizes these truths, detects these rhythms, in the sequence of every individual life.

The technique in both kinds of medieval religious drama is *illumination*: to make visible the invisible truths of time and the universe – as in manuscript illuminations and in the work of glaziers, woodcarvers, and stonemasons of the cathedrals. To consider fifteenth-century playscripts as medieval art is to find that medieval playmakers used the special properties of their materials (spoken language and dramatic action) with a comparable skill and directness, and to the same communal end.

Without rendering exaggerated judgments on its ultimate literary or theatrical value, it is now possible to see that the morality play,

like its counterpart, the Corpus Christi cycle, was ambitious in
theme, experimental in its dramaturgy, and, as drama, deserving
of the popularity which it seems to have enjoyed with fifteenth- and
sixteenth-century audiences. Moreover, unlike the Corpus Christi
play, the morality play would prove adaptable to new circumstances
and social conditions. It had at its basis, to begin with, an archetypal
human perception: the fall out of innocence into experience. The
centrality of this idea in the morality play is, perhaps, its defining
characteristic. The human predicament, both in a theatrical and a
theological sense, creates the morality play's plot and distinctive
structure.

A morality play sees life as a sequential process through which
every human being passes, by virtue of being human. The idea of
such a sequence is behind Jacques' mordant chronicle of humanity
in *As You Like It*:[6]

> All the world's a stage,
> And all the men and women merely players.
> They have their exits and their entrances,
> And one man in his time plays many parts,
> His acts being seven ages. At first the infant,
> Mewling and puking in the nurse's arms.
> Then the whining schoolboy, with his satchel
> And shining morning face, creeping like snail
> Unwillingly to school. And then the lover,
> Sighing like furnace with a woeful ballad
> Made to his mistress' eyebrow. Then a soldier,
> Full of strange oaths and bearded like the pard,
> Jealous in honour, sudden and quick in quarrel,
> Seeking the bubble reputation
> Even in the cannon's mouth. And then the justice,
> In fair round belly with good capon lined,
> With eyes severe and beard of formal cut,
> Full of wise saws and modern instances,
> And so he plays his part. The sixth age shifts
> Into the lean and slippered pantaloon
> With spectacles on nose and pouch on side,
> His youthful hose, well saved, a world too wide
> For his shrunk shank, and his big manly voice,
> Turning again toward childish treble, pipes
> And whistles in his sound. Last scene of all,
> That ends this strange eventful history,
> Is second childishness and mere oblivion,
> Sans teeth, sans eyes, sans taste, sans everything.

It may be noted that the pattern of Jacques' human 'history' is tragic. Beginning humbly, man rises through exercise of free will and appetite (as schoolboy, lover, soldier) until he reaches a plateau of illusory achievement. From this security, however, he is inexorably tumbled by physical decay into senility and finally non-existence.

The human drama of a morality play is an analogous, but crucially different, presentation of the life cycle. Beginning in innocence man falls by exercise of free will and appetite into a dilemma of his own making. From these depths, however, he is inexorably delivered by divine grace to achieve salvation and eternal life. The end of human life is not 'mere oblivion' but regeneration: never death, always a rebirth.

The Castle of Perseverance and *Magnificence* are in many ways stern exemplary discourses on human mortality and the wages of sin. But if they were merely that, such plays would end with 'mere oblivion' or its spiritual equivalent – damnation. This indeed is what will occur in the late sixteenth century, when the morality is reconstructed into the scheme of tragedy, and the result will be a play of tragic individuality, like Marlowe's *Dr Faustus*. In its original form, however, the morality play embodies a generalized and remarkably optimistic theatrical conception of the human condition. It moves to a rhythm even older and more fundamental than tragedy. It has the rhythm of the victory of life over death, the shape of enacted ritual.

2 Ritual and regeneration

'Ritual' in this context means a public observance of accepted truth; more specifically, a collective activity in which past action is imitated and repeated for a present purpose. I use the term 'ritual' in the sense of a series of significant collective *actions* (where myth, by contrast, is essentially verbal and narrative). These actions in primitive societies are public attempts to account for, and deal with, natural forces and phenomena. By means of ritual, primitive man seeks to establish a direct relationship between his society and the mysteries of nature so as to understand and control them. Claude Lévi-Strauss, Ernst Cassirer, and others who have studied the implications of these rituals see them to be among primitive man's strongest expressions of self-confidence, affirmations of his important position in the order of nature.[7]

In the action of the ritual, a collective articulation is being celebrated; from past experiences and individual responses, a collective attitude is formulated. The ritual action of the rain dancer re-enacts the coming of rain; by simulating rain he calls sympathetically for its fertility to come again. Continued drought may only mean that the ritual has been improperly performed, but the falling of rain will be taken to validate the ritual, its grasp of the truth. And the repetition of a ritual is a communal acknowledgment of the permanence and actuality of the concept. It serves, in Suzanne Langer's phrase, as 'a disciplined rehearsal of "right attitudes." '[8] By rehearsing in an articulated and formal sequence the correct attitudes, ritual causes the truth to 'come true.'

The celebration allows the believers to participate in its recurrence. In this way ritual seeks to control nature by imitating it. Thus the rituals of primitive man at the change of seasons are conceptual explanations of the decay of autumn or the rebirth of spring. They enact a logic for the events, in the image of a death or a revival. The forces of nature, represented in the form of dying or reviving gods, for example, come under human control.[9]

In the social rituals of primitive man, the life of the individual is brought into significant relationship with the totality of the society. The so-called *rites de passage* enact common attitudes adopted towards the sequence of life, celebrations of a pattern in which all participate. The power of such rituals is to convey to the individual life a general significance. As Joseph Campbell emphasizes:[10]

> the tribal ceremonies of birth, marriage, burial,
> installation and so forth, serve to translate the
> individual's life-crises and life-deeds into classic,
> impersonal forms. They disclose him to himself, not as this
> personality or that, but as the warrior, the bride, the widow,
> the priest, the chieftain. . . . The whole society becomes
> visible to itself as an imperishable living unit. Generations
> of individuals pass, like anonymous cells from a living body;
> but the sustaining, timeless form remains. . . .
> Rites of initiation and installation, then, teach the
> lesson of the essential oneness of the individual and the group.

Ritual, as it emerges from contemporary investigation, is a conceptual process. It functions by synthesizing general truths out of the particulars of human experience. It discerns an order, imitates the rhythm of the order, conceives its meaning. Above all it welds a connection – in terms of action – between this outer world of events and the inner world of feelings.

One theory is that all drama begins in the elaboration of such primitive ritual. Independent evidence from major civilizations, including India, Greece, and China, lends a basic plausibility to this theory. On the other hand, drama seems so much a part of human nature (e.g., disguise, mimesis, child's play, pageantry, game theory, dance, the whole idea of personality) that it may antedate any particular collective activity, such as ritual. In any event, primitive ritual is inherently dramatic and has in certain cultural instances produced a drama in which older, sympathetic-magical actions become clothed in the rationale of new myths, stories, or other narrative substitutions. Such a development, according to many accounts, brought about the evolution of Dionysian ritual into Greek tragedy.[11] In the present context, another less frequently noted example should be mentioned – the popular drama of ancient Egypt (based on the fertility rituals of Osiris) which staged in comic terms the birth and growth of Osiris' son Horus.[12]

There are indications that at least the structure of the morality play (as distinct from its intellectual substance, which is medieval and Christian) can be traced to similar origins in fertility ritual. The link which connects morality play and ritual is a folk ritual drama known as the mummers' play. Exactly what the mummers' play was like in the Middle Ages we cannot be certain, since it is an orally transmitted form (like the ballad) which went officially unnoticed until folklorists began to record it in the eighteenth century. However, three facts are abundantly clear: the mummers' play is an ancient outgrowth of fertility ritual; it existed in some form in medieval times; and it influenced the developing medieval drama.[13] Its central act, a battle of champions to the death, with a miraculous revival, reproduces the ritual battle of winter and summer, the rhythm of death and regeneration, the ritual burial of winter and the resurrection of life.[14]

The typical mummers' play, as E. K. Chambers reconstructs it, begins with a prologue introducing two champions (St George, 'Bold Slasher,' etc.). After considerable boasting and argument they fight; one is felled, but a widely-traveled doctor appears and cures the fallen warrior, often by a mock beheading. This action ends the drama proper, but a number of dancers enter (including one with a big head and one named Beelzebub) and the performance concludes with a collection of money (*quête*). The existence of this strange and widely dispersed folk ceremony (now known to have been performed at one time or another in over a thousand different localities in the British Isles)[15] can only be explained in terms of a widely observed folk ritual, a pre-Christian survival. Few scholars would today deny that a drama of this kind was indeed in existence and being performed throughout the Christian Middle Ages. The question is how, and to what extent, this folk tradition influenced the development of medieval religious drama.

W. K. Smart, writing in 1917, was first to point out the significant traces of the mummers' play to be found in the fifteenth-century morality play *Mankind*. These elements center in lines 426–68 which comprise, 'in a sense, a mummers' play.'[16] Three agents of temptation (Nought, New Guise, and Now-a-days) have been beaten up by Mankind; Mischief, their commander, offers to cure them of their ills by temporary decapitation. This episode recalls the mock cure of the mummers' play and refers to the folk tradition of magical beheading, best remembered from *Sir Gawain and the Green Knight*.[17] Later in *Mankind* the vices, summoning the demon Tityvillus to aid them, stop the play to make a collection from the audience, 'elles þer xall no man hym se.'[18] This event, which is often cited as the first incursion of commercialism onto the English stage, in fact suggests the inevitable collection (*quête*) of the mummers' play; it is likely that begging actors were no great novelty in the fifteenth century.[19] Tityvillus is described as 'a man wyth a hede þat is of grett omnipotens.'[20] He is very similar to the masked 'big head' character of the mummers' play.

The explanation of these similarities given by Smart – that the mummers' plays might be descended from moralities – is belied by what we now know of the pre-Christian origins of the mummers' play. Aside from sheer coincidence, the only other explanation for the folk elements in *Mankind* is that they were borrowed from the mummers' play in its fifteenth-century ritual form.

This relation of the moralities to a conjectural ritual drama has been explored in some detail. Baskervill found evidence of the magical beheading as a pagan 'Christmas game' of the Middle Ages, and pointed out that the castle in *Perseverance* could well have been a descendant of the tents, pavilions, and castles formerly erected on playing-fields for summer festivals.[21] In Redford's sixteenth-century play *Wit and Science*, the hero Wit fights with the giant Tediousness and is apparently slain until Lady Recreation and her followers appear and revive him miraculously with a song; in a later episode Wit triumphs over Tediousness by beheading him.[22] A few general resemblances have been noted by other critics, and echoes of the mummers' play prologue, with its invocation of the champions, have been found in the fifteenth-century morality play *Wisdom*.[23]

A caveat should here be entered against attempts to overstress the similarities of the morality play and the mummers' play. Medieval scholars are justifiably cautious about 'pagan' myth and ritual, and its supposed dominance in Christian works of literature. They recall the concerted attempt of a generation of folklorists (whose rise conveniently coincided with that of German National Socialism) to trace everything in literature to Germanic '*volk*' origin. Nevertheless, it is important in studying the early drama never to forget the advice of Pope Gregory the Great, who cautioned his missionaries that they must not destroy sacred places, but build upon them.[24]

An example may be seen in the earliest known morality, *The King of Life* (usually known as *Pride of Life*). This fragmentary play begins with a prologue of 112 lines summarizing the action to come. At the conclusion of the prologue the King of Life enters, boasting of his power and majesty. He is accompanied by Strength and Health, two guards sworn to defend him against all enemies. His Queen, however, warns him that he is a mortal creature; he ignores her warnings, and those of a Bishop and instructs his messenger to proclaim Life's domination of all the world and to challenge anyone, even Death, to fight if he would deny it. The messenger goes forth and is issuing the challenge to all (including the King of Death), as the manuscript breaks off.

The King of Life would seem to bear several previously unnoticed relations to the folk-play tradition. In the person of the King we possess a bragging champion to outstrip the St Georges and Bold Slashers, and yet to typify all that they might once have been. The King is a haughty and impressive figure, a worthy adversary for the King of Death. Their projected combat, like that of the mummers' play champions, is evidently to be the climax of the play.

Fortunately, the prologue gives a detailed summary of the action of the play and allows us to reconstruct the lost and concluding portion of *The King of Life*. The events can be outlined as follows:

1 The King of Life dreams that he will be killed by Death. (ll. 81–4)

2 Life and Death meet in battle; Death overcomes Life's guards and then Life himself. (ll. 85–92)

3 As Life dies his soul arises but is caught by fiends; the body and soul dispute over the blame, and soul bewails its fate. (ll. 93–106)

4 Through the intercession of the Virgin the soul of Life is freed from the fiends and allowed to ascend to heaven.[25]

The action of the play, then, follows the sequence of life, death, and rebirth. In this respect *The King of Life* is a typical morality play. We are accustomed to personified death in such a play, but the personification of a life force, once we examine it, suggests a distant and distinguished ancestry. For the King of Life belongs to the genre of dying and reviving kings who, as Frazer voluminously testifies, are found in the folklore and religion of so many cultures.[26] Like these representatives of the life principle, the King of Life is struck down in his prime and raised up by a higher power. In essence and in action he invites comparison with these archetypal ritual figures.

The similarities do not end with characterization; the dramatic structure of the play itself is ritualistic. In a series of actions the play presents an explanation – and a demonstration – of the fact of death.[27] Against the vaunting fact of Life this demonstration comes gradually nearer – first in the warning of the Queen, then in the Bishop's sermon, next in the King's dream, and finally in the actual combat. The moment of death finds the body racked with pain and the soul on the point of damnation. But the ultimate fact of death is the solution to it, explained and demonstrated in the revival of the King of Life. And the fact of death is expressed in a pattern which closely parallels that of the folk play: a combat between elemental forces, with challenges, direct battle, the apparent death of one participant, and a miraculous revival.

It seems highly likely that *The King of Life* is related to some primitive ritual drama (of which the mummers' play in turn preserves a dim memory). If we can ever in fact reconstruct this drama, perhaps it will be possible to prove the intriguing hypothesis that the morality play is the Christianized descendant of primitive fertility ritual. At the present time, however, evidence is insufficient to prove anything beyond a compelling parallelism.

Modern studies of primitive myth and ritual have opened new modes of understanding for the study of literature and drama. Although caution must be exercised in claiming anthropological ancestries and sources for all literary inventions, there is an equal danger in ignoring the available insights and pretending that modern man has rationally fabricated everything in literature. In a balanced judgment on this question, Frazer's latest editor emphasizes the general connections which can helpfully be established between ritual and literature:[28]

It may, for instance, be quite wrong to assume that
a particular ... myth, play, or epic actually goes back, in
point of literary genealogy, to an earlier ritual libretto;
but it may nevertheless be quite right to assume that this
particular type of composition was inspired or conditioned
in the first place by the standard pattern of seasonal rituals
and that its structure and conventions were determined
originally by those of the primitive performances. In other
words, what is really at stake is ... the parallelism
between a pattern of narrative and a pattern of ritual, or –
to put it in broad terms – the ultimate relation of a genre of
literature to a genre of ceremony.

A search for the origins of the morality play should begin with the perception that it is related in a variety of complex ways, to ritual and ritual drama. This relationship is *direct*, in the sense that faint textual links can be established between the morality drama and the action of ritual; it is also *analogical*, in the sense that the morality play appears to serve a ritual social purpose. Its primary function is to demonstrate and therefore to verify Christian doctrine.

The morality play, like a ritual drama (or a contemporary ideological play) is an extreme manifestation of one perennial impulse of theater, which is to embody, to verify, to create the acknowledged Truth. Every society creates verifications of its ideas, particularly any society with a systematic conception of truth, based on invisible but acknowledged higher principles (whether those of a fertility cult or Christianity or Marxist-Leninism is substantially unimportant for the moment). The ideological drama, the morality play, and the ritual play are demonstrative theatrical ceremonies of this kind. In each case we have a validating performance, a tangible substantiation of the higher principles. In each case the Truth comes true. In each case we have a drama of ideas, with a positive and reinforcing conclusion.

The morality play, an archetypal example of the theater of demonstration, is both didactic (in the sense of teaching Christian doctrine) and ritualistic (in the sense of 'proving' it). These interwoven strands of didacticism and ritual together provide the origins of the morality play.

3 The forgiveness of sins

To understand the origins of a dramatic form is not simply to establish its line of descent, but to reconstruct its original purposes. In some cases (e.g., Restoration heroic drama and *Commedia dell'Arte*) the idea may be highly uncertain; in others (e.g., Ibsen's social drama, Brecht's epic theater, and the morality play) the purpose is scarcely in doubt. The morality plays have a common theme and a practical (if theologically complex) moral: sin is inevitable; repentance is always possible. *Everyman*, and the other extant medieval morality plays (*King of Life, Castle of Perseverance, Wisdom, Mankind, Hickscorner, Youth, Mundus et Infans*) are about repentance – why it is necessary, how it may be carried out and what it will accomplish.

The morality plays have frequently been mistaken for naïve treatises on virtue. They are in fact the call to a specific religious act. If we are to understand the plays, we must clearly understand the action which they promulgate and ultimately represent. It is the acknowledgment, confession, and forgiveness of sin, institutionalized in medieval Christianity as the sacrament of penance.

In the early centuries of the Christian era penance was a public ceremony. It had come into being as a means of reconciling a wayward member of the Church; it was a ceremony representing renewal of the original act of baptism. By the third century a system had evolved whereby the aspirant wore special penitential garments and performed arduous duties of fasting and prayer. The public ceremony of reconciliation was traditionally performed near the end of the Lenten season, on Maundy Thursday.[29]

The ceremony of penitence, originally intended for pardoning the most serious offenses, was granted to the individual only once in a lifetime. Most early Christians understandably postponed the ceremony until the last possible moment, and deathbed confession became the common rule. For these reasons, the system proved ineffective and fell into gradual disuse.[30]

To supplement and replace these ceremonies another system arose in the sixth century in the Celtic Church, in which confession took place in privacy and secrecy. The sinner disclosed his transgressions to a priest, who questioned him at length to determine his spiritual condition and to set appropriate punishments. Such penance represented, on medical analogy, a prescription for the afflicted soul; the system was popularized through penitential books, instructing priests in their duties as confessors.[31]

The Celtic system of private penance spread eventually throughout the Carolingian empire. In this way private confessions came to replace public penitence in the Church of the Middle Ages. By the twelfth century Scholastic theologians such as Peter Lombard were promoting the recognition of confession as a sacrament.[32] Ancient authority for this position was elicited from recently discovered pseudo-Augustinian decretals which advocated individual reconciliation with God through the office of the priesthood.[33] The rise of private penance was thus connected with an increasing emphasis on ecclesiastical prerogative, symbolized in the doctrine of 'the power of the keys.' By this doctrine anointed priests (as Christ's successors) were granted the power to deal with sins in Christ's name and to 'loose' and 'bind' the sinner.[34]

A decree of the Fourth Lateran Council of 1215–16 confirmed the acceptance of this system, and proclaimed confession to be an obligatory sacrament. This decree of *Omnis utriusque sexus* represented the final step taken by Pope Innocent III in the establishment of penance as a sacrament of the Church, and the definition of its place in the life of every Christian. Henceforth, all adult Christians were required to confess their sins privately to their parish priest at least once a year, generally before communion at Easter.[35]

The difficulties of implementing such a wide-sweeping decree were considerable. Before sinners could be brought to confess their sins, they would necessarily require instruction concerning their new obligation. Which sins would they be asked to confess? What forms of punishment might they expect to receive? Who was authorized to hear these confessions? Above all, what were the demonstrable advantages of repentance, and what punishments were to be imposed on the unrepentant? The task of conveying such information to the largely illiterate rural populace of Christendom proved formidable enough, let alone the further imperative of enforcing compliance and detecting abuses within the system.

By the terms of *Omnis utriusque sexus*, the crucial responsibility for instituting confession was delegated to the individual parish priest. Unfortunately, the parish priest was normally unequipped for such responsibility, often ignorant of the basic doctrines of the Church and barely, if at all, literate. The seriousness of the situation in thirteenth-century England is documented in a series of episcopal constitutions drawn up to implement the terms of the Lateran Council decree. These constitutions provided instruction for the individual priest in hearing confession. The offenses with which he might be expected to deal were listed, generally organized under the traditional headings of the seven deadly sins. To these were added a summary of prayers and doctrines (Creed, Ave, Paternoster, Commandments, sacraments) in which the parishioners were to be instructed. At the Lambeth Council of 1281, as an outgrowth of these constitutions, Archbishop John Pecham established a program of mandatory instruction to be given by each priest four times yearly to his parishioners. In this way all members of the parish would be sufficiently informed to make adequate confessions.[36] All were to be supplied with a minimal body of prayers and orthodox beliefs to sustain their faith. Thus armed and informed concerning the kinds of sins which would put them in danger of damnation, individual Christians would be ready to seek forgiveness.

It was in support of these objectives that the numerous penitentials and shrift manuals of the thirteenth and fourteenth centuries were written and widely circulated. The more official penitentials, such as William of Pagula's *Oculus Sacerdotis*, were set forth in Latin. The doubtful Latinity of many parish priests, however, necessitated translations and vernacular adaptations of these manuals. Mirk's *Instructions for Parish Priests* (fifteenth century; adapted from the *Oculus Sacerdotis*) is typical of this variety of manual; nearly half of it is devoted to confession and penance.[37] The so-called 'Lay Folks Catechism,' which was itself intended for parish priests, describes penance in this fashion:[38]

The third sacrement is cald penaunce.
That is sothefast forthinking we have of our syn

Withouten will or thoght to turne ogayne to it.
And this behoves have thre thinges if it be stedfast.
Ane is sorrow of our hert that we have synned.
Another is open shrift of our mouth how we haf synned.
And the third is rightwise ammendes makyng for that
    we haf synned.
This thre, with gode will to forsake our syn
Clenses us and washes us of alkyn synnes.

In collections of sermons (such as Mirk's *Festial* or the *Jacob's Well* homilies) as well as in devotional works intended for a lay audience (*Cursor Mundi*, *Handlyng Synne*, *Aȝenbite of Inwyt*) and throughout early medieval literature, penance is almost constantly the matter at hand. It is, as W. A. Pantin observes, 'a theme which dominates or underlies most of the religious literature of the thirteenth and fourteenth centuries.'[39]

Associated with this movement in the Church, and contemporary with it, came the founding of the Dominican and Franciscan orders of friars. Committed to a kind of public monasticism, propagating the faith among the people, these zealous mendicants reached England early in the thirteenth century.[40] The friars brought instruction in penance to the general populace through vernacular sermons and shrift manuals. The encroachment of the friars on the prerogatives of parish priests (and bishops) led to a series of conflicting papal rulings during the thirteenth century, and the question of jurisdiction arose periodically thereafter.[41]

It is evident that the friars deserve considerable credit for popularizing the sacrament of penance. As priests (ordinarily) they had the power of the keys, could hear confessions, and give absolution. Moreover, as itinerants their commitment to secrecy gave small cause for concern, and they were never noted for demanding harsh acts of penance. 'It is probable,' A. G. Little concludes, 'that compulsory auricular confession would never have been enforced without the friars. A light penance which the people would perform was better than a heavy one which they would not.'[42]

The preaching of repentance was particularly prevalent during the season of Lent. The call to repentance was part of a plan for general spiritual cleansing in harmony with the season. Repentance and shrift were to be followed by a Lenten period of abstinence and good works, culminating in Easter communion. Preaching tending to this effect was traditional, and Chaucer freely alludes to its effectiveness:[43]

      But precheth not, as freres doon in Lente,
      To make us for oure olde synnes wepe.

The mendicant friars, living in many cases among the common people, seem typically to have phrased their call to repentance in terms of vivid denunciations of injustice and corruption in the various orders of society. Measuring the realities of this world against the ideals of Christianity, the medieval preachers stripped away pretenses, exposed abuses and called for amendment. Characteristically these preachers sought to relate theological formulations to the everyday world of peasants and townspeople. Abstractions were illustrated by means of homely and familiar *exempla*, proverbs, and folklore; at the same time men and institutions (including the Church) were subjected to rigorous moral scrutiny, expressed in complaint and satire.[44]

The mixture of doctrine and realism in the morality play has its origins in this preaching tradition, and the immediate sources of allegory in the morality play are almost invariably found in medieval sermon literature. For example, Owst has traced the evolution of the castle figure from an allegory of the incarnation to a pulpit commonplace employed as the 'toure of truth' in *Piers Plowman* and *The Castle of Perseverance* itself. A similar origin can be shown for an allegorical Trial in Heaven to decide the fate of mankind: in homily, religious poetry, and ultimately in drama.[45]

In medieval sermons the theme of the coming of death had a standard homiletic function of warning to the unrepentant sinner. This theme, which dominates *The King of Life* and *Everyman*, is prominent in *The Castle of Perseverance* and *Mundus et Infans*, and to a lesser extent in *Mankind* and *Wisdom*. The importance of this theme in medieval preaching is well recognized, particularly in its relation to the cult of death which swept fifteenth-century Europe in the wake of the plague. But the preaching of repentance by means of the figure of death was already commonplace in sermon collections of the thirteenth century; the *Summa Predicantium* of the Dominican friar preacher John Bromyard dwelt at length on the subject of death. The personification of death was familiar in the meditations of St Bernard, from which fourteenth-century English sermons drew their conception of death as a powerful tyrant, sparing no country or social estate. In several friars' sermons death is actually depicted as the sergeant or bailiff of God, come to arrest an errant mankind.[46]

The precise relation between the morality plays and the fifteenth-century Dance of Death remains somewhat uncertain. It now appears most likely that this literary and graphic convention (in which Death comes to take away Pope, Emperor, King, Cardinal) was itself derived from a dramatic or quasi-dramatic presentation. Seelmann asserted the precedence of Spanish and German verse texts of the Dance of Death based on a lost dramatic source.[47] Emile Mâle confirmed this theory with his discovery of a Latin poem probably intended for recitation by costumed representatives of the various estates, walking in turn to death. Besides this poem, which he compared '*à l'ébauche d'une moralité*,' Mâle summarized records of a lost fourteenth-century church play from Normandy in which kings and shepherds paraded to their death. He concluded that the Dance of Death was originally the mimed (or spoken?) illustration to a sermon on the inevitability of death.[48]

Fifteenth-century records tell of a performance of the Dance of Death under Franciscan auspices in Besançon in 1453. The connection of the friars with the Dance of Death is well documented, from the wall paintings of the Paris churchyard of the Innocents (where friars regularly preached) to Franciscan and Dominican friaries in Germany, Switzerland, and Italy.[49]

Like the morality play, the Dance of Death had its roots in preaching tradition; it seems to have originated as a demonstration accompanying a sermon. Its theme – the need for repentance in recognition of approaching death – is present in larger or smaller measure in all the early moralities. But the action of the Dance of Death – the procession of the various estates to their death – has no equivalent in the extant moralities. The personified character of Death is common to play and dance alike, but also to the sermon literature from which both are descended. The dramatic structure of morality drama, built on the pattern of innocence, fall, and redemption, bears no obvious relation to the Dance of Death. The moralities frequently allude to the Dance of Death, in their *ubi sunt* lists of 'Pope, Emperor, King, Cardinal,' but the obliqueness of these references, which are not dramatized, would seem to confirm the distinction. The play and the dance are most likely parallel but separate traditions of repentance drama.

A more substantial connection exists between the morality plays and that most typical of medieval traditions, the concept of the seven deadly sins. In his definitive study of the concept, Morton Bloomfield has carefully traced the development of this list of seven (originally eight) chief or cardinal sins from a monastic to a parochial instrument, by way of the Celtic penitential books, producing the mortal or deadly sins (sufficient to provoke damnation) which were required to be confessed within the sacrament of penance.

The medieval passion for correspondences demanded a set of virtues to match and oppose the seven deadly sins. But the traditional seven cardinal virtues did not correspond accurately to the deadly sins, since they had a separate derivation. To supply this lack, medieval homilists prepared a series of lists known as *remedia* or cures for the seven deadly sins. It is to this tradition that the 'virtues' of *The Castle of Perseverance* belong. Similar lists may be found in Chaucer's *Parson's Tale* or Passus V of *Piers Plowman*, where the castle of Truth is also defended by seven virtuous sisters who counter-act the deadly sins.[50]

In the penitential system of the Celtic Church, recitals of the Lord's Prayer were a commonly prescribed penance. The penitent repeating the prayer could fortify his soul against all the deadly sins, for which theologians discovered cures implicit in the Lord's Prayer. These *remedia* are the prayer's seven distinct petitions (1. hallowed be thy name, 2. thy kingdom come, 3. thy will be done, 4. give us daily bread, 5. forgive us as we forgive, 6. lead us not into temptation, 7. deliver us from evil). 'Hallowed be thy name' is a reminder to resist pride, 'thy kingdom come' warns against envy; and so forward through wrath, sloth, avarice, gluttony and lechery.[51] The relevance of the petitions to the sins is sometimes strained (e.g., 'give us ... daily bread' is a remedy for sloth), but these allegorical interpretations of the Lord's Prayer appear frequently in collections of medieval sermons and other penitential literature.

The esoteric *remedia* of the Paternoster against the deadly sins thus became public knowledge, as part of the educational campaign which sought to implement the institution of the sacrament of penance. The Paternoster was one of the few common possessions of all Christians, from the highest cleric to the most humble parishioner. Knowledge of the Paternoster, together with the Creed, Ave, and Commandments, gave the lowliest peasant a set of prayer-charms with which to ward off the devices of world, flesh, and devil, as well as a set of spiritual exercises to be performed as mild penance or repeated during Mass by those unable to follow the service.[52] Strings of beads to assist in prayer cycles (resembling the rosary) were known in the Middle Ages as 'Paternosters'; French records disclose the existence of guilds of Paternosterers who manufactured such beads.[53] The Lord's Prayer was a prayer for all men. Figuratively speaking, the *remedia* allegory had the effect of dramatizing the significance of the Lord's Prayer as an effective act of faith. And, as frequently happened in the medieval world, the figurative concept was not long in becoming literal and visible.

In *De Officio Pastorali*, a violent tract of the late fourteenth century castigating clerical abuses, John Wyclif demanded reforms, including the translation of the Bible into English. The friars were opposing this project as heresy, Wyclif noted, but they themselves had set a precedent for such a translation:[54]

& her fore freris han taught in englond þe paternoster in
englizsch tunge, as men seyen in þe pley of ȝork, & in many
oþer cuntreys. siþen þe paternoster is part of matheus gospel,
as clerkis knowen, why may not al be turnyd to englizsch
trewely, as is þis part?

Wyclif was no friend of the friars, but he did not pause to denounce
the play which they had made out of the Lord's Prayer; if anything,
he seems to have been satisfied with the translation. We must
regret this satisfaction, for it deprives us of a detailed account
of the famous York Paternoster play, of which this is the earliest
recorded notice.

Such a description would be precious indeed, for the text of the
York play, and all of its kind, disappeared in the course of the
suppression of religious drama in the sixteenth century. Of the
two-hundred-year dramatic history of the Paternoster play only a
few indirect records survive. Foremost among these is a summary of
the regulations and property of the organization responsible for
producing the play in York. From Wyclif's remarks we might have
expected this function to be performed by an establishment of
Franciscans or Carmelites, but production by 1389 was in lay hands.
The responsibility was vested in a guild which had been founded
explicitly to produce the play. Summarizing their regulations in that
year, officials of the guild explained its establishment as follows:
at some time in the past a play had been written on the subject of
the Lord's Prayer and performed in York; it had been so well
received that there was much sentiment to perpetuate the play,
'for the health and amendment of the souls, as well of the upholders
as of the hearers of it';[55] a guild was founded to perpetuate the tradition.

Of the nature of the play this document gives only a general
account. The subject of the play was the benefit of the Lord's Prayer,
and in it many vices and sins were denounced and virtues commen-
ded. The *remedia* of the Lord's Prayer are not specifically mentioned,
but lost records of the same guild apparently referred to a trans-
action '*in diversis expensis, circa ludum Accidie.*'[56] Since *accidie* is the sin
of sloth, it is therefore assumed that the York Paternoster play was a
dramatization of the seven deadly sins, and thus of the allegory of
the Lord's Prayer.[57]

Confirmation for this assumption comes from records of the nearby
Yorkshire town of Beverley where, on 1 August 1469, were performed 'the different pagends of Pater Noster.' Eight pageants were
listed, together with the guilds responsible for them. The first of
these was 'the pageant of viciose'; the remaining seven were
'superbie . . . luxurie . . . accidie . . . gule . . . invidie . . . ire.' In a
summary of players ('lusores') the seven deadly sins are once again
given, followed by 'vicious.'[58] The Beverley play was processional
in staging, with seven stations appointed for the successive performance of the pageants. Further evidence of Paternoster plays is
found in still another northern locality, in the records of Lincoln.
Paternoster plays are reported as being given on five occasions, in

the years 1397/8, 1410/11, 1424/5, 1456/7, and 1521/2 (as opposed to two performances of the Corpus Christi play and four of the saints' plays). The entry for 1397/8 carries the note 'lvi an,' which has been interpreted as indicating that the Lincoln Paternoster play was an annual event first given in 1342/3.[59]

The Paternoster play continued to be performed in York until late in the sixteenth century. Records show a performance on the Friday after midsummer 1488, another on Corpus Christi 1558, and a final showing in 1572. Indications are strong that the Paternoster plays, like the Corpus Christi cycles, did not precisely die of natural causes. In preparation for the performance of 1572 the mayor and council of York apparently altered the play so that it would give no offense. Nevertheless, Archbishop Edmund Grindal subsequently called in the playbook for examination, and the council agreed to furnish 'a true copy of all the said books, even as they were played this year.' That is the last heard of the York Paternoster play; it is probable that Grindal had the playbook destroyed.[60]

Grindal, appointed to the Archbishopric of York by Queen Elizabeth after the Earls' Rebellion of 1569, evidently conceived of his task as one of extirpating the last remnants of papist superstition in the North. He found the local peasantry clinging grimly to the customs of the past, particularly in praying for the dead and the souls of those in purgatory. He issued strict instructions forbidding such practices, which seem to have included praying on Paternoster beads:[61]

At burials no ringing any hand bells, no month's minds,
or yearly commemorations of the dead, nor any other
superstitious ceremonies to be observed or used, which tended
either to the maintenance of prayers for the dead, or of the
Popish purgatory . . . No persons to wear beads, or pray
either in Latin or English upon beads or knots.

Whether the original Paternoster plays contained or advocated prayers for the dead cannot be determined. We do know that one of the main functions of religious guilds such as the York guild of the Paternoster lay in commemorating and praying for the souls of the dead.[62] There is some emphasis on the efficacy of prayers for the dead in the early moralities. Central characters of *The King of Life* and *Perseverance* are apparently saved subsequent to their own death by heavenly intercession. *Mankind* makes strong dramatic use of the Paternoster and beads. Mankind begins to recite his Paternoster, but is distracted by Tityvillus and leaves the beads behind when he goes out. While he is off stage, Tityvillus gets rid of the beads, then proceeds to tempt Mankind into sin. Whatever the exact connection of the Paternoster play and the moralities, dramatizations of the customs of praying with beads and for the dead were not unknown in the early drama.[63]

In the absence of texts, the question of the nature of the Paternoster plays has provoked much speculation, particularly in its possible relations to the origins of the morality play. The available evidence is hardly self-explanatory. What, for instance, is the pageant of 'viciose' in the Beverley Paternoster play? Chambers identified this pageant with 'a typical representative of frail humanity,' the prototype of the mankind character.[64] Recently, Bernard Spivack has suggested that 'viciose' was the leader of the seven deadly sins, like the 'Vice' of Lydgate's *Assembly of the Gods*. Spivack also speculates that the Paternoster play may have staged a military battle between vices and virtues, resembling the *Psychomachia*. He cites as evidence for this theory an interesting passage in More's *Utopia* describing a mock battle of vices and virtues.[65]

Behind all these theories of the Paternoster play lies the assumption that the play had some founding connection with the morality tradition. Hardin Craig attacked this assumption as 'an ancient mistake' and put forward an alternative theory: the Paternoster play could have been a cycle of saints' plays illustrating virtue triumphant. M. D. Anderson, in a recent study relating medieval drama and iconography, examined Craig's theory closely. She concludes that contemporary church art indicated no traditional pairing-off of saints and sins.[66] Moreover, Craig's theory leaves unexplained the relation between the plays and the prayer – the Paternoster itself.

As we have indicated, the allegory of the Lord's Prayer had for centuries been associated in the sermon tradition with the call to the benefits of repentance. The concept of the deadly sins (whose pre-eminent role in the Paternoster play is incontestable) was popularized in the course of instituting the sacrament of penance. The Paternoster had been an instrument of repentance since the rise of the Celtic penitential system. It is therefore surprising that previous theories of the nature of the Paternoster plays have neglected the probable connection of this drama with the mechanism of repentance. A persistent difficulty of all such theories has been an insistence on seeing the seven deadly sins as evil forces, struggling against correspondent incarnations of virtue. The task of reconstructing the Paternoster plays must begin with the recognition of the seven deadly sins as incarnations, not of diabolical evil, but of human frailty.

Three particular medieval works seem to provide analogues for the possible staging of a Paternoster play. The first of these is a little noticed fourteenth-century French morality written in the Walloon dialect for the *Dames Blanches de Huy*. This play, the Liège

Moralité des Sept Péchés Mortels et des Sept Vertus has been dismissed by Grace Frank as 'an uninspired development of the *Psychomachia* type.'[67] In fact, however, it is a dramatic demonstration of the effectiveness of the sacrament of penance.

The Liège play begins with the speech of a hermit as prologue, initiating the action of the play by conjuring up Lucifer from the mouth of Hell. Lucifer seeks out on earth and introduces each of the seven deadly sins, in the person of seven ladies, emblematically dressed and carrying attributes of their nature (a sword for Wrath, a mirror for Lechery). Lucifer instructs his clerk to note down the sins carefully so that they will be on record at the Last Judgment. The hermit, pitying the fate of the seven ladies, prays to the Virgin to intercede on their behalf. The angel Gabriel comes to challenge the deadly sins and to lead them in turn to give up their vaunts and confess their sinfulness to the hermit. As each sin confesses, she is given absolution and a change of clothing to demonstrate her conversion from deadly sin to beneficence. It is noteworthy that the seven deadly sins become not the cardinal virtues but *remedia* (the names of the 'virtues' are almost identical with those of *The Castle of Perseverance*).[68]

At this critical point in the play Lucifer returns to the stage. He is infuriated at the sins' change of heart, but confident of gaining his revenge in any case, since he has the alarming evidence written down in his book. When he opens his book, however, the sins have been miraculously erased. He departs for Hell, quarreling with his clerk, amid general rejoicing; and the hermit draws the moral of repentance for the audience.[69]

The conversion of the deadly sins in the Liège play is not unique in medieval literature. It occurs most vividly, perhaps, in the great confession scene of *Piers Plowman*. Passus V (B Text) begins with the poet falling asleep over his prayers ('and so I babeled on my bedes ... þei broȝte me aslepe').[70] The dream vision takes the form of a sermon delivered to the 'field full of folk' by Reason, who castigates the various orders and estates of society for their misdeeds and instructs them in their duties. Following this sermon, Repentance appears and the deadly sins come forward one by one to confess to him. The repentances of Pride and Lechery are accepted without comment; the other sins (Envy, Wrath, Avarice, Gluttony, and Sloth) are closely questioned by Repentance and informed of the acts of penance and restitution which they must perform. When all have confessed, Repentance offers a prayer for God's mercy. He explains that man's sinful nature is, in the end, all for the best since it has brought God into the world to redeem these sins. Repentance describes the events of the Passion and Resurrection, concluding:[71]

if it be þi wille
þat art owre fader and owre brother/be merciable
   to us,
And haue reuthe on þise Ribaudes/þat repente hem
   here sore.

That this scene of the poem is a call to the merits of the sacrament
of penance has been amply demonstrated.[72] That this message is
depicted in terms of the seven deadly sins is, as we have established,
traditional. What is less obvious, but none the less present, is an
emphasis on the Paternoster. The scene begins and ends with
significant references (the poet falls asleep over his beads, and the
sermon concludes with 'þi wille' and 'owre fader'). In addition,
there are two other references – Gluttony's 'pissed a potel in a
pater-noster while,' and Sloth's excuse that he cannot confess
because 'I can nouȝte perfitly my paternoster, as þe prest it
syngeth.'[73]

The Paternoster was an essential and magical prayer, familiar to
all Christians, but to be spoken in good conscience only by those
who had repented of their sins. Something of the significance
which was attached to the Paternoster may be seen from its prominent place in Chaucer's *Parson's Tale*. In his sermon, Chaucer's
Parson advocates the use of the Paternoster as a penitential instrument for the forgiveness of sins, explaining,[74]

Whan thow prayest that God sholde forȝeve thee thy
giltes as thou forȝevest hem that agilten to thee,
be ful wel war that thow ne be nat out of charitee.
This hooly orison amenuseth eek venyal synne, and
therefore it aperteneth specially to penitence.
... It avayleth eek agayn the vices of the soule; for, as
seith Seint Jerome, 'By fastynge been saved
the vices of the flessh, and by preyere the vices of the soule.'

The same sermon concludes with a consideration of the reasons
which prevent men from confessing their sins: 'This is in foure
maneres, that is drede, hope, and wanhope.'[75] The dangers lie in
fear of receiving heavy penance, shame in admitting one's sins, hope
that confession is unnecessary, and despair that one's sins are
unforgivable. If all men are to be brought to confess their sins, they
must realize that the penalties are slight in comparison with the
risks, that all men are sinners whose sins are not hidden from God
in any case, that no man should forget that his hour of death is
always at hand (with damnation a possibility), and that no man
should despair since the mercy of God is equal to any sin.

Whatever it was in dramatic form, the Paternoster play was in substance a repentance drama. Such evidence as exists certainly permits us to conceive of the Paternoster plays as analogous to the Liège play and the confession scene of *Piers Plowman* in action and characterization. If we discern in all these penitential dramas a purpose approaching that of Chaucer's Parson, we will probably stand as close to the understanding of the play as is possible, short of recovering the texts.

If the deadly sins of the Paternoster play resembled their analogous counterparts, they were not abstract evil powers but rather human manifestations of sin. In the Liège play and in *Piers Plowman* the sins do not have any instrumental function of seducing humanity into sin. On the contrary, they have the representative function of showing human nature in its fallen state. The deadly sins are quite probably the ancestors of the mankind figures, the representative central characters of the moralities.

The forces of temptation are represented in the Liège play by the Devil and his clerk. The emphasis is not on seduction, however. The play begins with humanity in a fallen condition, expressed in the exaggerated form of the seven deadly sins. Here, and in *Piers Plowman*, the concentration is on displaying this fallen condition and showing how it can be altered by repentance. The virtuous characters of the analogues are not abstract virtues but advocates of repentance. In the Liège play it is the angel Gabriel who urges repentance and the hermit who hears the confession. In *Piers Plowman* the same functions are performed by Reason and Repentance.

The action of the Liège play is well designed to counteract the inhibitions to confession pointed out by Chaucer's Parson – to demonstrate that all men are sinners, and yet to point out the wages of sin. Fear of stringent penance is mitigated by the sight of a merciful and compassionate confessor. On the other hand, any false hope of salvation without confession is contradicted by the sight of the carefully kept book of sins. The deadly sins, representing sinful mankind, demonstrate the universality of sin, all-too-human, natural and well-nigh unavoidable. No man out of shame or hypocrisy need deny that he has sinned. No man, by the same token need despair that his sins are unforgivable. The deadliest of sins is forgivable, if it is repented.

In *Piers Plowman* the infectious gusto of the sins is only matched by the perfection with which their confessions proceed. In the case of Avarice, Repentance refuses to grant absolution until the ill-gotten gains are properly restored. Avarice is deeply moved:[76]

> Thanne wex þat shrewe in wanhope, and
> walde haue hanged him-self,

No hadde repentaunce þe rather. reconforted
   hym in þis manere,
'Haue mercye in þi mynde. and with þi mouth
   biseche it,
For goddes mercye is more þan alle hise
   other werkes . . .'

The Liège play and *Piers Plowman* demonstrate man's need for repentance, and attack the inhibitions which dissuade man from repenting. To show the universality of sin and the universal cure of repentance is the purpose of all these works. It was from this penitential tradition that there evolved, in the fifteenth century, the repentance drama we call the morality play.

Chapter II

Medieval plays:
the repentance drama
of early England

The extant English medieval morality plays, in approximate chronological order, are as follows:

1 *The King of Life* (published under the title, *Pride of Life*)
An ancient and fragmentary play, based on the contest between life and death, in which the King of Death is victorious, but the soul of the King of Life is saved. Lost sequences of the play can be reconstructed from the synopsis given in the prologue; it is written for performance on several scaffolds (including at least one which could be curtained off) and a connecting neutral acting area, by a cast of uncertain – but probably large – size. It was copied down and possibly composed in Ireland, conceivably as early as the mid-fourteenth century. 502 lines (fragmentary).

ed. Norman Davis, *Non-Cycle Plays and Fragments*,
EETS, S.T. 1, Oxford, 1970.

2 *The Castle of Perseverance* (1405–25)[1]
An outdoor spectacle of mammoth proportions, for performance in the round, with five scaffolds in a circle surrounding a neutral acting area and the centerpiece of an emblematic castle; probably performed originally in Norfolk by a traveling company of more than twenty actors. Its theme is the life of man, from birth to salvation. 3649 lines.

ed. Mark Eccles, *The Macro Plays*,
EETS, O.S. 262, Oxford, 1969.

3 *Mankind* (1465–70)
A popular and somewhat scatological little play, comic and didactic, written for rural audiences, and probably performed by a small professional troupe of no more than six actors. The central

figure, Mankind, is a yeoman beset by temptations, but saved by God's mercy. 913 lines.

> ed. Mark Eccles, *The Macro Plays*,
> EETS, O.S. 262, Oxford, 1969.

4 *Wisdom* (1460–70)

An elaborate blend of pageantry and theology, with satirical allusions which may indicate an origin in the London Inns of Court, for performance by a mixed cast of seven men and seven boys and (probably) six female dancers. It features Christ and Lucifer in contention for the Soul of Man and his Mind, Will, and Understanding. 1163 lines.

> ed. Mark Eccles, *The Macro Plays*,
> EETS, O.S. 262, Oxford, 1969.

5 *Everyman* (1495)

The most celebrated English morality, a dramatization of the coming of death; somber and in verse of unusual economy and high poetic quality, intended for performance by a company of about ten actors. The earliest morality extant in print rather than manuscript; four early editions, *c.* 1510–35; closely related to the Dutch *Elckerlijk*. 921 lines.

> ed. A. C. Cawley, Manchester, 1961.

6 *Mundus et Infans* (1508)

A radically compressed life-cycle play dramatizing the transformations of the seven ages of Man. It is designed for impromptu performance by a small traveling troupe – possibly as few as two actors. Printed in 1522. 974 lines.

> ed. J. M. Manly, *Specimens of the Pre-Shakespearean Drama*,
> New York, 1897, Vol. 1.

7 *Hickscorner* (1513)

Though built on the morality framework, this comic piece is primarily a satire on contemporary social abuses, with many references to the London underworld. Printed 1515 (?) for five or six actors. 1026 lines.

> ed. J. M. Manly, *Specimens of the Pre-Shakespearean Drama*,
> New York, 1897, Vol. 1.

8 *Youth* (1520)

A play with textual relations to *Hickscorner*, generally thought to be adapted from it, but possibly even its source in an early guise.[2] The human predicament is epitomized in the problem of youth in rebellion; for five or six actors. Printed 1557 (?), 1560.

> ed. J. S. Farmer, *Six Anonymous Plays*, London, 1906.

It seems particularly important to attempt to imagine the morality plays as physical events. From the late years of Henry IV to the early years of Henry VIII we possess fewer than eight complete texts (as such documents are known to scholars) or scripts (if one conceives of them as theatrical artifacts) of a distinctive and traditional kind of play, intended to catch the conscience of a medieval audience. As the summaries indicate, some of the plays are of epic proportions, and others rustic in their simplicity. All of them, however, have certain common theatrical characteristics. In style, they are presentational; in setting, they are microcosmic analogies; in the originating circumstances of their performance, they are communal calls to repentance.

1 Plays to catch the conscience

The moralities are acts of presentation rather than acts of illusion. Freely acknowledging the audience's presence, the plays customarily begin with a prologue in which the speaker (either a character in the play or a formal presenter) makes clear the argument of the play or sets the scene. Instead of asking the audience to imagine a fictional locality, however, the speaker is likely to allude directly to the playing area, suggesting that we equate it for the moment with the greater world. The speaker emphasizes that the events are contemporary rather than historical – they are occurring (as indeed they were, on stage) here and now. The first lines of *The Castle of Perseverance*, spoken by Mundus, illustrate the convention of a world-stage:

> Worthy wytys in al þis werd wyde,
>> Be wylde wode wonys and euery weye-went,
> Precyous prinse, prekyd in pride,
>> þorwe þis propyr pleyn place in pes be ʒe bent!
> Buske ʒou, bolde bachelerys, vndyr my baner to abyde
>> Where bryth basnetys be bateryd and backys ar schent.
> ʒe, syrys semly, all same syttyth on syde,
>> For bothe be see and be londe my sondys I haue sent,
>> Al þe world myn name is ment.
>
> (ll. 157–65)

Thus invoking the aid of the audience's imagination (in a manner to be borrowed definitively by Shakespeare in the opening chorus of *Henry V*), the prologue establishes the dual locality of the performance. The playing area, normally a market square or guildhall or

field, has become for the moment a model of the world – a microcosm. Members of the audience are not so much asked to suspend
their disbelief, as invited by the actors to participate in a theatrical
analogy.

> I pray you all gyue your audyence,
> And here this mater with reuerence,
> By fygure a morall playe.
> *The Somonynge of Eueryman* called it is,
> That of our lyues and endynge shewes
> How transytory we be all daye.
> This mater is wonders precyous;
> But the entent of it is more gracyous,
> And swete to bere awaye. . . .
> For ye shall here how our Heuen Kynge
> Calleth Eueryman to a generall rekenynge.
> Gyue audyence, and here what he doth saye.
>
>   (*Everyman*, ll. 1–9, 19–21)

In a purely theatrical sense the morality play is a drama of ideas.
The events which occur on stage in the course of the play are not
mimetic representations of life, but analogical demonstrations of
what life is about. The stage is the world; the time, the present.
Within this impromptu moment of time and space, the morality
playwright asks us to imagine a theatrical analogy of the human
condition.

From this ambitious pretext spring many of the virtues and most
of the defects of the plays. At their worst the morality playwrights
are betrayed by their analogies into the heavy didacticism and
hairsplitting abstractions proverbial in fifteenth-century devotional
literature. This tendency is compounded by discursive sermonizing
and by sonorous, frequently repetitive verse cadences – no worse
than the drab norm of fifteenth-century English verse, but not
noticeably better. With some exceptions, the language and poetics
of the moralities are workmanlike, but hardly intended for aesthetic
contemplation apart from the theatrical pretext. They are designed
for acting rather than reading. Literary concerns appear subsidiary,
as is so often the case in the drama, to more functional and practical
matters. The play, in the morality play, is the thing.

The theatricality of the morality play proves to be its saving grace,
given the necessity of holding and entertaining and significantly
moving its audience. At their best the morality playwrights work
with the eye of a skilled preacher or public speaker – balancing
rhetoric and earnestness against an awareness that the audience
must be surprised and delighted and mousetrapped into understanding.

33

The morality plays utilize at various times the full resources of medieval stagecraft, not merely the popular traditions of mime and traveling minstrels (see *Mankind* and *Hickscorner*), but also the courtly traditions of medieval pageantry. From pageantry come the elaborate visual designs of *The Castle of Perseverance*, and the sumptuous array of costumes bespoken for *Wisdom*:

> Fyrst enteryde WYSDOME in a ryche purpull clothe
> of golde wyth a mantyll of the same ermynnyde wythin,
> hawynge abowt hys neke a ryall hood furred wyth
> ermyn, wpon hys hede a cheweler wyth browys, a berde
> of golde of sypres curlyed, a ryche imperyall crown
> þerwpon sett wyth precyus stonys and perlys, in hys
> leyftehonde a balle of golde wyth a cros þerwppon and in
> hys ryght honde a regall schepter. (Opening stage directions)

The characters of the morality plays, though fitted out with abstract names, are impersonated by human actors. This obvious fact (generally the major discovery in any modern production) adds a dimension of humanity to the most theological of moralities. At the center stands a figure (or figures) representing humanity; to him, in turn, come auxiliary figures – persuasive agents of temptation and earnest agents of repentance. The pattern is such that both, in their ways, will be convincing. The sequential and linear nature of drama, presenting a series of actions in time, makes it an ideal medium for expressing the pattern of innocence, fall, and redemption.

Somewhere early in the typical morality play, Man discovers his freedom. By a process of identification the audience is invited to participate in the action, associating its own free will with that of all humanity and the character or characters who embody it. And the audience can only sympathize when Man, having discovered his freedom, decides to put it to a variety of pleasant and impious uses.

The irony of this course of action (and no doubt the source of much dramatic appeal for a medieval audience) lies in the mockery of established values which the logic of the drama permits. If all men are sinners, then man's rejection of sobriety and good order must be presented as sensible and at least temporarily inevitable. Virtue, for the moment, must appear barren and static; freedom must lead to sin, in the sense of pleasure and with the reinforcing implications of fertility. The protestations of reason (in the figure of Mercy, for example, in *Mankind*) must for the obligatory moment be overruled by misrule (as personified in the figures Mischief and New Guise in the same play).

> MERCY What how, Mankynde! Fle þat felyschyppe,
>   I yow prey!

MANKYNDE I xall speke wyth þe anoþer tyme,
   to-morn, or þe next day.
We xall goo forth together to kepe my faders ȝer-day.
   A tapster, a tapster! Stow, statt, stow!
MYSCHEFF A myscheff go wyth! here I haue a foull fall.
Hens, away fro me, or I xall beschyte yow all.
NEW GYSE What how, ostlere, hostlere! Lende ws a football!
   Whoppe whow! Anow, anow, anow, anow!

(ll. 726–33)

The presence of this saturnalian element in the morality plays
connects the form directly to traditions of comedy and satire. The
earlier plays satirize broad and universally recognized abuses of
society, in an imperfect world. In the later plays, such as *Hickscorner*,
the satirical target is often closer to home:

Loo, nought have I but a buckyll,
And yet I can imagen thynges sotyll,
   For to get monaye plenty.
In Westminster Hall every terme I am;
To me is kynne many a grete gentyll-man;
   I am knowen in every countre.

And I were deed, the lawyers thryfte were lost,
For this wyll I do yf men wolde do cost:
   Prove right wronge, and all by reason,
And make men lese bothe hous and londe;
   For all that they can do in a lytell season.

Feche men of treason prevyly I can,
And, whan me lyst, to hange a trewe man.
   If they wyll me monaye tell,
Theves I can helpe out of pryson;
And into lordes favours I can get me soone,
   And be of theyr prevy counseyll.

(ll. 214–30)

This satiric presentation of man's fallibility is very important to
the larger didactic and ritual purposes of the morality play. A
morality play which is to end with a call for repentance by the
audience must first produce the communal acknowledgment that
we are all human beings. It must define human beings as creatures
for whom the pleasures of the flesh will always seem more immediately attractive than the considerations of eternity. As members of the

audience, we are meant to acknowledge with laughter our recognition of the common weaknesses of humanity, which being general can scarcely be blamed. In this way the morality play is first of all a liberation from individual guilt; its initial attack is on the hypocritical pretension that any human being can be strong enough to resist being human.

Lured with vicarious pleasure into recognizing its own innate weaknesses, the audience is subtly prepared to accept the unfortunate and unpleasant consequences – physical, mental, economic, even philosophical – as a case of collective guilt. The enthusiasm with which the morality plays allow humanity free rein is only exceeded by the inevitability with which the plays bring the liberated creature to a reckoning. To the extent that the anguish of this dilemma is general and frightening, the solution of repentance will prove more compelling, both as a collective response to an individual problem and as an individual escape from the collective guilt. Thus the moralities argue by analogy, using an individual figure to demonstrate the general problem to motivate an individual act of repentance.

The audience, drawn together on a religious and communal occasion to be entertained and frightened by the caricature of its own behavior, is nevertheless verifying fundamental Christian concepts; each of the plays is an act of faith in life, considered as a process. The human predicament is imagined not as a static circumstance but a linked sequence of events – not as a portrait, but as a drama.

In greater or lesser degree the extant moralities persuade us that they were once the possession of an audience which found them both entertaining and moving. As communal works of art they are the relatively unpretentious acting out of a theological solution to the problem of evil. In addition, however, the plays are the acting out of a complex psychological experiment aimed at catching the conscience of the audience and evoking the repentance they advocate. This aim is made manifest in the closing speeches of the plays, with their transposition of the fictional analogy into the context of the real audience:

Wyrchepyll sofereyns, I hawe do my propirte:
    Mankyndye deliueryd by my fauerall patrocynye.
God preserue hym fro all wyckyd captiuite
    And send hym grace hys sensuall condicions to mortifye!

Now for hys lowe þat for vs receywyd hys humanite,
    Serve our condicyons wyth dew examinacion.
                              (Mankind, ll. 903–8)

And loke that ye forget not Repentaunce;
 Than to heven ye shall go the nexte waye,
Where ye shall se in the hevenly quere
 The blessyd company of sayntes so holy,
That lyved devoutly whyle they were here:
 Unto the whiche blysse I beseche God Almighty
To brynge there your soules that here be present
 And unto vertuous lyvynge that ye maye applye,
Truly for to kepe his commaundemente.

Of all our myrthes here we make an ending;
 Unto the blysse of heven Ihesu your soules brynge!
                                    (*Hickscorner*, ll. 1016–26)

2 Morality characterization and free will

Perhaps the best-known peculiarity of the medieval morality plays
is the fact that most of the characters have the names of abstract
qualities, rather than 'real' people. The literal-minded reader of a
morality text may conclude that he is being asked to imagine a
stage populated with abstractions: Mercy, Death, Fellowship, Good
Works, and Avarice, not to mention Almighty God. This convention, a function of the analogical nature of morality drama, has
perplexed generations of scholars and critics.

The eighteenth-century antiquarians who first discovered these
'abstract' characters found them peculiar and quaint, though something of a refinement on the blasphemous impersonations of
Biblical figures in the mystery plays.[3] Nineteenth-century scholars,
on the other hand, found the abstractions a step backward from the
realistic cycle play characters, and concluded they must be the
remnant of some primitive variety of allegory. German scholars
traced the characterizations of the moralities to the influence of the
Psychomachia (or 'War of the Soul'), a fourth-century Roman epic
poem. In this extended allegory by the Christian poet Prudentius,
female vices and virtues engage in a series of pseudo-Homeric single
combats. The outcome of each symbolic struggle is the same: the
Vice is slaughtered, amid much blood and clattering of armor.[4]

But Prudentius' warriors are more like Valkyries than figures in a
morality play. The beneficent characters of the *Psychomachia* are
conceived in heroic rather than human terms, and they do not
embody, much less practice, the quality of mercy. Their opponents
are even less typical of morality figures. The only approximations
to personified vices in the moralities come in appearances of the

37

seven deadly sins, but as we have seen in the previous chapter these figures have independent origins in early Christian mysticism and monasticism, and owe nothing to Prudentius. The influence, if any, is probably in the other direction.[5]

An analysis of the function of malevolent characters in the morality plays will immediately disclose the error in equating them with the personifications of Prudentius and describing the action of a morality play as a struggle between vices and virtues. Two of the moralities, for example, (*Everyman* and *The King of Life*), have no 'vicious' or evil characters whatever; instead, we find personal attributes (Goods, Strength) and agents of retribution (Death) who have the function of bringing the mankind character to a sense of his own situation. In the other early moralities there are malevolent characters who lead or attempt to lead the mankind character into sin. Though often mistaken for 'vices,' they are functional rather than abstract in their characterization. They do not epitomize; rather, they tempt. As Arnold Williams has observed, the important thing to note about these 'allegorical' characters is that they are not allegorical.[6] These tempters are very different from the death figures in *The King of Life*, *The Castle of Perseverance*, and *Everyman*, who precipitate the crisis of self-awareness on which the plays turn. The tempters have the opposite function of luring mankind into the state of sin in the first place.

With this distinction in mind we may observe that the tempters are depicted in terms of the three traditional temptations which frail mankind faces: the World, the Flesh, and the Devil. The Devil is represented in all three early plays preserved in the Macro manuscript: by Lucifer in *Wisdom*, Tityvillus in *Mankind*, and Belial in *Perseverance*. In *Wisdom* and *Mankind*, the Devil is the presiding agent of temptation; World and Flesh are also construed as present in *Mankind*[7] (the former in the person of the vices New Guise, Nought, and Now-a-days; the latter in Mankind himself); and World alone is the major tempter of *Mundus et Infans*. In *Youth*, two of the three tempters (Riot, Pride, and Lady Lechery) have the name of deadly sins rather than tempters, but there is an implicit attempt to equate them with the World, Devil, and Flesh, respectively.

We have observed, in considering penitential literature and the Paternoster play, that the seven deadly sins could be taken as representatives of frail humanity. In the case of *Perseverance*, however, the seven deadly sins play the role of temptations. They are subsidiary to the major tempters (World, Flesh, and Belial) and have something of a representative function of embodying sin, as well as urging Mankind into it. Pride, Wrath, and Envy are under the command of Belial, whereas Flesh rules over Gluttony, Lechery, and

Sloth. Avarice is accorded a scaffold of his own, befitting his ultimate success in seducing Mankind after his colleagues have all failed. There are additional tempters (Pleasure, Folly, and Backbiter), who take the role of dishonest servants to Mankind, as well as a bad angel who proffers a never-ending supply of bad advice.

In summary, the so-called 'vices' of the early moralities are more properly to be seen as agents of temptation, with the ritual function of leading mankind into a state of sin. The opposing function is performed by the so-called 'virtues' of the moralities, who have the role of instructing Mankind and leading him to repentance.

The virtuous characters of *Perseverance* are all directly associated with repentance. The good angel continually advises Mankind to repent, and the seven 'virtues,' vouchsafed to Mankind only after an act of repentance, endeavor to protect him from all temptations. The spiritual sins under Belial and the bodily sins under Flesh charge the castle, but are repulsed by this force of ladies who shower them with emblematic flowers. These lady virtues are Humility, Patience, Charity, Abstinence, Chastity, Earnestness ('Besyness'), and Largesse. Even their names, we may note, distinguish them from both the Psychomachian virtues and the seven cardinal virtues.[8] Rather, they are *remedia* or antidotes to the seven deadly sins. The two other 'virtuous' characters, Shrift and Penance, are explicit embodiments of the idea of repentance.

The functional scheme of characterization in *Perseverance* is repeated, with interesting variations, in all the early moralities. As agents of repentance, the virtuous figures have the office of instructing sinful mankind, and bringing about a reformation. Such is the sequence of duties performed by Knowledge and Confession, respectively, in *Everyman*. Like many of the other so-called virtues, Confession is given the dramatic identity of a priest; other 'virtues' who are in fact clergymen include the preaching 'clerk' Mercy in *Mankind*, the Bishop in *The King of Life*, the friars Conscience and Perseverance in *Mundus et Infans*, and the clerics Pity, Contemplation, and Perseverance in *Hickscorner*. Even in *Wisdom*, where the title character is presented as in one sense a figure of Christ, the repentance drama demands that in another sense he play the part of a priest admonishing the guilty faculties to repent, instructing them in the necessary procedure, and delivering a series of topical sermons (ll. 873–1116).

Morality characters are often perceived to be 'wooden,' but this quality is not so much a matter of abstraction as of relentless determinism. The tempters must single-mindedly tempt, the preachers must lead men to repentance, and death must have its day of reckoning. The formulaic world of the moralities determines this catalogue of roles, for all the persons of the drama – tempters as well as agents of repentance – are playing their parts in the necessary sequence of human life.

It is easy to conceive of repentance dramatized by means of an *exemplum* of the kind familiar in medieval sermons, or even by means of a Biblical play. Several examples of such plays are in fact extant, including the Digby play of *Mary Magdalene* and the numerous Continental dramatizations of the parable of the prodigal son.[9] What distinguishes the morality play, however, is a radically different concept of dramatic function. Instead of trying to particularize his idea of human nature, the morality playwright seeks to stage it directly: not through a manifestation of some instance of it (e.g., the sin and repentance of Mary Magdalene), but in a play about the nature of Man, epitomized in a central Mankind figure.

As twentieth-century readers we may have a tendency to imagine these Mankind characters in modern terms, as abstractions of everyday average man, medieval incarnations of Willy Loman. In doing so we are in danger of oversimplifying and even trivializing the plays. If Everyman were the medieval man on the street, merely a simple pawn propelled by forces beyond his ken, then the morality plays would indeed be as lifeless and hopeless as they are often reputed to be. In fact, however, the image of man in the morality plays is a medieval duality.

We can isolate two conflicting theories of the nature of man in the late Middle Ages. The more optimistic conception of man found its highest expression in Scholastic philosophy, in the image of man as the central figure of the universe. In one sense the world of the moralities imitates the orderly Scholastic universe in which man has a high appointed place. He is made in the image of God, to know and serve and love God. Rational yet sentient, man is the crucial link in the chain of being. He is, in himself, a microcosm. He is the appointed ruler of the Earth, carrying out the will of God on Earth.

At the same time, and with equal vigor, the late medieval world took an otherworldly, almost Gnostic view of man's earthly existence. The everyday life of man, the paragon of animals, was contemptible in the final analysis. The material world and all its devices were transitory and insubstantial; man himself, in so far as he had a body, was imprisoned in a futile bodily existence leading only to the grave. Based on this conception, the aesthetic and philosophical attitude of *contemptus mundi* reached the heights of its influence in the fifteenth century. As a view of man's existence (reinforced by the ruinous contemporary disaster of the plague), it was expressed in handbooks on the 'art of dying,' in the iconography of the Dance of Death, and, in literary terms, by medieval 'tragedy.' The futility of earthly glory was mirrored in the fall of princes, toppled from high eminence into misfortune.[10]

The simultaneous influence of these views of man's existence is present in the morality plays. Both views are represented; both, in fact, are necessary to the operation of the cyclical structure of the moralities. The doom-ridden world of the fall of princes, conjoined with the aspiring world of man the microcosm, expresses the fundamental paradox: man the sinner may yet be saved. The horizons of man in the morality are Temptation on the one hand, and Repentance on the other. In this little world mankind is a ruler over his own destiny, endowed with the decisive power of free will.

Of the medieval moralities, the only plays with multiple representatives of humanity are *Wisdom* and the relatively late *Hickscorner* (1513). With *Hickscorner* it is possible that we may possess a derivation from the Paternoster play, which featured multiple embodiments of human frailty and which was not suppressed until late in the sixteenth century.[11] *Hickscorner* commences with a lengthy sequence of sermons by three agents of repentance (Pity, Contemplation, and Perseverance) and proceeds to dramatize the sinful exploits of three representatives of humanity (Freewill, Imagination, and Hickscorner). Hickscorner inexplicably disappears, but the conclusion of the play finds Freewill and Imagination confessing their transgressions and undergoing conversion. There are no tempters in *Hickscorner*, and no need for any since the play begins with humanity already rampant in sin. *Hickscorner* presents its conception of mankind in a series of Breughel-like genre figures. Freewill and Imagination are not 'vices' or tempters. Rather, they are the faculties of mankind, whose free will and imagination often lead him astray but which, rightly instructed, impel him to repentance.

Wisdom provides a mutable multiple representation of mankind in the form of the soul and its three powers. While Wisdom (Christ) embodies ideal mankind, Anima and her powers (Mind, Will, and Understanding) represent the reality – mixed and changeable – of human nature. Anima's black and white clothing shows her mixture of reason and sensuality, and her maintenance in a state of grace depends upon the three powers. These powers, though well instructed by Wisdom, are tempted into sin by Lucifer. They adopt the clothing and behavior of town gallants, and continue in this way until Wisdom confronts them with an image of their own spiritual condition, in the changed person of Anima:

> Se howe ye haue dysvyguryde yowr soule!
> Beholde yowrselff; loke veryly in mynde!
> (Here Anima apperythe in þe most
> horrybull wyse, fowlere þan a fende)
>
> (ll. 901–2 and s.d.)

Anima's rehabilitation and that of her powers are effected by repentance, so that in the end all reappear in their original clothing with regal crowns.

As we have noted, the line of development in representations of Mankind may have begun in the multiplicity of the seven deadly sins. Following this hypothesis, *Hickscorner* and *Wisdom* might indicate an intermediate stage of integration in which the complexity of man's nature is demonstrated in a small group of personages. A further concentration would produce the single complex character representing all mankind. In chronological terms, however, this theory is open to question. In two early plays Mankind is represented in a specific (and notably powerful) figure. Those who assume that Mankind of the moralities is a generalized nonentity may recall that the central character of the earliest morality is not a pawn but a king.[12]

The King of Life (*Pride of Life*) emphasizes man's nobility within medieval limitations – appointed king over all creatures on Earth, yet subject to the higher monarchy of death. The King of Life is a proud boasting figure supported by his military retainers, Strength and Health. Ignoring the warnings of agents of repentance (Bishop and Queen), the king rashly challenges Death to a combat. In defeat, the perilousness of Life's human condition becomes apparent. The body returns to its natural elements, fiends come to menace the soul. Only divine intervention saves the high and mighty King of Life from the consequences of his self-deception.

In *Wisdom* Mankind is partly represented in the figure of a king. The regal costume of Wisdom is described at first entrance in considerable detail and includes a purple cloth-of-gold robe with ermine trim, jeweled imperial crown, orb, and regal scepter. Wisdom represents Christ; that is, he is both God and man:

> Therfor þe belowyde sone hathe þis sygnyficacyon
> Custummaly Wysdom, nowe Gode, now man.
>
> (ll. 13–14)

The majority of the morality plays are built around a less specific central figure. The obvious intention, and the principal aesthetic difficulty, is to confine all of the multiple and changeable aspects of human nature within the coherence of a single character. The morality playwrights approach this problem in a variety of interesting ways.

The early morality *Mankind* (1465–70) shows a consistent attempt to present humanity in the person of a single but mutable figure. The hero Mankind proclaims this nature from the outset:

My name ys Mankynde. I have my composycyon
Of a body and of a soull, of condycyon contrarye
Betwyx þem tweyn ys a grett dyvisyon.

(ll. 194–6)

As a result of his self-awareness, Mankind seeks the assistance of
Mercy, who advises him to be steadfast in prayer and labor and
thereby avoid the temptations of World, Flesh, and Devil. As a
token of his mortality (and mutability) Mankind adopts the Ash
Wednesday text reminding man that he is but dust (l. 314).

As an inheritor of Adam's sin Mankind must labor for his daily
bread. Continuing to say his prayers and toil in the field, he is able
to resist temptations and keep body and soul together. The Devil
leads Mankind into temptation by playing on his dual nature. He
attacks Mankind's material existence by casting a blight on the
fruit of his labors. When Mankind gives up laboring to pray for a
change of fortune, the Devil interrupts the spiritual exercises with a
reminder of physical necessity – which in this folk-rural play is a
bodily call of nature. By the time Mankind returns, the crop has
failed and as his efforts have brought no reward, he is willing to give
up his human responsibilities (prayer and labor) for the simple
animal comforts of food and sleep. He is quickly tempted into a
state of sin; without the atonement of Christ he is only another
Adam:

> Man onkynde, whereuer þou be! for al þis world
>   was not apprehensyble
> To dyscharge þin orygynal offence, thraldam
>   & captyuyte . . .
> . . . As þe fane þat turnyth with þe wynde, so
>   þou art conuertyble.

(ll. 42–3, 49)

The words are spoken by Mercy, denouncing the sins of Mankind,
but determined to save him from damnation. And Mankind is
indeed saved, for his better nature reasserts itself in the remorse
which Mercy is able to convert into repentance.

In comparing *Mankind* with *The King of Life* or *Wisdom*, we may
note the relatively inferior position in the social order which its
hero occupies; Mankind is Adam's descendant, and must labor in
order to live. On the other hand, despite the rusticity of the play,
Mankind is by no means depicted as a crude peasant; rather, he
appears as an honest, well-spoken yeoman tilling and planting his
land. His fall from grace is to some extent manifested by his adoption
of the crude and vulgar manner of the tempters. In the end, in the

state of repentance (and under the aureate influence of Mercy), his speech becomes Latinate and clerical.

The problem of displaying man's mutable condition (here somewhat crudely attempted in a linguistic device) has many potential solutions. One notion of mutability is expressed in the agricultural life cycle of germination, flourishing, and decay. Medieval sermons often related this cycle to the successive ages (whether three, four, or the traditional seven) through which man was seen to pass in his pilgrimage from the cradle to the grave. *The Castle of Perseverance* and *Mundus et Infans* have a common origin in this tradition.[13]

Both plays begin with their hero in a state of infancy, newly born and weak in a sinful world. Mankind in *Perseverance* is poorly clothed but attended by two companions, a good and a bad angel. For all his weakness, Mankind senses the dilemma:

> I wolde be ryche in gret aray,
> & fayn I wolde my sowle saue.
>
> (ll. 377–8)

The solution which the bad angel proposes is one of temporizing. If Mankind waits until old age to repent, he can become prosperous in the meantime. Mankind agrees to this scheme and joins the service of the World. After a fall into the clasp of the seven deadly sins, Mankind is rescued by penance and a premature repentance. He seems secure in the Castle of Perseverance until the assault of Avarice shows him to be in a weakened condition:

> I gynne to waxyn hory and olde.
> My bake gynnyth to bowe and bende . . .
> . . . .
> Age makyth man full unthende.
>
> (ll. 2482–3, 2485)

Thus Avarice persuades Mankind to leave the castle and spend his declining years in wealth. Mankind makes the choice of his own free will, and suffers the consequences. For a brief time he revels in senescent greed, but death comes unannounced to give Mankind's goods to a new young boy and carry Mankind away to perdition. Mankind dies, begging mercy and drawing the cyclical moral:

> Now, good men, takythe example at me.
> Do for ȝoureself whyl ȝe han spase . . .
> . . . .
> I bolne and bleyke in blody ble
> And as a flour fadyth my face.
>
> (ll. 2995–6, 2999–3000)

With the death of Mankind his dual nature is divided, and the soul emerges to be threatened with the punishment of Hell, from which, in the end, the soul is rescued by the mercy of God.

Perseverance delineates three ages in the life of its hero – childhood (characterized by weakness), a lengthy indistinct middle period (emphasizing strength), and old age (a time of renewed weakness). In *Mundus et Infans* the idea of a life cycle is more carefully explored in the structure of the play, though the length of the script has shrunk from 3600 lines to less than a thousand. As in *Perseverance*, the hero is first seen as a weak and naked infant. Appearing before the powerful King World he is uncertain of his proper name (though he can remember that his mother conceived of him as Dalliance). World gives the child clothes and christens him Wanton. In this role the hero relates his childish accomplishments:

> If brother or syster do me chyde
> I wyll scratche and also byte;
> I can crye and also kyke
> And mocke them all be rewe.
>
> (ll. 84–7)

At the age of fourteen Wanton appears before World once more and receives the new name of Love-Lust and Lykyng:

> All game and gle
> All myrthe and melodye
> All reuell and ribaudye.
>
> (ll. 140–42)

When he reaches the age of twenty-one he comes once again to visit World and is given new titles and apparel:

> Now, Manhode, I wyll araye the newe
> In robes ryall, ryght of good hewe
> And I praye the pryncypally be trewe
> and here I dubbe the a knyght.
>
> (ll. 196–9)

As Manhood he waxes proud, warlike, and defiant, acknowledging only the power of World and his seven tributary kings (the seven deadly sins). Prompted by Conscience, Manhood gives up his allegiance to these seven kings, but quickly falls into the hands of a tempter-servant named Folly. When he reappears, he has become Age, a groaning, staggering shadow of his former self. Folly has rechristened him Shame, but his affliction leads him not to sin (as in the case of *Perseverance*) but rather out of despair into repentance. Instructed in the meaning of his new name, Repentance transcends his own life cycle. His decline becomes the means of rebirth into a state of grace.

In both *Perseverance* and *Mundus et Infans* the period of old age is shown to be crucial, in the sense that it brings the physical decline of man and thus converts the question of man's spiritual health from a theoretical to an immediate one. It was the genius of the author of *Everyman* to remove this crucial moment from the inevitability of the life cycle and place it in the unsuspecting path of mankind at the height of his powers.

After a synopsis-prologue, the play begins with God's complaint over the state into which man has fallen. Mankind stands, in theory, little lower than the angels and destined to inherit the kingdom of Heaven. In God's view, however, he has become a blind, sinful, ungrateful creature who spends his time pursuing the seven deadly sins and worldly prosperity.

> Therefore I wyll, in all the haste,
> haue a rekenynge of euery mannes persone;
> For, and I leue the people thus alone
> In theyr lyfe and wycked tempestes,
> Veryly they will become moche worse than beestes,
> And now one wolde by enuy another up ete.
>
> (ll. 45–50)

The reckoning which takes place in *Everyman* is at once a summoning of recalcitrant Man to account, and a systematic analysis of Man's situation. The play proceeds by compiling the accounts on Man, his true assets and liabilities of the body and spirit. This reckoning begins with the greatest of man's liabilities, his mortality as a result of Adam's fall. It is mortality with which Death confronts the rich and unsuspecting Everyman. The necessity of an immediate reckoning is not pleasing to Everyman, who attempts to postpone the event at any cost, pleading for time to clear his accounts. Death refuses, pointing out to Everyman the numerous misconceptions which he has of his own nature – his money, power, and position are matters of indifference to universal death; he must be prepared for a reckoning at any time. Everyman's self-confidence has been misplaced:

> DETHE What, wenest thou thy lyue is gyuen the,
> And thy worldely gooddes also?
> EVERYMAN I had wende so, veryle.
> DETHE Nay, nay, it was but lende the;
>
> (ll. 161–4)

The early results of the reckoning are quite ominous. The external attributes of Everyman – his friends, relations, and worldly possessions – prove insubstantial. All that Everyman has to show for his stewardship on Earth are his good deeds, such as they are. Contemplating his blank book of accounts, Everyman solicits help from his crippled good deeds:

> Therefore helpe me to make rekenynge
> Before the Redemer of all thynge,
> That kynge is, and was, and euer shall.
>
> (ll. 511–13)

Everyman's confidence in his own worldly attributes has now given way to a recognition of the need for outside assistance. Although he has misused his life on Earth, all can still be redeemed. Through Christ, Everyman is a once-and-future king. The course of the play shows the process by which Everyman brings the cycle of his own life into consequence with the redeeming life, death, and resurrection of Christ.

Everyman's free will is an asset in this reckoning; though it has led him to the brink of disaster, his free will is still capable of choosing an alternative course of action. Once informed by Knowledge (in the specific sense of Christian doctrine), Everyman can find the way to repentance. By means of the sacrament of penance, his reckoning may ultimately be cleared.[14]

In the final scenes of the play Everyman becomes aware of his internal attributes (Beauty, Five Wits, Strength, Discretion) only to experience their final weakness and desertion. Everyman has counted these attributes as his best friends; their departure, properly understood, leads him not to despair but to a 'good ending.' He learns to be humble in the face of mutability; at the same time he discovers a higher conception of himself, not as an earthly creature but as a soul in harmony with God's will.[15]

> In to thy handes, Lorde, my soule I commende:
> Receyue it, Lorde, that it be not lost.
> As thou me boughtest, so me defende.
>
> (ll. 880–82)

3 Forgiveness as theater

The greatest danger for mankind in the moralities is not in falling into sin (for all men sin) or yet in delaying repentance (for that can be amended), but in despairing of the possibility of the forgiveness of one's sins. In demonstrating first the necessity for repentance, and then the fact of its efficacy, the morality playwright seeks the participation of his audience in a ritual verification of the whole concept of the forgiveness of sins.

This verification begins with an obligatory introduction of mankind into the state of sin which is his legacy from Adam. An ingenious example of this method in action may be seen in the mock trial of *Mankind*. The nonsensical preamble of the scene suggests a manorial court, but the body of the 'trial' is in fact an elaborate parody-reversal of the sacrament of penance.[16] Mankind is instructed in the six deadly sins (lechery is excepted), and admonished to practice robbery and gluttony. In token of his changed condition he is given a new garment (a gallant's jacket in this case). The scene ends as all repeat 'Amen' in unison and run off to seek their pleasures before Mercy can intervene.

Sin in the moralities is depicted as a necessary stage in the education of Mankind, immediately pleasurable and virtually unavoidable. As a result, the state of innocence is usually brief in the moralities, sometimes to the point of being largely theoretical. A play like *Wisdom* (nearly one-third of which concerns the state of innocence) is the exception rather than the rule. Mankind in *Perseverance* falls and repents, only to fall once again. In *Mankind*, the ribald blasphemy of Nought, New Guise, and Now-a-days expresses the inevitable temptations of the world in which Mankind finds himself. These characters' delight in their own evil is infectious, and once Mankind is seduced into sin by the Devil, he begs their forgiveness for previous injuries, repenting, like Faustus, of having thought of repenting.

The satire of the morality plays adheres to the conventions of medieval preaching tradition in exposing common social abuses. Clerical misconduct is denounced in *Everyman*, and Folly in *Mundus et Infans* is represented as a student of the law. In *Wisdom* the stage of sin is made specific in a pointed attack on abuses of the law and devices of maintenance, bribery, false indictment, perjury, and jury tampering. This matter is staged in terms of a delightful disguising with dancing, song, and minstrels' music.[17]

The sexual seduction of Mankind into sin is dramatized, either in a literal seduction scene (as with Mankind and Lechery in *Perseverance*) or by inference, with lemans, wenches, and brothels indicated just offstage. Only *Everyman* lacks these strong suggestions, and even here the offer by Kindred of her maid as a companion for Everyman (ll. 360–4) may possibly suggest a sexual diversion. As Lucifer expresses it in *Wisdom*:

Yowur fyve wyttys abrode lett sprede.
. . . .
Beholde how ryches dystroyt nede;
It makyt man fayer, hym wele for to fede;
And of lust and lykynge commyth generacyon.

(ll. 453, 458–60)

The moralizing of the moralities is not, then, a puritan denial of human nature; indeed, it is a dogmatic proclamation of the Adam in all men. And fortunately for all men, their sin may lead to remorse, that remorse may be converted to contrition, and thus they may be forgiven and saved. The dialectical thesis of the moralities, stated briefly, is that God has recognized human nature and carved out for it a path to salvation, through repentance.

In no two medieval morality plays is the presentation of repentance identically accomplished, but in all of them repentance is the climactic theatrical act. In most of the medieval plays an attempt is made to dramatize this transformation in the specific terms of the sacrament of penance.

In *The Castle of Perseverance* the component acts involved in taking the sacrament are delineated. The sequence begins when Mankind has thoroughly given himself up to the power of the World, embracing the seven deadly sins. Man's good angel laments the falling off, and Confession enters to offer assistance (l. 1298). Together they go to Mankind and urge him to repent. Mankind replies that they have come too soon, but Penance now enters (with a lance) and touches Mankind's heart, emblematically motivating the contrition necessary for repentance. The contrite Mankind begs Confession for mercy, and is informed of the choice which confronts him:

> If þou wylt be aknowe here
>   Only al þi trespas,
> I schal þe schelde fro helle fere,
> And putte þe fro peyne unto precyouse place.
> If þou wylt not make þynne sowle clere
>   But kepe hem in þyne hert cas,
> Anoþer day þey schul be rawe and rere
> And synke þi sowle to Satanas
>   in gastful glowyne glede.

(ll. 1455–63)

Mankind confesses his sins (ll. 1468–93) and, in consequence, is absolved by Confession. To make certain that he will continue repentance, Mankind takes refuge in the castle Perseverance, accompanied by the seven virtues. His act of repentance is complete, except for the necessity of proving (or satisfying) the act of repentance by steadfastness. On this point Mankind fails; he falls prey to the sin of avarice, and dies in a state of sin. By crying out for Mercy at the hour of his death, however, Mankind enables Mercy to plead:

> If he dey in very contricioun,
> Lord, þe lest drope of þi blod
> For hys synne makyth satisfaccioun.
> As þou deydst, Lord, on þe rode,
> Graunt me my peticioun!
> Lete me, Mercy, be hys fode,
> And graunte hym þi saluacion.
>
> (ll. 3367–73)

As a result, through a combination of his own merits and God's infinite mercy, Mankind's soul is saved.

We have only the outline of the climax of *The King of Life*, and thus cannot be sure of its precise details. However the prologue indicates that following the vanquishing of Life by Death, and before the saving of Life's soul, a sequence of repentance intervenes. In the first place,

> Qwhen þe body is doun ibroȝt
> þe soule sorow awakith;
> þe body is pride is dere aboȝt,
> þe soule þe fendis takith.
>
> (ll. 93–6)

The soul's contrition is the immediate cause of the intercession of the Virgin Mary and of the soul's consequent salvation; in this respect *The King of Life* resembles *The Castle of Perseverance*. A recent theory, indeed, suggests that in its original form *Perseverance* was resolved by intercession of the Virgin rather than by the present debate of the four daughters of God.[18] A likely and unnoticed analogue for this lost portion of *The King of Life* is the Welsh play *The Soul and the Body* which includes a disputation between the soul and the body over who is responsible for their sinful life. The soul is arrested by the Devil, but saved by the intervention of Christ.[19]

In *Wisdom*, the most carefully theological of the early moralities, the means of repentance is elaborately and precisely demonstrated. When the three faculties (Mind, Will, and Understanding) have fallen into sin, Wisdom reminds them of the sure approach of death and shows them the image of their disfigured soul. Realizing the peril of their common situation, the faculties and the soul call on God for mercy. Wisdom explains the process of ritual cleansing:

> By wndyrstondynge haue very contrycyon,
> Wyth mynde of your synne confessyon make,
> Wyth wyll yeldynge du satysfaccyon;
> þan yowur soule be clene, I wndyrtake.
>
> (ll. 973–6)

The power of contrition is demonstrated in the departure of the soul's afflicting demons. The soul remains in a state of sin, however; and Anima, singing a passionate lamentation, leaves to reconcile herself to the church by making confession, accompanied by the three faculties. When the soul returns from confession, she has resumed her original beauty and resplendent costume. She now recognizes Wisdom as Christ, without whom her sins would still be unredeemed. By the mercy of his passion, however, Christ has paid the price of her sins.[20] Through this satisfaction the sequence of penance is complete; Anima is now worthy of salvation:

> Ande now ye be reformyde by þe sakyrment of penaunce
> Ande clensyde from þe synnys actuall.
> . . . .
> Now ye haue receyuyde þe crownnys victoryall
> To regne in blys withowtyn ende.
>
> (ll. 1111–12, 1119–20)

It is one of the dramatic felicities of *Wisdom* that the divine basis for the soul's renewal (the passion of Christ) is presented without diverting the focus of the play from the soul's human situation. This purpose is emphasized in the soul's final speech, directed to the audience:

> Nowe ye mut euery soule renewe
> In grace, and vycys to eschew,
> Ande so to ende with perfeccyon.
>
> (ll. 1159–61)

In *Mundus et Infans*, as in *Perseverance*, the necessity of repentance is determined by the cyclical evolution of Infans into Manhood and thence into old age. The process is carried forward by Folly, who leads Manhood astray and later rechristens him Shame. In this condition Manhood shuns Conscience and its promptings. Indeed, he is on the brink of despair and suicide when he encounters Perseverance. It is the function of Perseverance to explain the forgiveness of sins:

> Be-ware of Wanhope, for he is a fo.
> A newe name I shall gyve you to,
> I clepe you Repentaunce;

51

> For, and you here repente your synne,
> Ye are possyble heuen to wynne,
> But with grete contrycyon ye must begynne.
>
> (ll. 855–60)

Manhood's shame, in so far as it leads to despair, puts him in danger of damnation. The same emotion, put to Christian use as contrition, can elicit the grace of God:

> For thoughe a man had do alone
> The deedly synnes euerychone,
> And he with contrycyon make his mone
> To Cryst our heuyn kynge,
> God is also gladde of hym
> As of the creature that neuer dyde syn.
> AGE Now, good syr, how sholde I contrycyon begyn?
> PER Syr, in shryfte of mouthe without varyenge.
>
> (ll. 862–9)

Repentance is thus the solution and denouement of *Mundus et Infans*. The play's final scene involves the instruction of Age in the twelve articles of faith and related knowledge which will help to confirm the transformation effected by the sacrament of penance.

Even in *Hickscorner* and *Youth*, which dwell heavily on the state of sin, repentance is the mechanism of the play's resolution. Youth forsakes his companions Riot and Pride, and is given a garment of repentance, 'beads for your devotion,' and a new name: Good Contrition. By the end of his play, the rascally Hickscorner has disappeared, but his companions in vice (Freewill and Imagination) are apprehended and brought to repent their ways. Freewill's conversion is, in fact, accomplished by means of mental and physical duress. Nevertheless, the formula is closely observed. Freewill begs mercy for his sins and receives a new garment in token of his repentance. He needs no change of name:

> For all that wyll to heven hye,
> By his owne frewyll he must forsake folye.
>
> (ll. 871–2)

Similarly, Freewill's colleague Imagination is led to repentance by imagining death and damnation. He, too, asks God's mercy and receives a new garment. In conclusion he acquires the more stead-fast name of Good Remembrance, and the moral is applied to all present:

And loke that ye forget not Repentaunce;
Than to heven ye shall go the nexte waye . . .
. . . .
Unto the whiche blysse I beseche God Almyghty
To brynge there your soules that here be present
And unto vertuous lyvynge that ye maye applye,
Truly for to kepe his commaundmente.

(ll. 1016–17, 1021–4)

Everyman, the most artistically successful of the moralities, is also the most imaginative and philosophical in dramatizing repentance in human terms. Here the consciousness of approaching death, which plays a part in the repentance scenes of *Perseverance*, *Wisdom*, and the other moralities, is expanded into a controlling metaphor for the human situation. Within this metaphor damnation and salvation are present possibilities; behind the grim aspect of death (as in other treatises on the 'art of dying') lies the exemplary atoning death of Christ. The problem which *Everyman* presents with such daring and subtlety is the effort of dying mankind to find a solution for death. The solution, as it is systematically discovered in the action of the play, is not to be found in either external relationships (Fellowship, Kindred, Cousin, and Goods) or internal attributes (Discretion, Strength, Beauty, Five Wits). Nevertheless, substantiated by external good deeds and informed by internal knowledge, it is possible for mankind to discover the theological answer to the dilemma. The solution leads, by way of repentance, toward putting the sequence of one's life and death in consonance with the redeeming life and death of Christ, and hence with the pattern of salvation.

The crucial transformation of Everyman is from a state of sin to a state of grace. This transformation is accomplished, in the central sequence of the play (ll. 463–654), by a closely detailed act of repentance. Everyman's repentance begins with contrition as a result of his estrangement from the external attributes upon which he had always depended – Fellowship, Kindred and Cousin, and Goods. With their departure he feels remorse:

Than of my selfe I was ashamed,
And so I am worthy to be blamed
Thus may I well my selfe hate.

(ll. 476–8)

Because of this remorse he is able to recognize the perilous weakness of his Good Deeds and to be directed thereby to seek Knowledge. Having achieved this consciousness of his own spiritual illness, Everyman is ready to receive the specific doctrine of repentance. Knowledge leads to a higher state,

Where thou shalte hele thee of thy smarte . . .

. . . .

Now go we togyder louyngly
   To Confessyon, that clensynge ryvere.

                    (ll. 528, 535–6)

In the 'house of Salvation' Everyman finds Confession, a 'holy man' who accepts his contrition and prescribes a remedy for his illness in the form of penance. Everyman is to scourge himself, in remembrance of Christ's sacrifice and in petition for God's mercy. In a lengthy prayer Everyman acknowledges Christ as his redeemer and asks the intercession of Mary.

      that I may be meane of thy prayer
      Of your Sones glory to be partynere,
      By the meanes of his passyon, I it craue.

                    (ll. 601–3)

Everyman completes the penance by scourging his body, in satisfaction of the sacrament. In doing so he makes the transition from a state of sin to a state of grace. The reality of this change is verified by three visible facts: first, Good Deeds, who has been hobbled by Everyman's sins, rises before the eyes of all to accompany Everyman on his journey; second, Knowledge provides Everyman with a penitent's garment in token of his contrition, which Everyman willingly puts on;[21] third, Everyman's book of reckoning, which previously had been rendered illegible by his sins, is now seen to be clear.

In full view of his audience, Everyman completes and demonstrates his repentance. The tension of the rest of the play lies in whether he will persevere in his state of grace or fall back into sin under the strain of approaching death. Everyman's inner attributes (Discretion, Strength, Beauty, and Five Wits) are revealed to him and as quickly taken from him. Even the counsel of Knowledge is ultimately lost to him. Everyman, denied (like Christ) by all, yet sustained by his good deeds, and bound (with Christ) in the sacraments, dies in a state of grace. His last thoughts are of Christ's redeeming death, and his last words (from the sacrament of extreme unction) are Christ's last words:[22]

      In manus tuas, of myghtes moost
      For euer, *Commendo spiritum meum.*

                    (ll. 886–7)

By contrast, the author of *Mankind* is less concerned with human repentance than with the divine mercy which makes it possible. There is relatively little emphasis given to the specific mechanism of the sacrament of penance – the sequence of contrition, confession, and satisfaction. Instead, the author of *Mankind* sees repentance as a kind of natural regeneration, in a world which is abundant with divine mercy. This identification is very carefully imagined in terms of the response of a particular audience.

Mankind was apparently written for performance by a touring company in rural Cambridgeshire and Norfolk.[23] On literary grounds, because of its lively and obscene low comedy and the aureate latinisms of its preaching, *Mankind* has frequently been mistaken for a degenerate text, and even regarded as an insincere travesty. 'Judged by the original standard of the morality play,' writes Pollard, 'it is about as degraded a composition as can well be imagined'; W. K. Smart concludes firmly that *Mankind* is 'only *a sham morality* – with a slight morality framework that offers an excuse for the production of the play.'[24] A further critical difficulty has been in accounting for the undigested 'popular' elements in *Mankind*. As previously noted, the play is replete with borrowings from the tradition of folk drama – suggestions of a beheading cure, masked actors, and a collection. But the presence of 'popular' elements in a drama demonstrating the efficacy of Christian doctrine is no more evidence of a corrupted text than is the effusive rhetoric of its sermon speeches. On the contrary, we should expect to find just this blending of elements in religious plays which moved a fifteenth-century rural audience. *Mankind* shapes itself to the thoughts of such an audience in its smallest figures of speech ('the corn xall be sauyed, þe chaffe xallbe brente,' [life] 'is but a chery tyme,').[25]

The care of Mankind's soul is dramatized in agricultural terms from the first, as Mankind conscientiously tills his land and chases off his idle tempters. Tityvillus begins his seduction of Mankind by invoking sterility. He hides a board in the earth to make the soil barren and strews weeds in the field to ruin the season's crop. As a result Mankind gives up his labor and falls into sin, where he remains until rescued by his act of repentance.

The unity and validity of *Mankind* as a religious play have been well documented in a study by Sister Mary Philippa Coogan, who found an immediate source for the sermon speeches of the play in the *Jacob's Well* homilies. The comic scenes of *Mankind*, examined with a medieval tolerance and ingenuity, proved to 'carry almost the entire burden of teaching Mankind through experience what Mercy has presented to him in theory.'[26]

It is a priest with the name of Mercy who warns Mankind in the beginning about the forces of evil. These forces nevertheless lead

Mankind into a life of sin, and in the process convince him that Mercy is dead. As a result Mankind concludes that there is no hope of salvation. When he hears that Mercy is in fact alive and looking for him, Mankind is overwhelmed with guilt. In shame he is ready to hang himself, with the assistance of Mischief and his colleagues in sin. The arrival of Mercy scatters the forces of Evil, but Mankind's remorse is such that he feels himself beyond redemption. Without a belief in the forgiveness of sins, Mankind is still in despair. Mercy, appearing, must convince Mankind (and the audience) of the reality and necessity for repentance. He explains the paradox by identifying mercy with natural regeneration:

> In þis present lyfe mercy ys plente, tyll deth
> makyth hys dywysion; ...
> . . . .
> Aske mercy and hawe, whyll þe body wyth þe sowle
> hath hys annexion; ...
> . . . .
> Be repentant here, trust not þe owr of deth . . . .
>
> (ll. 861, 863, 865)

In a sterile merciless world, Mankind would be damned; with Mercy he may be forgiven and saved. Understanding this abundance at last, through his own experience, Mankind acknowledges his sins. Mercy instructs him in the means of avoiding sin and the necessity of perseverance. Mankind departs with the blessing of Mercy, and extends the hope of forgiveness and regeneration to include 'þis worcheppyl audiens':

> Syth I schall departe, blyse me, fader, her þen I go.
> God send ws all plente of hys gret mercy!
>
> (ll. 899–900)

Thus the presentations of repentance which we find in the moralities differ in their emphasis. *Perseverance, Everyman,* and *Wisdom* tend to illuminate the particulars of the sacrament itself; *Mankind,* on the other hand, focuses on the spirit rather than the letter of repentance. One can even see in such differences the outlines of the two prevalent theories of penance in the fifteenth century – those of Alexander of Hales and Duns Scotus (emphasizing the letter of the law) and of William of Ockham (emphasizing the spirit).[27] Nevertheless, the unity of the plays is deep and specific. They are not documents of theological controversy but rather of a vernacular drama of ideas. Whatever their vast differences as works of art, *The King of Life, The Castle of Perseverance, Mankind, Wisdom, Everyman,*

Mundus et Infans, Hickscorner, and *Youth* are as one in their praise and demonstration of repentance. The medieval morality plays are a single act, variously celebrated.[28]

Thus the traditional morality play is not a battle between virtues and vices, but a didactic ritual drama about the forgiveness of sins. Its theatrical intentions are to imitate and evoke that forgiveness. In a morality play the events in the plot unfold, not with the tension and surprise of melodrama, but with the relentlessness of tragedy – toward a happy ending. It is a didactic drama, not in the melodramatic sense of containing a moral, but in the Brechtian sense of embodying one. Human life, in the sequential actions of the morality play, is a dialectical pattern, a linear problem which unfolds its own solution.

The morality play is acted out on the stage of a world where man is born to rule, bound to sin, and destined to be saved. To its audiences, and to their consciences, the plays reveal that the fall out of innocence into experience is unavoidable, theologically necessary, and solvable, through the forgiveness of sins. The action is thus an affirmation of the life process and the ultimate rationality of the human predicament.

Chapter III

Renaissance plays: Skelton, Medwall, and the morality of state

In sixteenth-century England the Renaissance and Reformation conjoined with a startling rise in national consciousness and power to produce a new world and a new drama. Acting evolved from an amateur or occasional occupation into a profession, as plays evolved from evanescent acts of faith into the professional entertainments of the public theaters. The dramatic methods which had originated in a religious context were gradually detached from that context and adapted to new purposes.

In the new social and intellectual world of Tudor England the morality play lost its original function as a repentance drama. A society increasingly preoccupied with the pursuit of wealth and power, and increasingly unable to agree in matters of religion, could scarcely continue to accept the microcosm of the medieval morality play as a true picture of the world. Yet the morality tradition – its structure, stage conventions, characterization and theatrical habit of mind – was assimilated into the new world. There the tradition survived and evolved in response to new conditions; the resulting plays were of many kinds and of widely varying significance. The following chapters are an attempt to discern, in the welter of influences and counter influences, a line of development for the English morality tradition from the Middle Ages to Elizabethan times.

The first and perhaps most decisive step in the evolution of the morality was its detachment from the practical religious function for which it was created. The occasion of this detachment was the assimilation of the morality into the sphere of courtly entertainment. Two substantial texts of the early Renaissance preserve the unmistakable evidence of such a development, the earliest moralities which we can plausibly connect with their 'compilers,' Henry Medwall's *Nature* and John Skelton's *Magnificence*.

Henry Medwall (fl. 1500) was a chaplain in the great household of Cardinal John Morton, Archbishop of Canterbury. As a cleric in minor orders he seems to have served the Cardinal in administering portions of the vast ecclesiastical and legal patronage of Canterbury. As a member of the Cardinal's household he was presumably in contact with the intellectual circle of John and William Rastell, John Heywood, and Thomas More.[1]

It was long believed that Medwall's reputation as a dramatist in his own day was a poor one. The basis for this judgment was one of the forgeries of J. P. Collier, who fabricated the account of an abortive Medwall play, 'The Finding of Truth,' to illustrate the obsolescence of morality plays at the court of Henry VIII.[2] The exposure of this fabrication, and the recovery in this century of the excellent *Fulgens and Lucrece*, the first English romantic comedy, have helped to clear Medwall's name.

Nature was probably written in the last decade of the fifteenth century during the period of Medwall's service in the household of Morton, who died in 1500. The only known edition of *Nature*, undated but presumed to be from the press of John Rastell, identifies the author as 'chapleyn to the ryght reverent father in god Johan Morton somtyme Cardynall and archebyshop of Canterbury.'[3] That the play was written for presentation in a noble household is evident from the text which is divided into two separate acts or portions to be presented on separate occasions. The conclusion of the first part explains that more is to come:

> To shew yt unto you after our guyse,
> When my lord shall so deuyse
> It shal be at hys pleasure.
>
> (sig. A2ʳ)

At the pleasure of 'my lord' (Cardinal Morton, presumably) and in the presence of a courtly indoor audience, *Nature* was originally presented near the turn of the sixteenth century.

The first speaker, Lady Nature, describes and embodies the order of the universe. By the ordinance of God she is minister over creation, maintaining harmony and degree between the elements. She is the cause of all natural and physical occurrences, from falling stars to the songs of birds. She reigns by the grace of God, yet with the understanding of

> ... Arystotell my phylosopher electe
> Whyche hath left in bokys of hys tradycyon
> How every thyng by heuynly constellacyon
> Is brought to effecte and in that maner wyse
> As far as mannys wytt may naturally compryse.
>
> (sig. A2ᵛ)

59

In this orderly universe there is, of necessity, a prescribed and central position for mankind, the chief creation. Nature explains the familiar interpretation of man's upright stance, befitting his status as paragon of animals. In support of this medieval commonplace, Nature cites 'Ovyde in hys boke cleped the transformacyon' (sig. A3ʳ). We are suddenly in a new world of ancient authorities.

Like Mankind in *Perseverance*, Man enters flanked by two contrary advisers – no longer depicted as good and bad angels, but identified as Reason and Sensuality. Also accompanying Man and representing his initial state of existence is the nurse Innocency. The state of innocence does not presuppose ignorance, however. Man's first speech shows that he fully understands his theoretical position in the scheme of things. He thanks God for creating him and making him sovereign over all earthly creation, for endowing him with wisdom, sense, and understanding, as befits a participant in all forms of being:

> Yet, for all that have I fre eleccyon
> Do what I wyll be yt evyll or well
> And am put in the hande of myne own counsell
> And in thys poynt I am halfe angelyke.
>
> (sig. A3ʳ)

On the other hand, Man acknowledges his mortality and the temporary scope of his dominion. Nature, departing, admonishes Man to obey his Reason and subdue Sensuality, and a lengthy debate ensues between these two advisers, which serves to remind Man of the uneasy divisions of his own mixed nature.[4]

Choosing Reason as his spokesman, Man makes his entry to the court of the World to begin his life. World has been informed of Man's impending arrival – Nature has long planned Man's dominion over the World. Yet World affects to be shocked at the appearance of Mankind, poorly attended and half-naked as he is:

> Ye must consyder thys ys not paradyse
> Ne yet so temporate by a thowsand fold.
>
> (sig. B2ᵛ)

As World points out, if Man is to live in the world he must apply himself to worldly things. World clothes Man in cap, girdle, and gown, in token of his new sovereignty, and salutes Man as ruler of the Earth. World dismisses the warnings of Reason and Innocency, and urges the retention of servants in numbers befitting Man's new high position. He recommends in particular one Worldly Affection, at the same time urging the discharge of the nurse Innocency. Man must become a Worldly Man – in his innocence he is unable to distinguish good from evil. Man agrees to World's advice, and his explanation is persuasive:

> I suppose there ys no man here
> Whatsoever he be
> That could in hys mynde be content
> All wayse to be called an innocent.
>
> (sig. C1ʳ)

The kindly nurse Innocency is dismissed.

In this first stage of the play, as Theodore Spencer noted, Mankind's ideal self-conception is carefully emphasized; *Nature* establishes in this way the standard against which Man's behavior in the context of experience will be judged.[5] The weak infant-figure of the life cycle symbolized Man's state of innocence as in *Perseverance* and *Mundus et Infans*, and the complexities of Man's situation, as in *Wisdom*. In harmony with the morality tradition, Man's passage to the obligatory state of sin becomes a natural development, the necessary response of Man to the world in which he must live. There are differences of degree, however. The emblematic Mankind hero of the moralities becomes, in Medwall's image, increasingly an autonomous creature of free will, more of a natural man.

In these scenes World, the familiar tempter of *Perseverance* and *Mundus et Infans*, plays his usual role. He disappears from the play, however, soon after Innocency's dismissal. Thereafter Man provides his own temptations, though his sinfulness is sustained by the crafty retainers who make their way into his service. The struggle of Reason and Sensuality continues, with Sensuality predominant. It is he who engages the ruffian Pride as Man's servant. Pride is quick to note the vulnerability of Man, which to some extent is due to his dangerously high self-conception:

> I wyll byd him thynk how he ye create
> To be a worthy potestate
> And eke that he ye predestinate
> To be a prynces pere . . .
> . . . .
> Specially I wyll commend hys wyt . . .
> . . . .
> He shall trust all to hys own brayne
> And then wold Reason neuer so fayne.
>
> (sig. C4ʳ)

The combined influence of Pride, Worldly Affection, and Sensuality overcomes Man's native devotion to reason, and soon he is off to his inevitable initiation into experience, conducted in this case at an offstage tavern. Sensuality soon recounts the particular delights of this experience, with an eye for evocative detail. A certain Kate and Margery have relieved Man of his virginity. He has answered the rebukes of Reason by felling him with a sword. Man is now the complete sinner. Pride's notorious six kinsmen have entered the service of Man under falsely respectable names.[6]

Soon Reason appears, complaining of the degradation of Man whom he now compares to a 'brute best that lakketh reson' (sig. E1ʳ). When Man reappears, however, he shows signs of regeneration and discharges Worldly Affection:

> Man without reson ys but blynde . . .
> I can well a dyfference fynde . . .
> By twyxt man and a beste
>
> (sig. E1ᵛ)

Shamefacedness now appears to Man in a brief scene, explaining that Man's regeneration must begin with a sense of shame for his misdeeds. Having led Man this far along the path to recovery, Shamefacedness (an auxiliary character directly in the morality tradition of agents of repentance) makes way for the re-entrance of Reason. Man asks for Reason's help and acknowledges his wrongdoing. Reason replies with words of comfort:

> If ye be contryte as ye pretend
> God ys mercyable yf ye lust to craue
> Call for grace and sone he wyll yt send.
>
> (sign. E2ᵛ)

This action concludes Part One of the play. There is in the repentance scene no elaborate demonstration of the workings of penance, beyond an insistence on the priority of shame to contrition, and none of the usual morality emphasis on the ultimate necessity of repentance. The sudden repentance is partly a practical matter; the division of the play into two parts was probably dictated by the time limits of the courtly occasion rather than by dramaturgic concerns:

> Here we make an end
> Lest we shuld offend
> Thys audyence as god defend.
>
> (sig. E2ᵛ)

The result is this abrupt repentance which has, in Ramsay's words, 'the air of being arbitrarily inserted to round off the ends of the fracture.'[7] So, too, the second part of the play begins with an abbreviated scene of innocence. In this way the familiar morality pattern is imposed upon both of the severed halves of Medwall's play. There could be few more vivid demonstrations of the vigor of the morality convention at the turn of the sixteenth century.

The performance of *Nature* seems to have taken place on two separate evenings, possibly three days apart. Reason, entering with the still contrite Man, points out that less than three days have elapsed since his repentance.[8] Reason preaches a brief sermon figuring Man as a besieged castle beset by his ancient adversaries, the World, the Flesh, and the 'Enemy.' This *contemptus mundi* view of Man, encircled by danger within his frail carcass, differs markedly from the prologue view of Man as the designated ruler of creation. As we have seen, however, both views are traditional and even mandatory in the dialectic of the morality. In this sense the state of innocence with which Part Two begins is fundamentally different from that of the opening scenes of Part One. Man's innocence is overshadowed by intimations of vulnerability, and the state itself is only a brief one. As Reason departs, Sensuality returns and the state of sin resumes almost immediately. Sensuality beguiles Man with a tale of misery; all his old acquaintances are languishing in sorrow at his repentance and will soon be at the end of their rope:

> yf ye endure
> In thys peuyche opynyon
> It wyll be theyre confessyon
> There ys none other remedy
> But for sorrow they shall dye.
>
> (sig. E4ʳ)

The impending confession and death of Man's companions recall the shriving of the seven deadly sins in the Liège play and *Piers Plowman*, and the conjectural action of the Paternoster play. But no such conclusion occurs in *Nature*; Man repents of his repentance on hearing of the fate of Margery, his erstwhile whore. She has demonstrated her anguish at Man's conversion by entering a 'Nunnery':

> And bycause she wold lyve in penaunce
> Her sorow for to quenche
> She hath entred into a relygyouse place
> At the grene frerys hereby.
>
> (sig. E4ʳ)

Man is dutifully impressed with the rules of this establishment, and after dallying with Bodily Lust sets off to visit Sister Margery. Amid the recurrent excursions and appearances of Man, we are entertained by the doings of the sinful household – Pride ordering elaborate clothes for the master, Sloth giving sermons on the virtues of inactivity, Gluttony apostrophizing his appetite, Wrath and Envy quarreling, and so on. There is talk of an armed clash with Reason who has gathered forces to recapture Man. But the battle never takes place, for Sensuality brings news of sudden change: Age has come upon Man, bringing physical disability and spiritual regeneration. Reason is once more his first counselor, Gluttony and Lust have departed to seek a new master, and Sensuality himself sees little future in prospect. On the other hand, Couvetise (Avarice) remains in favor with Man, who plans to conceal his presence from Reason. Nevertheless the fortunes of Sin seem to be on the wane, and Sensuality and Envy retire.

The state of Sin in *Nature* is dramatized traditionally in many respects. The offstage brothels and taverns are familiar; the mock penance of bawdy houses presents in parody the usefulness of experience, recalling in this sense the mock trial scene of *Mankind*. Similarly, the duration of the state of sin is directly related to the life cycle, as in *Perseverance* and *Mundus et Infans*. The particular appeal of Avarice to Old Age parallels the analogous events of *Perseverance*. Yet there are notable innovations in Medwall's depiction of sin, moving strongly in the direction of comic realism. The localization of the play in these scenes becomes distinct and specific, creating the sense of a great household staffed by those specialized retainers, the seven deadly sins. Whether Medwall derived this household figure from the actual scene of the play – the great household of Cardinal Morton – is conjectural. There are some mildly satirical gibes at clerics and lawyers, but no identifiable references to specific individuals. The particularity of this setting is of the first importance in the new development of the morality tradition. It supplies a natural locale for the satirical comedy of sin and a natural role for the mankind figure as the ruling lord, prince, or king of the household.

The state of repentance in *Nature* is brought about by natural causes. Man openly admits that his repentance is only logical since sensuality and old age are contraries. As long as possible he obeyed his lusts and appetites,

> Whyche now by the course and law of nature,
> And not of my polycye or good endeuoure
> Is taken fro me for euermore
> And so can I deserue no mede therfore.　　　(sig. H3ᵛ)

Reason instructs Man to discharge all his servants, beware of the dangers of despair, and use his own mind and will to cure himself of his sins. Likening himself to a physician, he proceeds to outline the remedies for Man's disorder. They are, not unexpectedly, the *remedia* for the seven deadly sins. Man asks where such remedies are to be found, and Reason explains that they must come from within. Here we may note Medwall's effort to internalize the drama to show man as a responsible creature. Reason leaves Man alone, urging him to take the allopathic treatment of curing by contraries.

One by one, the *remedia* appear to instruct Man, warning against specific sins and recommending remedial actions. In this fashion Meekness, Charity, Patience, Good Occupation, and Liberality present themselves. In some cases Man merely accepts their advice; in other cases he questions them. Liberality, for example, must instruct Man at some length in the proper use of his money. Mere almsgiving is no benefit if it is undertaken with wrongfully acquired wealth; Charity begins when all such wealth has been returned. On the other hand, excessive charity is mere prodigality; a balance between extremes must be sought, and gifts given in true charity rather than in self-seeking. Man is reminded that God will ultimately require a reckoning. The final two *remedia*, Abstinence and Chastity, come together to denounce Gluttony and Lechery. Man, after hearing their recommendations, asks to speak with Repentance.

As Man leaves the stage with the *remedia* to seek Repentance, Reason reappears. He is pleased to report that Man has discovered the *remedia* of his own volition. He credits the patience of God which allows even sinners prosperity and long life in hopes that they will eventually come to see the light. This interpretation of the workings of Providence is intended to explain the seeming inequities of this world, their subordination to the higher purpose and justice of God.[9]

When Man returns, Reason asks him whether he has done as he was instructed. Man's answer indicates that he has surpassed expectations and has cleansed himself of sin by means of the sacrament of penance:

> Ye that haue I don and what trow ye more
> I haue ben wyth repentaunce also
> Whyche fro my hart shall neuer go
> For he brought me unto confessyon
> And anon I was acquaynted with hartys contrycyon
> They aduysed and charged me to do satysfaccyon
> And so haue I don to my best power.

(sig. I4ʳ)

Reason responds to this news with joy in Man's present accomplishments, optimism for his future, and new insight into the significance of his sinful past:

> Than art thou fully the chyld of saluacyon
> Haue good perseuerance and be not in fere
> Thy gostly enemy can put the in no daunger
> And greter reward thou shalt therefore wyn
> Than he that neuer in hys lyfe dyd syn.
>
> (sig. I4^r)

In this paradox, affirming the precondition of sin to salvation, *Nature* is a thoroughly traditional morality play. The specificity of the state of sin – the realistic premise of the household – evaporates, like the law-court satire of *Wisdom*, to make way for a more general conclusion. Reason invites the audience to join in song and prayer, honoring the grace of God, through which Man's sins are forgiven.

For all his traditionalism, Medwall had pointed the way for those who would adapt the morality from its general religious context to various sixteenth-century secular functions. His introduction of philosophical and literary discourse into the early stages of *Nature* sets a precedent for humanist playwrights, notably John Rastell who was a printer, lawyer, Renaissance courtier, and brother-in-law of Thomas More. In the hands of Rastell and John Redford and their successors, the didactic form of the morality was employed in the service of the new learning.

Rastell's fragmentary *Four Elements* (1517), with a two-part structure apparently derived from *Nature*, presents its hero Humanity as a student.[10] Although instructed in the latest Renaissance cosmology and cosmography by *Natura Naturata*, Humanity eschews the counsel of Studious Desire and follows Sensual Appetite to the tavern. After much vacillation Humanity repents and returns to the study of Nature. Rastell thus translates the ritual formula of innocence, sin, repentance, and salvation into an account of the pursuit of knowledge, uncomfortably fitted into the morality structure. Similarly, though somewhat more artistically, Redford's delightful *Wit and Science* adapts the form to the story of Young Wit, who survives numerous ordeals and temptations to gain the hand of Science, daughter of Reason.[11]

Such allegorical transplantations, though interesting in showing the persistence of form, lead away from the natural development of the morality tradition, the beginning of which we observed in *Nature*. The accommodation of the morality to courtly circumstances, the localization of the morality microcosm in a great household, and the depiction of Mankind as a noble lord – virtually inevitable developments in the context of Tudor England – prefigured a new social and political role for the morality.

Like Medwall, John Skelton was both cleric and courtier. He had served at the court of Henry VII in the capacity of royal tutor to the King's second son. When circumstances brought about the accession of this son as King Henry VIII, Skelton returned to court, probably in 1511. He spent much of the rest of his life at court, serving his former pupil as secretary and court poet. It was during this period of service, in 1515 or shortly thereafter, that Skelton wrote *Magnificence*, his only surviving dramatic work.[12]

Magnificence is a considerably more specific play than *Nature*; its central figure is a noble prince whose court is infiltrated by dissembling intriguers. Under these influences the prince squanders his resources. He is rescued from miserable circumstance, repents of his misdeeds, and in the end determines to govern better. This play has sometimes been interpreted as a political allegory of the early reign of Henry VIII and a satire directed against the policies of Cardinal Wolsey. In this view *Magnificence* progresses toward realism by substituting the character of a particular prince for the generalized Mankind figure of earlier plays.[13]

The courtly setting and the king figure are, of course, familiar traditional elements of the morality. Those who see these factors as Renaissance innovations are possibly misled by the modern misconception of Everyman as a nonentity. In point of fact the role of humanity in the morality play is frequently compared to that of the ruler of a kingdom. Such a comparison, traditional in the moralities and elsewhere in medieval literature, is based on the familiar concept of the correspondent orders of cosmos, state, and individual. Man's position in the world is thus comparable to God's position in the universe or to a king's position in the state. Direct identifications of this sort can be seen in the earliest extant morality. In *The King of Life*, the position of kingship conveys a notion both of man's God-given power and responsibility in the world, and of his pride and self-conceit. Such in fact is the lesson contained in the action of the play, in which the King ignores good counsel, falls before the King of Death, and is saved only by divine intercession.

There are numerous instances of the king figure in the other medieval moralities. In *Wisdom* he is Christ as man and God; similarly in *Everyman*, where God is the angry 'Heuen Kynge' to whom Everyman (a subordinate lord) must submit his reckoning. God also appears in *Perseverance*, as 'Pater sedens in trono,' with his own royal scaffold. Though represented as the ultimate authority, God plays no part in the action until the last scene of the play, in which he saves Mankind from damnation. In the same play the tempters World, Flesh, and Devil are kings with a common purpose, which Flesh proclaims:

> Behold þe Werld, þe deuyl, and me!
> Wyth all oure mythis we kyngys thre
> Nyth and day, besy we be
> For to distroy Mankende.
>
> (*Perseverance*, ll. 266–9)

Indeed, World tempts Mankind into his service by offering to make him a king in his own right, with great riches and power. *Mundus et Infans* also represents World as the boastful vaunting king to whose court Man comes as a helpless infant. World patronizes the child during the period of his minority. When he reaches the age of twenty-one World dubs him a knight and gives him royal robes to wear. Manhood waxes proud and imperious as heir apparent to the World until Old Age teaches him humility. This traditional sequence appears, somewhat elaborated, in *Nature*. Man in his infant helplessness arrives at the court of World to be greeted as a long-expected lord. World is surprised to find a nobleman so naked and poorly attended (an analogy to the nativity of Christ is possibly intended), but quickly provides Man with worldly retainers and the rich clothing of a lord. As in *Mundus et Infans*, Man remains in this state of pride, power, and riches until the onset of old age.

The persistence of the king figure is such that it may be observed, practically unchanged, in *The Cradle of Security*, a popular morality of the 1570s. Although its text is lost, the play is vividly described in Willis' seventeenth-century account of a performance of the play in the Gloucester of his boyhood. It is one of the few eyewitness accounts of the moralities which have survived and as such, its description of the figurative setting of the play is particularly noteworthy:[14]

> The play was called the Cradle of security wherein was
> personated a King or some great Prince, with his Courtiers
> of severall kinds, amongst which three Ladies were in speciall
> grace with him; and they keeping him in delights and
> pleasures, drew him from his graver Counsellors. . . .
> This Prince did personate in the morall, the wicked
> of the world. . . .

This, then, was the tradition on which Skelton drew in composing a play around the figure of a prince. In this sense *Magnificence* does not represent a significant break with past practice but rather a logical, even predictable, development. We noted in *Nature* a tendency toward an increasingly specific court setting, possibly in response to the new courtly auspices of the plays, detached from their original popular and religious context. Like *Nature*, *Magnificence* was clearly written for evening indoor performance before an audience of the nobility.[15]

On his accession in 1509 Henry VIII had inherited from his cautious father a council of prudent conservative lords and a well-stocked royal treasury. By 1516 the influence of the old counselors had noticeably declined; in their place had come an untested flock of 'new men,' symbolized in the ascent of Cardinal Wolsey to the dual position of Lord Chancellor and Archbishop of York. At the same time, by a policy of unbridled expenditure at court and by a series of diplomatic misadventures abroad, the royal treasury had been woefully diminished. Foremost among the royal counselors whose influence had declined in the process was Thomas Howard, Earl of Surrey and later Duke of Norfolk. As Lord High Treasurer, Howard was leader of the conservative element within the council and a persistent critic of the extravagant policies of Wolsey.

Connecting the events of these years with Skelton's long-time devotion to the Howard family, Ramsay skillfully constructed a political interpretation of *Magnificence*. In this scheme Magnificence was a figure for the King himself while Measure, Circumspection, and the other virtuous characters of the play represented the party of Howard. The purpose of the play, Ramsay concluded, was a satirical attack on Wolsey and his allies thinly veiled within the play under the figure of Fancy, Folly, and other court intriguers who bring Magnificence to ruin.[16]

Was *Magnificence* in fact written to catch the conscience of Henry VIII? There is no proof that the play was ever presented at court, though Skelton's court position lends some support to the belief that it was. The response of Henry in that event remains also a matter of conjecture. Skelton's biographers, while generally accepting the play as a satire against Wolsey, differ markedly in their estimate of its relation to Henry VIII. William Nelson imagines that, 'If King Henry ever saw the play, he must have recognized himself and found it hard to forgive its author.'[17] On the other hand, Ian Gordon points out that the play might well have been presented at the household of the Howards and that in any case the satirical portraits are generalized rather than individual. 'Magnifycence himself is not a portrait study of Henry VIII. The King could view the pride and downfall of Magnifycence without feeling that he himself could be fooled so easily.'[18]

In the two recent extended studies A. R. Heiserman and William O. Harris challenge the view that *Magnificence* is primarily a political satire against Wolsey. Heiserman relates the play to Henry VIII in terms of the conventional *speculum principis* or advice to the prince on ruling wisely. Skelton did indeed present such a conventional *speculum principis* letter to his former pupil in 1511. Heiserman sees *Magnificence* as a similar offering in dramatic terms, using the form of the morality play to frame a letter of political wisdom. Harris, in a valuable study of Skelton's debt to the Ciceronian–Macrobian ethical tradition, supplies much additional evidence of traditional material in *Magnificence*. Seen in this light, Skelton's play becomes less a *pièce d'occasion* (much less Hamlet's 'mousetrap') and more a conventional compliment of advice to the ruler.[19]

Magnificence takes for its premise a paradox, stated by Felicity in the opening lines: the proper use of wealth is the true test of man's wisdom, yet this very wealth is most likely to cause a man to forget the insubstantiality of earthly things. As if to demonstrate the paradox, Liberty enters demanding a freedom of action which seems incompatible with Felicity's ideals of prudence and discretion. Measure arrives to mediate the dispute and solve the paradox – a measured use of wealth is possible: Liberty, while useful, must only be exercised within limitations. After some complaint, Liberty accepts the verdict and draws the moral:

> There is no prynce but he hath nede of us thre, –
> Welthe, with Measure, and plesaunt Lyberte.
>
> (ll. 159–60)

The prince in question enters almost at once, welcomes Liberty and Felicity to his service as 'conuenyent persons for any prynce ryall,' (l. 173) and appoints Measure his chief adviser to keep them in order. Liberty is taken away in the care of Measure.

If we compare this opening sequence with those of the earlier morality plays, certain immediate similarities are apparent. Like the sermon expositions of *Wisdom* and *Mankind*, this first scene of *Magnificence* establishes the principles upon which the action is to be judged. The hero is shown to be guided in the first instance by the counsel of virtuous figures. The conflicting views of Liberty and Felicity are ethical rather than theological, but none the less similar to those of the good and bad angels of *Perseverance* or of Reason and Sensuality in *Nature*. This sequence of *Magnificence* resembles, if it does not precisely duplicate, the morality state of innocence.

The paradox of wealth is analogous to the paradox of human nature. Traditionally wealth symbolizes earthly values, as in *Everyman*, where Man's disobedience is described in economic terms, or *Perseverance*, where the choice between good and evil is equated with a choice between virtue and riches. In *Magnificence*, on the other hand, wealth is a virtuous possession as long as it is administered with restraint. Like human nature, it holds high potential and high danger. By representing the problem of human nature in terms of the problem of wealth, *Magnificence* turns attention away from the ultimate questions of salvation and focuses the concern of its audience upon the duties of earthly stewardship. Its thesis is that every man, like each servant in the parable of the talents, receives a substantial gift of existence, for which he must take responsibility.

Critics have expended much ingenuity in attempting to demonstrate the derivation of this section of the play from Aristotle's *Nicomachaean Ethics*. Even more than *Nature*, *Magnificence* has a certain humanistic veneer; it has sometimes been mistaken for a full-blown philosophical allegory.[20] The explicit influence of Aristotle is in fact confined to the names of the characters, which may possibly be derived second- or third-hand from the *Ethics*. Ramsay traces the name Magnificence to the Aristotelian principle of suitable expenditure; nevertheless, as Ramsay himself points out, the term is in common fifteenth- and sixteenth-century use in the general sense of nobleness, culminating in Spenser's 'mistaken' use of the word in his remarks on the *Faerie Queen*: 'In the person of Arthur, I sette forth magnificence in particular, which virtue for that (according to Aristotle and the rest) it is the perfection of all the rest, and containeth in it them all.'[21] Similar Aristotelian origins can be found for Measure, Felicity, and Liberty; but, as Heiserman ably demonstrates, these terms are widely used in the drama and literature of Skelton's times and do not constitute, in a group, any specifically 'philosophical' allegory.[22]

The second phase of the play begins with the departure of Measure and the arrival of a new figure. He calls himself Largesse, though his true name is Fancy. His gallant manner arouses suspicion, but he produces a letter of introduction bearing the name (forged) of the revered courtier, Sad Circumspection. Fancy explains that although Measure is a good rule for merchants, Largesse is proper for those of high estate. In this fashion he wins his way into the service of Magnificence.

Following in Fancy's path comes a whole brigade of dissembling rogues – Counterfeit Countenance, Crafty Conveyance, Cloaked Collusion, Courtly Abusion, and Folly. They have come to gain service in the household of Magnificence. Their function is not to tempt Magnificence into sin, but rather to exemplify, in a sequence of comic scenes and satirical monologues, the vices of the day. To some extent these vices are specifically associated with court life (the mannered courtier Courtly Abusion provides one example); but in most instances the satire is directed at general foibles, as in the almost universal list of counterfeiters named by Counterfeit

Countenance. Fancy and Folly to some extent play the parts of the two recognized kinds of fool ('natural' and 'allowed'), as Ramsay observes.[23] The action takes place as if at a distance from the palace of Magnificence, and for a space of nearly a thousand lines Magnificence remains off stage. We hear of the growing influence of the rogues at court and of the fall of Measure from power; but it is not until 1375 that Magnificence re-enters and the plot of intrigue begins once again.

Magnificence, under the new influences, reverses his earlier decisions. Discharging Measure, he now puts Liberty and Largesse in charge of Felicity. For his own part, waxing proud and boastful, Magnificence launches into a monologue of self-conceit:

> For nowe Syrs, I am lyke as a prynce sholde be;
> I haue Welth at Wyll, Largesse and Lyberte
> Fortune to her lawys can not abandune me;
> But I shall of Fortune rule the reyne.
>
> (ll. 1457–60)

Like a proto-Tamburlaine, Magnificence populates the swelling stanzas with the illustrious kings and demigods whom he surpasses in power and glory – Cyrus and Darius, Hercules, Nero, Charlemagne, Hannibal, Alaric the Goth, and Alexander the Great. At the same time Magnificence remains an exemplar of the morality tradition – such boastful speeches may be found in the analogous situations of *The King of Life*, *The Castle of Perseverance*, or *Mundus et Infans*. There is no need to suggest, as does Heiserman, that Skelton created the character of Magnificence by combining the tyrant-Herod figure of the miracle plays with the 'simple' mankind figure of the moralities.[24] The combination is itself thoroughly traditional.

In the following scenes we are given a picture of the court of Magnificence, now decidedly in a state of disorder. The unctuous Courtly Abusion is seen flattering the prince and recommending to him the sexual delights of a mistress, whom he offers to obtain for a price. In a sententious speech which parodies the didacticism of grave counselors, Courtly Abusion instructs Magnificence in the various vices he must maintain:

> What sholde ye do elles? are not you a lorde?
> Let your Lust and Lykynge stande for a lawe.
> Be wrastynge and wrythynge, and away draw.
>
> (ll. 1606–8)

Measure, the deposed counselor, returns with Cloaked Collusion, who has promised to intercede for him in regaining the favor of

72

Magnificence. But Cloaked Collusion is interested only in soliciting bribes, and informs Magnificence of as much. Together they conspire to trick Measure, who comes before Magnificence expecting restitution, only to be dispatched unceremoniously and contemptuously. Magnificence now is persuaded to render all power into the hands of Cloaked Collusion and his fellow intriguers. Having done so, he awaits the return of his promised mistress and amuses himself with the foolish tales of Folly. But Fancy appears with disastrous news – Cloaked Collusion and his crew have abducted Liberty and Felicity, and Magnificence is ruined.

This concludes the second phase of the play, which corresponds to the state of sin in the earlier moralities.[25] As we have observed, this phase is devoted not so much to temptation as to a display of foolishness and intrigue. These comic scenes have a peripheral didactic intent, though their satire is frequently gratuitous and unconnected with the plot of the play. Skelton the playwright stands aside and allows free rein to Skelton the satiric poet. The resulting scenes are essentially outside of morality conventions and traditions.

With the return of Magnificence to the stage, however, the world of the morality is once again invoked. The instruction of Magnificence into sin parodies correct instruction (as in the mock trial scene of *Mankind*), and the prince's education includes the traditional initiation into sex. Magnificence shows his depravity both in his treatment of trusty (and untrustworthy) counselors, and in physical extravagance. Having angrily discharged Measure, Magnificence calls for a retching bowl to demonstrate his displeasure. The seven deadly sins, whose appearance at this stage of the morality is traditional (viz., *Perseverance*), do not make an overt entrance in *Magnificence*. Nevertheless, the conduct of Magnificence implicitly discloses an adherence to most of the deadly sins: Pride (in his boasting speech), Wrath (in dismissing Measure), Sloth (in giving up his proper responsibilities as Prince), Lechery (in desiring a mistress), and so forth. But Avarice (and, indeed, all but the most generalized economic satire) is notably absent. Those who would follow Ramsay in interpreting the play as a study of proper and improper policies must account for the lack of any overt demonstration of financial lavishness on the part of Magnificence.

The state of sin in *Magnificence* emphasizes, as in the earlier plays, the lessons which are learned only by experience and the vices to which man, poised between the animals and the angels, is heir. Angels and devils are absent from this play, but the sins of the flesh and the temptations of this world are dramatized. The particular setting of this segment of the play in courtly circumstances – a trend which we observed developing in *Nature* – is here advanced to the point that Mankind, the figurative ruler, has become the reigning prince, a figure of mankind. In crossing this distinction we find the future in the form of hundreds of plays with central king figures, spread suddenly before us.

The state of repentance is dramatized in *Magnificence* with a thoroughness that has mystified all those who have mistaken the play for a Henrician 'Murder of Gonzago,' contrived to discredit Cardinal Wolsey. If Wolsey were indeed the satiric object of this play, we would expect to find his figurative self suitably punished or perhaps converted before our eyes. Instead, the evil intriguers remain unregenerate and even mock the fallen Magnificence in his misery. The emphasis, as in earlier moralities, centers on the hero and the state of his being.

The sequence of repentance begins with an abrupt and dramatic change of fortune. Adversity appears suddenly and powerfully, like Death to Everyman or to the King of Life. He strikes down Magnificence and delivers a warning directly to the audience:

> For I stryke lordys of realmes and landys
> That rule not by Measure that they haue in theyr handys ...
> . . . .
> Take hede of this caytyfe that lyeth here on grounde;
> Beholde howe Fortune on hym hath frounde.
> For though we shew you this in game and play,
> Yet it proueth eyrnest, ye may se, euery day.
>
> (ll. 1938–9, 1946–9)

Adversity's sermon emphasizes mutability and fortune, as well as retribution for wrongdoing. In this way it substitutes the rationale of the Fall of Princes for the morality life-cycle rhythm. The inevitability derives not from individual frailty and mutability (as expressed in the onset of old age in *Perseverance*, *Mundus et Infans*, or *Nature*), but from a general and retributive mutability which fulfills God's providence. Skelton dramatizes this section of the play by bringing on a series of traditional agents of retribution (Adversity, Poverty, and Despair) to lead Magnificence to the brink of hopelessness.

Poverty rouses the fallen prince and explains that he must now go begging 'at euery mannes gate' if he expects to survive. Magnificence is overcome with shame over his changed condition, but Poverty points out the proper response to God's will:

> It is Foly to grudge agaynst his vysytacyon.
> With harte contryte make your supplycacyon

> Vnto your Maker. . . .
> . . . .
> Put your Wyll to his Wyll, for surely it is He
> That may restore you agayne to Felycyte. . . .
>
> (ll. 1990–92, 1997–8)

Thus Poverty, as an agent of repentance, counsels Magnificence to turn his sorrow to contrition by accepting God's will as his own. The willful Magnificence must learn to pray that God's will be done on earth.[26]

His repentance, however, is not so quickly achieved. At this stage he is content to blame fortune and bewail, in the fashion of an *ubi sunt* catalogue, his vanished grandeur. Liberty, his formerly trusted counselor, enters with further instruction. Magnificence's fault lies in confusing liberality (a noble and beneficial quality) with unmeasured extravagance. For his own part, Liberty is (like Freewill and Imagination in *Hickscorner*) ambivalently human:

> For I am vertue yf I be well vsed,
> And I am a vyce where I am abused.
>
> (ll. 2101–2)

The erstwhile courtiers Crafty Conveyance, Cloaked Collusion, and Counterfeit Countenance return, bragging of their success in fleecing their prince. Magnificence, now in rags, encounters them, identifies himself, and begs for help. They scorn and ridicule him as they exit to seek the pleasures of tavern and brothel.

Despair now visits Magnificence and (like Mischief in *Mankind*) informs him that he has sinned beyond hope, and that it is too late for repentance. Mischief comes bearing halter and knife, instruments of suicide. Taking the knife, Magnificence is about to kill himself when Good Hope intervenes, banishing Despair and Mischief.

Good Hope is the first of a series of agents of repentance who, like Shrift and Penance in *Perseverance* or Good Deeds and Knowledge in *Everyman*, lead the hero by degrees toward a state of grace. Good Hope reminds Magnificence that 'wanhope' and suicide are the worst of sins, and he describes himself as an apothecary bringing Magnificence the remedy of repentance. Under Good Hope's instruction Magnificence contritely begs God's mercy and submits himself to God's will. Redress questions Magnificence and, being satisfied, gives him garments betokening his new state of grace.

At this point, Sad Circumspection returns from his long absence to find Magnificence repentant but fallen from eminence. Hearing of Fancy's forged letter, Sad Circumspection admonishes Magnificence to be less credulous. Lastly and significantly, Perseverance now enters to complete the scheme of repentance, urging Magnificence to remain steadfast in the future. Harris points out that Perseverance is, in effect, the conventional princely virtue of fortitude as well as the traditional figure of religious steadfastness.[27] In ways such as this, the morality of salvation is subtly transformed into the morality of state.

The agents of repentance remind Magnificence (and the audience) of the inconstancy of worldly existence, as depicted in the action of the play:

> . . . this process brefly compylyd,
> Comprehengynge the worlde casual and transytory.
>
> (ll. 2505–6)

Thus instructed, Magnificence is informed that he has been restored to his former position and may return

> Home to your paleys with Ioy and Ryalte.
> CYRC. Where euerything is ordenyd after your noble
> porte,
> PERS. There to indeuer with all Felycyte.
> MAGN. I am content, my frendys, that it so be.
>
> (ll. 2562–5)

Though this portion of the play is remarkable for its traditionalism, we should note certain accommodations which link it to the less traditional earlier stages of the action. The specific relation of this sequence to the sacrament of penance is carried as far as the state of contrition, but no formal confession or act of satisfaction takes place, either on the stage or offstage. More significantly, the moralizing of the repentance figures converts the motif of fortune and the fall of princes into the specific didactic lesson, replacing the traditional call to timely repentance. The ideal of salvation is subordinated and confined within the allegory of the Prince's fall and restoration. Skelton brings the disloyal courtiers into this stage of the play and even gives them a function of unwittingly leading Magnificence to despair. Similarly, the entrance of Sad Circumspection renews the long-forgotten plot device of the forged letter.

Skelton's play is both more traditional and more revolutionary than has generally been recognized. The repentance sequence of *Magnificence*, in its complex blending of worldly and other-worldly elements, illustrates the adaptation of a religious structure to the political problem of government. But Skelton considers the problem only in a very abstract sense. Even the most persistent interpreters of anti-Wolsey satire in *Magnificence* are hard put to find specific political

76

allusions in this concluding portion of the play. The satire in any event attacks general and typical abuses, and consistently relates the behavior of Magnificence to considerations of the proper use of wealth. The Prince acts not as a leader or as an embodiment of national aspirations, but as the steward appointed to take charge of a portion of wealth. It is vital that we take account of the figurative sense of wealth in such an instance. As every man is steward of his own soul, so the Prince must discharge his responsibilities as guardian of the collective destiny of those whom he rules. This collective destiny is expressed in the concept of a commonwealth:[28]

> For Liberalyte is most conuenyent
> A prynce to vse with all his hole intent,
> Largely rewardynge them that haue deseruyd;
> And so shall a noble man nobly be seruyd.
>
> (ll. 2117–20)

With these considerations in mind we can better understand the nature of Skelton's accomplishment. We are prepared to see the play as an expansion of the morality concept, not as a mere borrowing of form for the purposes of topical satire.

In *Magnificence* the idea of the ruler expands the idea of Everyman. This development, rather than limiting the universal significance of the morality structure, gives it a new dimension of social significance. Whether we interpret this development as primarily a response to the new courtly auspices of the morality or as the logical development of the recurrent king figures in the early moralities, the result is a new drama expressing the old paradox of the human condition in the trappings of Renaissance statecraft. Man, far from being banished from the drama, is granted a loftier and more deeply ironic expression of his own potentialities for good and evil:[29]

> ... the ripest fruit of all,
> That perfect bliss and sole felicity,
> The sweet fruition of an earthly crown.

Chapter IV

Reformation plays:
Lindsay, Bale, Udall,
and the political morality

In the early decades of the sixteenth century the morality drama translates the individual problem of repentance and salvation into the collective problem of commonwealth and government. The central mankind figure emerges as an emblematic ruler and the auxiliary characters of the morality play assume their places easily in the microcosm of a courtly setting. Concurrent with this theatrical development, and related to it, come the historical rise of the Tudor monarchy and the revolutionary events of the English Reformation. Under these circumstances the morality play, like many another religious foundation, is diverted to political purposes.

We should recall, in this connection, however, that the involvement of politics and theater is no exclusive innovation of the Renaissance. Medieval theater could on occasion be highly political as in the case of the Tegernsee *Play of the Antichrist*; medieval politics, in the sense of its public ceremonies, may be described as traditionally theatrical. Behind the coronations, royal weddings, visitations, and progresses of medieval pageantry lay a dual function of honoring the sovereign and of reminding him of his responsibilities and limitations.

The pageants performed on these occasions, often on permanent and temporary structures along the route of the royal processions, were not merely decorative; they generally carried a specific instructive message for ruler and subjects alike.

Wickham has shown that theatrical pageants were already a part of public celebrations in thirteenth-century London. A series of thematically related tableaux and speeches on stages along the route presented an appropriate political lesson, 'an illustrated lecture in dramatic form on government and political philosophy.'[1]

Numerous accounts survive to show the continuity of this traditional mode of pageantry in royal processions of the fourteenth, fifteenth, and sixteenth centuries. There is, for example, Richard of Maidstone's poetic description of the ceremonies of reconciliation between the city of London and King Richard II in 1392, following a dispute over civic and royal prerogatives.[2] On this occasion, the civic artificers of pageantry framed their request for royal forgiveness in the form of an allegorical tableau featuring an angel who proffered a Scriptural text. In these pageants it was common to find Biblical, classical, allegorical, and even recent historical characters represented. Lydgate's pageant for the newly-crowned Henry VI in 1432 used spectacle and allegory to present a dramatic *speculum principis* for the benefit of the young ruler. A century and a half later the coronation procession of Elizabeth I manifested the same variety of *tableaux moralisés*, depicting in this case the symbolic union of the Houses of York and Lancaster and the causes of prosperity (and of ruin) in a commonwealth.[3]

Such presentations are directly related to the didacticism of the Elizabethan history play. Wickham sees an unbroken line of development from the pageants 'through Tudor Chronicles to plays like *Gorboduc*, *The Misfortunes of Arthur*, or *Endymion* with their expositional dumbshows and acutely personal allegory, and thus to Shakespeare's History Plays with their thinly veiled sermons on government.'[4] Yet however theatrically elaborate the royal pageants may have been, strictly speaking they never became dramatic. A series of tableaux, however allegorical, does not constitute a play. The didacticism of the Elizabethan historical drama can indeed be traced in part to the didactic historiography of Hall and Holinshed, but on its dramatic side the history play has a rich ancestry in the morality tradition.[5] It is in this traditional drama of ideas that Tudor political conceptions are first embodied in dramatic form.

The courtly morality of Medwall and Skelton takes the crucial initiative of stating the problem of humanity in terms of the problem of government, thus finding in the relationship of king and court a metaphor of wide significance. At the same time, records indicate an increasing use of theatrical shows at court to express political ideas. Hall's chronicle reveals numerous dramatic instances, beginning with the visit of Emperor Charles V of Castile to the court of Henry VIII in 1522. On that occasion entertainment was provided in the form of a symbolic taming of a horse, apparently representing Henry's and Charles' common enemy, the King of France.[6]

Five years later a play given in the Christmas season at Gray's Inn caused a political stir. The text of the play has not survived, but Hall's description indicates that it was a courtly morality in the Medwall–Skelton tradition: 'The effecte of the plaie was that lord governance was ruled by dissipacion and negligence by whose misgovernance and evill order lady Publike wele was put from governance.'[7]

The familiar figure of the ruler, his ruination at the hands of false courtiers, and the personification of the commonwealth are all typical of the morality in its courtly transformation. The play apparently concluded with the traditional overthrow of the false courtiers and the restoration of 'lady Publike wele,' but its repercussions were not so predictable. Cardinal Wolsey, seeing in the performance an attack on himself, had Master John Roo (a law sergeant who was the ostensible playwright) cashiered and imprisoned, together with one of the principal actors.

Hall relates this story to show the increasingly haughty behavior of Wolsey, but it should help to emphasize the nascent political possibilities of a traditional form. Wolsey himself seems to have learned from the experience. In the following year he sponsored the performance of a play at court depicting the current struggle of the papacy and the Emperor, and featuring a cardinal as hero. Hall characterizes the audience's covert reaction as follows: 'At this play wisemen smiled and thought that it sounded more glorious to the Cardinal than true to the matter in dede.'[8] The play, written by John Ritwise, a master of St Paul's school, and performed by his boy players, was remarkable in still another respect. It featured an attack on the 'herretyke Lewtar,' who appears, with his German *Hausfrau* and a host of allegorical, historical, and Scriptural characters in the dramatis personae of this lost play. Very few dramatic texts from this period have survived, but Hall's invaluable accounts of lost plays help us to measure the intellectual and dramatic climate of the court and to detect the stirrings of the Reformation. Gradually, then, in the 1520s, the drama seems to have become overtly political. Such a development is only appropriate for a decade which began with Henry VIII's acceptance from the Pope of the title of Defender of the Faith and concluded with his assumption of the title of Supreme Head of the Church of England in despite of the Church of Rome.

Henry VIII's break with Rome brought the fall of Wolsey and the rise of radical Protestant figures such as Thomas Cranmer and Thomas Cromwell. With their considerable assistance, English drama in the 1530s became an instrument of propaganda in the political and religious upheavals of Reformation. The acceleration of the trend is seen in a play of 1533 at court devoted to satire against 'certain Cardinals.'[9] Even the content of the old religious drama became a matter of political concern. The Pilgrimage of Grace, which rallied pro-Catholic support in the northern counties, was openly defended on more than one stage, and the first clumsy attempts at state censorship began.[10] An extant letter of Henry VIII specifically connects the performance of a saints' play with the occasion of uprisings in York.[11] At the same time the King and his supporters came to recognize the possibilities of the drama as a weapon in the battle. Henry permitted the performance of plays urging him to discipline the recalcitrant clergy, and such powerful figures as Cranmer and Cromwell expressed their views in public performance of anti-papal plays they had commissioned.[12]

The reverberations of such controversial drama in England had reached Scotland by the end of the decade. There in 1540 pro-English and pro-Reformation courtiers staged a play attacking the abuses of the clergy and calling for reform. In a letter to Cromwell one of these courtiers, Sir William Eure, explained the occasion:[13]

> By the Kings pleasour he being prevey therunto they haue
> hade ane enterlyde played in the feaste of the epiphanne of our
> lorde laste paste before the King and Quene at Lighgive
> [Linlithgow] and the hoole counsaile spritual and temporall
> the hoole matier whereof concluded vpon the Declaracion of
> the noughtinesss in Religion the presumpcion of busshops the
> collucion of the sprituall Courts called the concistory
> courte in scotland and mysusing of preistes.

The play in question is evidently an early version of *A Satire of the Three Estates*, written by the Scottish courtier, Sir David Lindsay of the Mount.

The performance at Linlithgow Palace took place on Twelfth Night in the presence of King James V of Scotland and his Queen, Mary of Guise. Lindsay had held positions of trust at the court from King James' earliest days. He had written much satirical and courtly poetry and devised royal pageantry.[14] Now, like Skelton, he was presenting a dramatic *speculum principis* to his sovereign.

No text of this early version has survived, but Eure enclosed a summary of the action of the play prepared by an eyewitness. This summary indicates a close identity between the 1540 'enterlyde' and Lindsay's *Three Estates*, which survives in two later rescensions representing the performance of the play at Cupar, Fifeshire, in 1552, and in Edinburgh two years later. In these later versions, the debt of Lindsay to the morality tradition is unquestionable. In the summary of the 1540 production, however, there are only limited references to morality elements. The protagonist is described as a poor man who denounces the repressive and corrupt spirituality and wins the support of the nobles and burgesses. The 'King in the playe' has a somewhat curtailed role, by morality standards. He is flattered by a group of courtiers and attended by representatives of the three estates, but apparently takes no part in the action; nor does he even speak until the conclusion of the play when he ratifies the judgment concluded against the bishop. Such a king has the representative position of the morality king figure, but his actions are restricted. He neither sins in any active sense nor does he repent. It would seem that these curtailments were the result of the presence in the hall of a reigning monarch.

The specific application of this play to James V is indicated in its dexterous approach to the problem of kingship. The poor man proclaims his loyalty to the king, yet bemoans his inability to bring his grievances before him. He declares that God is the one true king, to whom all earthly kings are mere officers subject to reckoning. When he is shown 'the man that was King in the playe,' he denies his kingship.[15]

And thene he loked to the King and saide he was not the king of scotlande for ther was an other king in scotlande that hanged John Armestrang with his fellowes and sym the larde and many other moe, which had pocified the countery and stanched thifte but he had lefte one thing vndone.

The player king, then, is doubly wanting as a monarch. He is not the king of heaven to whom all earthly kings are responsible; neither is he the true King of Scotland, the one present at the performance, renowned as the pacifier of the countryside. Lindsay uses the device of the player king to convey a warning to James against flattery, to remind him of his responsibility to God, to compliment him for his suppression of Armstrong and the rebellious lords, and last of all to persuade him that a further task remains uncompleted. Lindsay's representative of the poor bewails the state of the Scottish peasantry and lays the blame on the church and its consistory courts, its rack-renting land policies, corruption, and sexual depravity: 'All this was prouit by Experience, and alsoe was shewed thoffice of a Busshope and producit the newe testament with the auctorities to that effecte.'[16] The player king overrules the protest of the bishop, representing the spirituality. He sanctions majority rule by vindicating the opinions of nobles and burgesses and, indirectly, the peasantry.

The initial response of the King to this play must have been pleasing to Lindsay and his party:[17]

after the said enterluyd fynished the King of scotts Dide call vpon the busshope of Glascoe being Chauncelour and diuerse other busshops exorting thaym to reforme their facions and maners of lyving saying that oneles thay soe did he wold sende sex of the proudeste of thaym vnto his uncle of england.

But despite these threats James V did not follow the advice of the play (and the lead of Henry VIII) in seizing Church lands and disbanding monasteries. It seems clear that such were Lindsay's intentions in presenting the play. There has been some speculation that Lindsay himself was in league with the English Protestants. Harold Gardiner, for one, claims that Lindsay was one of Cromwell's patronized playwrights.[18] Whatever Lindsay's English connections might have been, his writings and those of his followers helped to prepare the way for the Reformation in Scotland. The actual event was long postponed by political considerations, including the blundering efforts of Henry VIII to coerce the Scots into adopting a joint position. Not until 1560, twenty years later, was the Scottish Reformation formally ratified at the Treaty of Edinburgh.

In the interim Lindsay apparently revised the play and greatly expanded it for presentation outdoors before a more general audience.[19] The result was a vast day-long entertainment, divested of its pressing topicality and enlivened with spectacle, comic interludes, and borrowings from the Continental traditions of *sottie*, farce, and *sermon joyeux*. At the same time Lindsay expanded the morality plot of the original. The *Satire of the Three Estates*, preserved in two versions of the 1550s, is an unwieldy and eclectic epic of satire, lately revealed as an authentic classic.[20]

The Bannatyne MS text, representing excerpts of the version played at Cupar, Fifeshire, on Whit Tuesday, 1552, includes a proclamation of Banns for the play, enlivened with a farcical interlude of broad slapstick and bawdry. The climactic scene of the Banns involves an old man and his young wife, a lusty fool, and a chastity belt. The actual performance is announced as beginning at seven in the morning, and patrons are advised to come early with their wine flagons full and their bladders empty 'vpone castell hill Besyd the place quhair we purpoiss to play.'[21] Like the Banns of *The Castle of Perseverance* or of the Chester Corpus Christi plays, these comic turns are designed to attract a crowd to the forthcoming performance. But the ribaldry of the Cupar Banns promises entertainment rather than worship. In this respect, the Banns are also more than a little misleading. Although the *Three Estates* contains its share of farce, the characters of the Banns interlude have little to do with the play proper.

But the ancient device of the Banns is indicative of the stage tradition within which the expanded *Three Estates* is conceived. Like *Perseverance* it calls for an immense cast and an elaborate outdoor setting, with numerous localized scaffolds.[22] Evidently these were arranged about a neutral *platea*, and possibly in the circular fashion of *Perseverance*. Flanking the *platea* was evidently a stream or ditch filled with water, recalling the 'watyr abowte the place' stipulated in the stage plot of *Perseverance*.[23]

The *Three Estates* divides itself naturally into three parts. Part one is a self-contained play which terminates with the calling of an intermission. After the interval, there occurs a farcical interlude of comic turns, followed by a final act in which the parliament of the three estates convenes. This rather disparate structure led Saintsbury to connect the *Three Estates* with the traditions of the French *sottie*. Anna Mill examined Lindsay's play in relation to contemporary French *sotties*, *moralités*, and farces, but found only general similarities.[24] Hamer's suggestion that the fool characters in the play were adopted directly from the feast of fools (known in Scotland as well as France) may provide a more sensible explanation for the 'Continental' elements of the play.[25]

In Part one of the *Three Estates* we find Lindsay's principal use of the morality tradition. No Continental sources need to be theorized for this portion, which is directly in the English tradition of Medwall and Skelton. A messenger opens the play, quieting the large open-air audience with a prayer for its welfare. He announces that a great king is coming, powerful yet merciful, to bring justice to the land. The messenger takes pains to point out that the performance will be a play only, and is not intended to apply to particular events or particular people. Completing this tongue-in-cheek Brechtian assignment, he bids everyone enjoy and behave himself:[26]

> Tak na mair greif in speciall
> For wee sall speik in generall
>   For pastyme and for play.
> Thairfoir till all our rymis be rung
> And our mistoinit sangis be sung
> Let euerie man keip weill ane toung
>   And euerie woman tway.

Lindsay is a satirist-entertainer of considerable skill, and his wit has a liberating effect on the deterministic shape of the morality. He infuses the form with a welcome human unpredictability, as well as a consistent satirical edge. Entirely at ease with his audience, Lindsay turns the presentational conventions of the morality to real effect, contriving with speeches and stage business to remind the spectators of their own presence and participation.

The action now commences with the opening prayer of King Humanitie, delivered from his own elaborate scaffold. We observe at once his deference to God, who has established him as ruler of the world. He prays for the grace to resist sin and fulfill his duties on Earth. Like the heroes of *Perseverance*, *Mundus et Infans*, and *Nature* he begins in humility and rectitude.

Humanitie is attended by three dissolute servants, Wantonness, Placebo, and Sandie Solace. The last brings news of the lovely lady

Sensuality, whose pleasures he puts at Humanitie's disposal. In rebuking his servant, Humanitie informs us of his particular state of innocence. Like his predecessors, he is an untried youth.[27]

> I haue bene to this day
> *Tanquam tabula rasa:*
> That is als mekill as to say
> Redie for gude and ill.

As in the earlier moralities Humanitie's state of innocence is brief and foredoomed. Lindsay further emphasizes this condition by excising from the scene any virtuous counselor, and putting in word and action a series of telling arguments against virtue. A saint in youth, the servants point out, often becomes diabolical in old age. Moreover, lechery can hardly be a sin; its exponents include priests, bishops, cardinals, and the papal court in Rome.

While Humanitie is considering this satirical instruction, Sensuality herself appears displaying her allurements and claiming all the kings of Christendom for her lovers. Sensuality's dissolute ladies in waiting gather to sing a song. One of them proclaims her unashamed delight in copulation and, turning on the audience, claims their tacit support:

> thair is ane hundreth heir sitand by
> that luifis geaping als weill as I
> Micht they get it in priuitie:
> bot quha begins the sang let se.

> (ll. 324–7)

The sweet sound of the music proves too much for King Humanitie, as he falls out of his brief and conventional innocence into the waiting arms of Sensuality.

Lindsay's alterations in the morality formulae are most instructive. He lifts the obligatory scene of sexual initiation out of its traditional demonstrative position (as an indication of the depravity of fallen man) and makes it a primary causative factor. At the same time he leaves the language of tavern and brothel to the servants, and couches the union of Humanitie and Sensuality in the language of Courtly Love. Thus the King speaks of Cupid's darts and of languishing in the 'death' of the lady's indifference, and Sensuality comes praising Venus and offering to cure the young man's distress. Lindsay sends the lovers to an offstage bower and ends the scene by pairing off two of the servants as well. The earthy bawdry of the male Wantonness and the female Hamliness is both parody and parallel to the main plot.

Only when the act of sin has indubitably taken place does Lindsay allow Good Counsel to enter, searching in vain for King Humanitie and bemoaning the unhappy fortunes of Scotland. Flattery follows close behind him, an apparent survivor from the wreck of the Ship of Fools. Two kindred companions soon join Flattery, and all decide to seek service at the court of King Humanitie. Accordingly they disguise themselves as clerics 'new cum out of France' and baptize one another with false names of respectability.[28] The King returns, in his morally decayed but physically enlightened condition, and falls easy prey to the flattery of the 'vices.'[29] The court of Humanitie, entrusted to these scoundrels, becomes an inhospitable place for virtue. As the vices drive Good Counsel away, the proud King retires to dinner, and Dame Verity enters, warning of disaster:

> Wo than, and duill be to ȝow Princes all,
> Suffer and the pure ones for till be opprest:
> In euerlasting burn and fyre ȝe sall
> With Lucifer.
>
> (ll. 1034–7)

She directs her strongest words against the Church, and when the vices hear of her arrival they go to the Spirituality and obtain permission to deal with Verity. They accuse her of plotting the King's overthrow and find proof of her iniquity:

> Quhat buik is that harlot, into thy hand,
> Out wallo way, this is the New Test'ment
> In Englisch toung, and printit in England,
> Heresie, heresie, fire, fire incontinent.
>
> (ll. 1144–7)

While the King pursues his own pleasures, the vices put Verity into the stocks. Lady Chastity arrives, forced into exile by the depravity of the Church. She is seeking shelter, but the Spirituality coldly rejects her, as do the Lords Temporal. Lindsay enlivens this scene of rejection once more by social comedy, as Chastity encounters a group of timid artisans and their shrewish wives. The wives' rejection of Chastity is both comic and ironic. Finally Chastity reaches the King, only to find him a willing slave of Sensuality. The vices remove Chastity from the court and place her in the stocks with Verity.

In this early part of the play Lindsay chooses to emphasize the humanity of the central figure rather than his kingship. It is only the King's delegation of power to the vices and to Sensuality that depicts him as a bad king. The political emphasis, as such, is rather on an increasingly pointed religious satire. Traditional elements of the morality – the disguise of the vices and the complaint of the virtues – take on the aspect of the contemporary struggle between Rome and Reformation. The satire of the *Three Estates* aims directly at one estate in particular. Its primary target is the Spirituality.

The entrance of a young boy heralds the turning of the action toward repentance. The boy announces the impending arrival of his master, the dread King Correction who executes God's reformation:

> Sumtyme with Sword and Pestilence
> With derth and povertie
> Bot quhen the peopill does repent
> And beis to God obedient
> Then will he gif them grace.
>
> (ll. 1490–94)

Lindsay characteristically ends this speech with a disclaimer, pointing out that everything now happening is 'all in the play.' But the vices know that reformation is on the way, and they make plans to escape – each will take refuge with one of the three estates. They steal the King's treasure box and depart, fighting over possession.

King Correction enters, warning of the fate which awaits tyrants and monarchs who forget their duties as deputies of God:

> Quhat is an King? nocht bot ane officer
> to caus his leiges live in equitie.
>
> (ll. 1606–7)

Correction greets Good Counsel, releases Verity and Chastity from the stocks, and marches toward the King's scaffold. The King's servants and Sensuality rouse him from his sleep to face the intruder, and Humanitie vaunts his best:

> Quha dois presume for till correct ane King?
> Knaw ʒe nocht me greit King Humanitie
> That in my Regioun Royally dois ring?
>
> (ll. 1709–11)

The confrontation of the two kings, recalling the similar episode in *The King of Life*, results in the expected victory of the agent of retribution (who, like Death in *Everyman* or Adversity in *Magnificence* is an indomitable agent of God's will). Correction warns Humanitie of the fate that has befallen tyrants such as Tarquin and Sardanapalus; he recommends as advisers Good Counsel, Verity, and Chastity. Humanitie submits to correction ('The King imbraces Correction with a humbil countenance' [s.d. following l. 1777]). Correction orders him to call a parliament of the three estates to redress all grievances. Correction urges him, in the meantime, to live in moderation. Chastity will take the place of Sensuality until such time as the King is properly married. Good Counsel directs a brief sermon in the *speculum principis* mode to Humanitie:

> Sir, gif ʒour hienes ʒearnis lang to ring
> First dread ʒour God abuif all vther thing.
> For ʒear bot ane mortall instrument
> To that great God and King Omnipotent.
>
> (ll. 1876–9)

In this first part of the *Three Estates* there is an easy accommodation of the morality play to political satire. The remainder of the play, although outside the morality form, makes use of certain morality conventions. Following the intermission and a series of comic satiric interludes, the parliament of the three estates convenes to consider the task of reformation. The two Kings, Correction and Humanitie, sit in judgment and assess penalties and rewards. As in the 1540 version, a representative of the exploited peasantry makes the accusations. Clad in rags, John Commonweal bursts into the august session and confronts his exploiters. Correction orders the vices put in the stocks and the Spirituality deprived of their attendants Sensuality and Covetise. The Temporality come forward and repeat their sins before King Correction and promise to defend the commonwealth in the future. Correction pardons the Temporality on that condition, but orders the offenders of the Spirituality unfrocked and replaced with learned (and presumably Protestant) clerics. John Commonweal receives new clothing and a place in the parliament. After a reading of Acts of Parliament curtailing the power of the Church, the vices are hanged. Falset, at the gallows, issues an invitation to all unwary monarchs:

> Cum follow me all catyfe covetous Kings
> Reauers but richt of vthers Realmis and Rings
> Togidder with all wrangous conquerours,
> And bring with ʒow all public oppressours.
> With Pharao King of Egiptians
> With him in hell salbe ʒour recompence.
>
> (ll. 4204–9)

We should note that the conventions of the morality drama, once the embodiment of orthodox Christian doctrine, have become a weapon for reform of those doctrines and the embattled institutions of the Church in the sixteenth century. The fall of mankind into sin translates almost effortlessly into the fall of a nation into the clutches of priestcraft. The king, embodying the nation as well as mankind, is the figure who makes possible the metamorphosis. The agents of temptation and repentance take on the identity of courtiers at cross purposes. The dramatic concept of the public good which is implicit in *Magnificence* bursts explicitly onto the stage of the *Three Estates* as a personified John Commonweal.

The steady trend toward explicitly political drama which we have observed in the plays of Medwall, Skelton, and Lindsay reaches its early Tudor culmination in the political moralities of Nicholas Udall and John Bale. In *Respublica* and *King John* the form and figure of the morality become an interpretive mirror of the events of the Reformation. The plays are in many ways remarkably similar. Both conceive the decay of the commonwealth in the figures of a poor widow and an impoverished peasant. The causes of the decay appear in dissembling vices who gain power in the state, and the resolution in each case is a reassertion of royal power, restoring the nation to felicity. In both plays the Reformation is a climactic event.

The difference, however, is in what the Reformation means as a dramatic event. To Bale, writing under the patronage of Thomas Cromwell in 1538, the Reformation appears as the cleansing time of national repentance; to Udall, writing under the patronage of Queen Mary Tudor in 1553, the same events are a national fall from grace, lately corrected, repented, and forgiven.

Respublica is a play about contemporary events, but these events are staged with great tact and circumspection:[30]

> not, as by plaine storye
> but as yt were in figure by an allegorye.

So Udall explains in his prologue, and so he proceeds in *Respublica*, not representing particulars of recent events but rather the abstracted meaning of those events. The Reformation lapse into schismatic Protestantism and secularism is, in *Respublica*'s morality scheme, only a prelude to repentance and forgiveness, with England received back into the body of the Church. The sin of despoiling Church lands and monasteries is not imputed to specific offenders, but rather is generalized and personified in the figure of Avarice, 'allias policie, the vice of the plaie.'[31]

Theatrical precedent, as well as prudence, dictated this figurative approach to contemporary political events. There could be no question in the mid-sixteenth century of representing such events undisguised on the stage.

It was a time of swift, and dangerous, shifts in the wind. Nicholas Udall had written verses for pageants at the coronation of Anne Boleyn and had even perhaps, like Bale, written plays for Cromwell. But where Bale was adamant in his politics, Udall seems to have been highly flexible. Although he had left his post as headmaster of Eton under a cloud of suspicion, he gained preferment at the court of Edward VI. At the accession of Mary he took service in the household of Bishop Gardiner, obtained the position of headmaster at Westminster, and wrote courtly entertainments for the new queen, of which *Respublica* and *Ralph Roister Doister* are the probable surviving examples.[32]

The occasion of *Respublica* was the confident first Christmas of Mary's reign, and Udall provided his boy-players with a witty, decorous, confident historical satire to fit the occasion. The prologue emphasizes the generality of the piece and its benign intentions, but it leaves little doubt of *Respublica*'s topical purposes:

> Soo for goode Englande sake this presente howre and daie
> In hope of restoring from hir late decaye
> We children to youe olde folke, bothe with harte and voyce
> Maie Ioyne all togither to thank god and Reioyce
> That he hath sent Marye our Soveraigne and Quene
> To reforme thabuses which hitherto hath been.
>
> (ll. 45–50)

We may suspect that the use of boy-players had its effects on Udall's approach to the morality tradition. The comic style is light and elevated, free of harsh satire and obscenity. The opening scenes introduce Avarice and three subordinate gallants (Insolence, Oppression, and Adulation) who are adopting disguises to gain entry to court. They rechristen themselves Policy, Authority, Reformation, and Honesty. In Udall's treatment this familiar conspiracy scene becomes a delightful comic interlude, essentially without sinister overtones.

In the same vein are the alterations which Udall effects in the central figure. Instead of a naïve young prince we find a noble widow (Respublica) in depressed circumstances. Stoically she recites an *ubi sunt* for all great civilizations which have declined, and points the moral:

> thus much is well seen
> That in Comon weales while good governors have been

All thing hath prospered, and where such men dooe lacke
Common weales decaye, and all thinges do goe backe.

(ll. 453–6)

Despite her misfortune and her representative function, Respublica
is no angry John Commonweal. Alone and unattended, she is
vulnerable, like the infant heroes of *Perseverance* and *Mundus et
Infans*, if not precisely innocent. To this unfortunate lady come
Avarice and the gallants, disguised as sober counselors and promising
to restore her fortunes. Respublica's fall under the domination of
these dissemblers is as inevitable as sin itself, but Udall divests the
occasion of its traditional aspect of moral choice. Respublica is not
a prince but a gentle lady, and no worthy advice or advisers are
present to be disregarded or discharged. The 'innocence' of
Respublica consists in her credulity, in placing her hopes for a better
future in the unworthy hands of the gallants.

The decay of commonwealth is thus linked to the rise of vice
characters to political power, as it similarly is in *King John*. In
Udall's play, however, these events become a satirical and comic
statement. Respublica, deceived by the vices' false names, is
convinced that their retention as her advisers has inaugurated a new
era of prosperity. Immediate evidence suggests that she is quite
correct. The advisers themselves fall diligently to work and quickly
wax rich and prosperous. The source of their revenue becomes
clear as the advisers meet to compare results: their new wealth has
been created by bleeding the rest of the country white. Policy
(Avarice) is so loaded down with bags of gold that he can hardly
drag them onto the stage. Reformation (Oppression) is almost
worn out with seizing ecclesiastical power and property:[33]

Feithe if I luste I maie were myters fowre or fyve
I have so manye haulfe bisshoprikes at the least.

(ll. 780–81)

Making an inventory of their gains, they sing gleefully ('Hey
noney nony hough for money'), resolving to make hay while the sun
shines and while Respublica remains credulously in the dark.

Enlightenment comes to Respublica, meanwhile, in the unlikely
shape of People, a rude and unlettered peasant. Though his expression is somewhat obscured by rustic idiom and a thick West Country
accent, his meaning is plain: the peasantry is being driven to ruin,
and the state of the country is 'As zoure ale in sommer, that is still
wurse and wurse' (l. 990). Respublica refers People's complaints to
her advisers, who ridicule People and insist that all will be well in
good time. Oppression swears on the gospel that the new laws could

not be better if he had made them for his own benefit. When Respublica leaves, reassured, the advisers chastise People and drive him from the court.

The unhappy state of the commonwealth depicted in the misapprehensions of Respublica and the distress of People is equivalent to the state of sin in which the traditional morality hero finds himself as a result of his own actions. What has been considerably deemphasized in *Respublica* is the moral responsibility of these representative characters. People is only an innocent victim of circumstances, and the fault for the deception of Respublica rests almost entirely with her deceivers. These alterations help to explain the events of Udall's fifth 'act,' which reproduces the state of repentance of the earlier plays.[34]

The solution of Respublica's dilemma comes through divine intervention in political affairs, heralded by the arrival of the four allegorical daughters of God.[35] Mercy enters to explain the Biblical precedents for God's intervention:

> In his mercie was Israell delivered
> From the gyptian thraldome and captivitee
> In his mercye the same throughe the red sea was led
> And through wildernesse to a lande of libertee,
> Syth that tyme all commonweales he hath protected.
>
> (ll. 1193–7)

The instance of divine intervention to which Udall is alluding here is most likely the death of the young King Edward VI, which brought the Catholic Mary to the throne and toppled the violent reformers (such as Bale) from their positions of power. The frailty and minority of Edward should help to explain why Respublica is shown in her earlier state of 'sin' as a widow not fully responsible for her actions. The absence of a king figure in *Respublica*, then, has an historical basis. England was, in effect, without a reigning male monarch from the death of Henry VIII in 1547 to the accession of James I in 1603. We may observe that the highly figurative rendering of Edward's death allows Udall to avoid details of the pathetic pretext for Mary's accession and yet show the event as an instance of divine providence. Such are the delicate uses of political allegory.

Two daughters of God come in the first instance to enlighten Respublica concerning her decay. The cause, as Mercy points out, rests with bad advisers. Though Avarice and his companions stoutly deny the charges, the accusations of Verity gradually convince Respublica of her true condition. Thus these figures serve as agents of remorse, like Adversity and Poverty in *Magnificence* or Penance in *Perseverance*. The remorse of Respublica is limited here

(as was her responsibility) to a hope for redress. This hope is
quickly granted, as Justice and Peace join their sisters and explain
the means of Respublica's salvation. Verity will determine the
truth of what has happened, Justice will administer punishment
(tempered by Mercy), and Peace will then be established.
Respublica pledges to carry out the daughters' instructions, and
they in turn promise to shield Respublica from her enemies. After
this sequence of instructions (closely reminiscent of the morality
scenes in which Mankind is instructed in the stages of sacrament of
penance) the daughters leave the stage to reclothe Respublica:

> MISERIC Nowe Sisters goe wee, and Respublica with vs
> to bee newe appareled otherwyse then thus.
> IUSTIC Come on Respublica with vs to wealth from wooe.
>
> (ll. 1425–7)

Despite the traditional seriousness of the repentance sequence in
the moralities, Udall manages to preserve the comic decorum of his
vices. Ignoring the impending doom Avarice continues to play the
miser, and Adulation the fool. Far from being afraid of the heavenly
visitors, the vices plot amorous intrigues with them. But their days
of misrule are over. Respublica returns in her new garments to
rebuke Avarice and discharge him. People in turn appears, wearing
a new coat of his own in token of prosperity. Now it is the turn of the
virtues to trap the vices, and Udall takes full comic advantage of the
situation, from the quick falling-out among thieves to the juxtaposition of mortals and daughters of God:

> AVAR Where is your dwelling?
> IUST In heaven and thens I came.
> AVAR Dwell ye in heaven and so madde to come hither?
> All our hucking here, is how we maie geate thither.
> IUST I bring heaven with me and make it where I am.
> AVAR Then I praie youe lett me bee your prentise madame.
> . . . .
> And ye cam downe from heaven too, I judge.
> MISERIC Yes sure.
> AVAR Why what folke are ye that cannot heaven endure?
>
> (ll. 1674–8, 1685–6)

Avarice is unmasked, however, when his bags of 'rye' are opened
and prove to contain the spoils of his maladministration. The
advisers are all unfrocked, revealing them as gaudily dressed
gallants.[36] Respublica, though convinced of their guilt, does not
prescribe punishments. The judgment of the offenders is left to a

further *deus ex machina* in the form of the goddess Nemesis, who now comes forth to set matters in order.

Nemesis, clearly representing the newly-crowned Queen Mary, passes judgment on the vices. She reproves the foolish Adulation, but pardons him in return for a pledge of loyalty to the commonwealth in the future. Avarice, on the other hand, is compelled to restore all that he has stolen, and is delivered into the hands of People, 'that he maie bee pressed, as men doo presse a spounge' (l. 1903).[37] Oppression and Insolence, who have carried out the Reformation, are to be imprisoned and tried for their crimes. Nemesis now counsels Respublica to accept the protection of the four daughters of God, then announces her departure:

> Well, I muste goe hens to an other countreye nowe
> That hathe of redresse the like case that was in youe.
> I leave you for thys tyme immortal thanks to geve
> To godde and your Soveraigne which doo youe thus relieve.
>
> (ll. 1926–9)

Thus, with prayers for Queen Mary and the commonwealth, this gently satirical play about the recent past concludes in the happy present, in the first Christmas of Mary's reign, with the Reformation seemingly banished forever from the Catholic commonwealth of England.

Writing some fifteen years earlier in the midst of the tumultuous 1530s, John Bale had also constructed a morality-play version of the contemporary political scene. Like *Respublica*, Bale's *King John*[38] is a figurative performance at a necessary aesthetic distance from contemporary reality. His innovation was to couch his apology for the Reformation in an historical figure – the distant events of the twelfth-century reign of King John. The mingling in *King John* of an historical king with auxiliary 'morality abstractions' like Clergy and Sedition is effortless, as is the frequent assumption by these 'abstractions' of temporary historical identities (Sedition becomes Stephen Langton, Archbishop of Canterbury). All, in fact, are figures in a contemporary political play. It is this secondary historical dimension of Bale's play which critics have ignored in their haste to designate *King John* the first English history play.

Bale's eventful and improbable career was a fitting preparation for the role of historical-political-religious playwright. Reared and educated by the Carmelites, he became a friar and studied at the universities of Cambridge, Louvain, and Toulouse, where he developed the voracious historical interests that made him one of the foremost antiquarians of his day. He served as prior of several Carmelite friaries until the influence of Lutheranism caused him to abandon the Carmelite order for a living in Thorndon, Suffolk. It is unclear whether Bale began to write plays at this time or whether he had written some previously while still a Carmelite. His self-compiled list of dramatic works includes a number of plays on traditional religious subjects (among them two plays on the Lord's Prayer and the seven deadly sins),[39] but these have not survived. All that is certain is that his new career as a parish priest was tempestuous, that during this period he took a wife, and that he was ultimately expelled from his living and imprisoned on a charge of heresy.[40]

From these difficulties Bale was rescued by Thomas Cromwell, the Lord Chancellor, under whose patronage he formed a company of actors and wrote a series of virulent anti-Catholic polemical plays. Unlike Udall, whose play was apparently intended solely for a court audience, Bale wrote evangelically and propagandistically for a popular audience. In so doing, he tried to turn the weapons of the enemy against themselves. In all his extant plays Bale works from within the conventions of Catholic religious drama, and of these two are clearly in the morality tradition.

The first, under its resplendent title of *A Comedy Concerning Thre Lawes, of Nature Moses, & Christ, Corrupted by the Sodomytes, Pharysees and Papystes*,[41] draws an elaborate parallel between Old Testament transgression against natural and Mosaic law and the corruption of the gospel by the Church of Rome. This parallel is contained within a morality framework which is both universal (the innocence, fall, affliction, and redemption of Man) and particular, repeated in the individual transgressions. The intervention of the vengeance of God brings the deliverance and fulfillment of the three laws.

Bale's major work in the morality tradition is *King John*. In its initial form this play was probably written in 1538 and performed at Christmas before the household of Thomas Cranmer, Archbishop of Canterbury. Records indicate that Cromwell paid for the performance; it is likely that the play was presented subsequently in public performances. Audiences evidently understood clearly the message of the play, and outbreaks of disorder occurred. One spectator remarked that 'it was a great pity that the bishop of Rome should reign any longer, for he would do with our King as he did with King John.'[42]

If *King John* was intended to urge Henry to adopt the extreme Protestant position, however, it failed utterly. Within two years Cromwell had been toppled from power and executed, and Bale had fled into exile. There he remained until the accession of Edward VI, when he returned to receive a living and ultimately to be named Bishop of Ossory in Ireland. Hardly had he taken up his duties of extirpating Catholic practices when in 1553 the young king died and

Mary Tudor became queen.[43] Forced to flee Ireland, Bale lost most of his possessions and was captured at sea by Flemish pirates; but he eventually reached the Continent where he passed a second period in exile. On the accession of Elizabeth he returned to England and became a canon at Canterbury Cathedral. He then revised the original *King John* for performance before Queen Elizabeth. It is quite possible that Elizabeth saw the play in Ipswich in 1561, before Bale died in 1563 at the age of sixty-eight.[44]

Like *Respublica*, Bale's *King John* has a courtly setting; its atmosphere, however, is strikingly different. Thus Bale's play begins not with the comic monologue of a vice, but with the vaunting entrance of a king bent on reformation:

> Iohn kyng of Ynglond, the croncyclys doth me call . . .
> . . . .
> By the wyll of God and his hygh ordynaunce
> In Yerlond & Walys, in Angoye & Normandye,
> In Ynglond also, I haue had the governaunce.
> I haue worne the crown, & wrought vyctoryouslye,
> And now do purpose by practyse and by stody
> To reforme the lawes and sett men in good order,
> That trew iustyce may be had in every bordere.
>
> (ll. 9, 15–21)

To this monarch appears a character very much like Udall's Respublica in outward attributes. Like Respublica she is a poor widow, representing the decay of the commonwealth. Her name, however, is Widow England, and rather than naïve innocence she brings a list of specific grievances and open accusations against her oppressors, the clergy.

Hardly has England begun her indictment when a courtier named Sedition intrudes upon the scene to bait England, scattering obscenities and praise of the Pope. Silencing the diversion the King promises England redress of her grievances. Meanwhile, Sedition makes clear his allegiance and lists for the King and the audience his multitude of disguises, his omnipresence in all clerical orders and nations, everywhere in the service of the Pope:

> For his holy cawse I mayntayne traytors and rebelles,
> That no prince can haue his peoples obedyence,
> Except yt doth stand, with the popes prehemynence.
>
> (ll. 218–20)

Warning King John that he will be deposed if he flaunts the Church's authority, Sedition leaves to assume one of his religious disguises.

Scorning Sedition's warnings, the King calls the three estates of society before him and castigates them for allowing England to have fallen into decay. Nobility and Civil Order (representing the Lords Temporal and the judiciary) agree to mend their ways. Clergy, on the other hand, demonstrates rebellious pretensions of grandeur and raises the ire of the King:

> CLERGY Yff yow continue, ye wyll holy chyrch confounde.
> KYNG IOHAN Nay, no holy chyrch, nor feythful congregacyon,
> But an hepe of adders of Antechrists generacyon.
>
> (ll. 491–3)

In the end Clergy submits to the King, who issues a call to the three estates to discharge their duties faithfully in the interest of the commonwealth:

> For the love of God, loke to the state of Englond!
> Leate non enemy holde her in mysrable bond
> Se yow defend her as yt becummyth nobilite,
> Se yow instructe her acordyng to your degre,
> Fournysh her yow wtth a cyuyle honeste,
> Thus shall she florysh in honor & grett plente.
>
> (ll. 527–32)

This opening sequence of Bale's play is traditional in many respects. It asserts the order of royalty against which the disorder of vice (in clerical garb) will be pitted. It establishes the King as, in one sense, a central figure of mankind. The King begins the play in some degree of innocence, to the extent that he holds an exaggerated view of his own actual power and a simultaneous unawareness of the true 'state of England.'

We can detect in Bale's play, however, some experimental modifications in the dynamics of morality characterization. Not all of these are entirely successful. The potential effectiveness of the play's beginning is marred by the premature (dramatically unmotivated) diatribe which colors every attack upon the Church. Such violent rhetoric is untraditional and unseemly for sympathetic representative figures like England and the King. Moreover, the traditional encounter of tempter and mutable humanity loses its effectiveness when the tempter, instead of dissembling, proclaims his viciousness for all to hear. Bale is more successful in splitting the role of the central mankind figure. The King, though embodying man (with the three estates as attributes), also acts as an agent of repentance. The part of human representative devolves on the three estates, to a significant extent. In a real sense this provides the play with two points of focus – the King as tragic hero, and the three estates as figures of commonwealth in the political morality play.

The troubles of England – caused by excessive power of the Church – reach a temporary solution with the departure of Sedition and the ostensible submissions of Clergy and the other estates. Like the King in *Wisdom*, John leads the three powers to repentance, but here there is no sense of finality – there is no reclothing of England to match the regeneration of Anima in the earlier play. There are, instead, intimations of a quick falling-off. The King has hardly left the stage when Clergy reasserts his authority over Nobility and plans a petition to Rome for assistance.

The second sequence of the play, corresponding to the con-spiratorial scenes of the state of sin in earlier plays, is considerably more traditional. A conspiracy of Clergymen – Sedition, Dis-simulation, Private Wealth, and Usurped Power – plot subversion, like the gallants of *Respublica* and the intriguers of *Magnificence*, and take up disguises and assumed names.[45] Instead of plotting to enter the service of a ruler, however, they are plotting his overthrow. And instead of disguising themselves as virtuous advisers, they gradually take up the identities of historical characters. Dissimulation is a messenger from the English Clergy, and he is amazed to see Usurped Power reveal himself as the Pope. Sedition, it develops, is Stephen Langton, newly-created Archbishop of Canterbury.

As Pope Innocent III, Usurped Power conducts on stage the cere-mony of King John's excommunication with bell, book, and candle. Private Wealth, now Cardinal Pandulphus, embarks as papal legate to threaten King John with further punishments. Sedition, alias Stephen Langton, departs to rally bishops and nobles to rebel against the King. Dissimulation, now named Raymundus, goes as messenger to the other Christian kings, with papal blessing, to order them to attack England and to depose the King.[46] Pope Innocent III remains in Rome to consolidate his tyrannical power. His next act, he announces, will be to call the Fourth Lateran Council of 1215; one of its heinous acts will be the installation of the sacrament of penance, making 'ear confession a matter necessary.'[47]

The usefulness of the new sacrament is quickly demonstrated in the assault of the Church against the power of King John. It is used in the subversion of the three estates. Sedition appears before Nobility, offering him a clean remission of all sins. Nobility agrees and begins humbly to confess, in considerable detail. Sedition shows no interest in such trivia, except to be assured that Nobility knows his prayers by rote and is uninfected by the 'new learning.' Before granting absolution, however, Sedition demands that Nobility take the Church's part and rebel against the King. Nobility at first refuses to consider such an act of rebellion, but he finally agrees under threat of damnation:[48]

> NOBILITY Than I submyt me to the chyrches reformacyon,
> SEDITION I assoyle the here from þe kynges obedyence
> By þe avctoryte of þe popys magnifycence:
> *Avctoritate romani pontyficis ego absoluo te*
> From all possessyons gebyn to þe spiritualte,
> *In nomine domine pape, amen.*
>
> (ll. 1183–8)

No sooner is Nobility gone than Clergy appears, bringing with him Civil Order, who offers to mediate the quarrel between monarch and Church. When Sedition offers him the blessing of holy relics and papal bulls, however, Civil Order admits to a dependence on church patronage and falls in with the rebellion. The subversion of the three estates is complete.

Now Pandulphus the papal legate comes to demand compliance from the King. When the King refuses, the legate declares him excommunicated and absolves John's subjects from obedience to him. The King turns for support to his three estates, but they deny him.

Here Bale effectively borrows the obligatory crisis scene of the morality. King John finds himself, like Everyman, abandoned by his attributes in the hour of need. His appeal for allegiance to Commonalty is also in vain, for this figure is led in, weak and blind, by his mother, Widow England. They, in their weakness, cannot help the King, nor can the King be of any help to them. England nevertheless proclaims her unswerving loyalty and explains the condition of Commonalty:

> His owtward blyndnes ys but a syngnyficiacion
> Of blyndnes in sowle for lacke of infomacyon
> In the word of God . . .
> . . . .
> Yf your grace wold cawse Godes word to be taw3t
>   syncerly
> And subdew those pristes that wyll not preche yt
>   trewly
> The peple shuld know to ther prynce þer lawfull dewty.
>
> (ll. 1582–4, 1586–8)

In this case, however, there is no time for such reform. The Cardinal returns to carry away Commonalty and to announce the open revolt of the three estates and the pending invasion of foreign powers from all sides. Fearing bloodshed and abandoned by all but England, John has no choice but to give up the crown (his last attribute of temporal power) and submit himself to the Pope's mercy. Meanwhile, Dissimulation arrives with a final plan: he proposes to poison King John. Langton supplies Dissimulation with the identity of Simon of Swinsett, a Cistercian monk, and absolves him of all sin.

King John re-enters, a beaten man, wishing to be relieved of the responsibilities of kingship. England tries in vain to comfort him, and Simon of Swinsett comes with a poisoned cup, which the monk contrives to have the King share with him. England returns to the King in time to inform him that he has been betrayed. Facing death, King John regrets his inability to discharge his office as king, asks the prayers of his people for God's mercy on his soul, and forgives those who have abandoned him:

> Your disobedyence I do forgyue yow all
> And desyre God to perdon your iniquyte.
> Farwell, swete Englande, now last of all to the;
> I am ryght sorye I coulde do for the nomore.
>
> (ll. 2176–9)

England, mourning for her king, follows him from the stage to see to his burial.

For all of its morality conventions, Part One of *King John* presents a fundamentally tragic action: the fall of the King from his position of eminence, a systematic decline which culminates in his deposition and murder. At the same time John is no raging tyrant, but the model of a Christian prince. Within limitations, Part One of *King John* is a Christian tragedy. The normal medieval concept of tragedy is providential, in the sense that it shows the working out of retribution or the cyclical turn of fortune. In *King John* this concept is modified by the direct political purposes of the play, and by Bale's apocalyptic interpretation of history. It seems clear that Bale believed literally in the Protestant identification of the Pope as Antichrist. This belief, based on an alleged pact of Pope Sylvester II with the devil in AD 999, sanctions the theory that evil has been ruling the world. King John is the tragic victim of the power of Antichrist.[49]

With Bale's experimental example at hand, it is easy enough to see the potentialities for tragedy inherent in the traditional falling action of the morality state of sin. The desertion of John's attributes recalls the similar events of *Everyman*, but also prefigures the deposition and murder scenes of Elizabethan political tragedy. The focus of this natural development, as we have seen, is the representative figure of the king. But *King John*, taken as a whole, is not a tragedy. The death of John is not the conclusion of the play, but the culmination of the state of sin and the beginning of the action which will bring about the regeneration of the commonwealth.

Between the first and second 'acts'[50] of *King John* (between the scenes of conspiracy and assault), Bale has inserted a speech explaining the topical intent of the play, the significance of King John's struggle with the Church:

> Ypon a good zele he attempted very farre
> For welthe of thys realme to prouyde reformacyon
> In the churche thereof. But they did hym debarre
> Of that good purpose, for by excommunycacyon
> The space of vii yeares they interdyct thys nacyon.
>
> (ll. 1093-7)

The 'interpreter' compares England to Israel, and King John to Moses attempting to lead her out of Pharaoh's slavery to the promised land, an event postponed

> Tyll that duke Iosue, whych was our late kynge Henrye,
> Clerely brought vs in to the lande of mylke and honye.
> As a stronge Dauid at the voyce of verytie,
> Great Golye, the pope, he strake down with hys slynge,
> Restorynge agayne to a Christen lybertie
> Hys lande and people, lyke a most vyctoryouse kynge.
>
> (ll. 1112-17)

Udall, writing in 1553, could depict the Reformation as a momentary political lapse. From Bale's standpoint, whether beforehand (1538) or afterward (1561),[51] the Reformation was not the temporary cause of England's misfortunes, but the permanent solution to them. It is this solution which he dramatizes in the final scenes of *King John* and to which the events of the historical reign of King John are as prologue. Like writers of history plays from Euripides to Brecht, Bale dramatizes events not primarily in the interests of reconstructing the past but with the idea of illuminating the present. Thus King John's quarrel with the Church prefigures, and motivates, the Reformation.

With the exit of England and the dying King, the play dissolves out of its historical figure into a contemporary setting. Verity enters to assess King John's sixteenth-century reputation, citing numerous authorities who speak well of his actions, despite Polydore Virgil and other biased detractors. The view of John as a wicked king is expressed by Nobility, Clergy, and Civil Order, entering (in their sixteenth-century reincarnations) to question Verity's conclusions. Verity rebukes the three estates both for present irreverence to royalty and for past actions:

> I am Veritas, that come hyther yow to blame
> For castynge awaye of our most lawfull kynge.
> Both God and the Worlde detesteth your dampnable
> doynge.
>
> (ll. 2282–4)

Like his namesake in *Respublica*, Verity thus functions as a traditional morality agent of remorse, moving the three estates to repentance by confronting them with the truth of their condition.[52]

Hardly have Nobility, Clergy, and Civil Order begged and received forgiveness from Verity when a figure of retribution enters to confront the three estates. It is Imperial Majesty, who represents the full regeneration of the English monarchy in its sixteenth-century vigor:

> And how do they lyke the custome they haue vsed
> With our predecessours, whome they haue so abused,
> Specyally kynge Iohan? Thynke they they haue done
> well?
>
> (ll. 2321–3)

Nobility, Clergy, and Civil Order kneel, ask pardon of the King and pledge to have nothing further to do with Sedition, Private Wealth, Usurped Power, or Dissimulation.

Bale makes imaginative use of morality conventions in this scene, bringing present truth (Verity) to bear on the three estates, causing them to repent of their past betrayal of the monarchy. The three estates play the traditional role of the mankind figure (in multiple form, as in *Hickscorner* and *Wisdom*). To give historical continuity, Bale uses the three estates with a fine medieval disregard for simple chronology, linking their past responsibility for King John's death and their present sixteenth-century need for repentance and obedience. The figure of Imperial Majesty compels their repentance and embodies its goals – a reformed commonwealth, a revived and reincarnate monarchy. Imperial Majesty succeeds, where King John failed, in carrying out the necessary reformation. The terms of this reformation are political and, as Verity points out, sanctioned by Scripture. The King is sovereign, under God:

> For in hys owne realme a kynge is iudge ouer all
> By Gods appoyntment . . .
> . . . .

> He is a mynyster immedyate vndre God,
> Of hys ryghteousnesse to execute the rod.
> I charge yow, therfor, as God hath charged me,
> To gyue to your kynge hys due supremyte
> And exyle the pope thys realme for euermore.
>
> (ll. 2347–8, 2356–60)

When Imperial Majesty rephrases Verity's statement into a royal proclamation, Clergy offers to arrange for Imperial Majesty to become Supreme Head of the Church. He is rebuked for presumption, such powers being already bestowed on a king by God and not the Clergy's to give away. Nobility pledges his loyalty to the King, and Civil Order offers a petition concerning the Pope:

> Of the Christen faythe playe now the true defender;
> Exyle thys monster and rauenouse deuourer.
>
> (ll. 2427–8)

Imperial Majesty bids the three estates to rule, speak, and judge in the name of the Holy Scriptures. They pledge to exile Usurped Power and Sedition, to hang Dissimulation, and to expel Private Wealth from the Monasteries.

The identification of Imperial Majesty with Henry VIII, and these events with the English Reformation, is obvious. Where Udall discreetly clothed the accession of Mary Tudor in allegorical conceits, Bale is, as always, blatantly direct, even in his use of contemporary terminology. The notion of a *true* defender of the faith could only be intended to recall the title Henry had received from Pope Leo X in 1520; the term 'Supreme Head of the Church,' grudgingly allowed to Henry by the clergy in 1530, had been confirmed without qualification by the Act of Supremacy in 1534. The final act of breach with Rome – the suppression of the monasteries (1536) – also finds its place in *King John*, as we have seen. What is missing, of course, is any reference to Henry's quarrel with the papacy over his divorce. Imperial Majesty, unlike his prototype, ordains the Reformation with impersonal objectivity.

The repentance of the three estates and the new felicity of the commonwealth are quickly tested by the reappearance of Sedition. The three estates demonstrate their change of heart by offering to execute him posthaste. Pleading to the King for his life, Sedition promises a full confession, including the secrets of the confessional. He warns Imperial Majesty that many clerics are not carrying out the spirit of the Reformation and that the uprising in the North (the Pilgrimage of Grace of 1536) will not be the last:

> In some byshoppes howse ye shall not fynde a testament,
> But yche man readye to deuoure the innocent,
> We lyngar a tyme and loke but for a daye
> To sett vpp the pope, if the Gospell woulde decaye.
>
> (ll. 2548–51)

Humored this far by Imperial Majesty, Sedition goes on to admit that he has plotted 'to haue serued yow, lyke as I ded Kynge Iohn' (l. 2528). Though Imperial Majesty has previously promised immunity for Sedition, he now condemns the confessed traitor to be hanged and quartered, and his head displayed on London Bridge. Despite the severity of this sentence Sedition has intimations of immortality:

> Some man tell the pope, I besyche ye with all my harte,
> How I am ordered for takynge the churches parte,
> That I maye be put in the holye letanye
> With Thomas Beckett, for I thynke I am as wurthye,
> Praye to me with candels, for I am a saynt alreadye.
>
> (ll. 2587–91)

The accession of Imperial Majesty and the condemnation of Sedition bring this study to an indicative juncture. The act of confession, which once led the sinner to salvation, is now the prelude to an execution. The act, in demonstration of which the morality play had its beginnings, has now become, in England, a discredited relic of superstition. The morality play, freed from its original purpose, moves toward a new identity. Mankind, the religious hero of the morality drama, is now a political creature of the Elizabethan Age.

Imperial Majesty urges the three estates to profit by the example of Sedition. He accepts their repentance and proclaims his intention to institute such reforms as will fully suppress the powers of Antichrist. The actors pay tribute to the Queen, who has shown her godly ways by encouraging the English Bible and suppressing heretics. The play ends with prayers for a long and prosperous reign for Queen Elizabeth and her descendants.

Chapter V

Early Elizabethan plays in the morality tradition

The traditional morality play had both an immediate and a delayed influence on the Elizabethan drama. In the ultimate sense it provided the inherited mythic idea of a theatrical treatise on the human condition – a fabric of dramatic assumptions out of which great plays of the order of *Dr Faustus*, *Henry IV, Part One*, *Measure for Measure*, *Othello*, *Volpone*, and *King Lear* could be created. In the direct sense, however, the morality play appeared to the Elizabethans as a set of traditional stage conventions of plot and character that could be put to many useful and contemporary theatrical purposes in the emerging popular drama. The nearly thirty years that separate Elizabeth's accession from the staging of Marlowe's *Tamburlaine* constitute a formative and confusing period of change in English drama, and an examination of the existing corpus of plays from that period shows how central the morality tradition is to the process of change. Of the sixty-one extant English plays from the period 1558–86, some twenty-eight can be plausibly connected with the morality tradition and they are of many sorts: moral interludes, tragedies, 'youth' plays, academic allegories, satiric comedies, neo-classical legends, Biblical plays, histories, and romances:[1]

Year	Plays in morality tradition	Total extant plays	Summary of other extant plays, by genre
1558	*Mary Magdalene*	2	1 tragedy
1559	*Patient and Meek Grissell* *The Longer Thou Livest, the More Fool Thou Art*	3	1 tragedy
1560	*The Disobedient Child* *Enough is as Good as a Feast* *Tom Tyler and His Wife*	5	1 tragedy, 1 May game play
1561	*Pedlar's Prophecy* *Cambises*	3	1 tragedy
1562	*Gorboduc*	1	
1563		1	1 tragedy
1564	*Appius and Virginia*	2	1 comedy

Year	Plays in morality tradition	Total extant plays	Summary of other extant plays, by genre
1565	King Darius	2	1 tragicomedy
1566		7	6 tragedies, 1 comedy
1567	Horestes	3	1 tragedy
	Trial of Treasure		
1568	Free Will	3	
	Like Will to Like		
	The Marriage of Wit and Science		
1569	Virtuous and Godly Susanna	1	
1570	Misogonus	3	1 romance, 1 comedy
1571	New Custom	1	
1572	Conflict of Conscience	3	1 tragedy, 1 masque
1573			
1574	Interlude of Minds	1	
1575	Glass of Government	2	1 tragedy
1576	Tide Tarrieth No Man	2	
	Common Conditions		
1577	All For Money	1	
1578		1	1 comedy
1579	Marriage Between Wit and Wisdom	1	
1580		1	1 pastoral
1581	Three Ladies of London	3	1 pastoral, 1 tragedy
1582	Triumphs of Love and Fortune	1	
1583			
1584		4	3 comedies, 1 dialogue
1585		1	1 comedy
1586		3	1 dialogue, 1 history, 1 tragedy

In this profusion of experiments three early Elizabethan dramatic inventions based on the morality emerge as of particular interest and importance. They are the nascent traditions of moral comedy, the political history play, and homiletic tragedy.

1 Moral comedy

The numerous printed texts of Elizabethan moral interludes from the 1560s and 1570s document the emergence of a didactic and ethical drama, concerned with problems of everyday human behavior and earthly justice rather than ultimate questions of salvation. Recent critics such as Alan Dessen, Edgar Schell, and J. D. Shuchter have reconstructed a theatrical context for this 'transitional and experimental drama,'[2] apparently devised largely by Elizabethan clerics and schoolmasters for pedagogic purposes. These early Elizabethan amateur playwrights, writing in serviceable if unpoetic verse, applied Humanistic and Calvinistic interpretations to contemporary social conditions. Using the morality theater as a pulpit, they attacked ignorance, injustice and corruption in the increasingly prosperous and complicated Elizabethan society. In the process, they gradually molded the conventional morality comic devices of plot and character into the tradition of Jonsonian corrective comedy.

The process of adaptation may be observed very distinctly in the extant series of 'youth' plays written over a sixty-year period preceding the opening of the public theaters. The interlude of *Youth* (1520), still firmly within the medieval morality tradition, employs rebellious Youth as a theological figure of speech, to dramatize for its audience the innate fallibility of individual mankind, and the 'maturity' of salvation which is possible if man repents. In later plays this figure of speech becomes increasingly literal. The sixteenth-century plays which follow *Youth* come more and more to depict juvenile behavior as a troublesome social phenomenon. In the Protestant polemic *Lusty Juventus* (1550) the youthfulness of the hero (in *Youth* merely the *occasion* of sin) becomes the *cause* of his misbehavior. In the state of sin Juventus is misled by gamey (and Roman Catholic) vices; in the state of repentance he is called to a puritanical rejection of his misspent youth, and salvation by faith rather than good works.[3]

Nice Wanton (1550), a didactic case study of three adolescents, 'twoo naught, and one godlye,'[4] carries the process a significant step further. Here the admonitory possibility is raised that erring youths may stray too far from God's mercy to escape justice, at least in the earthly sense. In *Nice Wanton* the three young people are raised in a dangerous state of innocence, propelled toward sin by an all-forgiving mother. Two of the three, Ishmael and Dalilah, throw away their books (*Nice Wanton* being an early instance of the social gospel of education) and follow the Vice Iniquity into a delightful and dramatically effective sequence of debauchery. From the wages of this prodigality they are *not* saved; their virtuous (and noxious) brother Barnabas lives to see his erring brother and sister come to a bad end: Dalilah sickens and dies of the pox; Ishmael turns thief, is caught, tried, and taken off to be executed and hanged in chains as a public display. The sequence of repentance in this grim little object lesson of a play has become vestigial and subsidiary: before she dies, Dalilah passes across the stage in rags lamenting her upbringing, Ishmael implicates and denounces the Vice Iniquity, *en route* to the scaffold; and the Mother is saved, on the point of remorseful suicide, by her virtuous and scolding son:

> Beware what ye do! fye, mother fye!
> Wyl ye spyl your-selfe for your own offence,
> And seme for-ever to exclude God's mercy?
> God doth punysh you for your negligence.
> Wherefore take his correction with pacience.
>
> (ll. 489–93)

For all of its moralizing, however, *Nice Wanton* has a comic exuberance which transcends the admonitions. This aspect of the play, particularly evident in performance, has been noted by Glynne Wickham who recalls it as 'a stunning vehicle for clowns . . . an entertainment within the tradition of the Feast of Fools and the Lord of Misrule.'[5]

In *Nice Wanton* and Thomas Ingeland's *The Disobedient Child* (1560) the morality is frankly adapted to the purposes and occasion of a school play. The imagined audience of parents and children is lectured on the dire consequences of youthful sin, and the necessity of parental discipline. In the process original sin has to some extent been redefined as a social malady. The preoccupation of the Elizabethan moral comedies and much of their entertainment quotient is in the vivid portrayal of wrongdoing. As Bernard Spivack has shown, the machinations of the principal Vice become correspondingly more prominent and ironic; in the resulting 'comedy of evil' the villainous protagonist serves to engineer the punishment of malefactors.

Two later examples of the youth morality tradition, George Gascoigne's prose comedy *Glass of Government* (1575) and the spirited manuscript play *Misogonus* (1570) show the ease with which the traditional morality could be fused with classical elements into neo-Terentian prodigal son comedies, complete with pithy quotations from Horace, mistaken identity plots and regular five-act structure, no longer teaching the concept of Everyman, but rather the injunction of 'spare the rod and spoil the child.'

It is in this fashion that the untidy dramatic genre of early Elizabethan moral comedy comes to evolve, with its unique jumble of intellectual and theatrical elements: admonitory satire, stage horseplay, morality figures, the Vice, classical allusions, and Calvinism. Where once the morality featured a single and mutable central figure, the moral comedies begin to multiply and differentiate their heroes.

Though fairly new to the English stage, multiple and multi-fated central figures are not by any means a sixteenth-century Calvinist innovation. A prominent series of French dualistic moralities, including *Bien-Avisé, Mal-Avisé* (1439) and *L'Homme juste et l'Homme mondain* (1476) feature parallel and contrasted heroes: the repentant achieving redemption and the unrepentant, damnation. What the English Calvinist playwrights add is a decisive change in the odds. In Ulpian Fulwell's *Like Will to Like, Quoth the Devil to the Collier* (1568) there are six predestined reprobates and only one persevant hero. The theme of the play is set in its appended subtitle: 'Wherein is declared not only what punishment followeth those that will rather follow licentious living than to esteem and follow good counsel: and what great benefits and commodities they receive that apply them unto virtuous living and good exercises.'[6] Yet the texture of Fulwell's play is unmistakably comic, from the opening monologue of the Vice, Nicholas Newfangle, to its gallows humor ending, with the dispatch of Cuthbert Cutpurse and Pierce Pickpurse by a jovial hangman, and the departure for hell of Newfangle, riding on the back of Lucifer.

What begins to take shape in the early years of Elizabeth's reign, then, is a tradition of corrective comedy, derived from the didactic dramaturgy of the morality play, but also proceeding from humanistic interpretations of comedy (in the footsteps of Plautus and Terence) as moral philosophy. These plays seem puritanically obsessed with the omnipresence of evil. Corruption lurks in every alley, usually perceived in terms of economic and social abuses.[7] In the anonymous *Trial of Treasure* (1567) the familiar morality scene of temptation blends sexual and economic connotations with classical allusions:[8]

INCLINATION But hark you, Master Lust, if I may do you pleasure, Whisper, whisper.
LUST　　　　　She is called Treasure.
O, my heart is on fire till she come in place.
INCLINATION O Master Lust, she hath an amiable face
A tricker, a trimmer, in faith that she is
The goddess of wealth, prosperity and bliss . . . .
LUST Sith that the apple of Paris before me is cast
And that I may deliver the same where I will

I would Prometheus were here to holp me hold fast
That I might have a forewit with me ever still.

Cautiously and often ineptly, early Elizabethan comedy begins to probe the materialistic hypocrisies of a society in which Christian theory and middle-class practice were becoming more and more at odds. In the hands of a Jonson, a Fielding, or a Brecht such dramatic *exposés* can produce superb comic theater; in the 1560s and 1570s, however, the result is inexplicable dumb shows, satirical invective, a scattering of hilarious moments, and an habitual belaboring of the obvious.

The difficulties of reconciling realistic dissections of social condition and a morality plot are evident in George Wapull's *The Tide Tarrieth No Man* (1576).[9] The Vice Courage functions during the bulk of the play as a master of ceremonies, preaching the doctrine of *carpe diem* to assorted representative figures of contemporary misbehavior, including a would-be courtier, a greedy moneylender, a charming young thing called Wilful Wanton, and her ne'er-do-well husband Wastefulness. Late in the play agents of repentance (Christianity and Faithful Few) enter for the first time and conclude the festivities with a highly traditional and sententious morality repentance sequence. But the balance of the playwright's emphasis has of necessity shifted decisively toward satire and comedy. Wapull is one of a number of dramatists in the period who are writing, as David Bevington has demonstrated, for the early and rudimentary professional companies of 'Four men and a Boy.'[10] For these traveling players, Wapull and his colleagues provided plays moral enough to please local authorities, and comic enough to entertain local audiences. The expedient doubling of parts in such plays transmitted yet another morality tradition from the medieval to the Elizabethan stage.

A Moral and Pitiful Comedy, entitled All For Money (1577), the work of Thomas Lupton, illustrates quite well the morality play in its late stages of comic transformation. Lupton, principally known as a writer of tracts, begins his play with a lengthy prologue, looking backward to *Nature* and forward to *Faustus*, in which the arts and sciences, including Medicine, Music, Cosmography, Astrology and Theology, are placed in a moral hierarchy, in opposition to the pursuit of worldly gain. Instead of dramatizing this conflict, however, Lupton embarks on a series of *tableaux moralisés*. First we are shown personified figures (Science, Art, Theology and so forth) disputing in learned terms, trading lengthy collections of pithy Latin epigrams. There follows a scene, consciously and rather laboriously allegorical, in which personified Money, falling ill, pretends to vomit up a series of odious vices (e.g. Prest-for-Pleasure, Swift-to-Sin, and 'snottynose' Satan with his two sons, Gluttony and Pride).

Following this scene, in conformity with the play's music hall structure, there ensues a lengthy dispute between the various possible combinations of Learning and Affluence (i.e. Money without Learning, Learning without Money, Learning with Money, and Neither Money nor Learning). The dialogue consists once more of exchanges of proverbs and sententiae:[11]

> LEARNING-WITH Your wise words have brought this
> sentence to mind,
> > Written in *Tertio Tuscalorum*,
> > where you may it find:
> > *Omnes, cum secundae, tum*
> *maxime secum meditari oportet, quo pacto*
> *adversam aerumnam ferant.*
> > It is meet for all men when they
> be in prosperity
> > to meditate how to suffer trouble
> in adversity.

The skeptical reader of the playscript may well be tempted to suspect that the drama is, on one level, simply a mnemonic device to teach schoolchildren their Cicero. Whatever the truth of this suspicion, the size of the cast and lack of doubling makes a schoolboy cast quite likely. There are significant elaborations of the original idea of a morality play in *All For Money*, not merely in thematic terms, but also in stage action: All for Money 'aparelled like a ruler or magistrate' humbles himself before Money, then sits in majesty accepting bribes from a series of figures representing human frailty: thieves, bigamists, professional litigants, lecherous itinerant preachers and others, culminating in the figure of 'Mother Croote,' a repulsively goatish rustic anticipation of Mrs Malaprop. The dramatic occasion which such a summoning of humanity provides is generally missed in *All For Money*, but we are only something more than a generation away from the comic rogues-galleries of Ben Jonson, and the scent of possibilities is already in the air. *All For Money* ends with crashing incongruity, as Sin, the Vice of the play, introduces two attested residents of Hell, the Biblical figures of Judas and the rich man Dives, who are suffering 'all' for Money. They are driven back into hell by Damnation, to the strains of an *ubi sunt*:

> (Here he speaketh to Judas)
> Where is now thy money wherefore soldest thou thy master?

(Here he speaketh to Dives)
Where is now thy fare, wherin thou hadst thy pleasure?

(ll. 1406–7)

The audience is instructed to mediate on their punishment, repent of all avaricious practices, and pray for Queen Elizabeth, her Council, 'And all the high estates and commons of this region,' (l. 1470).

2 Political drama and the history play

Overtly political drama, which had flourished amid the controversy of the Reformation struggle during the reigns of Henry, Edward, and Mary Tudor, quickly expired in the moderate environment of the Elizabethan compromise. *King John* and *Respublica* were among the last of their polemical kind.[12] One of Queen Elizabeth's first official acts with respect to the drama, in a proclamation of May, 1599, was to order the suppression of controversial plays. Henceforth no plays whatever were to be performed unless licensed by local authorities, who were instructed 'that they permyt none to be played wherein either matters of religion or of the gouernaunce of the estate of the common weale shalbe handled or treated.'[13] This act, the culmination of a trend which began in the early days of the Reformation, established the precise limitations of subject matter within which the Elizabethan drama would operate. By sanctioning a suppression not only of political plays but also of the popular religious drama, governmental policy helped to bring into being, in the form which they ultimately took, Elizabethan secularized professional drama and the public theaters of the last quarter of the sixteenth century.[14]

The prohibition of political and religious controversy on the stage had its inevitable effects on the morality play which had been from the beginning a drama of religious ideas. Its original didactic purpose of calling the sinner to repentance had evolved into socio-political purposes in the plays of Medwall, Skelton, Lindsay, Bale, and Udall.

The official suppression of stage polemics had the effect of blunting and diverting this development of the morality play at a crucial moment. The king figure, and the moral allegory of commonwealth in which he existed, could no longer be presented as thinly veiled representations of contemporary political intrigue. Instead it was now legally necessary to differentiate the worlds of theatrical fiction and political fact. The paths followed by the morality were the ones anticipated in the tragic and historical setting of Bale's *King John*. Political issues could be disputed and staged within the relatively safe context of far-off historical events, subtly linked to the contemporary moment by analogy. Past tragedy could be viewed as present lesson. The central and mutable king could be seen as a tragic and representative figure of the body politic, and ultimately, by a logical extension, as a figure of the human condition. The path of the Elizabethan morality leads ironically and brilliantly back to the paradox of mankind and the political microcosm, thanks in interesting measure to Elizabethan attempts at censorship of political controversy on the stage.

By the late 1580s there is an established genre of English history plays, built on the foundations of morality structure and typically embodying contemporary political implications. Two notable plays, *Jack Straw* (1591) and *Woodstock* (1591) use the historical figure of Richard II's reign, and the conventions of the morality play, to make political statements about Elizabethan conditions. *Jack Straw* deals unsympathetically with the Peasants' Rebellion of 1381 and commends loyalty to the monarchy, in the person of a saintly King Richard.

Woodstock, by contrast, emphasizes the pernicious influence of bad advisers in the early years of Richard's reign, leading to the murder of Thomas of Woodstock, the Earl of Gloucester; its aim is to warn an Elizabethan audience of the same dangers, and it does so, as A. P. Rossiter has shown, by distorting historical fact to suit the structure of a political morality play. These plays, the culmination of a tradition that goes back to Skelton's *Magnificence*, are the immediate predecessors of Shakespeare's history cycles. *Woodstock* is now acknowledged to be a direct and crucial influence on Marlowe's *Edward II* and Shakespeare's *Richard II*.[15]

The complex transition from *Magnificence* to *Richard II* is achieved through an Elizabethan dramatic form – the history play – which develops in large measure logically and directly out of the morality tradition. The important transitional works here are two very different histories of the 1560s: *Gorboduc*, a blank verse pseudo-Senecan object lesson to Elizabeth on the dangers of diversion in a kingdom, and *Cambises*, a 'mungrel tragy-comedy' about a young king who blossoms into an oriental tyrant.

Gorboduc (1562) was written by two young and influential members of Queen Elizabeth's parliament: Thomas Sackville, author of the best-remembered portions of the *Mirror For Magistrates*, and Thomas Norton, Protestant reformer and translator of Calvin. The play tells the story of an old king who divides his kingdom, on the advice of bad counselors, between his two sons Ferrex and Porrex. The result is murder, civil war, social revolution and the ultimate political tragedy of chaos in a leaderless kingdom. There are many obvious anticipations of the tragedy of *King Lear*: an old king, a division of the kingdom, a resulting civil war, and the interesting precedent that both Lear and Gorboduc are legendary historical kings of ancient Britain. From the point of view of the evolving morality tradition, two characteristics of *Gorboduc* are most significant: its literary quality, and its subtle adaptation of the conventions of the political morality play.

Gorboduc is written in verse of a sophistication unknown in previous exemplars of the morality tradition. That it is in *blank* verse (and as such the first Elizabethan blank verse tragedy) has perhaps tended to obscure the more significant fact that it is in very *good* verse – or at least verse good enough to catch the ear of Sidney, who mentions the play favorably in his otherwise unfavorable account of the drama of the early Elizabethan decades, 'mungrel tragy-comedy mixing Kings and Clowns.' The following example, a speech by the tempter Hermon, urging the Prince to murder his brother, is characteristic. If the verse is hardly as good as Shakespeare's (or Sidney's) it is a great deal better than that of any morality since *Everyman*:[16]

> But, if the feare of goddes and secret grudge
> Of nature's law, repining at the fact,
> Withholde your courage from so great attempt,
> Know ye that lust of kingdom hath no law: . . . .
> Murders and violent theftes in private men
> Are hanious crimes and full of foule reproach,
> Yet none offence, but deckt with glorious name
> Of noble conquests, in the handes of kinges.

Gorboduc's reputation for being a neo-Senecan tragedy, which is deserved only in such superficial respects as act division and the presence of a recurrent chorus, has impeded a perception of the degree to which the play belongs to the tradition of the political drama as a Tudor variation on the original morality idea. *Gorboduc*, like the plays of Lindsay, Udall, and Bale which we examined in a previous chapter, is written for an identifiable occasion and political purpose. It was first presented in the legal and highly political context of the Inner Temple of the Inns of Court, of which Sackville and Norton were both members; more important, it was subsequently presented by members of the Inner Temple before Queen Elizabeth herself, at Whitehall on 18 January 1562. The historical narrative of civil disorder in Gorboduc's ancient Britain is, in the exact manner of Bale, an elaborate figure by which a contemporary political statement may be advanced. Sackville and Norton dramatize the danger of an uncertain succession to the throne; they present in fictional terms the real threat of civil war which existed in Elizabeth's reign in the absence of an heir or a parliamentarily-approved line of succession.[17]

The devices of the morality play prove as useful and politically transferrable for Sackville and Norton as they had for their predecessors in this tradition, from Medwall to Udall. The central king figure inherits the representative and mutable function of the Mankind character, and his malicious and virtuous advisers offer temptation and the possibility of repentance, respectively. The good adviser Eubulus survives his king and the civil war to prophesy, out of the ruins of the tragedy, a better day for England. Eventually, since God is just,[18]

> . . . must God in fine restore
> This noble crowne unto the lawfull heire;
> For right will alwayes live and rise at length,
> But wrong can never take deepe roote, to last.

Thus *Gorboduc*, for all its tragic action, is a politically optimistic play. Sackville and Norton transpose its final moment out of the figurative past into the potentiality of the present, in a manner most reminiscent of Bale's *King John*. Fundamentally a political morality play in blank verse, *Gorboduc* illustrates the ways in which that tradition will help to define the presentation of politics and history on the Elizabethan stage of Marlowe and Shakespeare.

From a literary point of view *Cambises* (1561) is in every way a lesser piece of work than *Gorboduc*. Written in plodding 'fourteeners' by Thomas Preston, an otherwise uncertain figure, *Cambises*' contradictions of dramatic form arc infamously summed up in the full title of the first printed edition: 'A Lamentable Tragedie mixt full of pleasant mirth containing the Life of Cambises King of Percia, from the beginning of his kingdome unto his Death, his one good deede of execution, after that, many wicked deedes and tyranous murders committed by and through him, and last of all, his odious death by God's Justice appointed. . . .' This panoramic tale requires thirty-eight speaking parts, deftly arranged for eight busy professional actors. The ranting style of the verse is bad enough, and popular enough, to have come to Falstaff's mind when he prepared to impersonate a monarch in the 'play extempore' scene of *Henry IV, Part One*, promising to deliver his lines 'in passion, and I will do it in King Cambises vein.'[19] The vein is short on grace, but long on bombast and syllables:[20]

> Thou cursed Iill, by all the gods I take an
>   othe and sweare,
> That flesh of thine these hands of mine in
>   peeces small could tere. . . .

Like *Gorboduc*, *Cambises* adapts the devices of the political morality drama and the pretext of an historical setting, in this case an Elizabethan hyperbole of ancient Persia. Once more we have a central, mutable king figure with good and bad advisers. The latter group of tempters includes Ambidexter, the Vice and dissembling rogue who brings all the characters in the play to a bad end. It is he, ironic moralizer, who presides over the operation of God's justice, the ultimately triumphant force whose victory is promised from the beginning on the title page.

Thus the 'plesant mirth' of *Cambises* is by no means completely extraneous to its 'Lamentable Tragedy.' The temptations and responsibilities of royal power – those characteristic themes of Marlovian and Shakespearean tragedy – are already fully developed in *Cambises*, and the lures and snares of bad advice are demonstrated more fully by the quick-witted Ambidexter than by all the malicious courtiers of *Gorboduc*. For all of its crudeness, then, *Cambises* looks ahead theatrically. Ambidexter the tempter functions as an ambiguous moral force, foreshadowing such complex figures of the late stage as Mephistophilis, Bosola, and Iago. These Elizabethan and Jacobean tempters have their antecedents in the discoveries of a transitional play like *Cambises*, with its dawning comprehensions of the true ambiguity of evil.

The fall of King Cambises is 'tragic' mainly in a homiletic sense; that is, its meaning is not to be found in the inward tragedy of a wayward king, but in the lesson which that fall should provide, to the wise listener. The *speculum principis* convention of the political morality play gives Preston the obligation to relate his theatrical figure to the contemporary situation of the reigning monarch. His play, like so many of its generation, ends with a prayer (and implicit admonition) for Queen Elizabeth:

> And for her Honorable Councel, the truth that
>   they may use,
> To practice iustice and defend her Grace eche day;
> To maintain Gods woord they may not refuse,
> To correct all those that would her Grace
>   and Graces lawes abuse.
> Beseeching God over us she may raigne long,
> To be guided by truth and defended from wrong.
>
>   (ll. 1214–19)

The unspoken moral is, of course, that political tragedy will result if good counsel and just advice are not tendered, or heeded. Behind *Gorboduc* and *Cambises* stand a set of historical assumptions about the punishments which Divine Providence inflicts on tyrants and irresponsible rulers. These assumptions, implicit in the dramatic terms of the political morality play, will become explicit in Elizabethan history plays which evolve from it.

3 Homiletic tragedy

For so long as the central figure of the morality play represents all mankind, a tragic ending is ritualistically impossible. Mankind, fallen with Adam but redeemed by Christ, must needs repent and be saved. It is when dramatists begin to individualize, qualify or multiply Mankind, and place him in a particular human situation, that the logical possibility of tragedy occurs. Mankind must be saved, but kinds of man (the unrepentant sinner, the Worldly man) may be damned; Everyman must be saved, but a Faustus will be damned.

The increasingly pointed social satire of Elizabethan moralities produces a greater individuality and variety of vices, and in turn these individual sins and crimes demand correction and punishment. The shift of focus to the behavior of individual men on earth creates the moral imperative for comedy and tragedy. These kinds of drama for the Elizabethan (as for the Greek before him) are not diametrical opposites but complementary dramatic exemplifications of a single idea of justice.

The historical evidence to support this observation, for the Elizabethan drama, is in the hybrid moralities of the 1560s and 1570s. Once the figure of mankind is reduced to individual human terms, justice insists that reward, correction or retribution be carried out, according to the circumstances. Corrective comedy and retributive tragedy are thus born in a state of coexistence, often within a single awkward play of the homiletic kind which Sidney labeled 'mungrel tragy-comedy.'

As we have noted, early Elizabethan plays such as Fulwell's *Like Will to Like* (1568) explore both correction and retribution to their logical conclusions, while remaining moral comedies in most significant respects. There are similar plays of the period which present these comic and homiletic elements in the opposite configuration, emphasizing retribution. Like the moral comedies, these dramas are didactic and corrective. They show the punishment of vice according to the orthodox prescription of catechism and homily. They are intended as admonitions, proofs of the punishment which awaits the unrepentant kind of man or individual, and they end with episodes of despair and hellfire. For this reason, though they also contain without exception, comic characters and scenes, and even partially happy endings, we can discern them as an emerging genre of homiletic tragedy.[21]

William Wager's *Enough is as Good as a Feast* (1560) inherits most of the traditional elements of the morality play, beginning with a central mutable figure called Worldly Man, attended by agents of temptation and agents of repentance. Like the heroes of *Mankind* and *Mundus et Infans*, Worldly Man is called to an early and rather perfunctory repentance under the guidance of a figure called Heavenly Man,[22] and then subjected to an overwhelming series of temptations. Three tempters enter, disguise and rechristen themselves in a manner very reminiscent of their counterparts in *Magnificence* or *Respublica*, in order to trap Worldly Man. A rhetoric of Ciceronian tags does not obscure the medieval familiarity of the action:[23]

> COUVETOUS While you live, take heed; strive not against policy.
> The best of them all are glad of policy,
> Yea in Westminster Hall they use much policy.
> WORLDLY MAN *Prudentia noscit omnes* saith the noble man Tully;
> Policy knoweth all things both good and ill truly.

Worldly Man's sinfulness is expressed in economic terms, in his exploitation of a rustic tenant and an unpaid hireling. He has only just finished dismissing their suits with contempt when agents of repentance appear, a Prophet threatening hellfire and God's Plague bringing sudden retributive disasters on a scale recalling Job or Everyman.

It is at this point that Wager's alteration of the traditional morality rhythm begins. Though tormented with fears of death and damnation, Worldly Man does not become Mankind. He remains worldly, attended by Couvetous and preoccupied with his goods and possessions:

> O Policy, if I might not die, what a fellow would I be!
> In all this country should be none like unto me
> Sirrah, what a goodly turret have I made in my hall!
> But yet my banqueting house pleaseth me best of all.
> O, O, alas what a pang is this at my heart.
>
> (ll. 1325–9)

Despite the ministrations of a Physician, who gives theological as well as medical prescriptions, Worldly Man remains to the end an economic creature. He sets about writing his will and planning how his wife will deal with his creditors, but dies without having repented of anything, or ever having mentioned God's name. The vicious advisers withdraw, leaving the stage free for Satan to enter triumphantly, point the homiletic moral, and bear the body of Worldly Man off to hell. Nevertheless the play concludes with a reassertion of divine order, as agents of repentance re-enter, denouncing covetousness and praising God's mercy to those who will keep the faith, and economically speaking be satisfied with 'enough,' rather than a feast.

In the medieval morality play, the concluding stage convention of repentance and salvation gains something of its dramatic power from the unstaged alternative – the grim understanding that in any actual individual case another sort of ending always threatens. Wager's innovations begin with particularizing his central figure, and end in staging this grim alternative of retribution, while acknowledging and comprehending the old rhythm of forgiveness. Though its ending is uncompromising, there is nothing in Wager's play to suggest any questioning of the divine order. Thus it would be premature to see darkness and doubt in the tragedy of Worldly Man. *Enough is as Good as a Feast* may best be imagined as the photographic negative of a medieval morality play, a definition of the light by means of its shadows.

There are other plays of the period in which particularized descendants of the Mankind figure come to a 'tragic' end. Wager's other confirmed dramatic work *The Longer Thou Livest, the More Fool Thou Art* (1559) administers such a punishment to Moros the fool, in order to underline the dangers of rejecting knowledge and discipline. *Trial of Treasure* (1567), also possibly Wager's work, recounts the adventures of a young gallant named Lust, who refuses the entreaties of his companion character Just and reaps the ultimate reward of being carried off by Time.[24] The homiletic tragedians of the 1560s and 1570s moved experimentally from general cases to the particular, from Worldly Man to spectacular or legendary examples of worldly or sinful men. In doing so these playwrights invented what Bernard Spivack has called 'the Hybrid Play,' an adaptation of morality conventions to the biography of an historical or legendary character.[25] John Pickering found material for the homiletic stage in the legend of Orestes, as medievalized in Caxton's *Recuyell of the Historyes of Troye*. Pickering's *Horestes, an Interlude of Vice* (1567)[26] is provided with a central mutable hero and a Vice who is Revenge in disguise. Tempted by the Vice, Horestes wreaks his vengeance on Egistus and Clytemnestra, his father's murderers.

Though he killed his mother, Horestes is forgiven on the grounds that he has only carried out the will of the gods. The ending of *Horestes* avoids tragedy by reverting to the traditional rhythm of the morality play (and also of course to the original resolution of the Orestes legend in the *Oresteia* and Caxton) but with significant ambiguities. The play raises but does not resolve the issue of whether murder is justified by the duty of revenge. Moreover Horestes' forgiveness is not bought by repentance. By focusing on the crime of Egistus and Clytemnestra, Pickering is able to conclude a tale of homiletic and tragic punishment with the semblance of a morality ending.

A feature of the evolving morality tradition in the early years of Elizabeth's reign which has not been sufficiently noted is the sequence of plays with female central figures. Lewis Wager's *The Life and Repentance of Mary Magdalene* (1558) easily adapts the career of this famous repentant sinner to the dramatic sequence of the morality play, with Magdalene tempted but ultimately victorious over the Vice Infidelity.[27] In most of these plays, however, the prototype is not a fallen Magdalene but a persevering Griselda. This legend is dramatized by John Phillip as *Patient and Meek Grissell* (1559), and mirrored in two Biblical plays: the anonymous *Godly Queen Hester* (1527), which is about Esther, and Thomas Garter's *Virtuous and Godly Susanna* (1569), which stages the story of Susanna and the Elders.[28] In both of these plays, the feminine virtues and reward of the heroines are contrasted with the masculine perfidies and punishments of their tempters. In this sense the plays contain, within their dramatic structures, subordinate homiletic tragedies. There are a number of interesting ways, as Bernard Spivack has noted, in which these 'hybrid plays' point forward to the sexual tragedies of Shakespeare and Webster.[29]

Yet another play of this genre, *Appius and Virginia* (1564), illustrates quite effectively the curious state of development of homiletic tragedy as of the year of Shakespeare's birth. The author, identified on the title page only as 'R. B.,' calls his play a 'Tragical Comedy . . . Wherein is lively expressed a rare example of the virtue of Chastity by Virginia's constancy in wishing rather to be slain at her own Father's hands, than to be deflowered of the wicked Judge Appius.' The story comes from Livy by way of Chaucer's *Physician's Tale,* and this earliest Roman play is easily fitted into a morality framework. Haphazard the Vice successfully tempts Appius to 'detain' the young girl, despite the protests of Justice and Conscience. Virginia evades the Judge by demanding death before dishonor; she is killed by her Father, who is himself kept from despair by the intervention of Comfort. When Appius claims his right he is presented by the Father with the severed head of his intended victim. Appius summons Justice to punish the Father, but instead Justice seizes bombastically upon Appius:[30]

> O gorgon judge, what lawless life hast
> thou most wicked led!

> Thy soaking sin hath sunk thy soul, thy
> virtues all are fled.

Appius is carried off to prison and an offstage suicide, and Haphazard is caught and hanged by the Father as the virtuous ladies three (Justice, Reward, and Fame) praise the name of constant Virginia. In *Appius and Virginia* as in *Horestes,* there is a certain ambiguity in the justice of the ending; the lecherous Judge dies in despair while the Father, who actually performs the killing, becomes a triumphant figure of retribution. The increasing specificity of homiletic tragedy, its staging of historical and legendary events, makes complications of this kind unavoidable; in such instances a tension naturally arises between the ritual sequence of the morality plot on the one hand and the facts of the 'fable' on the other. A pattern begins to appear: the more tragic the events, the less ritualized must be the action.[31]

The trend of serious moral drama of this early Elizabethan kind is toward 'fable' and tragedy, and hence away from ritual structure. The pattern of Innocence/Fall/Redemption continues to be felt strongly in theory, but is confined to offstage events. It becomes the ideal norm, the hopeful expectation against which increasingly abnormal and particular tragic actions are played out on the later Elizabethan stage.

A late example of the persistence of the formal morality structure is Nathaniel Woodes' *The Conflict of Conscience* (1572). This homiletic tragedy, whose close associations with Marlowe's *Dr Faustus* have been explored by David Bevington, is a dramatization of the life of Francesco Spira, an Italian Protestant converted, under the pressure of the Inquisition, into an apostate. Spira is given the less particularized name of Philologus (lover of talk), and his persecution often takes on the shape and appearance of a traditional temptation by Vices. The latter part of the play is an extended debate over the possibility of repentance and salvation. 'Philologus' (the allegorical Spira) adopts a theological view which is strongly suggestive of Faustus, and Calvin:[32]

> I am refusèd utterly; I quite from God am whirled;
> My name within the Book of Life had never residence;
> Christ prayed not, Christ suffered not my sins to recompence,
> But only for the Lord's elect, of which sort I am none.

The ending of this play, first published in 1581, evidently caused Woodes some moral uncertainties. 'Philologus' leaves the stage in the company of two agents of repentance but in a questionable state of grace. Visions of devils torment him, to the point that he is crying out for a sword with which to end his life. It is left for a messenger to report the ultimate homiletic outcome:[33]

> O doleful news which I report and bring into your ears:
> Philologus by deep despair hath hanged himself with cord.

This ending is, indeed, historically correct and true to the 'fable' of Spira's life. Yet, since 'Philologus' is in most ways a sympathetic character, it violates the moral expectations of an audience anticipating the old sequence of repentance and forgiveness. Later writers of tragedy, including Marlowe, would discover in this violation a powerful dramatic mechanism. But for Woodes, who had moved the scene offstage to begin with, the tragic conclusion was obviously troubling. With intriguing ambiguity, and with an economy of construction that has never failed to amaze his critics, Woodes published later in 1581, within months of the original edition, a second version of *The Conflict of Conscience*, with the critical messenger's speech rewritten:[34]

> Oh joyful news which I report and bring unto your ears!
> Philologus, that would have hanged himself with cord,
> Is now converted unto God, with many bitter tears.

The wonder of this textual feat is not that morality structure can so easily be interchanged with tragedy, as Bevington seems to suggest.[35] Rather it is the persistence of that morality structure – its reassertion here of a pattern of salvation upon a tragic contemporary biography. Such a resolution answers to what is evidently the unspoken wish of an Elizabethan audience – not merely to see justice done, but to see mercy intervene, blessing him that gives and him that takes.

In this way *Conflict of Conscience* looks ahead to a new and greater Elizabethan drama. Woodes, writing only five years before the opening of the public theaters, struggles with his audience's traditional expectations, and ultimately fulfills them. The Kyds, Marlowes, and Shakespeares of the next generation will find powerful ways of moving an audience by denying and violating these medieval certitudes. In the tragic rhythm of every Elizabethan hero's fall is the counterpoint, expressed or unexpressed, of Everyman's forgiveness.

Chapter VI

Marlowe, Shakespeare, Jonson: the apotheosis of the morality play

The audience for popular drama in the age of Shakespeare inherited from medieval drama its concept of what a play performance is fundamentally about. The stage is a quintessential version of the world; the players are images in flesh of what is true but obscure; the act of performing is a way of interpreting or mirroring reality, to enable humanity to perceive itself. Hamlet reminds his actors of

> the purpose of playing, whose end, both at the
> first and now, was and is, to hold as 'twere
> the mirror up to nature, to show virtue
> her own feature, scorn her own image,
> and the very age and body of the time
> his form and pressure.
>
> (III, ii, 22–7)

Central to the experience is the response of the audience. Those who perform 'virtue' and 'scorn' have come to evoke recognitions and move an obligatory set of spectators, 'You that look pale and tremble at this chance/That are but mutes or audience to this act' (*Hamlet*, V, ii, 345–6). Beneath this idea of drama as a collective act of recognition, in the universality of the action, and in the imagined psychology of the audience, are the roots of the morality tradition.

Yet it is evident that the actual plays of the Elizabethan and Jacobean theater, with their elaborate and intricate plots, striking language and characterizations, and complex philosophical statements, are altogether different from their medieval archetypes. The richness of the best plays, indeed, lies in the startling new effects which they can achieve with the old conventions, in how far beyond the simple affirming rituals of religious drama the playwrights can carry the medieval idea of a theatrical experience. When a Macbeth

123

or an Angelo struggles with his conscience, or when a Iago deceives an Othello, or when a Cordelia or an Enobarbus speaks the truth, we are invited to watch familiar moral events as interested – indeed, implicated – spectators. The characterizations, however complicated, have their basis in common conceptions of human nature, expressed through theatrical convention. These Shakespearean characters, and dozens of other Elizabethan stage figures, inherit the functions of conventional morality characters: the central and mutable hero, the agent of sin and temptation, and the agent of repentance and good counsel. In the same way, many otherwise inexplicable bits and pieces of Elizabethan plays, and a whole series of basic varieties of scene have their original rationale in stock episodes of the morality play, for example:

The moral prologue which outlines the whole of the play's action in advance (e.g. the prologues to *Romeo and Juliet* and *Pericles*).

The instruction of the hero by good counsel (e.g. Gaunt to Richard II, Polonius to Laertes).

The conspiracy of vice, disguising itself as virtue (e.g. Richard III and Buckingham, the Witches in *Macbeth*).

The initiation of the naïve hero into experience (e.g. Brutus in *Julius Caesar*, Troilus in *Troilus and Cressida*).

Virtue unjustly cast out (e.g. Adam in *As You Like It*, the Soothsayer in *Julius Caesar*).

The delinquent hero's recognition of his state of sin (e.g. Antony in Egypt, Clarence's dream in *Richard III*).

The providential intervention of God's mercy (e.g. the rebirth of Hermione in *The Winter's Tale*, Portia in *The Merchant of Venice*).

The formal confession and repentance of the hero (e.g. Kate's recantation in *The Taming of the Shrew*, Richard II in the tower).

The unmasking and punishment of disguised vice (e.g. Malvolio in *Twelfth Night*, Iago's unmasking by Emilia).

The moralizing epilogue, implicating the audience (e.g. Feste in *Twelfth Night*, Prospero in *The Tempest*).

In this sense, then, it can be said that the morality play furnishes a kind of stage mythology upon which much of Elizabethan drama is based. It would be a mistake wilfully to ignore these medieval implications in Elizabethan dramatic performance; it would be an equally unfortunate mistake to attempt to reduce the multiplicity of a Shakespearian tragedy to the simple formula of a morality play. The genius of Marlowe, Shakespeare, Jonson, and their contemporaries is in probing the limitations of the old drama, and challenging its optimistic definitions of human action while not rejecting its theatrical premises. Upon the foundations of certainty, the greater Elizabethan and Jacobean playwrights could build structures of aspiration, doubt, mockery, and the emerging irony of an image of the human predicament which is true only in the abstract.

The convention and myth of the human predicament as a morality play seems to have occupied a place in the mind of Marlowe or Shakespeare very similar to the place which Scribe's convention of the well-made play holds for Ibsen or Chekhov. In a formal sense, it is the assumed pattern of events which may both be copied, for the sake of the audience's delight, and violated, for the sake of shock and effectiveness. What remained of the old dramatic assumptions, and how the new dramatists transformed them, may be observed in the textual circumstances of any number of Elizabethan and Jacobean plays. I have chosen five – *Dr Faustus, Henry IV, Part One, Hamlet, Volpone, King Lear* – which seem together to define the full range and complexity of this transformation.

1 Four levels of *Dr Faustus*

Marlowe's monumental play is structurally, intellectually, and textually difficult to perceive as a whole, and these problems are made more obscure by the intervening forests of the Faust myth. To return to *Dr Faustus*, perhaps the most frequently read Elizabethan tragedy outside the Shakespeare canon, is to encounter disjointed artistic parts – conjurations of black magic, cosmological debates, a picaresque master and servant, comic devils, soaring blank verse soliloquies of despair, horseplay and parlor tricks, and hellfire and damnation – through which one must search for a defining unity.

One intrinsic source for this unity, given the highly subjective texture of *Dr Faustus*, is in the mind of Christopher Marlowe himself. The renowned ambiguities of the play obviously derive at least in part from conscious overlapping and contradictions. For this reason it is tempting to accept the image of Marlowe, contriving in a single act of will, out of his own uncertainties, an archetype for the predicament of Renaissance Man. Whether or not this notion is demonstrable the question remains: from what materials is such a novel and yet representative piece of work as *Dr Faustus* constructed? On this point the acknowledged connections of the play with the morality tradition supply a most crucial body of evidence. *Dr Faustus* is a new kind of Renaissance psychological tragedy built on the successive foundations of at least three other earlier kinds of play. Thus the apparent disunity of *Dr Faustus*, is, structurally speaking, a multiplicity of dramatic levels. It is like an overlay of battle plots across a single terrain of subject matter, or an archeological cross-section of an ancient city site.

At its most primary structural level, *Dr Faustus* is a medieval morality play in the tradition of *The Castle of Perseverance*, based on the theoretical concept of the human predicament as a sequence of innocence, fall, and redemption. *Dr Faustus* is a play about a single representative hero who is initiated into worldly experience, gaining knowledge and power at the price of deadly sin. The action leads toward a crisis of repentance, in which, in the traditional morality play, true divine knowledge drives out illusory worldly knowledge. This idea of a morality play antedates and predetermines the structure of *Dr Faustus*; its conventional framework conditions a set of responses and expectations on the part of Marlowe's audience. The appeal to these traditional responses is made obvious in the play by employment of familiar stage conventions of the old drama. Faustus is supplied with a Good Angel and a Bad Angel, after the fashion of *Humanum Genus* in *The Castle of Perseverance*. Though these counselors of grace are relatively ineffective and choric, in comparison with their medieval originals, the effect is to show the audience that Faustus is, on one level at least, the old figure of mutable humanity. That this level is a vestigially theoretical and ideal one is crucial to the play's dynamics. As David Bevington observes, 'the tension between what could be and what actually takes place is the primary source of conflict in Faustus' spiritual biography, and owes its power to the morality heritage.'[1] The Good and Bad Angels alone would perhaps suffice to suggest this tension, but *Dr Faustus* includes many other conventional morality characters. Marlowe's comic caricatures of the seven deadly sins have more in common with their predecessors in *Perseverance* than has sometimes been assumed. The main function of the sins, in the old moralities and in *Dr Faustus*, is to epitomize human frailty rather than tempt humanity. Faustus' formal introduction to the sins is an articulation of his human nature, a sight which he declares to be 'as pleasing to me as paradise was to Adam the first day of his creation.'[2] Morality agents of temptation are vestigally represented in *Dr Faustus* by the conjurors Valdez and Cornelius, who lure Faustus to necromantic studies – and as quickly disappear. More systematic use is made of the Old Man, a perfectly rendered example of the morality agent of repentance. In a scene which leans heavily for its effect on the traditional climactic morality tableau of counter-poised hope and despair, the Old Man materializes to urge Faustus to repent:

> O stay, good Faustus, stay thy desparate steps.
> I see an angel hovers o'er thy head.
> And with a vial full of precious grace
> Offers to pour the same into thy soul.
> Then call for mercy and avoid despair.
>
> (V, i, 60–64)

The accompanying stage direction (*Mephistophilis gives him a daggar*) completes the picture of a classic, and decidedly old-fashioned theatrical moment.[3] Faustus indeed seems to choose the traditional path to repentance: his acknowledgment of sin ('Leave me a while to ponder on my sins,' V, i, 67) is the vital first step in the process. The audience is prepared by this sequence of events to be surprised and even shocked by the diabolical reversal Marlowe immediately imposes upon it:

> MEPHISTOPHILIS Thou traitor, Faustus, I arrest thy soul
> For disobedience to my sovereign lord.
> Revolt, or I'll in piecemeal tear thy flesh.
> FAUSTUS I do repent I e'er offended him.
> Sweet Mephistophilis, entreat thy lord
> To pardon my unjust presumption.
>
> (V, i, 74–9)

This counter-repentance foreshadows the tragic ending of the play, which will depend for its shattering effect on reversing the hopeful expectations of a morality ending.[4] In such ways as these, *Dr Faustus* includes, beneath and within its larger structure, a traditional morality play. The characters and actions of the old drama are brought onto the stage, like sacred objects of a superstitious past, to be mocked and atavistically wondered at, and ritualistically destroyed.

Overlaying the fragmentary morality play of *Dr Faustus* are at least three other kinds of play: a homiletic tragedy, a blasphemous and heroic anti-morality play, and a psychological tragedy of despair. The homiletic tragedy is implicit in Marlowe's literary source, the German 'Faust Book,' which surveys 'the damnable life and deserved death of Doctor John Faustus.' To this prescription need only be added the stage requisite of 'mixt' full of pleasant mirth' to indicate the nature of this second Faustus play. Its hero is the embodiment of intellectual pride, directly compared with Icarus and indirectly with Lucifer, who rejects conventional knowledge to seek forbidden experience. He exists in order to be

E*

punished, and the method of his overthrow, like the web of circumstances in a revenge tragedy, involves delay, mounting suspense, and multiplying irony. In *Dr Faustus* this irony is achieved by means of Faustus' worldly success as a magician – a success which is at once total and trivial, affording the superficial comic tide of pleasant mirth which sweeps the play along through its middle scenes toward the catastrophe of Act V. Here the punishment, delayed for twenty-four years, is carried out in earnest, and a homiletic epilogue is pronounced over the mangled corpse:

> Cut is the branch that might have grown full straight . . .
> Faustus is gone, regard his hellish fall,
> Whose fiendful fortune may exhort the wise
> Only to wonder at unlawful things,
> Whose deepness doth entice such forward wits
> To practice more than heavenly power permits.
>
> (Epilogue, 1, 4–8)

The punishment is as homiletic as the death of Worldly Man in *Enough is as Good as a Feast*. But the enunciated moral is clearly inadequate to the life of Faustus, and wholly anticlimactic to his great and horrifying death scene. For the heroic dimension of Dr Faustus has required a heroic Faustus play, and Marlowe has supplied it, in *addition* to the homiletic tragedy.

Faustus' rebellion against the Christian idea of man's fate is superhuman in its proportions. In the apostrophes to power and the magical conjurations which dominate the early portions of the play, and return with ironic force in the tragic finale, we encounter what seems the particularly Marlovian level of the play. The blasphemous cosmic ambition of Faustus, a theological variant on the royal ambition of Tamburlaine or the economic and Machiavellian schemes of Barabas the Jew of Malta, is presented in a deliberately appealing light as magnificent villainy. It is Marlowe's characteristic artistic statement, as a man of his time. As C. L. Barber says, 'In presenting a search for magical dominion, Marlowe makes blasphemy a Promethean enterprise, heroic and tragic, an expression of the Renaissance.'[5] This level of the play's action, which almost fades from view in the middle sequence of the play, gains much of its drama from the medieval certitudes of morality play and homiletic tragedy which it so effectively mocks. Linking beauty, spirit, magic and art in the famous Helen of Troy scene, Marlowe almost persuades the beholder that the immortal game is worth the damnation. The audience, to the extent that it is captivated and awestruck by Faustus' blasphemous free will, is participating in a desecration of medieval pieties, and divinely-ordained limitations.

At its highest dramatic level, however, *Dr Faustus* is a new kind of psychological tragedy which stages in its own questioning terms the old morality paradoxes of life and death, sin and forgiveness, hope and despair. It begins where a Calvinist biographical drama like *The Conflict of Conscience* leaves off, probing the mind of a believer whose God is terrible, just, and unforgiving to the unsatisfied. Despair, the unenacted threat in a morality play, becomes the impulse for Faustus' every tragic action, from his rejection of humane and divine studies to his obliterating unforgiven death. Repentance, the easy remedy for despair in a morality play, becomes the unattainable tragic ideal:

> FAUSTUS When I behold the heavens, then I repent
> and curse thee, wicked Mephistophilis . . . .
> . . . I will renounce this magic and repent.
> GOOD ANGEL Faustus repent, yet God will pity thee . . . .
> FAUSTUS Yea, God will pity me if I repent.
> BAD ANGEL Ay, but Faustus never shall repent.
> FAUSTUS My heart is hardened, I cannot repent.
> Scarce can I name salvation, faith, or heaven,
> but fearful echoes thunder in mine ears:
> 'Faustus, thou art damned!'
>
> (II, ii, 1–2, 11–12, 16–21)

What Icarus-Faustus encounters, in his soaring transcendence of the old limitations, is not the heat of the sun, but the coldness of an inhospitable universe in which man, unlike mankind in a morality play, is held absolutely responsible for his actions, and estranged from forgiveness.

The myth of Faustus, then, is no subjective accident. It emerges out of the overlapping dramas of old certainty and new ambition, old punishment and new despair. It is built over the ruins of the old myth of a forgiving universe. It is the first, and in some ways the greatest, of the Elizabethan religious tragedies.

2 *Henry IV, Part One*:
variations on a political morality

The relationship between historical drama and the morality tradition comes to full maturity with Shakespeare's second tetralogy, four plays of the 1590s about three succeeding fifteenth-century kings. We have traced the connection between kingship and drama back to the earliest extant morality, *The King of Life*, and followed in successive chapters the development of the king from an emblem of humanity into a characteristic central figure of Elizabethan political tragedies and histories. Shakespeare inherits this tradition, and consciously makes use of it to enlarge the historical meaning of his Lancastrian cycle. The characters of Richard II, Henry IV, and Henry V are variations on the theme of the royal Everyman, in the direct line of ascent from *Cambises*, Bale's *King John*, and *Magnificence*.

It is usually assumed that Shakespeare, artistically a more 'advanced' playwright than Marlowe, made correspondingly less use of the conventions of medieval dramaturgy. However, a study of Shakespeare's *Richard II* in relation to Marlowe's *Edward II*, its principle direct influence, suggests otherwise. Shakespeare's Richard resembles Marlowe's Edward in being a flamboyantly incompetent king who evokes pity in his overthrow; the dissimilarity is in the dramatic causation. Edward's fall proceeds logically and inexorably from flaws of character; Richard's fall, by contrast, is shown to be an act of will. Shakespeare, drawing directly upon his other principal source, the anonymous historical morality *Woodstock*, gives Richard's career and dilemma the defining shape of a morality play. Poised between grave counselors (John of Gaunt) and flattering vices (Bushy, Green, Bagot) Richard makes the traditional wrong choices and suffers the chastening results. It is not merely our pity that redeems Richard in the final act, but his knowledge of his own humanity, achieved at the cost of his kingdom:[6]

> But whate'er I be
> Not I nor any man that but man is
> With nothing shall be pleased till he be eased
> With being nothing.

The instrument of Richard's correction, Henry Bolingbroke, becomes in his own turn a figure of royal morality. The final tableau of *Richard II* juxtaposes the body of Richard with the triumphant and troubled figure of Henry, securely crowned at the cost of Richard's life. The moment of contrition which in the traditional morality sequence leads directly on to repentance is employed by Shakespeare as a superbly ironic ending, pointing forward to 'the unquiet time of King Henry the Fourth.'

Henry plays the role of a king-penitent in the two Shakespearean plays that bear his name. In guilt he plans a pilgrimage of repentance to the Holy Land, but pressures of royal office prevent him from carrying it out. His title is uncertain, and constantly under challenge. The powerful nobles who helped him to the throne abandon him at the moment of greatest need and plot his overthrow. The years of his reign are consumed in a civil war which proves as much of a morality object lesson as the tragic disorders in *Gorboduc*. Henry preserves his crown, only to discover in the moment of victory late in the fourth act of *Henry IV, Part Two* that his strength, health, and five wits are deserting him.

> And wherefore should these good news make me sick? . . .
> I should rejoice now at this happy news,
> And now my sight fails, and my brain is giddy.
>
> (IV, iv, 102, 109–10)

He dies, confessing the sins for which his life has amply proved an expiation:

> God knows, my son,
> By what bypaths and indirect crooked ways
> I met this crown, and I myself know well
> How troublesome it sat upon my head. . . .
> All these bold fears
> Thou see'st with peril I have answered,
> For all my reign hath been but as a scene
> Acting that argument.
>
> (IV, v, 184–7, 196–9)

Once again Shakespeare has deliberately sought out morality images to give shape to the historical plot, and once again the moment of transition is vivid with ironic and penitential overtones. Henry is bequeathing his title to a man whose very life has been a further punishment to him. The new king is his prodigal son Hal.

The man who becomes Henry V is the evolving focus of Shakespeare's tetralogy. By the end of the cycle he is the resplendent 'mirror of all Christian Kings,' victorious and chivalric in adversity on the battlefield of Agincourt, and happily united to the daughter of the King of France whom he has overcome; at the beginning of the cycle, in *Richard II*, he is the offstage 'unthrifty son' of Henry Bolingbroke, who sends after him:

> . . . at London, 'mongst the taverns there;
> For there, they say, he daily doth frequent
> With unrestrained loose companions,
> Even such, they say, as stand in narrow lanes
> And beat our watch and rob our passengers.

> Which he, young wanton and effeminate boy,
> Takes on the point of honour to support
> So dissolute a crew.
>
> (V, iii, 5–12)

A principal question which the cycle poses is how, since 'miracles are ceased,'[7] such a change can really have occurred. The answer is partly to be felt in the pressure of the historical events in which the Prince finds himself. Yet Shakespeare takes pains to show that the change is both willful and premeditated on Hal's part, a conscious alteration of previous modes of behavior, a step deliberately and dramatically taken. The change is perceived by distant observers to have occurred spontaneously, and the Archbishop of Canterbury in *Henry V* compares it to a death and rebirth, or the repentance scene in a morality play:

> But that his wildness, mortified in him,
> Seemed to die too. Yea, at that very moment,
> Consideration like an angel came
> And whipped the offending Adam out of him,
> Leaving his body as a paradise
> To envelop and contain celestial spirits.
> Never was such a sudden scholar made,
> Never came reformation in a flood
> With such a heady currance, scouring faults.
>
> (I, i, 26–34)

Yet long before, in the depths of his supposedly wanton youth, carousing in the taverns and plotting robberies in *Henry IV, Part One*, Hal had paused to imagine just such a transformation for himself:

> So when this loose behaviour I throw off
> And pay the debt I never promised
> By how much better than my word I am,
> By so much shall I falsify men's hopes.
> And like bright metal on a sullen ground
> My reformation, glittering o'er my fault,
> Shall show more goodly and attract more eyes
> Than that which hath no foil to set it off.
>
> (I, ii, 231–8)

These contradictions, particularly apparent in *Henry IV, Part One* in the crux of Hal's development, have brought into question the sincerity of the Prince's conversion. Romantic critics from Morgann and Hazlitt to Bradley have contrasted a calculating, imperious, seemingly hypocritical and ultimately ungrateful Hal with the more warm-blooded and instinctive characters of *Henry IV, Part One*, in particular with Falstaff, the 'undiscovered hero' of the play.

It was J. Dover Wilson, endeavoring to restore a balance to the twentieth-century understandings of Hal and Falstaff, who first made careful note of the connections of *Henry IV, Part One* to the morality tradition. Dover Wilson had been impressed, in seeing a revival of the interlude of *Youth*, with its proto-Shakespearean overtones.[8] Youth, the central figure, and Riot, the principal Vice, seemed to be conceived and related to one another in the precise manner of Hal and Falstaff. This experience of a performance led Dover Wilson to reinterpret *Henry IV* in light of the sixteenth-century 'youth' moralities and prodigal son plays. He identified Hal with the prodigal Youth, the Court and the Lord Chief Justice with sober virtue, Falstaff with the Vice, and the plot with the prodigality of a young prince leading logically to a welcome repentance, evidenced by a rejection of vice.[9]

In short, the Falstaff-Hal plot embodies a composite myth which had been centuries amaking and was for the Elizabethans full of meaning that has largely disappeared since then: which is one reason why we have come so seriously to misunderstand the play. . . . *Henry IV* was certainly intended to convey a moral. It is, in fact, Shakespeare's great morality play.

Dover Wilson's reading of the play, contributing one of the earliest sophisticated discussions of Shakespeare's debt to the morality tradition, suggests the freedom with which Shakespeare uses the old conventions. Hal is not just a prodigal son, but a prodigal prince; Falstaff is not simply a tempter into vice, but a walking argument (in physical terms at least) for reformation; the Lord Chief Justice is not merely sober virtue, but an ambiguous symbol of responsibility, an object of ridicule whose sternness entails the sober realities of government. Dover Wilson's perception of the morality play tradition in *Henry IV* thus vindicates Shakespeare's rationale in the conception of his characters, and the shape of the events in which they take part.

In the years since Dover Wilson's views were published much has been learned about the morality tradition, and a reconsideration of *Henry IV, Part One* in this context if anything strengthens the original interpretation – though it suggests some re-evaluations within it. The tradition out of which *Henry IV, Part One* emerges seems not so much that of 'youth' plays as of the political morality. Skelton's *Magnificence* and Medwall's *Nature* provide the dramatic premise in the figure of the world as a court, and the Prince as an inexperienced hero subject to good counsel and temptation. This idea of a play, transformed in the generation of Bale, Lindsay, and Udall to overt political purposes, and reconverted to more subtle political guises by the early Elizabethans from Sackville and Norton to the author of *Woodstock*, seems in Shakespeare's mind throughout the tetralogy.

Henry IV, Part One can be seen as essentially a series of stunning variations on the theme of a political morality. Reversals of this tradition, such as the relatively sympathetic characterization of Falstaff, are frequent and powerful in effect. Naïve and blatant morality notions of evil are present in the audience's theatrical memory, as Shakespeare reminds us in the names he gives Hal to call Falstaff, in the extempore play scene:

> There is a devil haunts thee in the likeness of an old fat
> man. . . . That reverend vice, that gray iniquity, that father
> ruffian, that Vanity in years . . . that villainous abominable
> misleader of youth, Falstaff, that old white-bearded Satan.
>
> (II, iv, 498–500, 508–9)

Shakespeare uses these expectations as both a model and a foil for the real Falstaff, who must be rejected as forcefully by Hal in the end as is Sedition by Bale's King John, or Counterfeit Countenance by Magnificence.

Falstaff's religious and political ambiguity, which has its basis in the disguised Vice of the political morality, is a crucial source of his strength and prodigious resiliency as a dramatic character. Though Hal describes him as a set of hyperboles, Shakespeare draws Falstaff as a set of religious and political contradictions. The religious Falstaff is the unrepentant young old man who embodies the fulfilled temptations of the flesh and moralizes from one end of the play to the other his long-delayed repentance:

> Now am I, if a man should speak truly, little better than one
> of the wicked. I must give over this life, and I will give it over.
>
> (I, ii, 104–7)

> If I grow great, I'll grow less; for I'll purge, and leave sack,
> and live cleanly as a nobleman should do.
>
> (V, iv, 167–9)

The political Falstaff is a nobleman turned outlaw trying shamelessly and without much energy to find his way back into courtly favor, intrigued with the possibilities in Hal's accession of a utopia of misrule, a chivalric anarchy of nature:

> When thou art King, let us not that are squires of the night's body be called thieves of the day's beauty. Let us be called Diana's foresters, gentlemen of the shade, minions of the moon. And let men say we be men of good government, being governed as the sea is, by our noble and chaste mistress the moon, under whose countenance we steal.
>
> (I, ii, 26–33)

Propelled by events into the middle of an actual political conflict, Falstaff pursues his self-interests (survival and enrichment) with as little regard for the issues of the war or the lives of soldiers as Ambidexter in *Cambises*. And like Ambidexter, he is irresponsible enough and sufficiently detached to deliver Shakespeare's satiric epitaph on the failed peace parley of Act V: 'What is honour? A word. What is in that word honour? What is that Honour? Air. A trim reckoning! Who hath it? He that died o'Wednesday.' (V, i, 135–9). Falstaff is, finally, what he seems to be – a colossal threat to religious and political respectability. He embodies all and more of the mockery of established values which the morality play traditionally presents, in justification of human frailty.

In dramatizing the life of Henry V, Shakespeare is writing his own version of a popular myth, the story of a heroic king in the legendary mold of Richard the Lion-hearted and King Arthur. Shakespeare is free to embellish the story with fictional characters and incidents, as for instance in the case of Falstaff, but the quality of his hero is dictated by the audience's traditional expectations. Henry V had been a legend in his own time, and hagiographic accounts of his career dating from the fifteenth century contain the full heroic outline, climaxing in the victory at Agincourt, but beginning with a misspent youth in which the hero 'yntended gretly to ryot, and drew to wyld company; and divers Ientylmen and Ientylwommen folwyed his wylle.'[10]

Shakespeare is dealing with a hero whose life had been perceived for nearly two centuries as a metamorphosis, with the basic pattern of a morality play. Yet it is an interesting fact that the direct stage source of *Henry IV, Part One*, the popular Elizabethan chronicle play known as *The Famous Victories of Henry V*, has little or no connection with the morality tradition. It dramatizes the young Hal's wild behavior, but only as a series of unconnected picaresque incidents.[11] The morality structure and characterizations of the tetralogy are not, in fact, vestiges of early stage versions retained by Shakespeare to please the groundlings. On the contrary they are apparently consciously imposed by Shakespeare upon the stage action, or more precisely discovered to be implicit in the legendary interpretations given Henry V's life by the medieval chroniclers. Here again, as in the case of *Richard II*, Shakespeare proves to be more of a morality playwright than his immediate predecessors; he knows and consciously utilizes the old rhythms of action and the conventional figures to achieve new effects of his own devising.

In the case of his hero, Shakespeare accepts the spectacular changes in Hal's life as a given and interesting dramatic fact. Where the writer of a political morality would be content to stage this series of changes, however, Shakespeare probes more deeply. On the one hand he looks for explanatory circumstances in Hal's life; on the other hand he considers the inner logic of the parable of the prodigal son, and the morality formula. If innocence and inexperience are qualities of weakness, and if there is indeed more joy in heaven over one that repenteth than for ninety and nine who do not sin, then experience is a prologue to better understanding, and a great king is made, not born. The ceremony of experience which is enacted in a morality play requires a mutable hero who will learn from *all* of his experiences, and ultimately benefit from encountering the worst as well as the best advisers and examples.

Prince Hal is just such a mutable potential hero, and his beneficent exposure to the full range of experience is the argument of *Henry IV, Part One*. His participation in the plot and counterplot of the Gadshill robbery is not an act of desperation by a destitute prodigal (as in, say, *Nice Wanton*) but rather a game of consummate deception, playing on human nature, and by no means irrelevant to an eventual career of royal warfare and political manoeuvre. The battle of Agincourt is won on the playingfields of Gadshill.

What most distinguishes Henry V from his predecessors the secretive Henry IV and the aloof Richard II is his feeling for the psychology, not merely of the commonwealth, but of the common subject. Hal has learned his trade of leadership the hard (and pleasant) way, in the Boar's Head Tavern in Eastcheap:

> I have sounded the very base string of humility. Sirrah I am
> sworn brother to a leash of drawers, and can call them all
> by their Christen names, as Tom, Dick, and Francis. They
> take it already upon their salvation that though I be but
> Prince of Wales, yet I am the king of courtesy, and tell me
> flatly that I am no proud Jack, like Falstaff, but a
> Corinthian, a lad of mettle, a good boy, by the Lord, so they
> call me, and when I am King of England I shall command all
> the good lads in Eastcheap.
>
> (II, iv, 5–14)

And lest we assume that Hal's ceremony of initiation i
exception or a unique case, Shakespeare reminds us of his d
hero's pedigree: 'I am now of all humours that have
themselves humours since the old days of goodman Adam t
pupilage of this present twelve o'clock at midnight.' (II, iv, 104–

Hal becomes capable of becoming king in the course of *Henry IV*,
Part One. Many have noted his stated intention of transforming
himself into a great monarch, in his soliloquy at the end of Act I,
but few would claim that he is at that moment able to do what he
contemplates. Hal must first be tested, as a human being, a son,
and a warrior, and he must learn from what happens to him. Like
the heroes of *Magnificence* or *Respublica*, he learns even – in fact,
especially – from being momentarily deceived.

If we contrast Hal, who learns consistently from experience and
advisers (whether Falstaffs or Lords Chief Justices) and Hotspur,
who listens to no one and learns nothing, Shakespeare's point is
reinforced. Hotspur corresponds to no stock figure in the morality
tradition, with the possible exception of a predestined reprobate in a
dualistic morality of the late Calvinist sort – an antitype to the hero
who lives, learns, and is saved. Hotspur is fated by the immutable
complexion of his character, by the stars he does not believe in, to
understand almost nothing which happens to him. The passionate
imagination with which he conceives of a haphazard plan of
rebellion that 'cannot choose but be a noble plot' is carefully contrasted with the shrewd and cautious planning Hal lavishes on a less
exalted plot against Falstaff. When Hal, reformed and in armor,
bests Hotspur in single combat, we may be moved with pity for
Hotspur but are not really surprised. Shakespeare allows Hal an
instant of recognition over the dead bodies of Falstaff and Hotspur
as if assimilating what he has survived: Hotspur's 'great heart' and
Falstaff's 'old acquaintance.' Just as surely, Shakespeare allows
Falstaff to upstage Hal's triumphal exit with a comic resurrection
act, reminding his audience of what they undoubtedly remembered,
that the Falstaff in human nature cannot, and theologically should
not, be abolished from the unfinished morality play. The political
and social threat of Falstaff must survive to be rejected with finality
by the new King Henry V.

The historical comedy of *Henry IV, Part One*, as it emerges from
such an interpretation, is not a play about the friendship of Falstaff
and Hal, but a less romantic and more incisively thoughtful play
about a man becoming a prince, stressing the dependence of individual 'character' upon the interaction of circumstances and free
will. As such, the play at once fulfills and transcends the idea of a
political morality play. Falstaff in the tavern is a wit; as a robber
he is the cause of wit; on the battlefield in command of human

; as the mascot of victory he is something else
uosity is comic in its performance, and tragic
Hotspur personally and for the society that he
Hal's willful change of character is, unsenti-
realistic and sympathetic study of the effect
ces on a mutable individual. Born to be an
n, Hal becomes heir apparent as a result of
a man of arms by way of defending his
inheriting his father's responsibilities. The
character are decisive and circumstantial.

In *Henry IV, Part One*, Shakespeare discovers new psychological reality in the old dynamics of medieval characterization, and his art looks ahead to the interests of modern fiction. The play is indeed in many respects 'Shakespeare's great morality play,' but it is also perhaps Shakespeare's first novel – a *Bildungsroman* of a young man's education which explores in the special circumstances of a destined political leader, the perennial and difficult questions of innocence, experience, and responsibility.

3 *Hamlet:* the morality play within the play

For plays as different as *Dr Faustus* and *Henry IV, Part One*, the morality tradition provides a basic structure of action; in *Hamlet* the idea of a morality play has much more limited and specific uses. It arises out of the action of the play-within-the-play, as an exorcism of the guilt of Denmark. The old morality theater of sin and penance is utilized by Shakespeare to suggest the illusory possibilities of a way out of Hamlet's dilemma.

The appearance of players at the Danish court provides Hamlet with an unexpected instrument of justice. As the first player speaks his 'Hecuba' speech, Hamlet reflects on its power to move the imagination. It is a description of a murder, and the compassionate response of those who witness it – Hecuba herself, and all the other possible spectators, human and divine, who can imagine both the act itself and Hecuba's horror at it. The tears of the first player are proof that an imaginary scene can have the force of a fact. Hamlet, impressed, puts the players in the safe keeping of Polonius, calling them 'the abstract and brief chronicles of the time' (II, ii, 549–50). He speaks of them, with what seems at the time an inexplicable reference, in terms of justice and mercy:

> Use every man after his desert and
> Who shall 'scape whipping?

> (II, ii, 554–5)

The emotional soliloquy which follows the players' departure should not obscure the fact that Hamlet has indeed come upon a plan. Briefly forgotten as he compares himself unfavorably to the actor, the idea of the plan returns to mind:

> About my brain! Hum, I have heard
> That guilty creatures sitting at a play
> Have by the very cunning of the scene
> Been so struck to the soul that presently
> They have proclaimed their malefactions.
>
> (II, ii, 617–21)

This plan has its basis in the idea of drama as a mechanism which may evoke recognition in the audience of its own sins. In the morality play this recognition leads to confession and repentance. Hamlet, however, proposes to utilize the power of drama for his own purposes, to furnish proof of his stepfather's guilt, confirming the Ghost's allegations and justifying Claudius' punishment. He alone, among the projected audience, will recognize the illusion as the representation of a fact.

> I'll observe his looks,
> I'll tent him to the quick. If he but blench,
> I know my course . . . .
> The play's the thing
> Wherein I'll catch the conscience of the King.
>
> (II, ii, 625–7; 633–4)

The Murder of Gonzago is not a morality play, but a domestic-homiletic tragedy, interrupted early in its course. If allowed to continue it would eventually have wrought punishment on the poisoner, whose thus-far successful act of murder and usurpation brings Claudius to his feet and terminates the performance.[12] Shakespeare, however, by halting the play at this crucial juncture, has sprung the mousetrap prematurely and given it the function of a morality play. The play has *worked* as a call to repentance. Claudius rises, not in anger, but in fear and trembling, as Hamlet's comments indicate ('What, frighted with false fire,' 'Why, let the stricken deer go weep,' III, ii, 277, 282). Though Rosencrantz mistakes the King's humor for 'choler,' and though Claudius is able to function sufficiently to order Hamlet's dispatch to England, the play has truly frightened him, and he is wracked with guilt.

In soliloquy Shakespeare presents Claudius as the central figure of the morality play, confronted inescapably with the dilemmas of sin and repentance. Claudius is contrite ('Oh my offence is rank, it smells to heaven,' III, iii, 36) and aware of the traditional role of divine mercy in such circumstances ('Whereto serves mercy/But to confront the visage of offence,' III, iii, 46–7). But Claudius is utterly alone, unprovided with a morality agent of repentance to lead him to confession. Moreover he is admittedly unwilling to give up the possessions his sins have won him, and his position therefore remains unforgivable, if perhaps temporarily viable in a corrupt world. He is as lost as Faustus:

> What then? What rests?
> Try what repentance can. What can it not?
> Yet what can it when one cannot repent?
>
> (III, iii, 64–6)

He kneels, and as if on cue a figure enters to confront him. But it is not Mercy, the agent of repentance; it is Hamlet. The ironies in Shakespeare's reversal of this familiar morality repentance scene are bold and devastating. As Claudius kneels in vulnerability, Hamlet advances with sword drawn, in revenge. He is the wrong character in the wrong play. Hamlet's stratagem has so caught the conscience of the King (or so it seems) that Claudius has repented. To kill him now, in an apparently repentant state of grace, would be to give him salvation; Hamlet refuses to play the role of Death which the scene has contrived for him. On the other hand he is not about to speak words of consolation to Claudius in the role of the Good Angel in *Dr Faustus*. The further irony is that if he did so, he would find a despairing and unrepentant Claudius, fit for his purposes. He passes on, vowing to find Claudius

> When he is drunk asleep, or in his rage
> Or in the incestuous pleasure of his bed . . .
> . . . Or about some act
> That has no relish of salvation in 't.
>
> (III, iii, 89–90, 91–2)

Claudius is left behind, pardoned unawares, contemplating the failure of his repentance:

> My words rise up, my thoughts remain below.
> Words without thoughts never to heaven go.
>
> (III, iii, 97–8)

The consequences of the play-within-the-play do not stop with Claudius. The question which Shakespeare raises in this sequence of actions is a profound one – is it possible that conscience, in the sense of recognition of sin,[13] will enable the crimes of the Danish court to be resolved through repentance rather than bloodshed? The question involves not merely Claudius, but Gertrude, and indeed Hamlet himself. Gertrude's sins are less serious than those of Claudius, and her actions during the play-within-the-play give the audience some cause to believe that her conscience has also been caught. When the player queen makes extravagant vows to Heaven and earth that if widowed she will never remarry, Gertrude recognizes the hyperbole ('The lady doth protest too much, methinks,' III, ii, 240). If there is only the wisdom of an ex-widow's experience in this remark, Hamlet's contemptuous answer ('Oh but she'll keep her word,' III, ii, 241) drives home the implied comparison and contrast. The player queen will not remarry.

If Hamlet is telling the truth about the player queen's role, then she is scheduled to resist the poisoner's blandishments and perhaps even take a part in his punishment. Claudius' suspicious response to Hamlet's statement ('Have you heard the argument? Is there no offence in 't?', III, ii, 242–3) indicates that he too may already have made some kind of connection between Gertrude and the player queen. If the play had continued, he would likely have observed her become a Griselda or a Penelope or a Bel-Imperia of a widow, instead of a Gertrude. But once again Shakespeare's disruption of the play leaves the moral position of the player queen as ambiguous as that of her actual counterpart, whose response to the episode of the play is 'great affliction of spirit.' Or so Guildenstern reports, summoning Hamlet:

ROSENCRANTZ Your behaviour hath struck her into amazement and admiration.
HAMLET Oh wonderful son that can so astonish a mother. But is there no sequel at the heels of this mother's admiration? Impart.
ROSENCRANTZ She desires to speak with you in her closet, ere you go to bed.

(III, ii, 338–44)

It is at this point that Hamlet apparently sets his mind on playing the part of an agent of repentance to Gertrude; it is the 'sequel' of repentance he seeks now to effect. His first task is to make her aware of her sin, and thus genuinely contrite; he recognizes that this will involve harsh words, if not harsh actions. He pledges to himself that he will not use the weapons of some matricidal revenger, but daggers of the mind.

The so-called 'Closet scene' is predominantly a tragically aborted repentance scene. Gertrude, confused and distracted by the last-minute promptings and bestowings of Polonius, attempts to play the role of an irate mother with a prodigal son. Hamlet, mocking her formal speeches, strikes to the heart of his purpose in coming:

> Come, come, and sit you down. You shall not budge,
> You go not 'till I set you up a glass
> Where you may see the inmost part of you.
>
> (III, iv, 18–20)

Hamlet, with his sword drawn[14] acts the role of retributive scourge, shocking the sinner into a recognition of his true state. This is a familiar and crucial scene in the medieval morality plays; for example, in *The Castle of Perseverance*, Mankind is resisting the arguments of Confession, when Penance appears, armed with a symbolic weapon:[15]

> Wyth poynt of penaunce I schal hym prene
> Man's pride for to felle.
> Wyth þis launce I schal hym lene
> Iwys a drope of mercy welle . . . .
> Wyth my spud of sorwe swote
> I reche to þyne hert rote.

It is this violent but merciful act that Hamlet seeks to perform. In forcing Gertrude to contemplate her true self, Hamlet is attempting to initiate the self-recognition scene of a morality play, where, as in *Wisdom*, the unrepentant mind is forced to witness:[16]

> WYSDOM . . . See howe ye have dysvyguryde yowr soule!
> Behold yowrseleff; loke veryly in mynde!
> Here ANIMA apperythe in þe most horrybul wyse,
>   fowlere þan a fende.

In *Hamlet*, however, the obligatory scene of contrition is interrupted by a disaster. Gertrude's fear rouses Polonius. Hamlet mistakes the voice for Claudius, and changes instantaneously from agent of repentance to revenger. He kills what he thinks to be the no-longer repentant Claudius, in Gertrude's bedchamber. Once more, and fatally, Hamlet in switching between 'rival moralities'[17] has been deceived by appearances, and this time he has killed an innocent man.

With Polonius' body dead on the floor, Hamlet resumes his role of bringing Gertrude to repentance. He preaches with bizarre self-assurance and great skill, evoking 'sweet sorrow,' wringing Gertrude's heart with an unfolding and unlovely picture of her true state. And Gertrude begins to recognize her sins:

> Oh speak to me no more,
> These words like daggers enter in my ears.
> No more, sweet Hamlet!
>
> (III, iv, 94–6)

Hamlet persists, like Chaucer's Pardoner, in finishing the sermon of repentance, though his own guilt lies visible to everyone:

> Confess yourself to Heaven.
> Repent what's past, avoid what is to come . . . .
> Forgive me this my virtue,
> For in the fatness of these pursey times
> Virtue itself of vice must pardon beg . . . .
> Assume a virtue if you have it not.
>
> (III, iv, 149–50, 152–4, 160)

Hamlet sweeps on to an optimistic morality play conclusion: a resolution to all the misfortune is possible; for those who can sincerely repent, there is the blessing of forgiveness:

> Once more, good night.
> And when you are desirous to be blest
> I'll blessing beg of you.

With the turn of the final phrase, the focus of the scene comes to rest on Hamlet's own quandary. The real dilemma mocks Hamlet's sermon on guilt and forgiveness. The fact of his own tragedy is a dead body on the floor:

> For this same lord,
> I do repent. But Heaven hath pleased it so,
> To punish me with this, and this with me,
> That I must be their scourge and minister.
> I will bestow him, and will answer well
> The death I gave him.
>
> (III, iv, 172–7)

The morality play within the play in *Hamlet* is initiated insincerely, as a device of revenge, and it ends in failure, in the perception of incipient tragedy. The escape which the old device seemed to offer, of the resolution of guilt through recognition and repentance, proves thoroughly illusory. The players are banished from the script, their function performed in vain, and the guilt remains 'Unhousled, disappointed, unaneled,/No reckoning made' (I, v, 77–8). Its resolution now involves Hamlet, Claudius, Gertrude, Ophelia, Laertes and the rest in an older, crueler, and deadlier ritual of expiation.

4 *Volpone* as a Jacobean *Everyman*

GOD I perceyue, here in my maieste,
How that all creatures be to me unkynde,
Lyuynge without drede in worldly prosperyte . . . .
Therefore I wyll, in all the haste,
Have a reckenynge of every mannes persone;
For, and I leve the people thus alone
In theyr lyfe and wycked tempestes,
Veryly they will become moch worse than beestes . . . .
Where art thou, Deth, thou myghty messengere?[18]

Volpone is a comedy of death; the threat and promise of mortality gives Jonson's great play its special gamey odor, its elemental and biting humor of the graveyard. The folly of mortal, animal man is observed by Jonson with quasi-divine detachment, impatience, and contempt; humanity is rendered in the woodcut caricatures of a medieval *danse macabre*, as modified by Jacobean cynicism and the full exuberance of Jonsonian wit. If *Volpone* is among the greatest comedies of its age, it is also among the strangest – an amalgam of beast fable, *commedia dell'arte*, courtroom farce, Italianate intrigue, topical satire, the feast of fools and a sermon *de contemptu mundi*.[19]

Like its great predecessor *Everyman*, *Volpone* turns morbidity to art, and finds satirical drama in the uncertainty of the human response to certain death, juxtaposing materialism and mortality. The categorical differences between the two works are a good measure of the century (*Everyman* 1495; *Volpone* 1606) that separates them; the basic and sometimes mocking similarities are evidence of the tenuous living traditions of drama that connect them. *Volpone* is a Jacobean *Everyman*: a rich, savage theatrical treatise on human nature, as defined by the eventuality of death.

The original *Everyman* studies the materialism of a dying man, exploring the qualifications of his impending death on his sense of values and self-definition. *Volpone* takes its premise from a sham and mockery of the same extreme situation: a thriving materialist pretends, to his profit and delight, to be a dying man. The social response which Everyman's dying produces is abandonment. He finds himself mortally and progressively abandoned by friends, relatives, possessions and eventually physical and mental powers. In the case of Volpone, of course, the news of impending death does not drive acquaintances and possessions away, but rather attracts them. A childless man is suddenly besieged by new-found friends, would-be heirs, and augmented possessions. Where Everyman is forced by his abandonment to redefine his life in spiritual terms, in order to save it, Volpone is lured by wit and greed to prolong the hour of his 'death' through five acts of intrigue before he too is brought to a reckoning. To see *Volpone* in the perspective of the morality tradition is to explain, at least in important measure, the ferocious seriousness of this very funny play.

The basic pattern of the early scenes of *Volpone* – the successive attraction of 'comforters' to the deathbed of Volpone – is a mirror-perfect reversal of the progressive estrangement of Everyman from the selfish unconcern of Fellowship, Kindred, and Cousin. Jonson's borrowing of the Roman legacy-hunting motif provides the new material for this fresh and greatly more sophisticated satire on the operation of human self-interest in another's misfortunes. The greed of old men, axiomatic on the stage since the days of *Perseverance*, is manifested in the frustration, the abortive poisoning schemes and nervous hovering of a feeble, deaf bird of prey like Corbaccio.[20]

> VOLPONE 'Tis true, 'tis true. What a rare punishment
> Is avarice to itself!
> MOSCA   Ay, with our help, sin.
> VOLPONE So many cares, so many maladies,
> So many fears attending on old age.
> Yea, death so often called on as no wish
> Can be more frequent with 'em. Their limbs faint,
> Their senses dull, their seeing, hearing, going,
> All dead before them; yea, their very teeth,
> Their instruments of eating, failing them.
> Yet this is reckoned life!

Alan Dessen has convincingly shown that Jonson's birds of prey are stage figures representing the 'estates' of society, descended from the morality tradition.[21] In the exposure of their avarice and morality, Volpone, the epitome of avarice, plays a crucial satiric part. But the real focus of the play, as it emerges in the middle acts, is on exposing the vices of the Vice. The subtle transition of Volpone into a central mutable character corresponds to the gradual rise of his servant Mosca to the position of chief tempter.

The temptation of Volpone by Celia, the wife of Corvino, is one of Jonson's most inspired dramatic mechanisms. It is built on the ancient foundation of two stock morality play episodes – the initiation of the hero into experience, and the appearance of God's mercy to the afflicted and despairing mankind. When Mosca first describes Corvino's wife to Volpone, it is in the alluring terms of Flesh once used to describe Lady Lechery (in *Youth*) or Abominable Living (in *Lusty Juventus*), raised to Jonsonian extremities:

> O, sir, the wonder
> The blazing star of Italy, a wench
> O' the first year! a beauty ripe as harvest!
> Whose skin is whiter than a swan, all over!
> Than silver, snow, or lillies! a soft lip,
> Would tempt you to eternity of kissing!
> And flesh that melteth in the touch to blood!
> Bright as your gold! and lovely as your gold!
>
> (I, v, 107–14)

Volpone is tempted, and abandons the disguise of his deathbed for the disguise of a mountebank, vending disease- and death-cheating medicines beneath the window of his heavily-guarded prize as a trick to gain a look at her. He suffers the penitential blows of frustration and Corvino's angry beating, but they only whet his sexual appetite. When Mosca proposes a remedy, and Volpone responds, it is in terms which deliberately parody the traditional stage devices of mercy and despair:

> VOLPONE Dear Mosca, shall I hope?
> MOSCA   Sir, more than dear,
> I will not bid you to despair of aught
> within a human compass.
> VOLPONE   O, there spoke
> My better angel.
>
> (II, iv, 18–21)

The remedy which Mosca contrives, with Vice-like dispatch, is the conveying of Celia to Volpone's bedchamber. Presenting her to Volpone, disguised in the role of the dying man once more, Mosca announces Celia's function 'to be your comfortress, and to preserve you' (III, vii, 80). Beneath this morality play fiction, of course, are intricate and multiple levels of intrigue. Mosca has convinced Corvino that the gift of a woman to Volpone is necessary to fulfill a doctor's prescription. Corvino has convinced himself that the gift of his own wife will prevent the loss of Volpone's legacy, that the gift will be negligible since Volpone is probably impotent, and that even if Celia proves sufficiently tempting to prove Volpone otherwise it will not matter, since the whole affair is to be conducted in strict privacy. He tells the horrorstruck Celia that, in the special circumstances, she will be acting virtuously:

> I grant you. If I thought it were a sin
> I would not urge you . . .
> . . . but here, 'tis contrary,
> A pious work, mere charity, for physic
> And honest policy to assure mine own.
>
> (III, vii, 56–7, 64–6)

In fact, Celia *does* tempt Volpone; her innocent beauty is as attractive to him as the virtue of Isabella is to Angelo in *Measure for Measure*, and in a similar way the temptation of Virtue lures the hidden Vice out of his disguise. In Volpone's case this disguise is the semblance of a dying man who has abjured the temptations of the flesh. His transformation, staged by Jonson with brilliant theatricality, sees Volpone leaping from his deathbed to proclaim his reborn sensuality. The roles are now reversed, and Volpone revived miraculously, as he claims, by the sight of Celia ('thy beauty's miracle,' III, vii, 146), becomes the glib tempter. With rhetoric, song, and glittering emblematic treasures Volpone contrives to lure her; his arguments are flowing and logical, but Celia's innocence (and some measure of ignorance) preserves her:

> CELIA Good sir, these things might move a mind affected
> With such delights; but I, whose innocence
> Is all I can think wealthy, or worth th'enjoying,
> And which, once lost, I have nought to lose beyond it,
> Cannot be taken with these sensual baits.
> If you have conscience –
> VOLPONE   'Tis the beggar's virtue.
>
> (III, vii, 205–10)

Celia's perseverance is crucial; it forces the Vice Volpone to expose his true nature yet further. Behind the mask of the sensualist lies a disagreeably ugly vanity of will, a spiritual deadness:

> Think me cold,
> Frozen, and impotent, and so report me?
> . . . I should have done the act, and then have parleyed,
> Yield, or I'll force thee.
>
> (III, vii, 260–1; 265–6)

The surprising realism and crudity of this action carries the scene beyond its comic bounds; the all-too timely intervention of the hidden Bonario ('Forbear, foul ravisher! libidinous swine!') returns it instantly to its comic perspective.[22] Mercy has rescued the steadfast heroine from the jaws of a painted devil. We are back in a world of morality play morality, where salvation through divine mercy is the mandatory ending and vices are hoist on their own petard.

Things cannot realistically remain in this fictional moral condition for very long. Jonson's constant artistic problem in *Volpone* seems to be one of reconciling a true-to-life portrayal of the triumphs of vice with his stated intention of fulfilling 'the office of a comic poet to imitate justice.'[23] He solves this problem in the traditional theatrical (and indeed judicial) manner. Though justice is finally not denied, it is systematically delayed. Like the *Castle of Perseverance*, *Volpone* is a two-part play in which the initial ending in justice proves illusory, necessitating a second series of actions and a second and finally conclusive ending.

It is the stern justice of this final ending which has troubled many readers of Jonson's play, and caused adapters such as Stefan Zweig to supply a more lighthearted and pleasing conclusion to the action.[24] But Jonson the moralist is interested in his audience seeing poetic justice done. Some comprehension of the morality tradition is a necessary prologue, I believe, to understanding Jonson's own notions of a just comic ending, and measuring the degree to which justice has been successfully carried out.

The final sequence presents two contiguous actions – the legal vindication of Volpone, and the 'death' of Volpone. The first action necessitates the suborning of the Venetian law courts, the bribery of false witnesses, diabolically truth-twisting legal arguments by a corrupt lawyer, and the discrediting of Celia and Bonario. It is one massive act of injustice, and it is very amusing – to the extent that no one is ultimately going to get away with it. It prepares the way for – indeed absolutely necessitates – an ending in which the shufflings of earthly injustice are reversed by the higher court of Divine Justice. What is required, in short, is the happy ending of a morality play.

The concluding portion of the play, involving the 'death' of Volpone, fulfills this traditional moral function by releasing a series of tensions which have been operative since the play began. In the hero's 'death' another inspired comic mechanism is set in motion which scourges one by one all who are deserving of being punished – which in the quaint and rotten byways of Jonson's Venice is practically everyone.

The scourging action begins with the determination of Volpone to see justice delayed no longer on the birds of prey, who have been circling his carcass relentlessly since Act One. He decides to present them with his dead body at last (or rather the semblance of it), and with it the news that he has disinherited them all. To do this he must vacate the deathbed, take on another disguise, and compose a will as selfless as Everyman's, leaving everything to his loyal servant Mosca.

The jest is ingenious, and it works perfectly; with Mosca's help, the avaricious birds of prey are trapped and penitentially scourged, as Volpone (in hiding) points out to the audience:

> My advocate is dumb; look to my merchant
> He has heard of some storm, a ship is lost,
> He faints; my lady will swoon. Old glazen-eyes
> He hath not reached his despair, yet.
>
> (V, iii, 23–6)

There are practical complications, however. For one thing, Mosca the trusty servant is not to be trusted. He will quickly discover the advantages in taking Volpone's 'death' seriously.

> Since he will needs be dead afore his time,
> I'll bury him . . . . This is called the fox-trap.
>
> (V, v, 13–14, 18)

Moreover, the disappointed would-be heirs, mocked by the disguised Volpone and expelled from false hopes by Mosca, the agent of retribution ('Go home, be melancholic too, or mad . . . . Go home, and die, and stink . . . best go home and purge, sir,' V, iii, 60, 74, 101), have occasion to contemplate the error of their ways. In consonance with the morality formula (and hypocritically, in Jonson's comic rendering, out of jealousy for Mosca) they begin to confess their sins.

Voltore, rising to address the *Scrutineo* at the sentencing of Bonario and Celia, launches into an unexpected, 'emotional' and exemplary confession:

> O my most honoured fathers, let your mercy
> Once win upon your justice, to forgive –
> I am distracted . . .
> I know not which t'address myself to first,
> Whether your fatherhoods, or these innocents . . .
>   . . . whom equally
> I have abused, out of most covetous ends –
> For which, now struck in conscience, here I prostrate
> Myself at your offended feet, for pardon.
>
> (V, x, 3–12)

To convey the general sensation, Jonson neatly juxtaposes the naïve apostrophe of Celia ('O heaven, how just thou art!') and the gallows humor realism of the disguised Volpone ('I'm caught in my own noose,' V, x, 13–14). A sequence of confessions has begun which will indeed carry the play to a just and comic conclusion.

Volpone, cornered but fox-like, contrives an apparent way of escape; convincing Voltore that the 'master' is still alive, he swiftly persuades him to recant the confession.[25] Voltore has just arisen from a supposed 'possession' to announce that the confession is false, when Mosca enters like a redeemed morality hero, re-clothed in the garments of a *clarissimo*. This exquisite theatrical moment brings Mosca and Volpone, both disguised, into a final confrontation. It is Volpone's turn to beg, and what he must plead for, ironically, is his own life ('Say I am living,' V, xii, 54). Mosca's answer (closely recalling the retort of the new King Henry V to Falstaff in *Henry IV, Part Two*) is the obligatory rejection of vice:

> What busy knave is this? Most reverend fathers,
> I sooner had attended your grave pleasures,
> But that my order for the funeral
> Of my dear patron did require me.
>
> (V, xii, 55–8)

The Vice is dead; long live the Parasite. Volpone, unable to strike a bargain with the arrogant Mosca, and about to be whipped and humbled for his pains, now is driven to his own bizarre act of repentance:

> Soft, soft. Whipped?
> And lose all that I have. If I confess,
> It cannot be much more .... I must be resolute:
> The fox shall here uncase.
>
> *He puts off his disguise.*

His confession is at once an accusation of his numerous accomplices in avarice, and a plea for mercy:

> I am Volpone, and this is my knave;
> This his own knave; this, avarice's fool;
> This a chimera of wittol, fool, and knave.
> And, reverend fathers, since we all can hope
> Nought but a sentence, let's not now despair it.
>
> (V, xii, 89–93)

To the judge's astonishment ('the knot is now undone by miracle!'

V, xii, 95) and Bonario's sententious relief ('Heaven could not long let such gross crimes be hid,' V, xii, 98) justice is indeed served by the confessions and counter-confessions of the entangled guilty. The sum of the actions resembles the concluding scene of *Respublica*, in which Avarice and his subordinate vices are trapped in their own accusations:[26]

ADULATION Nay Madame, the cause of all this was Avarice.
He forged us new names, and did us all entice.
OPPRESSION We neither did nor could work but by his advice!
ADULATION Because I got no more, he chid me once or twice!
INSOLENCE Madame, only Avarice made us all to fall.
AVARICE Yea? Fall to peaching? Nay then will I tell all.
Madame, ere I had taught these merchants any while,
They were cunninger than I, all men to beguile.

Corvino and Voltore 'beg favor,' Celia, playing her part as an innocent minister of grace, urges 'mercy.' And mercy, in the sense that no capital sentences are imposed, tempers the justice of an ending that sees the presumptuous Mosca cast down to be a galley slave, the 'dying' Volpone 'mortified' as a shackled prisoner, the law-twisting Voltore disbarred, the decaying Corbaccio sent to a monastery to learn to die properly, and the wife-pandering Corvino exhibited as a public laughing stock and deprived of his ever-innocent wife. The first *Avocatore* will hear no appeals:

Now you begin,
When crimes are done and past, and to be punished,
To think what your crimes are. Away with them!
Let all that see these Vices thus rewarded,
Take heart, and love to study 'em.

(V, xii, 146–50)

In Jonson's comic perspective, the difference between mercy and justice is only the time of day. The ending of *Volpone* draws a moral connection between the protesting, too-late repentant Venetians of his play, and the implicated Londoners of the audience. The fools and knaves of the play are brought by the comedy to a timely reckoning; the audience is reprieved, instructed to take to heart what it has delighted in, and warned to change its ways of living while there is still time. The *Avocatore*'s speech echoes, with interesting changes of emphasis, the final call to repentance of a morality play. The call traditionally draws a hopeful connection between judged actors and the yet-unjudged audience, as in the Angel's final address to Everyman and his audience:[27]

151

> Now thy soule is taken thy body fro,
> Thy reckenynge is crystall-clere.
> Now shalte thou in to the heavenly spere
> Vunto the whiche all ye shall come
> That lyueth well before the daye of dome.

The ending of *Volpone*, a supreme example of what Brecht meant by the 'alienation effect,' turns this conventional appeal into an ironic warning. The fictional sinners have been punished, but the real sinners have escaped thus far. The stern ending of *Volpone*, like the play itself, weighs humanity in the balance and finds it living badly, and expecting (in the absence of poetic justice) to get away with it.

5 The summoning of King Lear

King Lear is Shakespeare's supreme, metaphysical, idiosyncratic morality play – a work of Gothic dramatic architecture that takes premises, structure and characterizations from medieval precedent, and makes of them something utterly unprecedented. It is an exploration of pain, separation, cruelty, incomprehension, madness, and futility, conducted in the guise of a spiritual pilgrimage, and it ends in tragedy.

Shakespearean critics from the time of Bradley have recognized that many of the conventions of *King Lear* may be traced to the morality play.[28] Its patterned cast of characters – a generalized central figure, set about with 'virtuous' and 'vicious' subordinate figures – is unusually symmetrical and old-fashioned. Many of the highly stylized and emblematic scenes of *King Lear* – the humiliation of the loyal adviser Kent, for example, or the reunion of the penitent Lear and his gracious daughter – recall thoroughly traditional pieces of morality play stage business. But to examine and identify these familiar devices is not to convert *King Lear* into a morality play; that would be reductive vision in the extreme. The keener historical truth is to discover how a morality play has been transformed into *King Lear*.

Like *Henry IV, Part One*, *King Lear* is an extension into new philosophical and dramatic regions of the political morality tradition. The roots of the tradition are deep in the Middle Ages. Indeed, the earliest extant morality *The King of Life* (*Pride of Life*, fourteenth century) utilizes the figure of a King to represent humanity. This figural idea, a commonplace in numerous medieval sermons, is at the core of the ancient story in the *Gesta Romanorum* (itself derived from Geoffrey of Monmouth) on which *King Lear* is based. Its 'moralite,' or moral, is expressed as follows:[29]

> MORALITE Dere Frendis, thes Emperour may be callid ech
> worldly man, the which hath thre doughters. The first
> doughter that seith 'I loue my fadir more than myself,' is the
> worlde . . . the second doughter, þat lovith her fader as
> moche as her self, is þi wife, or þi childryn, or þi kyn . . . .
> And the thrid doughter, þat lovith the as moche as þou art
> worthi, is our lord god, whom we lovith to littell. But if we
> come to him in tyme of oure nede with a clene hert and mynde,
> without doute we shull have help of him . . . and he shal sette
> us in our heritage.

In construing the story of *King Lear* as a morality play, then, Shakespeare is following the spirit of his earliest sources as well as a long tradition of plays about kingship – the medieval repentance drama as adapted to courtly and political statement by sixteenth-century playwrights. *King Lear* (1606) is the culmination of a dramatic idea already well developed in *Mundus et Infans* (1508) where the mankind figure is a boisterous and proud ruler, riding for a fall:[30]

> I am worthy and wyght, wytty and wyse,
> I am ryall arayde to reuen vnder the ryse,
> I am proudely aparelede in purpure and byse,
> As golde I glyster in gere.

In his pride the hero of *Mundus et Infans* is misled by Folly, and falls into sickness, old age and near-despair, from which he is rescued by agents of repentance. This pattern of action, repeated and refined in various ways by the authors of such plays as *Nature*, *Magnificence*, *King John*, *Respublica*, *The Three Estates*, *Gorboduc*, *Cambises*; and *Woodstock*, is the plan on which Shakespeare's play and his audience's expectations are ultimately based.

The opening scene of *King Lear* is dense and swift. In a space of 312 lines, eleven important characters are introduced, including all the major characters of the play except Edgar and the Fool; the ritualistic love test is made, Cordelia is banished and betrothed, Kent is dismissed, the King resigns his power, the kingdom is divided, and Goneril and Regan join forces against their father. This remarkable series of actions, whose enactment occupies a large portion of the attention in earlier versions of the Lear story,[31] are here played as a decisive prologue. That the scene is unbewildering is due in part to its archetypal familiarity; there is about it the ritualized formula of a chess opening, with matched and well-defined sides and stereotyped responses. Kent's speech of warning to Lear specifically identifies the cast of characters and the argument:

> Thinkst thou that duty shall have dread to speak
> When power to flattery bows? to plainness honour's bound
> When majesty stoops to folly.
>
> (I, i, 149–51)

From the political morality tradition Shakespeare borrows not merely the central king figure, but also the subordinate character groups. There is, first of all, a loyal and truthful group of advisers (Kent, Cordelia) who are soon to be ignored or discharged. In opposition to this group, and in the ascendant, are a parallel company of flattering advisers wearing the disguise of virtue (Goneril and Regan and their husbands).

The discharge of virtuous advisers and the preferment of disguised vices is the opening gambit of the political morality tradition from *Magnificence* to *Richard II*. The rash, disastrous (and highly predictable) choices which Lear makes in the opening scene initiate a very familiar kind of play about the consequences to the commonwealth of a ruler's mistakes. This is underscored in the second scene by the elaboration of a subplot in the same configuration. Gloucester, a loyal subordinate duke, is given a particular kind of bastard son in Edmund, who persuades him to banish his legitimate son Edgar. Bernard Spivack has carefully traced the characterization of Edmund to its sources in the morality Vice tradition, noting 'his gay alacrity in deception and dissimulation, the breach his stratagem achieves between father and son, and, beyond anything else, his absolute awareness of the moral position.'[32]

The figure of Kent is almost as traditional in his virtue as is Edmund in vice. Acting the role of duty and honor, like Measure in *Magnificence*, he speaks plainly to a ruler and is discharged for his frankness. Like Reason in *Nature*, he does not abandon the ruler who has rejected him. Like Charity in *Youth*, Pity in *Hickscorner*, and Verity in *The Three Estates*, he is put in the stocks for his pains. His soliloquy ('Fortune, good night. Smile once more, turn thy wheel!' II, ii, 180) is a moving lament for what will happen to Lear; it follows the well-established pattern of concern expressed by virtue in disgrace in the earlier plays.[33]

In the traditional sequence of the political morality play the ruler's mistakes are followed quickly and logically by providential retribution. In *Magnificence* Skelton confronts his errant hero with a series of agents of rebtribution (Adversity, Poverty, and Despair) who punish Magnificence and lead him to the verge of damnation. The retributive process which Shakespeare arranges to afflict

Lear and Gloucester has its origins in just this idea of dramatic justice. Like the comparable sequences in *Richard II* and *Macbeth*, however, the retribution in *King Lear* leads the audience inward to the psychology and suffering of its victims. In this way an old and potentially mechanical series of stage actions can be reimagined as vividly believable human experience.

Shakespeare's variations on the traditional formula of retribution serve the cause of greater complexity and tragic action. Unlike typical political morality heroes, Lear and Gloucester do not have the excuse of youth or inexperience. Gloucester has two grown men for sons, and Lear, the father of three daughters, is 'forescore and upward' (IV, vii, 61). Lear's irresponsible prodigality is the more tragic for being unseasonable and inappropriate, as the Fool continually reminds him; Gloucester's rash credulity in distrusting Edgar is rationalized by 'heavenly compulsion,' as Edmund wryly points out (I, ii, 128 ff.). Lear and Gloucester are held responsible, from the beginning, for their own exercise of free will. Nor are they allowed the traditional period of temporary euphoria which follows the commission of sin in the old morality play. The retribution begins at the beginning. The ceremony of initiation into experience in *King Lear* is in all these ways a most unusual one, performed on the unlikely persons of mature men who should, by the course of nature, have known better. The tragedy accepts no excuses; as the Fool tells Lear, 'thou shoulds't not have been old till thou hads't been wise' (I, v, 48-9).

The question of identity, which is posed by the tidy circumstances of a morality play like *Everyman* or *Mankind*, and answered in orthodox theological terms, is rephrased by Shakespeare to fit the unruly and expanded ideological world of *King Lear*, with its strange intimations of pagan determinism, medieval hope, and seventeenth-century skepticism.[34] Gloucester and Lear, perceiving themselves to be the injured fathers of ungrateful children (Edgar and Cordelia), are in fact the duped fathers of untrustworthy children (Edmund, Goneril, and Regan). These misconceptions of identity are fundamental, and can only be corrected by bitter experience.

The slow and painful series of discoveries which Gloucester makes systematically alienate him from the King, from the daughters and their husbands who brand him a traitor and torture him, and even from the son whom he trusted. Regan's commentary on the credulity of the blinded Gloucester is definitive:

> Thou call'st on him that hates thee. It was he
> That made the overture of thy treasons to us,
> Who is too good to pity thee.
>
> (III, vii, 88–90)

This revelation, intended as further torture, brings Gloucester pain and insight. His eyes forcibly closed to the false appearances of things, Gloucester sees distantly his real identity, his crime, and his only remaining hope:

> Oh, my follies! Then Edgar was abused.
> Kind gods, forgive me that, and prosper him!
>
> (III, vii, 91–2)

Regan's response forecasts the pilgrimage to despair, and beyond it, that Gloucester must now travel:

> Go thrust him out at gates and let him smell
> His way to Dover.
>
> (III, vii, 93–4)

For Lear, the discovery of his own loss of identity comes more quickly, and even more disastrously. Gloucester has lost his sight, but Lear will lose his faculties of reason. Like Everyman summoned to death's reckoning, Lear finds in his abdication that he has been abandoned by everything with which he had hitherto defined himself. In this discovery he learns in pain what Regan and Goneril have known from the beginning. ('Yet he hath ever but slenderly known himself,' I, i, 297). Arriving at Goneril's as a king in name only, he is treated accordingly:

> LEAR . . . Who am I, sir?
> OSWALD My lady's father.
>
> (I, iv, 86–7)

When Goneril does indeed treat him as a mere father, the effect is to disorient him completely:

> LEAR Doth any here know me? This is not Lear.
> Doth Lear walk thus? Speak thus? Where are his eyes?
> Either his notion weakens, his discernings
> Are lethargied – Ha! Waking? Tis not so.
> Who is it that can tell me who I am?
> FOOL Lear's shadow.
>
> (I, iv, 246–50)

Clutching at conflicting thoughts of doubt, contrition, and revenge, Lear is being summoned to a cruel self-reckoning that can only make the abandonments of Everyman by friends and family seem kind, dispassionate, and merciful by contrast. There may be,

Shakespeare suggests, some fates very much worse than death. Lear, leaving Goneril's without his kingship, is a lost and tormented creature who has only begun to suffer. On arrival at Gloucester's he encounters a further series of shocks, beginning with the sight of Kent in the stocks, and leading to the recognition that his daughter's cruelty is somehow his own odious fault:

> But yet thou art my flesh, my blood, my daughter,
> Or rather a disease that's in my flesh
> Which I must needs call mine. Thou art a boil,
> A plague sore, an embossed carbuncle
> In my corrupted blood.
>
> (II, iv, 224–8)

The scene culminates in a ritual stripping from Lear of his worldly goods, symbolized by the one hundred knights of his following. Goneril and Regan, joining forces, carry out the ritual with a vengeance:

> GONERIL ... What need you five and twenty, ten, or five,
> To follow in a house where twice so many
> Have a command to tend you?
> REGAN What need one?
>
> (II, iv, 264–6)

Lear's reply demonstrates how thoroughly his own self-conception has been based on these external possessions, and how little will be left of the old Lear when they are taken from him:

> Oh reason not the need. Our basest beggars
> Are in the poorest thing superfluous.
> Allow not nature more than nature needs,
> Man's life's as cheap as beast's.
>
> (II, iv, 267–70)

Begging for patience, abjuring womanish tears, vowing revenges, prophesying his own madness, Lear leads himself defiantly away into the storm and civil war, attended by his alter-ego the Fool. Shakespeare's stage of the imagination, expanding to contain the vastness of an uncertain cosmos and magnify the depths of a tormented mind, carries the idea of the medieval world theater to its logical and somewhat awesome conclusions. The old pathway through adversity to knowledge appears, in this transmogrified vision, more painful and uncertain than the compilers of repentance dramas like *Wisdom* seem ever to have imagined possible.[35]

157

> All þe penance þat may be wrought,
> Ne all þe preyer þat seyde be kan,
> Wythowt sorowe of hert relesyt nought;
> That in especyall reformyth man
> Ande makyt hym as clene as when he begane.

For Gloucester, blinded, guilt-ridden, and led haltingly by an old man toward Dover, regeneration is no longer possible in the physical sense. The damage has been done. The pathetic sight of him makes another unfortunate outcast realize that there are depths of misery beyond his previous imagining. This outcast, chosen by Shakespeare to play the role of agent of repentance to Gloucester, is his son Edgar. He has, since the play began, been betrayed and slandered by his brother, falsely accused of capital crimes by his father, forced into hiding in the disguise of a Bedlam beggar. As such, Edgar seems in every way *un*like the stereotypical morality agents of repentance. He has little in common with the stock piety and hollow preaching of Shrift in *Castle of Perseverance*, or Charity in *Youth*, or Mercy in *Mankind*.

He does, however, bear some resemblance to the homiletic figure of Good Deeds in *Everyman*, who is crippled by Everyman's sins. In Edgar's decay Gloucester's sins are made visible; in the possibility of his restitution lies the only hope for Gloucester's peace of mind. Gloucester has previously seen 'Poor Tom' as a companion of Lear, and been moved by the sight. Edgar has maintained the disguise out of fear, and kept his distance. Now, when Edgar, described as 'madman and beggar too,' approaches his father, the blind man seems to sense a horrible connection between the beggar's misery and his own son's downfall:

> I' the last night's storm I such a fellow saw,
> Which made me think a man a worm. My son
> Came then into my mind, and yet my mind
> Was then scarce friends with him. I have heard more since.
> As flies to wanton boys are we to the gods,
> They kill us for their sport.

(IV, i, 34-9)

The context of these lines is crucial and ironic. In bringing comfort to Gloucester, Edgar has brought him perilously close to despair. Edgar must remain disguised to prevent Gloucester from confirming his worst suspicions, of how thoroughly he has ruined Edgar's life. It will only be much later, when Gloucester has passed his crisis of despair and Edgar is on the verge of vindication, that Edgar will be able to confirm the accuracy of Gloucester's tragic intuition.

In the world of *Everyman*, agents of repentance freely announce themselves, and a simple process of penance on the hero's part clears his book of sin and restores Good Deeds. In the harsh world of *King Lear* it is more difficult.

Edgar, disguised from Gloucester by a mutuality of injuries, painfully attempts to help Gloucester to cleanse his soul. Edgar has no sooner blessed his father than the blind man reciprocates by offering him all of his remaining goods. He asks to be led to Dover.

> There is a cliff whose high and bending head
> Looks fearfully in the confined deep.
> Bring me but to the very brim of it . . . .

(IV, ii, 76-8)

For the stock stage emblems of despair, the rope and the dagger, Shakespeare has substituted a cliff's edge of the mind.[36] That it is imaginary, an opiate figment of Gloucester's mind from beginning to end, is crucial to the staging of the scene of Gloucester's attempted suicide. Edgar leads him to safe ground, and this plan ('Why I do trifle thus with his despair/Is done to cure it,' IV, vi, 33-4) is a penitential one. Edgar rhetorically supplies the steepness, the sounds of the sea and the vast perspective; Gloucester supplies the moving and even convincing justification for self-slaughter:

> O you mighty gods!
> This world I do renounce, and in your sights
> Shake patiently my great affliction off.
> If I could bear it longer and not fall
> To quarrel with your great opposeless wills,
> My snuff and loathed part of nature should
> Burn itself out. If Edgar live, oh, bless him!

(IV, vi, 34-40)

Out of Gloucester's imagined act of desperation Edgar fashions a 'miracle' of providence. Pretending to be a man on the shore below, rousing the 'fallen' Gloucester from the 'dead,' Edgar presents him with a new lease on his undervalued life:

> But thou dost breathe,
> Hath heavy substance, bleed'st not, speak'st, art sound.
> Ten masts at each make not the altitude
> Which thou hast perpendicularly fell.
> Thy life's a miracle.

(IV, vi, 51-5)

Casting off affliction, like Good Deeds after Everyman's repentance, Edgar has presented the vulnerable Gloucester with a consciousness of his attributes of life (Discretion, Strength, Wits, etc.). At the same time Edgar has changed his own disguise. The Bedlam beggar has been left behind on the imaginary cliff's edge, and the blame for despair unjustly shifted to him by Gloucester:

> Henceforth I'll bear
> Affliction till it do cry out itself
> 'Enough, enough' and die. That thing you speak of,
> I took it for a man. Often 'twould say
> 'The fiend, the fiend.' He led me to that place.
>
> (IV, vi, 75–9)

Intruding into this fictitious scene of repentance wanders the mad and visionary figure of Lear. Shakespeare has used the illusory happy ending of Gloucester's redemption to introduce a scene of grotesque irony. The two central once-powerful figures – a madman and a blind man – make what sense they can of what is left of one another.

Gloucester recognizes the King's voice. Lear, unintentionally wounding Gloucester with references to Edmund's bastardy and the culpable adultery in which Gloucester conceived him, comes gradually to recognize the blind man, and preaches him a brilliant sermon on justice. Lear's *exempla* (the thieving Justice, the farmer's dog, the lusting whore-whipper, the usurer-hangman, the fur-gowned vice, the gold-plated sin, the blind politician) are a catalogue of the world's injustices, and they lead him to an elemental conclusion about the life process:

> LEAR I know thee well enough. Thy name is Gloucester.
> Thou must be patient, we came crying hither.
> Thou know'st the first time that we smell the air,
> We wawl and cry. I will preach to thee. Mark.
> GLOUCESTER Alack, alack the day!
> LEAR When we are born, we cry that we are come
> To this great stage of fools.
>
> (IV, vi, 181–7)

Instructed by the spectacle as well as the preaching of Lear, Gloucester asks the gods for death, but prays he will not be tempted again to kill himself. His somewhat qualified repentance and Edgar's removal of the Poor Tom disguise brings them closer together, with their worst afflictions apparently in the past. They are not yet father and son, however, and more obstacles remain to be overcome.

Oswald's sudden appearance with sword drawn suggests the resurgence of despair; it is a seeming answer to Gloucester's plea for a quick death. Offering himself willingly to be killed, Gloucester is all but a suicide once again. Though Edgar defends him successfully, Gloucester shows no gratitude, and the letters which Oswald is carrying to 'Edmund, Earl of Gloucester' reveal that Gloucester's bastard son has usurped his father's title and plotted the murder of the Duke of Albany from adulterous motives. Gloucester finds in these events a counsel of despair. He wishes that he were insane like Lear and therefore unable to comprehend what he is experiencing.

The son and father wander through the battlefield of what is for them an almost irrelevant civil war, as Edgar searches for an opportunity to challenge Edmund, while attempting to keep Gloucester from despair.

> GLO. No farther, sir. A man may rot even here.
> EDGAR What, in ill thoughts again? Men must endure
> Their going hence, even as their coming hither.
> Ripeness is all.
>
> (V, ii, 8–11)

Gloucester's answer ('And that's true too.') is his final line in the play, and it sums up the equivocal and unorthodox philosophical position which he has reached as a result of suffering. He accepts the necessity of enduring, but he also points out the uselessness of it. Ripeness is one truth about the human predicament; it is as true as rottenness.

When Gloucester's two sons have fought and one of them lies dying, the punishment of Gloucester and his vindication have been completed. There is little sense of the triumphant, however. Speaking to the dying Edmund, Edgar hazards an unsettling retributive explanation for what they all have suffered:

> The gods are just, and of our pleasant vices
> Make instruments to plague us.
> The dark and vicious place where thee he got
> Cost him his eyes.
>
> (V. iii, 171–4)

It is suddenly apparent that Gloucester and Edgar are no longer together. Edgar expresses for the first time his belief in the guilt of the man he has rescued from despair, and his understanding of the terrible justice of events.

> ALBANY How have you known the miseries of your father?

EDGAR By nursing them, my lord. List a brief tale
And when 'tis told, oh, that my heart would burst.

(V, iii, 180–2)

In victory, as Gloucester's champion, Edgar is a changed man.
His acceptance of deterministic retribution and his wish for death
are reminiscent of his father's resigned attitude, and quite unlike
his own earlier statements of hope. They express the concluding
pessimistic qualifications with which Shakespeare differentiates the
meaning of Gloucester's life from the stereotypes. In the 'brief tale'
of Gloucester's death there is a semblance of a morality play,
modified by the inadequacy of a mere morality play to explain away
the problem of evil, and the fact of suffering. There has been no
homiletic scene of death-in-despair, but also no transcendent
deathbed repentance, no formalized 'good ending.' With enigmatic
self-understanding, Gloucester has reached a conclusion of reconciliation. Despite and because of Edgar, his pilgrimage has ended
where he lived, in a painful ceremony of knowledge:

> And in this habit
> Met I my father with his bleeding rings
> Their precious stones new-lost, became his guide
> Led him, begged for him, saved him from despair,
> Never – oh fault! – revealed myself unto him
> Until some half-hour past, when I was armed.
> Not sure, though hoping of this good success,
> I asked his blessing, and from first to last
> Told him my pilgrimage. But his flawed heart –
> Alack, too weak the conflict to support!
> Twist two extremes of passion, joy and grief,
> Burst smilingly.

(V, iii, 188–99)

Gloucester's pilgrimage to an ambiguous understanding is parallel
and subordinate to another, and very different story – the tragedy
of King Lear. In interpreting the Lear story, many critics have
noted its traditional morality play motifs and Christian imagery,
and used them to 'demonstrate' the optimism of the play's conclusions:

> Should we not be at least near the truth if we called this
> poem *The Redemption of King Lear* . . . .[37]

We watch, not ancient Britons, but humanity; not England,
but the World. Mankind's relation to the universe is the

162

theme of Lear and Edgar's trumpet is as the universal
judgment summoning vicious man to account . . . . It is a play
of creative suffering. Mankind are working out a sort of
purgatory . . . . The good are sweetened, purified by
adversity.[38]

. . . a sublime morality play . . . set against a backdrop of
eternity . . . . Man's endless search for spiritual values,
rewarded, in this case, by the final discovery of them just
before he must answer Death's awful summons.[39]

If one thinks again in terms of the moral play, it is as though
Lear loses the world only to save his soul by confession and
penitence.[40]

Lear's pathway into the storm and what lies beyond it, is a more
frightening, less certain journey than these critical reassurances
would seem to suggest. The tormentors of the King are horrible
magnifications of the old enemies of mankind: the world (the
pitiless elements of earth, air, water, and fire), the flesh (the bare
weakness of unaccommodated man), and the devil (the terrible
possessions of madness). Lear, 'in his little world of man' (III, i, 10)
is summoned to a reckoning:

> Rumble thy bellyful! Spit, fire! Spout, rain! . . .
> Then let fall
> Your horrible pleasure. Here I stand, your slave,
> A poor, infirm, weak and despised old man.
> (III, i, 14, 18–20)

As the central figure in a play from the political morality tradition,
Lear is also suffering a storm in the 'little world' of the state, where
civil war and foreign invasion disturb the political order as a direct
consequence of his intemperate actions. Yet Shakespeare relegates
these matters to the background, in order to project and consider
the greater inner conflict. It is there, in the byways of his own
wounded mind, that Lear's deepest torments and trials occur.

Lear interprets the storm as a premonition of divine punishment,
being visited upon those who deserve it, and causing those who are
guilty at heart to be fearful, to tremble, to reveal themselves.
His initial exultation in the storm and his refusal to seek shelter,
are an expression of his insistence that he has nothing to fear from
such a summons.

> Close pent-up guilts,
> Rive your concealing continents and cry

These dreadful summoners grace. I am a man
More sinned against than sinning.

(III, ii, 57–60)

But the storm and subsequent events are gradually instructive to Lear. Innocent of his own injustices, Lear is to be informed of the reality of evil and his participation in it, initiated into the suffering and misery of the human race. His instructors are carefully and grotesquely chosen; they are not conniving vices, but friends and comforters, more unfortunate even than he.

At first there is only the Fool, urging Lear to seek shelter by the common sense of proverbs and ballad-snatches. Disconnected and indicative of mental confusion as the Fool's scraps are, they have a common theme: human life is harsh and uncertain, people are untrustworthy, justice is unavailable, the rain rains every day. Kent, banished and ruined himself by Lear's unjust folly, now arrives in his guise of loyal servant, Lear's second emblematic companion in the storm. Urging Lear to take cover, he tells him that the storm is unbearable by 'man's nature.' What is true for a fool and a servant is also true for a king, who is first of all a man.

Lear's earliest recognition of the ceremony in which he is involved had been a passing thought that the elements might be in league with his daughters; seeing the Fool's response to the storm he discovers a bit of himself:

How dost, my boy? Art cold?
I am cold myself.

(III, ii, 68–9)

As Lear reaches the threshold of shelter, he realizes that his disregard of the storm was not out of guiltlessness, but rather out of preoccupation. The tempest in his mind was simply stronger, and it continues to obsess him. In this affliction he is able to imagine another set of victims of the storm, not the unpunished guilty but the unguilty punished. For these victims he feels a new and royal sympathy:

Poor naked wretches, whereso'er you are,
That bide the pelting of this pitiless storm,
How shall your houseless heads and unfed sides,
Your looped and windowed raggedness, defend you
From seasons such as these? Oh, I have ta'en
Too little care of this.

(III, iv, 28–33)

This sentiment, while touched with insight, is highly generalized. The next of Lear's instructors, emerging with a rush from the hovel, makes the misery of such wretches individual and visible. It is Edgar, victim of Edmund's and Gloucester's injustice, disguised as a fiend-obsessed shivering beggar. Lear's instant response shows a recognition of common misfortune that is by no means as mad as it sounds:

> Hast thou given all to thy two daughters
> And art thou come to this?
>
> (III, iv, 49–50)

Poor Tom's story, as it unravels amid warnings against the fiend and indiscriminate blessings, is a confession of sins culminating in a riddle-definition of Man, the 'paragon of animals':[41] 'False of heart, light of ear, bloody of hand, hog in sloth, fox in stealth, wolf in greediness, dog in madness, lion in prey.' (III, iv, 94–6). Lear responds with what is, for him, a 'philosophical' discovery. In Poor Tom he has found an answer to the still-pending question 'Who is it that can tell me who I am?'

> Why thou wert better in thy grave than to answer
> With thy uncovered body this extremity of the skies.
> Is man no more than this? . . . Here's three on's are
> sophisticated. Thou art the thing itself. Unaccommodated man
> is no more but such a poor, bare, forked animal as thou art.
> Off, off you lendings! Come, unbutton here.
>
> (III, iv, 104–6, 109–13)

In this way Lear's instruction by ministers of grace, in a grotesque tragic parody of the morality play sequence, leads him to a perception of truth which is insupportable. In his madness Lear attempts to conduct a trial and pass sentence *in absentia* on his unnatural daughters, with the Fool, Kent, and Edgar as officers of the court. But the imaginary defendants easily escape Lear's imagination and we learn that in the real world Lear himself is under sentence of death. Earthly power and justice have parted company, as multiplying examples confirm – Kent's banishment, Edgar's disgrace, Gloucester's blinding, Goneril's adultery, Edmund's rise to power – and Lear, knowing nothing directly of these events, seems to intuit them. His madness can be defined as a malignant perception of total injustice.

The comfort and instruction which Lear's companions provide, is, despite their best intentions, a counsel of despair. That it is also, perhaps, the truth is a possibility that Shakespeare deliberately asks his audience to ponder. There are no easy evasions of the chaotic darkness in *King Lear*. This is particularly true because its orthodox alternative – the possibility of a redeeming divine justice that transcends earthly injustices – is also fully articulated.

There is, for example, a certain justice or logic in even the most unjust occurrences in the play: Cordelia is abrupt, Lear rash, Edgar and Gloucester credulous. That they are punished in the earlier portions of the play is understandable; it is only the degree of punishment which seems excessive, and the likelihood exists for the audience that the play will be resolved in their favor.

As is often noted, all Shakespeare's precedents in earlier versions of the Lear story dictated a happy ending to the play, with Lear restored to the throne and reunited with Cordelia. The impulse which led Nahum Tate in 1671 to reconstitute a happy ending of *King Lear* is deep in the dramatic logic of the play, and completely true to medieval precedents. That Shakespeare chose otherwise is a fact which is profoundly important to any interpretation of the meaning of *King Lear*.

The possibilities of an untragic resolution of the play are embodied in a resurgence of forces in opposition to Goneril, Regan, Cornwall and Edmund. That all these characters are dead by the end of the play is testimony to the degree to which *King Lear* is completely tragic. The resurgence of good is sufficiently successful to punish evil, but not to secure justice. Albany, a character too easily overlooked in the text of *King Lear*, though crucial to any performance of the play, is the harbinger of such a resurgence. As early as Act I he expresses uncertainties about the way Lear is being treated, and by Act IV he has taken Lear's side against his wife and Regan:

> Tigers, not daughters, what have you performed?
> A father and a gracious aged man
> Whose reverence even the head-lugged bear would lick
> Most barbarous, most degenerate, have you madded!
>
> (IV, ii, 40–3)

Albany's change of sides is motivated at least in part by his wife's contemptuous unfaithfulness. Nevertheless he speaks with conviction and prays for divine intervention:

> If that the Heavens do not their visible spirits
> Send quickly down to tame these vile offences,
> It will come.
> Humanity must perforce prey on itself,
> Like monsters of the deep.
>
> (IV, ii, 46–50)

The words recall in interesting ways the opening speech in *Everyman*, spoken by God:[42]

> For, and I leve the people thus alone
> In theyr lyfe and wycked tempestes,
> Veryly they will become moch worse than beestes . . .
> Where art thou, Deth, thou myghty messengere.

Albany's words are indeed followed by events which seem the expression of divine providence. When the news of Cornwall's death in the course of blinding Gloucester reaches Albany, he proclaims:

> This shows you are above,
> You justicers, that our nether crimes
> So speedily can venge.
>
> (IV, ii, 78–80)

Following immediately on this scene comes news that Cordelia has returned to England. That she comes with the army of her husband the King of France to effect the political restoration of Lear is a fact of the story which, again, Shakespeare relegates to the background. Instead the focus is on foreshadowing the reunion of father and daughter, and it is made abundantly clear in the imagery of the speeches ('holy water,' 'heavenly eyes,' IV, iii, 32) that Cordelia can be regarded as a minister of Christian grace. Lear is depicted in the traditional guise of the as-yet unrepentant sinner:

> These things sting
> His mind so venomously that burning shame
> Detains him from Cordelia.
>
> (IV, iii, 47–9)

The foreshadowing continues in the following scene, with Cordelia's appearance, searching for the mad King. Pledging Lear's restoration to health and kingdom, as well as her love for him, she seeks a cure for his soul. Once again there are telling Christian references ('O dear Father/It is thy business that I go about,' IV, iv, 23–4).

But the promised reconciliation of Lear and Cordelia is delayed by Shakespeare to permit the juxtaposition of mad Lear and blind Gloucester. 'Fantastically dressed with wild flowers,' Lear is a lost soul, quenched of pride but also of hope. His growing conviction that the world contains no justice is laid bare, together with a furious attack on women, laced with sexual disgust. The diseases of the soul from which Lear suffers are pitilessly exposed, once more foreshadowing his need for Cordelia. He runs from the scene, pursued by Cordelia's attendants, and soon to be apprehended, but quite unlike the sinner frightened of repentance. He is rather the mad-man, frightened of reality.

When Lear is next seen he has been given medicines and, during a long sleep, reclothed in the garments of a king. This action, the traditional morality play ceremony of reclothing the penitent hero,[43] is Cordelia's way of reconstructing Lear's identity in its original rank, but in chastened form. The drama of the scene, as Lear awakes, is in the difference between the actual Lear and the man whose clothes he is wearing:

> CORDELIA How does my royal lord? How fares your Majesty?
> LEAR You do me wrong to take me out o' the grave.
> Thou art a soul in bliss, but I am bound
> Upon a wheel of fire that mine own tears
> Do scald like molten lead.
>
> (IV, vii, 44–8)

The reconciliation of Lear and Cordelia is intensely and visibly moving for many reasons. It fulfills, seemingly, Lear's original intentions in dividing the kingdom. It restores, seemingly, a lost soul from perdition. But it is also moving because it is ominous, in the unchanged reality of the play's world. The Fool's earlier warning ('Let go thy hold when a great wheel runs down a hill, lest it break thy neck with following it,' II, iv, 72–4) applies to Cordelia. It is a fatal reconciliation.

Lear, revived as if from the dead, becomes the emblem and cause of France's army, and a pawn of complex power politics. Albany, who has no choice but to oppose such a foreign invasion, intends no harm to the King; his ally Edmund, however, leaves no doubt of his plan to circumvent this reprieve:

> As for the mercy
> Which he intends to Lear and to Cordelia,
> The battle done, and they within our power,
> Shall never see his pardon.
>
> (V, i, 65–8)

Shakespeare thus foreshadows the outcome of this ill-sided battle, and the merciless tragedy that will occur as a result. When next Lear and Cordelia appear on stage they are prisoners of Edmund. Their illusions of reconciliation are the more heartbreaking for being illusions. Their anticipated scene of blessing and forgiveness belongs to an older and more innocent drama:

> Come let's away to prison.
> We two alone will sing like birds i' the cage.
> When thou dost ask me blessing, I'll kneel down
> And ask of thee forgiveness. So we'll live,
> And pray, and sing, and tell old tales and laugh
> At gilded butterflies . . .
> And take upon's the mystery of things
> As if we were God's spies.
>
> (V, iii, 8–13, 16–17)

Edmund's instructions to the captain re-evoke the kind of world in which they are actually living:

> Know thou this, that men
> Are as the time is, to be tender-minded
> Does not become a sword.
>
> (V, iii, 30–32)

The Captain's answer ('If it be man's work, I'll do it,' V, iii, 39) prepares the audience for the last scene of Shakespeare's essay on mankind. When Albany demands the prisoners, Edmund can answer that they are in safe keeping, ready to be summoned for trial.

When Lear re-enters, many things have changed. Edgar has challenged and wounded Edmund to the death, Gloucester is reported dead, Goneril and Regan have quarreled and one is poisoned, the other a suicide. But what has changed most is the lifeless body in his arms. Cordelia, the minister of grace and forgiveness and regeneration is dead. The image of the old man and the dead body poses for those who remain alive a simple question – what does a dead Cordelia signify? To Kent, Edgar, and Albany it means the end of the world:

> KENT Is this the promised end?
> EDGAR Or image of that horror.
> ALBANY Fall and cease.
>
> (V, iii, 263–4)

Newly dead, there is the illusion in her body that she could revive. Lear's senses scan the possibility, his mind the meaning of a resurgence of life over death:

> If it be so
> It is a chance which does redeem all sorrows
> That ever I have felt.
>
> (V, iii, 265–7)

His senses examine, his mind ponders the alternative conditions and the blame. When Kent speaks of Goneril's and Regan's suicide, and tells him 'All's cheerless, dark, and deadly,' Lear answers 'Aye, so I think' (V, iii, 290, 292).

Out of the ruins of so many lives the semblance of a just and moral ending is suggested by Albany – Lear will rule for his lifetime with Edgar and Kent restored to places of honor:

> All friends shall taste
> The wages of their virtue, and all foes
> The cup of their deserving.
>
> (V, iii, 302–4)

The idea of resurgent order, of youth in succession to age, and a last judgment in which good and evil are rewarded, glitters for an instant in Albany's speech. It is perhaps what one ought to say under such circumstances, what one does say even if it cannot be true. Lear answers it in the negative:

> No, no, no life!
> Why should a dog, a horse, a rat have life
> And thou no breath at all? Thou'lt come no more,
> Never, never, never, never, never!
>
> (V, iii, 305–8)

In Lear's last moments Shakespeare admires the beauty of the idea that there is somewhere beyond hopelessness a solution to the human predicament. He allows it to flicker, in the evil negation of the world, into the knowledge of which King Lear has been summoned. Then he extinguishes it. In a merciless world, Death is a mercy for King Lear. Shakespeare gives the last words to Albany, who speaks more soberly now, as if an idea had died.

> The weight of this sad time we must obey,
> Speak what we feel, not what we ought to say.
> The oldest hath borne most. We that are young
> Shall never see so much, nor live so long.
>
> (V, iii, 323–6)

Chapter VII

European plays: the morality tradition from the Middle Ages to Calderón

Early medieval drama, like medieval music, painting, and architecture, is international. The texts of liturgical dramas, whether from France, Spain, Germany, Hungary, or wherever in Western Christendom, are in Latin and almost indistinguishably of one tradition in their literary texture and implicit theatrical conventions. With the coming of vernacular drama, local characteristics become more apparent: the English development of creation-to-doomsday cycles offers some contrast to the characteristic Continental elaboration of the Passion play, for example. Nevertheless, the common religious institutions of the West continue to produce a religious drama with common underlying assumptions – dramatic as well as theological.

We should therefore expect to find that the morality play is not an exclusively English phenomenon, but rather an English manifestation of a more widespread dramatic tradition. That, in fact, is what seems to be the case; there were evidently many distinct manifestations in many localities. The search for a European morality tradition leads through Celtic and Germanic texts from Wales, the Netherlands, and Germany to scattered evidence in fifteenth-century Italy, a significant and in many cases unstudied corpus of texts from fifteenth- and sixteenth-century France, and a unique flowering in seventeenth-century Spain, where historical developments brought the morality tradition into the hands of writers of genius, including Lope de Vega and Calderón de la Barca.

1 Celtic

Court records of King James IV of Scotland relate that on 13 August 1503, 'after dynnar, a Moralite was played by the said Master Inglishe and hys companyions, in the Presence of the Kyng and Qwene, and then daunces war daunced.'[1] What this lost play was like cannot be determined, but the record of its performance indicates that a later and more celebrated Scots morality play, Sir David Lindsay's *Satire of the Three Estates* (first performed in 1540 before King James V) is no isolated instance.[2] There are no examples surviving in the Irish language, but the earliest morality in English – *The King of Life* (*Pride of Life*) – was preserved in an Irish manuscript in the archives of the Priory of the Holy Trinity, Dublin. On the basis of linguistic affinities, the most recent editor of this fragmentary play has concluded that the text was not merely copied down in Ireland, but was probably composed there.[3]

Among the handful of medieval plays in the Welsh language is a perfectly preserved example of a morality. This brief yet dramatically effective little play, *The Soul and the Body*, was edited and translated by Gwenan Jones in 1918, but has almost entirely escaped notice. When the play begins, the Body is already dead. From this vantage point, awaiting punishment, he warns the audience of the wages of sin. The Soul enters and the two dispute over which one is to blame for their common misfortune in death. The Soul blames the Body for its former appetites, and the Body blames the Soul for failing to exercise its rightful command. As the Soul parts from the Body, the Angel Michael and the Devil (armed with bow and arrow) come to dispute over which has claim to the Soul. In the course of the dispute the opposing sides are augmented by two more devils on one hand, and the Virgin Mary on the other. The Virgin, interceding, takes the case before Jesus, sitting in Judgment as God the Son. She summarizes the Soul's condition:[4]

> He said psalms
> And showed repentance in the hour of death,
> And received thy consecrated Body.
> I ask that with him
> I may place my Pater Nosters.

Jesus grants Mary's petition and the Soul is saved. The Body, left behind, laments its fate; however, it too fulfills a penitential function. A Strong Man, seeing the weakness of the Body, is drawn from pride to repentance. The play ends with an exhortation by the Angel to the audience, preaching the power of mercy and the necessity of repentance and good works.

The Welsh playwright who composed *The Soul and the Body*, probably sometime early in the sixteenth century, is quite certainly working in the same tradition of repentance drama as his English contemporaries. He blends a variety of familiar motifs (the debate of the body and soul, the Trial in Heaven, the coming of Death) into a coherent dramatic action. The play, though lacking verbal comedy and subtleties of characterization, is well-structured and economical in its rhetoric. *The Soul and the Body* assumes an easy relationship with its audience and makes telling use of direct address. Aside from its own content, the play may be valuable in reconstructing the lost conclusion of *The King of Life* (*Pride of Life*) in which the Body and Soul debate and the Virgin intercedes to save the soul of the King.

2 Netherlands and Germany

There are several interesting fifteenth-century religious plays from the Netherlands, including one which seems an amalgamation of all the traditional 'types' of medieval drama. The *Eerst Bliscap*, or *First Joy of Mary*, is, to begin with, a 'Miracle of the Virgin' play; however, it comprehends all previous human history in its attempt to account for the historical *necessity* of Mary. It is here that elements of the morality tradition appear. In the postlapsarian world of the play, the laments of Adam and other Old Testament patriarchs provoke two auxiliary characters, Distress and Prayer, to beg Heaven for redress. These petitioners win the ear of Mercy, and thus initiate a Trial in Heaven (cf. *Castle of Perseverance*) in which Mercy and Justice contend over the fate of Man. God's decision to save Man by means of the incarnation necessitates the creation of Mary.[5] The *Eerst Bliscap* shows vividly the microcosmic fore-shortening of the morality, the sense in which it seeks to imitate in miniature the large pattern of Christian history. This aspect of the form is, by general agreement, achieved most completely in the late medieval play, *Everyman* – or, as it is known in a contemporaneous Dutch version, *Elckerlijc*.

Whether *Elckerlijc* or *Everyman* is the original work will perhaps be disputed for as long as the moralities are studied. The texts are a pair of twins, and they have been scrutinized by philologists and argued over by the scholars of half a dozen nations since 1865, when Karl Goedeke first challenged the originality of *Everyman*. The battle has been fought first on nationalistic and ultimately on reverse-nationalistic lines, with the best modern arguments for the primacy of *Everyman* given by H. de Vocht of Louvain, and for *Elckerlijc* by E. R. Tigg, an Englishman.[6] Critics championing *Elckerlijc* note the greater regularity of its versification, list instances of 'mistranslation' in *Everyman*, and find a practical explanation of the dual texts in the nature of the Anglo-Dutch book trade; the partisans of *Everyman*, on the other hand, cite the greater coherence of the play with the English dramatic tradition, quote instances of 'superiority' in the text of *Everyman*, and find linguistic blunders in the names of characters, and even the title of the Dutch play.

In this tangle of opinions, the supporters of *Elckerlijc* currently hold a slight argumentative advantage. My own belief that *Everyman* is probably the original play rests on two primarily non-philological grounds: the literary quality of the play, and the determination of its date. The argument that *Everyman* must be a translation is, *prima facie*, unconvincing. Its language and versification are 'plain English' of a very high order, as T. S. Eliot has pointed out. If *Everyman* is not the original work, it is that literary miracle of poetry, the translation which transcends the original. The arguments for the priority of *Elckerlijc* necessitate, as the most recent editor of *Everyman* has pointed out, that the date of *Everyman* be moved forward from 1495 to 1518–25.[7] To do so would require us to project the composition of this indisputably medieval work of art forward a crucial two decades into the age of Luther and Machiavelli. An earlier date and an English origin remain, to my mind, the more probable, on literary grounds.

Whatever its parentage, *Elckerlijc* is certainly the best known Dutch play in the morality tradition. It belongs to a group of dramas and other literary works which were produced in the formal Chambers of Rhetoric, or *Rederijkerskamer*. These official cultural associations, modeled on French literary guilds, flourished in cities throughout the Netherlands in the fifteenth and sixteenth centuries. At first the *Rederijkers* produced civic performances of religious plays; later they came under humanistic influence and ultimately produced neo-classic comedies and tragedies.[8]

The indications of a more popular Flemish morality tradition are to be found in the contemporary drawings of Breughel. In an allegorical sequence on vices and virtues, this great artist shows how such human qualities might have been represented before popular audiences. In his drawing of 'Temperance,' Breughel shows an actual performance in progress. The setting is a simple temporary booth stage with a curtain, perhaps erected at a fairground. The actors are wearing, attached to their costumes, signs which give the names of the characters they represent. A courtier named Hope discourses with Lady Faith. A fool, or other figure representing misrule, is about to enter the action. This Breughel drawing and a similar one called '*Elck*' (or Everyman) have led many to conclude that such signs were an ordinary part of morality costumes. Whether or not this was the case, Breughel's drawing may preserve a unique visual record of a morality play in contemporary performance.[9]

In the sixteenth-century drama of the Netherlands it is possible to observe a transition from medieval didacticism to Renaissance allegory and symbolism. This change is expressed in increasing emphasis on a literal and 'realistic' story, in which the surface of bourgeois life is represented, with the meaning or moral of the piece to be discerned by discovering its hidden allegorical meaning. Thus in the *Tspel van der Cristenkerke* (1540) the theological struggles of the Christian Church are represented by a love story: Faith is nearly seduced by a false lover (Self-Opinion), but she is saved from a bad fate by the intervention of a true love (Loving Heart). In the *Spiegel der Minnen* (*c.* 1550), the main plot is a bourgeois tale of a rich merchant and a poor seamstress. The morality figures play auxiliary roles (Desire, Fear, Jealousy) and operate the machinery of the melodrama.[10]

With rare exceptions the true morality play is not found in medieval Germany. A Latin liturgical play, the Tegernsee play of the *Antichrist* (*c.* 1160) from Kloster Tegernsee, Bavaria, includes such abstract auxiliary characters as Hypocrisy, Heresy, and Synagogue, though its theme is political and apocalyptic rather than penitential. It is designed for spectacular mansion-and-place staging in the round, in a fashion similar to the Cornish Plays and *The Castle of Perseverance*.[11] A fourteenth-century German play, *Das Spiel von den zehn Jungfrauen*, shows the evolution of a repentance drama from Biblical materials, with Christ sitting in judgment on the fate of the five wise and five foolish virgins of the parable. This play, performed in 1322 at Erfurt, is reputed to have so upset a distinguished nobleman in the audience that he suffered a stroke and later died.[12]

The fifteenth-century German Shrovetide plays (*Fastnachtspiele*) show some relation to the morality tradition. At Lükbec, little besides the names of the plays have survived, but these are indicative: e.g., a 1439 'Play of the Four Virtues,' and a 1466 'Play of the Old World, the New World, Vindication, his daughter Faithful, his brothers Truth and Moderation.'[13] The *Fastnachtspiele* were originally earthy folk dramas probably evolved from seasonal ritual; later, in the hands of Renaissance figures like Hans Sachs, they became bourgeois secular plays in the Dutch manner.

In Germany, as in the Netherlands, schoolplays devoted to the problem of Youth became popular in the sixteenth century. These 'humanistic' plays, derived on one hand from Terentian comedy and, on the other from the morality tradition, were written in Latin at first, and later in the vernacular. The parable of the Prodigal Son, which originally had been dramatized as a call to repentance, could also be interpreted as a stern admonition to rebellious youth. It became an almost inevitable subject in this genre, of which the Dutchman Macropedius and the German Burkard Waldis are among the numerous successful practitioners.[14]

Through such accommodations the relatively weak morality tradition in Germany and the Netherlands is subsumed into bourgeois theater, not to reappear in its undiluted form on the stage until the time of Hugo von Hofmannsthal and Max Reinhardt, some four hundred years later.

3 Italy

In Italy, where drama and music have never been firmly separated, the earliest vernacular dramatic texts are unquestionably intended to be sung rather than spoken. These *Laude*, or sung dialogues, were apparently the creation of the penitential societies which enjoyed a considerable vogue in fourteenth- and fifteenth-century Italy. Out of the fanaticism and religious zeal of these societies came lyric evocations of the nativity, passion, and martyrdom of saints, and also the seven deadly sins. Here, and in other records of fifteenth-century dramatic activity, there are clear indications of an indigenous morality tradition. A *Lauda* of the *Disciplinati di Orvieto*, intended for performance at Carnival, illustrates 'how the seven deadly sins may be led to contrition.'[15] In a dramatic debate *Il Vivo e Il Morto*, of the *Disciplinati dell'Umbria*, a living man and a dead man dispute over the forgiveness of sins, in the manner of the debate between the body and soul. A dance of the virtues and vices was performed at a banquet in Rome, in which vices dance with swords, and virtues ('dressed in feminine manner, with counterfeit painted faces') overcome them.[16]

The *Sacra Rappresentazione*, which follows from the *Lauda* in the evolution of dramatic forms in Italy, is in many ways equivalent to the early religious plays in the English and French traditions. Dialogue comes to be spoken, though the plays retain many musical features. Though most of the *Sacre Rappresentazioni* are dramatizations of saints' lives and Biblical events, some show morality features. For example, in a fifteenth-century cycle of plays intended for performance in Bologna, we find the *Redenzione del Genere Umano*, a drama about the forgiveness of sins, conceived in terms of the Trial in Heaven. The qualities of Mercy and Justice dispute before the high Judge of Heaven, and the Virgin; various saints also take part. The play is notable for its pointed and satiric references to alleged sins of its Bolognese audience.[17]

In *La Rappresentazione del'Di del Guidizio* (1490) by Feo Belcari and Antonio Avaldo, the day of judgment becomes the setting for a stern repentance drama in which seven sinners, whose names are derived from the seven deadly sins – 'Proud,' 'Envious,' etc. – stand in contrast to seven virtuous characters, with similarly derived names – 'Humble,' 'Charitable,' etc. – who dispute with them in turn. Christ, coming in judgment, rebukes the sinners (and an unrepentant king), and condemns them to hellfire. Their virtuous counterparts, on the other hand, are saved, and an angel ends the play with an appeal to the congregation (i.e., the audience) to remember its Paternoster, Ave Maria, and Salve Regina, pray to the Virgin, and consider that her son will one day come to judge the quick and the dead.[18]

The most compelling evidence of an Italian morality tradition, however, lies in a play which was not published until 1575, though critics have speculated that it is of an earlier date. Francesco de Sanctis, the dean of nineteenth-century Italian men of letters, devotes a lengthy essay to the *Commedia Spirituale dell'Anima* in his *Storia della Letteratura Italiana*. He apparently regarded it as a crucial formative influence on Dante's *Divine Comedy* – no mean feat for a work published in the last quarter of the sixteenth century. De Sanctis explained that the *Commedia Spirituale dell'Anima*,[19]

> is one of the very ancient liturgical mysteries, touched up, polished, modernized, and given a laic character in the time of Lorenzo de' Medici or later. . . . But if the weft is modern, the stuff is very ancient indeed. . . . This spiritual comedy of the soul, of which we have endeavoured to give as exact a summary as possible, is the code of the thirteenth century.

The *Commedia*, whatever its original date (the thirteenth century is far too early, but the sixteenth seems far too late) is to all appearances an archetypal medieval morality play, reminiscent of the English *Wisdom* and *Perseverance*. The focus of the play is on the Soul, furnished by God with natural powers and theological virtues, beset by the Devil, seduced by Sensuality, saved by the Cardinal Virtues, struck down by illness, and *in extremis* disputed over by Angel and Devil. The decisive moral is spoken by the Angel:[20]

> *Umana cosa è coscar in errore,*
> *e angelica cosa è il rilevarsi. . . .*
> *Sol diabolica cosa è star nel vizio*

> It is but human to fall into error,
> and angelic to raise oneself again . . .
> It is only devilish to stay in Vice

The soul is ultimately saved, and sent hopefully on its way to heaven by a chorus of the heavenly choir, in the manner of *Everyman*.

Mention of two Italian dramas of the early seventeenth century will suffice to illustrate that in Italy the stage traditions of the morality clearly endured through and beyond the Renaissance. *Anima e Corpo*, a dramatization of the body-soul contention performed in Rome in 1600, is frequently mentioned as among the early formal examples of the opera. Giambattista Andreini's *Adamo* (1613) stages the creation and fall of Adam and Eve, but carries the action on to the fallen world where Adam is assaulted and tempted by World, Flesh, and Devil. In the end Adam is given assurances of his salvation, and that of the race, by the angel Michael. Numerous Miltonic parallels have suggested to many critics a relationship between this work and *Paradise Lost*; it is possible that Milton saw *Adamo* while in Italy and adapted from it such details as the personification of Sin and Death, when, years later, he came to write his own account of the Innocence, Fall, and Redemption of man.[21]

4 France

The morality play as a French stage tradition has had a long history of association with the development of secular comedy. Thus we find in the regulations of the University of Orléans in 1447 an announcement that students are henceforth prohibited from presenting comedies, 'even in the form of morality.'[22] Something of the ambiguous critical response to the French moralities is epitomized in this prohibition. The relation of the voluminous French moralities to the other forms of fifteenth- and sixteenth-century drama in France remains ill-defined; most French historians of the theater have marshaled them, rather uncertainly, under the rubric of secular drama.[23] There, together with the *sotties* (plays featuring a licensed fool) and *farces* (secular folk comedies), they can be seen as among the evolutionary predecessors of 'regular' neo-classical comedy.

The catalogue of Petit de Julleville lists fifty-eight examples of extant French moralities; of these thirty carry the subtitle '*moralité*' on their title pages, nine others are called '*morales*' or '*dialogues morales*.' The other plays, despite differing generic titles (*mystère, tragecomedie*, etc.) are grouped with the moralities on the basis of form. Petit de Julleville defines the essence of the morality form as its didacticism and moralizing spirit; abstract characters and allegory are seen as secondary yet contributing features. Freely admitting the looseness of the term '*moralité*,' which was used in fifteenth- and sixteenth-century France for all kinds of didactic poems – non-dramatic as well as dramatic – Petit de Julleville and his followers nevertheless discerned the morality tradition as a particular but somewhat inexplicable genre of plays.[24]

The recent work of John S. Weld, who has greatly expanded the canon of Petit de Julleville in identifying and analyzing the plays of this tradition, is a prologue to much-needed critical re-evaluation of the French morality and its relation to English practice.[25] While such a task is outside the scope of the present book, it is nevertheless important to discern the crucial characteristics of this neglected body of *moralités*.

Indications are that the French plays, like the English, have their origin in a penitential tradition. The oldest examples of the French morality, not discovered until 1909 and therefore unrecorded by Petit de Julleville, are three plays in the Chantilly MS 617.[26] One of these, the Liège *Moralité des Sept Péchés Mortels et des Sept Vertus*, has possible connections with the English Paternoster plays, as pointed out in an earlier chapter. Both this work and the *Moralité du Pèlerinage de la Vie humaine* are classic medieval morality plays – repentance dramas recapitulating the Fall and Redemption in terms of the life of the individual Christian. A third play from this manuscript, the *Moralité de l'Alliance de Foy et Loyalté*, features pastoral characters and an allegorical marriage, but its main action involves the repentance of Faith and Loyalty. These plays, dating in most critics' calculations from the early half of the fourteenth century, are among the earliest of their kind in any vernacular, though there are records of a 1390 performance in Tours of '*Gieux des sept vertuz et des sept pechiez mortelz.*'[27]

The great majority of the French moralities are the product of the fifteenth and earlier sixteenth centuries. Here, as in England, the didactic message of repentance and the ritual action of rebirth comprise the basic substance of the drama. There are, however, some peculiarly French developments of the tradition. One of these is what might be termed the dualistic morality, featuring twin central figures. Two of the best known earlier French moralities, *Bien-Avisé, Mal-Avisé* (1439) and *L'Homme juste et L'Homme mondain* (1476), are built on this dichotomy, with a double plot to match. Each play's thesis is embodied in a virtuous central figure who repents and is redeemed; the antithesis in a parallel but depraved figure who sins, fails to repent, and is condemned to hellfire. The mechanical symmetry of such a demonstration – particularly when carried on interminably (*Bien Avisé, Mal Avisé* is 8000 lines in extent, more than twice as long as *The Castle of Perseverance*) – tends to vitiate its dramatic effectiveness. A more successful elaboration of the idea may be seen in the *Moralité très singulière et très bonne des Blasphémateurs du nom de Dieu* (1530?) in which three central figures are featured. The three *Blasphémateurs* are young gallants who carry on a wild and riotous existence, culminating in a scene in which they torture a crucifix, making a macabre game of recrucifying Christ. Struck down in a state of sin, the blasphemers reach separate conclusions: two die in despair and are carried off by devils; one repents and is saved.[28]

There are several French repentance plays of this period with single central figures more closely approximating their English counterparts. Among these may be mentioned *l'Homme pécheur* (1494), a massive spectacle performed at Tours and Orléans, and *Charité* (early sixteenth century), a sharp satirical essay on the uses and abuses of wealth. In *Mundus, Caro, Daemonia* (1520) the familiar figures of the World, the Flesh, and the Devil are the principal agents of temptation. Even here, however, there are interesting variations from English usage. The central figure is called *le Chevalier Chrétien* (a superficial element of allegorical romance, unknown in the English plays), and the 'play' is really a debate: after an opening prayer by the Knight, all the other characters appear at once, the three tempters on one side, an agent of repentance (*l'Esprit*) on the other. The remainder of the play is a verbal duel of wits, concluding in the successive departures of the Devil, the Flesh, and the World (who refuses to repent of worldliness). In this early example one can perhaps observe a national characteristic of taste in theater – the notorious French preference for dialogue and rhetoric as opposed to stage action – beginning to predominate.[29]

As in England, the French morality tradition produces secular offshoots, plays which borrow the method and conventions of the morality to deal with questions of less finality than spiritual life and death. It is in these plays, logically, that the obvious connections with comedy, and critics' confusion about the nature of the morality form develop. It is also in these plays that national characteristics achieve further expression. Who could imagine, for example, an English morality 3650 lines in length taking as its subject the temptation and dangers of gourmandizing? *La Condamnation des Banquets* (1507), perhaps the most widely known of French moralities, features a company of human central figures (including I-Drink-to-You and Sweet Tooth) who attend a Dinner, followed by a Supper, followed by a Banquet. There they are set upon by diseases and most are overwhelmed. Those who survive reach Experience and secure the arrest of their tormentors. Dinner and Supper are disciplined and separated, and Banquet, after repenting and confessing his sins, is executed.[30]

The later French morality is put to a variety of admonitory sixteenth-century uses, including warnings to the disorderly young (*les Enfants de maintenant, l'Enfant ingrat, l'Enfant de perdition*), homiletic and domestic tragedy (*l'Empereur qui tua son neveu*), and reformation polemics (*l'Eglise et le Comun, l'Homme justifié par Foi*). It vanishes from the stage as a discernible form before the end of the century.

Though the French morality tradition produced no major work to equal the English *Everyman*, or even *The Castle of Perseverance*, it is an unjustly neglected body of plays far more varied and numerous than its English counterparts, if apparently considerably less influential.[31] Many circumstances combine to limit the immediate impact of the *moralité* in its own time. The greater genius of French medieval drama is expended elsewhere, in the elaborate Passion plays and of course in the farce tradition. Moreover, the French moralities play less of a role in determining the course of French drama than their English counterparts, since early neo-classic domination of French theater effectively disrupts the native tradition.

Nevertheless today French critics increasingly place the morality among the important formative influences on French comedy. It is quite possible to look ahead and detect the descendants of Avarice and Hypocrisy, thinly disguised as the characters Molière called Harpagon the Miser and the Reverend Tartuffe.

5 Spain and Portugal

The most substantial and influential morality tradition in European drama, with the possible exception of that in England, is to be found in Spain. It is a very different tradition from that of any other country, for a variety of cultural, political, and social reasons, and it has been unaccountably neglected by critics of the drama. There is no space in the present context to do anything more than survey the general topography of its splendid development, which is deserving of much wider study than it has yet received.

In England the morality tradition flourished in the fifteenth century, adapted itself to the Renaissance and Reformation in the sixteenth century, and eventually found its way into the moral assumptions and conventions of the secularized Elizabethan drama. But what might have happened to the medieval morality if it had not encountered these intellectual and political changes of climate, if it had instead been allowed to develop in its generating neo-medieval Catholic environment alongside the new secular drama? The answer would seem to be that it did so, in sixteenth- and seventeenth-century Spain. And where the transmuted English morality tradition may be discerned just beneath the surface of the Elizabethan drama, in Spain true moralities were being written by the major playwrights of its *Siglo de Oro* – by Lope de Vega, Shakespeare's contemporary, and even Calderón de la Barca, the contemporary of Milton.

Historians have frequently alleged that Spain never experienced the Renaissance, let alone the Reformation. From the point of view of the history of drama, however, it might be more accurate to observe that Spain never truly experienced the Middle Ages. There is an astonishing lack of authentic dramatic texts before 1500. Only scattered evidence of any early mystery plays has come to light, and our evidence for a medieval morality tradition is even more fragmentary. One fifteenth-century text of a Dance of Death has been preserved, in which the various estates (Pope, King, commoner, etc.) are led away by Death; there are strong doubts as to whether this piece was intended for performance, and it does not in any event dramatize repentance.[32]

Another quasi-dramatic fifteenth-century text is the Catalan *Mascarón*, surviving in a narrative version of the Trial in Heaven, but probably based on a lost dramatic version. Here Christ sits in judgment and a devil named Mascarón brings charges against all mankind, calling Justice and Truth as witnesses; the Virgin Mary acts as Man's advocate, calling Mercy and Peace, and also claims to represent all Mankind.[33]

At the turn of the sixteenth century, without any particular foreshadowing, the first major Hispanic playwright emerges. He is Gil Vicente, goldsmith and poet to the court of Portugal, in that brief brilliant period when its navigators were mapping and claiming large portions of the world. Vicente, who is acknowledged today as one of the very great Spanish and Portuguese poets, provided plays for ceremonial occasions at court, more than forty of which are extant. They are of bewildering variety for their time – farces, courtly romances, allegories, mystery plays, and anticlerical satires in both Spanish and Portuguese, as well as a highly original series of morality plays.

The first of these, indeed, was published under the title *Auto da Moralidade*,[34] though it is better known as the *Auto da Barca do Inferno* (the Ship of Hell), first performed in 1516. The dramatic idea of this play is that two ships await the souls of dying men. Accommodation on the Ship of Heaven is difficult to obtain, but the Ship of Hell has room for all varieties of people; the list of passengers includes a usurer, a friar, a female pimp, a corrupt judge, and a proud nobleman. In two succeeding plays, *The Ship of Purgatory* (1518) and *The Ship of Heaven* (1519), Vicente explores the dramatic possibilities of his metaphor, giving this trilogy something of the shape of a theatrical *Divine Comedy*. *The Ship of Purgatory* opens with a song, sung by three angels, that seems to epitomize the lyric medievalism of Gil Vicente:[35]

> *Remando vam remadores*
> *Barca de grande alegria:*
> *O Patrao que a guiava*
> *Filho de Deus se dizia;*
> *Anjos eram os remeiros*
> *Que remavam a profia;*
> *Estandarte d'esperanza*
> *O quam bem que parecia!*
> *O masto de fortaleza*
> *Como cristal reluzia*
> *A vela com fe cosida*
> *Todo o mundo esclarecia*
> *A ribeira mui serena*
> *Que nenhum vento bolia!*

> Rowers now are rowing
> A boat of great delight;
> The boatman who was steering it
> The Son of God is hight;
> And angels were the rowers
> Rowing with all their might;
> Its flag the flag of hope
> O how fair a sight!
> Its mast the mast of fortitude
> And as crystal bright
> The boat's sail, sewn with faith,
> To all the world gave light.
> Upon the waters calm
> No breath of wind may light.

The characters of this second play, from the lower orders, go through the process of purging themselves of their relatively minor failings. In the third play, the characters summoned by Death are of high rank: Pope, Emperor, King, Cardinal, etc., and their sins are considerable because of their power. The angels who man the Ship of Heaven reject the petitioners and set sail for Heaven without them. As the ship leaves, the now-humbled noblemen kneel in prayer to Christ, who appears to carry them – not by their power, but by his sacrifice – to Heaven.

Of Vicente's other moralities, the *Auto da Alma* (1519)[36] is perhaps of greatest interest. Written during the same period as his ship trilogy, this play depicts the Soul as a vulnerable and beautiful female pilgrim tempted by two devils but guided by her guardian angel to Mother Church, where she is introduced into the mysteries of Christianity and addressed by Fathers of the Church – St Augustine, St Ambrose, and St Jerome. The states of sin and repentance are represented, as so often in the English plays, by changes of costume; the play takes a mystic and solemn turn in its final scene, with a visually-effective unveiling of religious emblems of Christ's passion (including a crown of thorns and a crucifix) and the singing of the *Te Deum*.[37]

The morality tradition which Gil Vicente begins finds few successors in Portugal, but is extended, if not necessarily surpassed, in sixteenth-century Spain. The *Farsa del Mundo y moral* (*c.* 1518), written by Hernán López de Yanguas, is an Assumption of the Virgin play incorporating a morality plot. The author, in a unique preface, explains that the play is based on the Biblical text, *Hic est victoria qui vincit Mundum fides nostra*, and that it is written for four actors:[38]

> The first is the same world; the second is a shepherd called Appetite; the third a hermit; the fourth is Faith. It is the intention of the author to show the cunningness of the world; how it takes in every one of us who gives sway to his appetites; next to this, how by the Hermit (who is preaching and religion), we come to Faith, and by it are victorious as the text declares. In the end the Assumption of Our Lady is related; in the which there is good to be seen and not to be seen, because the eyes cannot comprehend it. It concludes with music in good order. Dedicated to the very illustrious and magnificent lady Señora Doña Juana de Cuñega, Contessa de Aguilar. The World should be dressed as a King, Appetite as a shepherd, the Hermit as such, Faith as a noble lady, a green branch in her hand.

Other earlier sixteenth-century Spanish moralities include the *Farsa de la Concordia* (1529) also by López de Yanguas, and the *Obra del Pecador* (1530) by Bartholomé de Aparicio. The first is a dramatization of the Trial in Heaven, adapted to celebrate a contemporary historical event – the Peace of Cambray, concluded on 15 August 1529, ending the war between France and Spain on terms favorable to the Spanish. Aparicio's play begins as a morality concerning a sinner threatened by Justice and saved by Mercy; after the sinner's repentance, however, the play is suddenly transformed into a Nativity, with Joseph and Mary and Shepherds and Angels. In the end the sinner goes off with the rest to Bethlehem to worship the Christ Child.[39] These dramas can be seen as early examples of the *auto sacramental*, a genre of short plays generally written for civic performance at the Feast of Corpus Christi. These sacramental plays, whether Biblical, pastoral, or allegorical, whether called *farsa* or *auto*, are characteristically joyous public celebrations. The Spanish moralities are written chiefly within the convention of the *auto*, and are influenced by its celebrative atmosphere.[40]

Diego Sánchez de Badajoz, the most significant figure of the Spanish drama in this period, was a curate in the town of Talavera who composed religious plays for performance on Christmas, Corpus Christi, and other festival days. His twenty-eight extant plays were probably written between 1525 and 1547, and they include six *farsas* (or plays) in the morality tradition, not to mention a Dance of the Seven Deadly Sins. These remarkable texts, published by an admiring nephew shortly after Diego Sánchez' death, preserve the largest number and variety of surviving morality plays written by a single author. Moreover, as Bruce Wardropper has recently pointed out, Diego Sánchez is a genuinely gifted poetic dramatist.[41] As a result we possess a group of plays of great significance, which have been insufficiently studied and appreciated outside Spain.

The most conventional, and perhaps the most dramatic, of Diego Sánchez' moralities is entitled *Farsa dicha Militar, en que principalmente se ablaba la Sacra penitencia*. It has the plot and cast of characters of a traditional repentance drama despite its military title. The central figure, in a nice twist of irony, is a Friar. He is equipped with a guardian angel, but pursued and tempted by the enemies of Man: 'Lucifer in the form of a fierce beast, World in the dress of an old Man of Affairs, Flesh in the habit of a woman of small honesty.'[42]

Lured into sin, the Friar abandons his friar's habit, but is saved by his guardian angel at the point of death. His change of heart becomes, in characteristic morality style, the author's call for general repentance, implicitly assuming that the play has touched the conscience of its audience.

In two other plays, *Farsa Moral en que se representan las Quatro Virtudes Cardinales* and *Farsa del juego de cañas*, Diego Sánchez blends Biblical and folk elements with morality action. The *Farsa Moral* has for its central figures the four cardinal Virtues (Justice, Prudence, Fortitude, and Temperance) who are threatened by a vice figure named Perversity – actually a stock shepherd character of the sort Diego Sanchez favors for prologues – half-earthy sinner and half-redeemable. The auxiliary characters include, in addition to the shepherd, 'Job with his patience, his servant, King Nebuchudnezar with his pride, Our Lady with a child in her arms.'[43] Job and Nebuchudnezar function as positive and negative exemplars, and the ultimate appearance of the Virgin with Christ confirms the defeat of Perversity. Like the *Farsa Moral*, the *Farsa del juego de cañas* involves a confrontation between vices and virtues. Here the characters are drawn from the tradition of the prophets play, with Adam, Noah, Isaiah, Jeremiah, and the Sibyl taking parts.

Somewhat less interesting than these plays, and rather more specifically didactic, are Diego Sánchez' *Farsa Racional del libre albedrio* (Free Will) and *Farsa de la Iglesia*. These plays are devoted to theological exposition and stock debate – in the first case, the Body and the Soul, in the second, Church and Synagogue. Another play of the same variety, the *Farsa de la Muerte* features Youth and Old Age (the one rich, the other poor) visited in turn by Death, 'Who can be shown with a skull-mask, with a quiver full of arrows and a bow in his hand, with a harpoon.'[44] In the most unusual text of the *Danza de los Pecados*, the central figure is Adam, who dances in turn with each of the seven deadly sins (all apparently female), after they beg him to join them with various blandishments:[45]

> PRIDE O Man, Tall, Perfect
> Of such extreme loftiness . . .
> You know no superior.
> GLUTTONY Neither is there pleasure without
> Eating and drinking
> O Adam, my first friend.
> LECHERY My delights and pleasures
> Work with potent force
> On the wise and valiant,
> Made subject to women.

After having his turn with each of them, and being tripped up by them, Adam is struck with contrition, rises up and, driving away the sins, makes a public repentance to the audience. He urges them to partake of the sacrament.

The morality tradition is heavily represented in the *Codice de autos viejos*, a manuscript collection of ninety-six plays of the late sixteenth century. One critic's estimate is that thirty-three of the ninety-six have a 'tendency toward allegory and symbolism;'[46] as I have read only a portion of them, I am unable to confirm this figure. It is indisputable, however, that many of these plays have pronounced morality characteristics, though there is a free blending of other elements, as in the earlier plays of López de Yanguas and Aparicio. The *Codice* plays are anonymous and undated, but they reveal an increasingly sophisticated *mise en scène*; where earlier plays called for no particular stage machinery, or perhaps a single pageant wagon set, the *Codice* plays in most cases stipulate two pageant wagons, drawn up facing one another with a stage in between.[47] One of these plays, the *Auto de los hierros de Adan,* has Adam for its central mankind figure, in the manner of Diego Sánchez' *Danza*; another, the *Auto de la Resedencia del Hombre* is a pure morality incorporating the World, Flesh, and Devil and a Trial in Heaven with an exemplary confession at the end; a third, the *Farsa del Sacramento de las Cortes de la Yglesia,* adapts the Trial motif to an impassioned exposition of the excellence of the Spanish Inquisition! Faith, Hope, and the Church sit in judgment on such errant characters as Hypocrisy, World, and Novelty. Besides these *Codice* plays, there are several other moralities of interest from this period of the sixteenth century, including Juan de Pedraza's *Farsa llamada Danza de la Muerte* (1551), which features a shepherd as its central mankind figure,[48] and the anonymous *Comedia Sesta y Auto Sacramental del Castillo de la Fee* (1590). The *Castillo de la Fee* is focused, like *The Castle of Perseverance,* around an emblematic castle. A lord has it given to Faith who journeys to the castle and occupies it, together with Care and Prayer. When they fall asleep a heretic soldier routs them from the castle, but they rally Catholic forces, recapture the castle, and convert the heretic.[49]

The prodigious achievements of Lope de Vega (1562–1635), by most accounts Spain's greatest playwright, coincided with the transition of Spanish drama from an amateur to a professional basis, and the evolution of a theater for entertainment rather than religious celebration. Yet the old religious theater was not by any means abolished; on the contrary it too flourished throughout the golden age of Spanish imperial power: *autos* were still required for feast-day performances, and the utterly remarkable Lope de Vega, who found time for everything (he played the violin, fathered ten illegitimate children, fought with the Spanish Armada, became a judge in the Inquisition, took Holy Orders, and, by the most conservative estimates, wrote over 700 plays of all descriptions),[50] also found time to write sacramental morality plays.

As the staging of *autos sacramentales* became more and more elaborate in prosperous early seventeenth-century Spain, the artistic problem for the playwright became more complex. The difficulty was to find ways of staging the old stories while avoiding the tyranny of spectacle for its own sake; to find spectacular ways of speaking simply. Of Lope's numerous *autos*, one in particular will illustrate the extraordinary fashion in which he revivified the tradition.

El Viaje del Alma, of uncertain date but published in 1604, is loosely adapted from Gil Vicente's ship trilogy of nearly a hundred years earlier. The play begins with a lengthy history of the world and its great historical figures – Biblical, classical, historical, and mythological. The world is seen to be operating on an apocalyptic timetable; the 6000-year-old world has 400 years left; it will end on schedule in the twentieth century. The Soul, central figure in the play, is a girl dressed in white who is tempted aboard the good ship 'Delight' by a fast-talking Devil-Captain who says he will take her to the New World:[51]

> DEVIL Those islands of great riches!
> There you see flourish
> Highest beauty –
> Pure gold and silver,
> Elegance of an age,
> Delicate youth in gowns
> Of a thousand frills
> Flows in the aroma
> And perfume of feasts,
> Of baths, of games, and love.
> Famous and beautiful, my ship
> Is called *the Delight*
> Come inside, beautiful lady,
> For I am her Captain
> Her pilot-to-fame.
> Here Caesar sailed –
> Marc Antony and Masinisa,
> Mesalina, Dido, Elisa.

Before the play is over, the Ship of Delight has been exposed as a Ship of Fools *à la* Hieronymus Bosch, with the seven deadly sins on deck, and the Soul has found her way to the Ship of Penitence, manned by Angels, Saints, and the Pope, decorated with religious emblems, a gold chalice, and red silk ropes; there Christ, the ship's captain, takes her for a wife. In turn these elaborate ships, each built upon its own pageant wagon, are said to enter the sight of the audience and anchor at opposite sides of a neutral playing area, in what must have been a truly spectacular demonstration of the Spanish technique of multiple staging.

Lope's other moralities are equally strange and wonderful – at once very baroque and very touching. *La Siega*, for example, has a rural setting, and the basic metaphor is a harvest. After a struggle the vices are defeated and fertility triumphs amid much music and dancing. *Los Dos Ingenios* rings unexpected changes on the familiar motifs of the good and bad angels, and the Trial in Heaven – the pilgrimage of life passes through Babylon, and there are lunatics and highwaymen to be encountered *en route* to a dinner invitation (allegory: the Sacrament) from Christ the Redeemer. Lope has been criticized for his indiscriminate packing of the *auto* with stock comic devices, but there were never such infectious and convincing religious plays before or since. Only a Malvolio, in such circumstances, would be an unbeliever.

Lope and his seventeenth-century contemporaries consciously blended secular and religious traditions, enriching celebration with comedy. It remained for the last significant Spanish writer of moralities to carry the tradition with him in the direction of tragic and philosophical speculation. Pedro Calderón de la Barca (1600–81) lived in the age in which the Spanish empire was coming to pieces, through defeat abroad and rebellion at home. In his hands the neo-medieval *autos sacramentales* reached their greatest heights as an art form. His most celebrated autos include *La Cena de Baltasar* and *La Vida es Sueño* (not to be confused with the Comedia of the same name). But none is more significant than *El Gran Teatro del Mundo*.[52]

This *auto*, first performed in Madrid in 1649, is constructed upon the metaphor of the world as a stage, and dependent on the morality tradition of a stage as all the world. The Author (who is in one sense the author of everything, and in another, the actual director-playwright-manager of a theatrical company) summons World to prepare for a play. World explains how history has proceeded thus far in the great theater of the world – from *Natural Law* and Adam's Fall through Noah's flood to the *Written Law* of Moses to the *Law of Grace* by Christ's sacrifice, under which law the theater now exists. In this theater, with one entrance (the cradle) and one exit (the grave) there are many parts to be played – all significant. With this established, the Author calls in his company of actors and gives them their parts. Beauty is pleased with her role, the Laborer says he has been miscast, the Rich Man and the King are delighted, the Beggar complains, and so forth. The World provides the actors with appropriate costumes and trappings; the name of the 'play' will be, 'Do good, for God is God.' There will be no rehearsal; the play begins now.

The action of *El Gran Teatro del Mundo* consists in the actors first 'living' their parts, then coming to question whether their 'lives' have any meaning, and finally seeing their lives become parts once again, as the performance comes to an end and their costumes are collected from them. Calderón has thus redefined the duality of mankind in theatrical terms. Men are not mixtures of 'good' and 'evil'; rather they are at once 'men' and 'characters.' Those whose lives are most fortunate – the King and the Rich Man, for example – are the least able to grasp this discrepancy, and therefore the most in danger of living only for 'themselves' (which is to say, for an illusion).[53]

BEGGAR Your part is finished now.
Down here in the dressing room,
the grave, everyone is equal.
What you were doesn't mean a thing.
RICH MAN How could you forget that yesterday
you begged me for help?
BEGGAR How could you forget that
you didn't give it to me?
BEAUTY You forget the respect you paid to me
Since I was richer and lovelier.
DISCRETION Here in the dressing room
We all look alike.
There's no particular class distinction
in winding sheets.
RICH MAN How dare you go ahead of me!
LABORER Forget those foolish pretensions.
Finally dead,
From the sun that you were
you have become a shadow.

In the end, like actors, men will be judged by their performances and
not for their parts. And in the end, since there is an author, they
will find in self-knowledge the possibility of repentance and a
happy ending.

The accomplishment of Calderón's great play is in the harmony of
its complexities, which lift the morality play to a level of high art.
The texture of life, the infinite varieties of human thought, action,
pretension, and emotional response are acknowledged and even
glorified – yet they are only an enrichment, in the end, of a general
concept of humanity. This concept, obviously, is the idea of
Christianity – taken more seriously by Calderón than is ever
comfortable. The result, as Alexander Parker has pointed out, is
that *El Gran Teatro del Mundo* is not merely an artistic *tour de force*,
but a radical social document.[54]

If we recall that the morality has its roots in the preaching
tradition, with its definition of man's life as a sequence of inevitable
stages, and its warning against pretension to illusory permanence,
then Calderón's attack on materialism is both highly traditional and
highly contemporary for a seventeenth-century audience. The
message of this play, like Donne's 'no man is an island,' is the vanity
of private defenses against eternity, and its moral is the ultimate
responsibility of being human. Calderón's denunciation of blind
privilege and self-seeking should be viewed in the context of the
increasingly accepted theory of his own day, that every man is pre-
eminently an economic and social island unto himself. *El Gran*

Teatro del Mundo examines this idea, and finds it to be an illusion.

Like many a modern psychologist, Calderón is ultimately skeptical about the separate existence of the individual. *El Gran Teatro del Mundo*, written in a century in which individualism had begun to find respectable philosophic justification, is a defense of the general priority and the finality of the human condition. Calderón asserts, against the dying of the light of medieval civilization, the unity of Man.[55]

Chapter VIII

Rediscovering the evidence:
1660–1914

In the year 1660 the English morality play had ceased to exist as a fact and did not yet exist as an idea. As a medieval dramatic tradition it had long since been subsumed in Elizabethan drama: as an event in literary history it had not yet been discovered. The non-existence of even a concept of the morality play at this point in the seventeenth century is understandable. There can hardly be a concept if there is neither evidence to suggest it nor a question for which it can supply a useful answer. There were in 1660 no such questions and no visible signs of a medieval drama; any direct link with current theatrical tradition had been lost with the closing of the theaters in 1642. Yet much evidence remained, scattered and undisturbed in various archives. There, in black-letter pamphlets and illegible manuscripts, it had survived the upheavals of Reformation and Civil War. There the texts and documents remained, reduced to raw material for which a use had not yet been devised.

All the direct evidence which we possess of the moralities today (together with much that may have been lost in the meantime) was in existence in 1660. If all this evidence had been uncovered at once, and evaluated from the same point of view as we presently occupy, there would be no need for this chapter. In point of fact, however, the texts and documents came to light slowly, haphazardly, and unsystematically over a period of 300 years. Thus the idea of the morality play has a history of its own.

Literary scholarship in the seventeenth century was to some extent impeded by a lack of interest in the immediate past, the dark ages from which (or so it seemed) 'modern' civilization had so recently emerged. The usefulness of the past lay in its ability to inspire achievements in the future. For this purpose the likely models were not medieval remnants but the pinnacles of high art reached in ancient Greece and Rome.

The study of classical languages and literature had, at least from the time of the Humanists forward, a prescriptive rationale; Greek values and Roman accomplishments were intended to inspire students to emulate and re-establish high civilization in the modern world. Neo-classicism, in this sense, was an endeavor to see history repeating itself, with civilization in the ascendant.

Thus the origins of classical drama were of modern as well as ancient significance. Tragedy and comedy were not ephemeral genres but universal types, and Elizabethan critics were fully aware of the theory that these forms had evolved by degrees from religious celebrations;[1]

> . . . mingling much pleasant myrth wyth theyr graue
> Religion, and feasting cheerefully together wyth as great ioy
> as might be deuised. But not long after (as one delight
> draweth another) they began to inuent new persons and newe
> matters for their Comedies, such as the deuisers thought
> meetest to please the peoples vaine: and from these they began
> to present in shapes of men the natures of vertues and vices,
> and affections and qualities incident to men, as Iustice,
> Temperance, Pouerty, Wrathe, Vengaunce, Sloth, valiantnes,
> and such like, as may appeare by the ancient workes of
> *Aristophanes.* There grewe at last to be a greater diuersitye
> betweene Tragedy wryters and Comedy wryters.

In Restoration times apologists for the theater began to draw modern parallels to this formula of the ancients, and in doing so became the first historians of the English stage. The origins of modern comedy and tragedy were traced to analogous religious sources; a similar period was seen to intervene, characterized by abstract, instructive types. It was this neo-classical analogy which determined the earliest modern conception of the morality play.

1 The neo-classical preconception 1660–1760

Charles II's sanction of the theaters by royal patent in 1660 had ended an eighteen-year period of official suppression. The early histories of the stage should be viewed in the context of this act, as briefs in defense of the legitimacy of the stage, by appeal to precedent. Thus Richard Flecknoe, publishing his play *Love's Kingdom* in 1664, appended an historical essay emphasizing the parallel characteristics of the ancient and modern drama.

Flecknoe had scant knowledge of the origins of modern drama. He knew only that drama had fallen into decay in Roman times, 'From which time to the last Age, they Acted nothing here, but Playes of the holy Scripture, or Saints Lives, and that without any certain

theaters or set Companies till about the beginning of Queen
Elizabeth's Reign.'[2]

Thomas Rymer, writing thirty years later, worked from much the
same vague impression of a medieval drama, but reached more
intemperate conclusions. In ancient times the ultimate falling-off
from classical grandeur had come in the abandoning of the stage to
strolling players 'who wandered up and down, acting Farce, or
turning into Farce, whatever they acted. Castelvetro tells us that
even in Rome in his time *Christ's Passion* was so acted by them, as
to set all the Audience a laughing.'[3]

Rymer noted with approval the sixteenth-century suppression of
religious plays in France. Such action he deemed a necessary
prelude to the rise of the classical French theater. Turning to
England Rymer recalled Stow's account of religious plays staged
by the parish clerks of London in 1391 and 1409. He expressed his
shock at finding that plays of this sort 'were the ordinary entertainment on the Stage, all Europe over, for an hundred year or two, of
our greatest ignorance and darkness.'[4] Some remedy for this state of
affairs had come with the revival of learning (Heywood's interludes,
Gascoigne's translations, and *Gorboduc*), but the result, unfortunately,
was Elizabethan tragedy.

Rymer's famous attack on Elizabethan tragedy in general and
Othello in particular concludes with these observations on the
pernicious influence of medieval stagecraft:[5]

> But the ground of all this Bedlam-Buffoonery we saw in the
> case of the French Strollers, the Company for Acting Christs
> Passion, or the Old Testament, were Carpenters, Coblers, and
> illiterate fellows; who found that the Drolls and Fooleries
> interlarded by them, brought in the rabble and lengthened
> their time, so they got Money by the bargain. Our Shakespear,
> doubtles was a great Master in this craft. These Carpenters
> and Coblers were the guides he followed. And it is then no
> wonder that we find so much farce and *Aprocryphal Matter* in
> his Tragedies. Thereby un-hallowing the Theatre, profaning
> the name of Tragedy; And instead of representing Men and
> Manners, turning all Morality, good sense, and humanity into
> mockery and derision.

The earliest sympathetic account of the medieval drama came in
the last year of the seventeenth century, in James Wright's pamphlet
Historia Histrionica. It was written in the form of a dialogue between
two old cavaliers, recalling the great years of the Elizabethan and
Jacobean drama, its actors and playhouses. Responding to the
anti-theatrical pamphleteering of Jeremy Collier, Wright invoked

the usual classical precedents. But he was also at some pains to show that the English stage had an illustrious past of its own.

Kings and nobles of the realm, Wright pointed out, had attended the religious plays mentioned by Stow. Defending the *Ludus Coventriae* Corpus Christi plays, he noted the scope of the cycle, described its supposed staging on pageant wagons, and published excerpts from three of the plays.[6] Wright was also the first chronicler of the English drama to see the importance of pageantry in the development of the stage; he quoted illustrative descriptions and dialogue from the Royal street pageants of 1456 and 1474 in Chester and of 1505 in London.[7] Concluding the survey with a neo-classical flourish, Wright observed that 'plays in England had a beginning much like those of Greece, the Monologues and Pageants drawn from place to place answer exactly to the cart of Thespis.'[8]

Thus for Wright the Corpus Christi plays were reminiscent of the formative period of the Athenian drama and its legendary first actor. In this way the medieval street theater could be seen as the prelude to tragedy, comedy, amphitheaters on the London Bankside, and Shakespeare the English Sophocles.

Other neo-classicists were less certain. Artless Shakespeare, warbling his native woodnotes wild, appeared more the English Thespis. The real and 'regular' accomplishments were yet to come, in the view of such theorists as Charles Gildon, whose 'Essay on the Art, Rise, and Progress of the Stage in Greece, Rome and England' appeared in 1710 as an appendix to Rowe's edition of Shakespeare. Gildon was chiefly interested in setting forth the proper laws of tragedy for the contemporary playwrights who would soon surpass the uncouth Elizabethans. He summarized the progress to date: 'In England Plays began at the very Bottom of the People, and mounted by degrees to the state we now see them in, the yet imperfect Diversion of Ladies and Men of the first Quality.'[9]

Gildon said nothing (and knew perhaps as much) of the medieval drama, but he restated a notable critical commonplace of the time, the theory that the drama was ideally in the nature of allegory:[10]

> the action ought to be general and Allegoric, not particular . . .
> so ought all Heroes of Tragedy to be . . . the Drama consults
> not the truth of what any particular person did say or do,
> but only the general Nature of such Qualities to produce such
> Words and Actions. 'Tis true that *Tragedy* employs true
> Names, but that is to give a credibility to the Action, the
> Persons still remaining *General* and *Allegoric*.

All this was written, it should be emphasized, in complete ignorance of any morality tradition. The medieval allegorical drama, when it came to be discovered, little resembled such a pristine exposition of generalities. Among other things, it lacked the elegance of a thin disguise. Nevertheless, to the eighteenth-century view, its allegorical characteristics would when discovered, seem to be indicative of *art*.

Gradually the neo-classical expectations of a pure English drama (on the French model) faded. Shakespeare, seen with increasing perspective, was at last established as *the* classical English dramatist. Once this appointment had been confirmed, Shakespeare's line of predecessors assumed their Thespian role in the neo-classical analogy, and two centuries of critics and scholars would henceforth refer to the English medieval drama as 'Pre-Shakespearean.'

Perhaps the first published critical speculation on the moralities came by way of explicating an obscure simile in *Richard III*:

> Thus, like the formal vice, Iniquity,
> I moralize two meanings in one word.

(III, i, 82–3)

Theobald, pondering this entry in his 1733 edition of Shakespeare, provided the following comment:[11]

> By Vice, perhaps the Author may mean not a *Quality* but a
> *Person*. There was hardly an old Play, till the period of the
> *Reformation*, which had not in it a Devil, and a drole
> character, a Jester; (who was to play upon and work, the
> Devil;) and this Buffoon went by the name of a *Vice*.

Theobald's source was probably a passage in the works of Bishop Harsenet: 'It was a pretty part in the old church-playes when the nimble Vice would skip up nimbly like a Jack-an-apes into the Devil's necke, and ride the devil a course, and belabour him with his wooden dagger, till he made him roar, whereat the people would laugh to see the Devil so Vice-haunted.'[12] Such dramatic incidents are, like the Vice character himself, more typically Elizabethan than medieval.[13] But Theobald supposed that he was dealing with exceedingly primitive matters. He also realized that he had only cleared up part of the obscurity of the passage. So much for the 'Vice,' what about 'Iniquity'? Theobald's explanation was, in itself, an elaboration of the theory of a 'rise and progress'[14]:

> This was the constant Entertainment in the Times of *Popery*
> whilst Spirits and Witchcraft and Exorcising held their own.
> When the *Reformation* took place, the Stage shook off some
> Grossities, and encreased in Refinements. The Master Devil
> then was soon dismissed from the Scene; and this Buffoon was

chang'd into a subordinate Fiend, whose Business was to range
on Earth and seduce poor Mortals into that personated
vicious Quality, which he occasionally supported; as, *Iniquity*
in general, *Hypocrisy, Usury, Vanity, Prodigality, Gluttony*, &c.
Now as the Fiend (or *Vice*) who personated Iniquity (or
Hypocrisy, for Instance) could never hope to play his game to
the purpose but by hiding his cloven Foot, and assuming a
Semblance quite different from his real Character; he must
certainly put on a *formal* Demeanour, *moralize* and prevaricate
in his Words, and pretend a Meaning directly opposite to his
genuine and primite Intention.

Theobald was evidently aware of a kind of 'old play' in which
'poor mortals' were seduced into vice by evil characters, who
sometimes took the part of vices or deadly sins. But whether he
knew more than he told may be doubted. If he had consulted any
such plays at first hand, he would very probably have mentioned
them by name. His theory, nevertheless, had some basis in fact.

One thing which Theobald certainly lacked was a generic term
for such plays. In the early eighteenth century none was available.
Such sixteenth-century terms as 'moral play' or 'interlude' had
long since become extinct, along with the plays themselves. This
lack in terminology was remedied within eight years after the
publication of Theobald's theory by the invention of a modern
term. The inventor, in fact, seems to have been the English translator of a book in French by an Italian who had never seen or heard
of any of the English plays in question.

Luigi Riccoboni (1674–1753) was an itinerant Italian actor-
manager and theatrical reformer who attempted, with limited
success, to restore classical and 'regular' plays to the Italian stage in
the early eighteenth century. After his retirement from the stage in
1731 Riccoboni wrote a voluminous series of books on theatrical
subjects.[15] One of these books, *Réflections historiques et critiques sur les
différents théâtres de l'Europe*, was published in Paris in 1738, and
translated into English in 1741 as *An Historical and Critical Account of
the Theatres in Europe*.

In this book Riccoboni gave an account of the progress of the
theater, particularly in Italy, Spain and France, from medieval
religious plays to the neo-regularity of the eighteenth century. He
discussed the Spanish *autos sacramentales* and French medieval plays
of various kinds, including the *moralités*. His anonymous and literal-
minded translator, in rendering the latter term into English, caused
Riccoboni to speak of such plays as 'Pieces of Piety and Morality,
under the common title of moralities.'[16] An English critical term was
born.

Riccoboni did not use the term *moralité* in his discussion of the English theater; indeed he was unaware of any English plays to which the term might be applicable. He criticized the backwardness of English scholarship and admitted that the only sources he had found for an English medieval drama were passing references to Corpus Christi plays by historians such as Stow. Besides these 'moral representations of the Old Testament' (in the translator's phrase), Riccoboni was unable to discover any 'prophane pieces' in England prior to the performance of a translation of Plautus at Greenwich in 1520, as mentioned by Holinshed.[17]

The name of Riccoboni's English translator has not been established, but it may be significant that one of the English publishers of the book was Robert Dodsley, bookseller, playwright, collector and ultimately anthologist of the early drama. A year after the publication of the Riccoboni translation Dodsley co-published the Charles Jarvis translation of *Don Quixote*. In this edition appeared a 'Supplement to the translator's preface,' mainly an extended gloss on Cervantes' allusions to Corpus Christi plays. Unsigned, and apparently added to the book as an afterthought, it bore the notation 'communicated by a learned writer, well-known in the literary world.' This essay traced the history of Scriptural plays on the Continent, culminating in their prohibition in sixteenth-century France. 'Upon this prohibition, the French poets turned themselves from Religious to Moral Farces. And in this we soon followed them. . . . These Farces they called MORALITIES.'[18]

Discussing the French *moralités* at some length and outlining the plot of Pierre Gringore's solemn *La Moralité de l'Homme obstiné* (in which the obstinate hero is inexorably damned), the writer contrasted them with the more farcical *sotties*, dominated by their fool characters. The development of the English medieval drama was seen as a corruption of the French forms:[19]

> But we (the English) who borrowed all these delicacies from
> the French, blended the *moralité* and *sottie* together, so that . . .
> the clown or fool got a place in our serious *moralities* . . . But the
> French, as we say, keeping these two sorts of farces distinct,
> they became in time the Parents of Tragedy and Comedy;
> while we, by jumbling them together, begot in an evil hour,
> that mungrel Species, unknown to Nature and Antiquity,
> called Tragi-Comedy.

Thus the writer was able to deduce the modern origins of comedy, tragedy, and tragi-comedy from the transitional drama which had taken the place of the forbidden Scriptural plays. Although we may admire the writer's imagination we should note (as in the case of

Theobald) the vagueness of all references to English 'moralities.' Indeed, in attempting to account for obscurities in *Measure for Measure* and *Love's Labours Lost*, the writer betrays his singular notion of what these plays had been like:[20]

> in these *Moralities*, the Fool of the piece, in order to shew the inevitable approaches of *Death*, (another of the *Dramatis Personae*) is made to employ all his stratagems to avoid him; which, as the matter is ordered, bring the *Fool*, at every turn, into the very Jaws of his Enemy: So that a representation of these Scenes would afford a great deal of good mirth and morals mixed together.

Patent fabrications of this sort demonstrate both the lack of factual evidence of the early drama and the almost desperate need for some piece of literary engineering to bridge the gap from the Corpus Christi plays to Shakespeare. From such manifestations an important conclusion emerges. In English literary history the category of 'morality' was not created to explain the common characteristics of various plays; it was first of all a theory. The plays which were to belong to this category were discovered afterwards.

It would be helpful to establish which moralities were actually known to exist at this moment in the mid-eighteenth century. In attempting to do so, we must begin by pointing out that there can of course be no definitive canon of moralities. It would be as hopeless to compile such a list as to make a precise account of all tragedies, comedies, tragi-comedies or any other alleged genres of drama. We are dealing, after all, not with ironclad categories but with multiple traditions; any conscientious attempt to divide plays generically ends in the Polonian bathos of pastoral-comical, historical-pastoral, tragical-historical, and tragical-comical-pastoral-historical.

The moralities are a tradition and not a rigid type. Nevertheless, some forty-five extant English plays are substantially within this tradition, of which approximately twenty were written before the accession of Queen Elizabeth. In determining the extent to which this body of plays was known in the eighteenth century, our chief source of information is the series of early play lists which were appended to printed plays of the Commonwealth and Restoration periods. Though they purported to be lists of all printed plays in English to date, they were more strictly rare book lists than bibliographies. They are nevertheless of considerable aid in the tracing of texts.[21]

On the evidence of these lists the earlier morality plays were virtually unknown; only two of the ten earliest plays are listed –

Dickscorner (*sic*) and *Four Elements*. On the other hand the Elizabethan moralities (apart from plays known only from manuscript) are listed very much as we know them today.

The dependability of these lists should not be overstressed, however. Gerard Langbaine, the first English dramatic bibliographer worthy of the name, gives us a more honest idea of the true state of knowledge. Writing in 1691, he printed the titles of many plays from the early lists, but freely admitted that he had never seen copies of them. Of all the plays in the morality tradition, he had personal knowledge of the existence of only eight: one pre-Elizabethan play (*Youth*), and the rest Elizabethan (*The Disobedient Child, Glass of Government, Mary Magdalene, Conflict of Conscience, Like Will to Like, Tom Tyler*, and *New Custom*).[22]

Thus the most persistent antiquarian could only uncover a small fraction of the extant plays, and even these were rare copies scattered through various collections, intrinsically interesting to no one. For this reason the early eighteenth-century scholars had few specific examples at hand when they spoke of the early drama. In fact, when the first anthology of old plays came to be compiled, and the editor wished to include a representative English morality, there was difficulty in finding a single one.

The main purpose of Robert Dodsley's *Old Plays* was to reprint Elizabethan and Jacobean classics, including *Edward II, The Jew of Malta, Friar Bacon and Friar Bungay, The Malcontent*, and *The White Devil*. Dodsley, influenced by the new historical attitude toward the drama, decided to include in addition specimens of the earlier drama, by way of comparison. He added, as a dignified afterthought, a 'Short Historical Essay on the Rise and Progress of the English Stage.'[23]

Here, leaning heavily on Riccoboni, Dodsley summarized the similar beginnings of the modern theater in the various countries of Europe. His account of the early drama in England was disparaging, but with the view of glorifying the Elizabethan accomplishment. He expressed this judgment in a metaphor of gradual illumination, beginning in the depths of the miracle plays:[24]

This period one might call the Dead Sleep of the Muses.
And when this was over, they did not presently awake, but
in a kind of morning Dream, produced the Moralities that
followed . . . in these Moralities something of design appeared,
a Fable and a Moral; something also of Poetry, the virtues,
vices, and other affections of the mind being frequently
Personified.

Dodsley, examining the moralities with neo-classical critical tools, found them to be an improvement over the miracle plays in many respects. Instead of mere representation (dramatized Scripture) there was a didactic purpose ('Moral') and a fictional pretext ('Fable'). Allegorical characters exemplifying the rhetorical device of personification were an artistic advance, an artifice. In apology for not substantiating these critical generalizations, Dodsley explained:[25]

> I should have been glad to be more particular; but where Materials are not to be had, the Building must be deficient. And to say the Truth, a more particular knowledge of these things, any farther than as it serves to shew the Turn and Genius of our Ancestors, and the progressive Refinement of our Language, was so little worth preserving, that the Loss of it is scarce to be regretted.

Dodsley explained that the first volume of his collection would present six early plays, in the original spelling and in chronological order, to show 'the progress and improvement of our taste and language.'[26] There can be little doubt that he encountered difficulty in finding early specimens. The Scriptural drama is represented by Bale's *God's Promises*, a belated and atypical example, but 'the only specimen I have been able to find of the Mysteries.'[27] He was unaware, apparently, of any of the English Corpus Christi cycles, including the *Ludus Coventriae* from which Wright had quoted, and from which excerpts had recently been published elsewhere.[28]

Dodsley's information on the moralities was only slightly less deficient. Though he spoke as if from wide experience, the best example of a morality he could find to reprint was *New Custom*, a barren controversial piece of the 1570s, which he called 'one of the most remarkable of our ancient moralities, as it was wrote purposely to vindicate and promote the Reformation.'[29] It would be difficult to know which other moralities Dodsley had in mind; apart from quoting the cast list of *All For Money*, he mentions none.

The explanation for these unrepresentative choices would seem to lie in the fact that Dodsley compiled the anthology not from all possible sources but from material at hand, that is, the Harleian collection which he had recently acquired. Despite its imposing bulk, this collection was not rich in early plays. It contained, besides *New Custom*, only three morality plays. Two of these were poor examples indeed: *Glass of Government* was of late date, written in tedious prose, and heavily disguised with neo-Terentian trappings; *Tom Tyler and His Wife* was a much altered piece, not printed until Restoration times. The third play, Lindsay's *Satire of the Three Estates*, over 4600 lines in length and written in Scots dialect, was hardly an ideal anthology piece. In any case there is no evidence that Dodsley had discovered the *Three Estates* copy, which was listed as poetry rather than drama in the Harleian catalogue.[30]

Thus, by process of elimination, *New Custom* became the first morality to appear in a modern edition. It is significant that the play's more distinctive characteristics – its controversial background and its explicit acting instructions[31] were pointed out in a brief headnote, but not in Dodsley's prefatory essay on the rise of the stage. Such characteristics did not well agree with the historical distinctions and generalizations to which the essay was devoted. After Dodsley's anthology, thirty years elapsed before another morality was printed in a modern edition; and in the meantime, quite unaffected by the particularities of *New Custom*, the theoretical process of defining the moralities continued.

In the next important edition of Shakespeare Theobald's remarks on the Vice character drew a response from the editor, William Warburton, Bishop of Gloucester. Theobald's theory had been that the Vice, beginning as a buffoon, had evolved into a seducer who impersonated evils to lead men to follow them. Warburton disagreed:[32]

> That the buffoon, or jester of the old English farces, was
> called the Vice is certain: and that in their moral
> representations, it was common to bring in the deadly sins, is
> as true. Of these we have yet several remains. But that the
> Vice used to assume the personages of these sins is a fancy
> of Mr. Theobald, who knew nothing of the matter.

With these authoritarian words 'the formal Vice, Iniquity' was banished, not merely from the transitional place which Theobald had given him, but from the text altogether. Warburton's certainty impelled him to one of his most fantastic emendations:

> Thus like the formal-wise Antiquity [*sic*]
> I moralize. Two meanings in one word.

To explain this position, Warburton referred the reader to a further discussion of the subject at the conclusion of the play. Here was printed a full 'general account of the rise and progress of the modern stage.' It was, in fact, a direct copy, with minor deletions and additions, of the 'supplement to the translator's preface' of Jarvis' *Don Quixote*. Warburton gave no source for the essay, and later commentators have assumed that it was his own. This seems unlikely, however, for it contradicts the very opinion expressed in support of the emendation and declares that the mingling of buffoonery and evil forces is particularly characteristic of the English moralities.[33] Its inclusion might perhaps be explained as false pedantry, a peculiar eighteenth-century vice.

Of a piece with Warburton's scholarship was that of William Rufus Chetwood, sometime prompter of Drury Lane and the author of the pretentious volume *The British Theatre*. This book contains its own prefatory 'Short View of the Rise and Progress of the English Stage,' cribbed wholesale from Dodsley. It is notable only for compounding a confusion of Dodsley's so as to suggest that moralities were designed as amateur theatricals for the gentry.[34] In the same decade Thomas Wilkes published *A General View of the Stage*, containing a brief history of the theater. Here, too, there were unacknowledged debts to Dodsley, as well as to the Jarvis essay. Though hardly the master of his material, Wilkes had strong opinions:[35]

> When the Roman empire was overwhelmed by the invasions of the northern nations, when Gothic barbarity and Monkish ignorance darkened the world . . . then monstrous fictions of giants, champions and distressed damsels, were spun out in monasteries by dreaming monks; and, to the destruction of reason and common sense became the most favorite amusements of the people.

2 The recovery of *Everyman* and the Macro MS 1760–1835

Robert Dodsley disposed of the Harleian collection of plays soon after the publication of his anthology gleaned from it. It would appear than he sold many if not all of the plays to David Garrick. Later quarrels between Dodsley and Garrick have obscured their relationship in the 1740s and 1750s, but the facts appear to be as follows: in the first edition of the *Old Plays* (1744) to which Garrick was a subscriber, Dodsley noted that he was in possession of the Harleian plays;[36] in the second edition (1780) this note was removed, and the editor remarked that 'the present Volumes were originally compiled from the only collection then known to exist, that which had been formed by the Earls of Oxford. This afterwards came into the possession of the late Mr Garrick, and, with great additions, hath since been bequeathed by him to the *British Museum*.'[37]

Garrick's collection included two moralities of far more importance, and far earlier date, than *New Custom*. It appears that these pieces were never in Dodsley's possession but came to light twenty years after the publication of the first edition of the *Old Plays*. Confirmation lies in a series of letters written by Bishop Thomas Percy, then in the process of collecting material for his *Reliques*, to the antiquarian Thomas Astle. In a letter of 15 January 1763 Percy mentioned an 'old fragment printed by Wynkyn de Worde' which Astle had dispatched to him, and said that he would be sending several other curiosities in exchange for it. Apparently Astle wrote back demanding the return of the fragment, for Percy answered ten days later, regretting that the fragment did not belong to Astle, and affirming his willingness to buy it if the price were right. Percy described the fragment as being 'in very shattered condition' and containing the following: 'six tracts, of which only three are perfect, viz. 1. The History of Robert the Devil; 2. Secretary of Jalousie; 3. Cock Lorrel's Bote; 4. Parliament of Birds; 5. Hickscorner; 6. Every Man. The whole volume does not exceed the size of a 12 penny pamphlet.'[38]

No further negotiations are recorded. It seems possible, however, that Astle ultimately made a present of the 'fragment' to David Garrick. Percy spoke of a gift to Garrick in a letter to Astle dated 12 May 1763: ('When he has got your late present to him new bound as he intended, you must provide me another sight of it.')[39]

In any event the Garrick collection came to include copies of *Everyman* and *Hickscorner*, and Percy acknowledged that he had consulted these copies in the preparation of his essay 'On the Origin of the English Stage.'[40] This essay is usually seen as the outgrowth of Percy's decision to include in his collection of 1765 a section on ballads used by Shakespeare. The letters to Astle throw a somewhat different light on the essay and suggest that Percy may have been stimulated at least in part by his discovery of two unknown plays in a black-lettered fragment which he nearly succeeded in obtaining for his own library.[41] Though the essay is prefixed to the section of the *Reliques* dealing with Shakespeare and the ballad, it is essentially independent of these considerations. Using all the available and reputable sources, Percy comes to the brink of a revolutionary conclusion: that Shakespeare's plays (particularly the histories) have rules of their own and are therefore not to be judged by neo-classical rules. Percy's direct familiarity with the early drama may well have influenced the formulation of this concept.

Percy shows scant interest in the medieval Biblical drama. To explain the process of transition from these plays to more advanced forms, however, he sets forth ideas of his own:[42]

As the old mysteries frequently required the representation of some allegorical personage, such as Death, Sin, Charity,

Faith, and the like, by degrees the rude poets of those
unlettered ages began to form compleat dramatic pieces,
consisting intirely of such personifications. These they
intitled MORAL PLAYS, or MORALITIES.

The moralities, then, are seen as a direct development from, and
an improvement upon the 'inartificial' plays from Scripture; by
contrast the moralities are 'not devoid of invention'.[43] Thus far
Percy took a standard neo-classical view, in line with Dodsley. But
he proceeded to a more original conception: 'I have now before me
two [moralities] that were printed early in the reign of Henry VIII,
in which I think one may plainly discover the seeds of Tragedy
and Comedy; for which reason I shall give a short analysis of
them.'[44]

Percy begins his oft-quoted impression of *Everyman* as a Greek
tragedy:[45]

... not without some rude attempts to excite terror and
pity ... in this old simple drama the fable is conducted upon
the strictest model of the Greek tragedy. The action is a
simple one; the time of the action is that of the performance.
The scene is never changed nor the stage ever empty.
Every-man, the hero of the piece, after his first appearance
never withdraws except when he goes out to receive the
sacraments, which could not well be exhibited in public; and
during his absence Knowledge descants on the excellence and
power of the priesthood, somewhat after the manner of the
Greek chorus. And indeed, except in the circumstance of
Every-man's expiring on the stage, the 'Samson Agonistes'
of Milton is hardly formed on a severer plan.

This, the first extended critique of a morality, could scarcely be
more neo-classical. By way of contrast, twentieth-century observers
commonly see *Everyman* as the very opposite of tragedy, as a kind of
divine comedy illustrating, with its 'fable' of Everyman, the 'moral'
of salvation.[46]

Percy is, perhaps, doing no more than describing by analogy the
moral unity, high seriousness, and restraint of *Everyman*. By expressing his regard for the play in the rigid terms of classical tragedy,
however, Percy diverts attention from the particularities of
Everyman. In this context, condemned to re-embody ineptly the
classical forms and to foreshadow primitively the Elizabethan
achievement, the moralities can hardly amount to anything in
themselves.

In *Hickscorner*, the other morality at hand, Percy professes to find the beginnings of modern comedy. Though the play is no Terentian intrigue, its manner and satiric purposes are correct; and he terms it 'a humorous display of some of the vices of the age . . . its chief aim seems to be to exhibit characters and manners.'[47] Thus Percy provides specific English plays to support the argument, first proposed from French analogies in the Jarvis essay, that the moralities constitute the roots of comedy and tragedy. He acknowledges the essay, and prints without comment its suggestion that tragi-comedy arises from the same source.[48]

Ironically, Percy's important conclusions in this essay, vindicating Shakespeare from attacks by neo-classical purists, are based on a dawning consciousness of the differences, rather than the parallel development, of the ancient and modern genres. Indeed, Percy seems to recognize the limitations of the theory that the morality represents embryonic tragedy and comedy. Besides *Everyman* and *Hickscorner* he mentions three other moralities known to him, but he makes no attempt to incorporate them into the theory. Of *Four Elements* he observes that it is about science and natural philosophy; of *Lusty Juventus*, only that it seems to be the first play with stage directions.[49] The date of *New Custom* (1573) is observed to overlap the coming of the regular drama (*Gorboduc*, 1565). Percy's solution for this difficulty is to connect the moralities with yet another dramatic genre: 'at length they assumed the name of MASQUES, and with some classical improvements became, in the two following reigns, the favourite entertainment of the court.'[50]

Both *New Custom* and *Lusty Juventus* have an obvious connection with the religious controversy of the Reformation, but of this Percy says nothing in the essay proper. Later in the *Reliques*, by way of introducing a controversial ballad, he proposed another theory. Such plays were Protestant tracts, attacking the Roman Catholic church and its superstitions, just as *Everyman* and similar plays defended Catholic institutions. Without exploring the chronological difficulties of this theory, Percy drew a significant moral, nearer to the truth than he perhaps realized: 'so that the stage in those days was what wise men have always wished it – a supplement to the pulpit.'[51]

Whatever Percy's theories about the moralities, it was mainly necessary for readers to take his word for them. The plays themselves were unavailable, except in rare copies; and there was no great rush to remedy the situation. In 1771, six years after the publication of the *Reliques*, Thomas Warton approached Garrick on behalf of one Thomas Hawkins, who wished to examine Garrick's collection with a view to publishing an anthology of old plays. Garrick agreed cheerfully enough but wondered to Warton whether such a project were not 'rather too inferior an office for a gentleman who deserves the character you give him .... Does not Mr. Hawkins think that the old plays are in general more matters of curiosity than of merit.'[52]

Nevertheless Hawkins, who had been led into the study of the early drama by attempting to edit Thomas Hanmer's Shakespeare, persisted and gathered together a far more representative selection of early plays than Dodsley's. Hawkins died suddenly in 1774, before the collection could be published, but it appeared posthumously in the following year. *The Origin of the English Drama* is 'illustrated in its various species, viz., MYSTERY, MORALITY, TRAGEDY, AND COMEDY,' and begins with a theoretical essay. Hawkins contends that drama is a spontaneous product of numerous civilizations and that modern drama is not a rebirth of a classical idea, but a new growth entirely. He therefore concludes that Shakespeare must not be judged by 'his obedience to the RULES of the ANCIENTS, which probably he did not know, but certainly did not mean to follow.'[53] Hawkins follows earlier critics in his low opinion of the Corpus Christi plays, but he is at least familiar with the existence of the Chester and *Ludus Coventriae* cycles; he reprints the Digby play of the *Slaughter of the Innocents*, and compares its ranting Herod favorably with the flat characters of 'regular' French tragedy. And despite his critical opinions he observes the now-traditional progression: 'One of the first improvements on the old MYSTERY was the Allegorical Play, or MORALITY, in which the Virtues and Vices were introduced as Persons of the Drama, for the purpose of instilling moral truth, or inculcating some useful lesson for the conduct of life.'[54]

We should note, besides the inevitable projection of rise and progress, the characteristic assumption of the time that allegory, fleeing particulars, expresses general sentiments. Here lies the origin of the strange belief that the moralities are, if nothing else, at least elevated. On the subject of the relation of the moralities to other genres, Hawkins seems to take issue with Percy. He relates these plays only to comedy. 'These moral plays having for their end to divert, as well as to instruct the populace, were for the most part of comic turn, and therefore naturally led the way for COMEDY: which it should be seen was introduced into our language before TRAGEDY.'[55]

Hawkins reprints three specimens of the morality; in fact he subtitles each of them (*Everyman*, *Hickscorner*, and *Lusty Juventus*) 'a morality.'[56] His texts are based on the Skot edition of *Everyman* and the Vele edition of *Lusty Juventus* from the library of Lincoln Cathedral (which he had collated with the copies in the Garrick collection), and the Wynken de Worde edition of *Hickscorner* from the Garrick collection. Excerpts from Percy's essay are printed as introductions to the individual plays. Whether Hawkins died before he could complete his own introductions, or whether the Percy excerpts were a part of the original plan, is uncertain. In some respects (for instance, the designation of *Everyman* as a tragedy) the opinions are at a variance with those expressed in the general preface.

Hawkins' editions of 1773 were the last modern editions of moralities to be published in the eighteenth century; there were in fact no others for nearly fifty years. But in the interim, criticism continued unabated. The last quarter of the eighteenth century brought two significant discussions of the early drama. The first of these, Thomas Warton's four-volume *History of English Poetry*, is not primarily a history of the stage. Perhaps because of this fact Warton seems less interested than his predecessors in discovering causal chains of development or genres of drama. He tends to regard the moralities as merely one manifestation of the popularity of allegory. Thus he considers the traditions of allegorical figures in street pageants as an interesting parallel to the morality personifications. Warton sees these traditions of public performance as a formative influence on the taste for poetry of the English people and on the rise of the school of Spenser. 'By means of these spectacles, ideal beings became common and popular objects: and emblematic imagery, which at present is only contemplated by a few retired readers in the obsolete pages of our elder poets, grew familiar to the general eye.'[57]

It is possible to detect here the beginnings of a new attitude toward the literature of the Middle Ages. Within a generation the Romantic movement conceived a brighter image of the medieval period, and the old clichés of monkish darkness gave way to the new clichés of chivalry and romance. Allegory, the most characteristic of medieval literary expressions, was patronized for its picturesque quaintness; the moralities, didactic and unpicturesque, became the object of a new, and greater, misconception. Critics in search of individuality, sentiment, and self-expression found them indistinguishably dull, theological, and anonymous. Where once the neo-classicists had seen unity of moral purpose as an artistic advantage, an improvement over mere storytelling, the new age found this moralizing vapid and tediously inartistic. At the same time, and for different reasons, the crude humor of the moralities was less acceptable than ever. Yet tradition, and the exigencies of chronology, served to perpetuate in spite of everything, the now-illogical theory that the moralities were a development from, and an improvement on, the Corpus Christi plays.

Warton's version of the theory was thoroughly traditional, indeed a close paraphrase of Percy's remarks.[58]

It is certain that these MIRACLE-PLAYS were the first of our
dramatic exhibitions. But as these pieces frequently required
the introduction of allegorical characters, such as Charity,
Sin, Death, Hope, Faith or the like and . . . at length plays
were formed entirely of such personifications. These were
called Moralities.

The heterogeneous volumes of the *History* contain, side by side with
such venerable theory, a striking amount of new information. But
Warton makes no systematic use of this material – indeed, most of
his specific references to the moralities are in passing, in the *History*'s
labyrinthine footnotes. Sometimes Warton is merely repeating
Percy, as when he pairs *Everyman* and *Lusty Juventus* as competing
works of controversy. Elsewhere, however, he deals at length with the
controversial aspects of Bale's *Three Laws*, and mentions for the first
time in English criticism two important plays – Lindsay's *Satire of the
Three Estates* and Medwall's *Nature*. His knowledge of the latter plays
is largely bibliographical, but at least he makes their existence a
matter of public record.[59]

Warton was also the first modern observer to identify John
Skelton as a writer of moralities. He had come across a copy of
Skelton's *Magnificence* in the Garrick collection and appended a plot
outline of the play, commenting that 'there is often much real
comedy in these ethic interludes, and their exemplifications of
Virtues and Vices in the Abstract convey strokes of character and
pictures of life and manners.'[60] But Warton's most renowned
contribution to Skelton studies was his infamous account of a play
called 'The Nigramancer.'

Noting that a copy of the play 'printed by Wynkin de Worde
[*sic*] in a thin quarto in the year 1504,' belonged to the poet William
Collins, Warton explains that the copy disappeared after his death.
Since he saw the copy before its disappearance, however, Warton is
able to point out that the play involved the trial of two vicious
characters, Simony and Avarice, with the Devil as judge. In the
play the Devil (who had been conjured up by the necromancer for
whom the play is named) sentenced the accused to damnation
amidst much horseplay.

Warton's account of 'The Nigramancer' has been carefully studied
and is now generally discredited. No trace of the play has ever been
found, and it resembles no extant play of the period. Rather it seems
to be derived from contemporary misapprehensions of the supposed
drollery of Devils and Vices on the early stage. The consensus is that
Warton invented the whole story as a piece of bogus scholarship.[61]

Warton's motives for such a fabrication may perhaps be expressed
in a little noticed passage of the *History*. He apologizes for the tedium

of such dry material as 'that very rude species of our drama, called the MORALITY.' Beginning a digression (which closely follows his account of 'The Nigramancer') he explains, 'In this respect I shall imitate those map-makers mentioned by Swift who[62]

> O'er inhospitable downs
> Place elephants for want of towns.'

The other important critic of the time to deal with the early drama was Edmund Malone. His essay was prepared as prefatory material for his edition of Shakespeare, issued in a fragmentary form in 1780, and finally ten years later published as an 'Historical Account of the Rise and Progress of the English Stage.' Malone inherited from his predecessors a low opinion of the artistic merit of the early plays, of which he says 'the Titles are scarce known, except to antiquarians; nor is there one of them that will bear a second perusal.' He also accepts the traditional theory of transition and development, and quotes with approval the formula of Warton which, in turn, was derived from Percy.[63]

Despite this theoretical conservatism, Malone's practical criticism brings to light much new information. He examines, for instance, the fragmentary 'plot' of the lost Jacobean play *The Seven Deadly Sins* and notes its relation to the moralities. At the other end of the chronology he records his conclusion that the Corpus Christi plays and the moralities are contemporary rather than consequent. With one hand he defers to Percy's accounts of *Everyman* and *Lusty Juventus* as offering, on the moralities, 'a perfect notion of this kind of drama'; with the other hand he supplies in a footnote an unprecedented list of fifteen other moralities.[64]

The most important piece of new evidence here is drawn from Willis' *Mount Tabor*, published in 1639. The author, an exact contemporary of Shakespeare, describes an event of his boyhood – the performance of a play called *The Cradle of Security*. It is an eyewitness's recollection of the performance of a morality; and it emphasizes, not the crudeness, but the *impressiveness* of the play. At the very least, its suggestions of elaborate staging, costumes, and music call for some elaboration and explanation; but Malone merely prints the piece, with the comment that it will 'give the reader a more accurate notion of the old moralities than a long dissertation on the subject.'[65] Like the rest of Malone's new material it is added to the sum of knowledge rather than analyzed or applied to the line of development of the English drama.

Thus it is that the definitions of eighteenth-century critics survived despite the discoveries of eighteenth-century scholars. The increasing extent of the evidence, combined with a fundamental lack of interest in its significance (as opposed to its utility in charting the 'rise and progress'), produced increasing vagueness. The unfashionable didacticism of the plays, once thought of as evidence for progress, became an unfortunate and persistent flaw. Equally distasteful were the strange allegorical characters. What remained nevertheless to the moralities was a chronological function, the bridging of the gap between Scriptural and 'regular' drama. In the absence of other meaningful distinctions the category of moralities becomes neutralized and almost useless, a critical no-man's-land.

The first year of the new nineteenth century brought *A Complete History of the Stage* in five volumes. Its author, the Reverend Charles Dibden, presented this concept of the moralities: 'The subjects were sometimes holy, and sometimes prophane; but as their general tendency was morality, everything was permitted.'[66] The term 'morality' is used by Dibden as a catch-all for non-Scriptural sixteenth-century plays populated by personifications. However debatable this usage it is still chronologically possible, since no earlier moralities were yet known to exist. Dibden leads the reader through a maze of contradictory platitudes about the moralities: since they must have been too tedious to be endured they are, therefore, disfigured with low comedy to amuse the ignorant groundlings, except that many of them are written for amateur performance in the houses of the gentry, for which they are quite unsuitable.

Dibden is particularly distressed to find so many of the plays unclaimed and anonymous. He is not merely at pains to discover authors for the plays but to provide moralities for any likely authors. He examines the list of John Bale's plays (which he affects to know intimately, though nearly all of them were lost) and pronounces four of them moralities.[67] He gleans the name of Richard Tarleton from Malone and pronounces him the author of a morality.[68] He calls George Gascoigne's *Supposes* 'a morality from Ariosto,' though it is in fact a scrupulously 'regular' comedy; and when he still finds anonymous plays to be accounted for, he has a solution: 'John Rastell, a famous typographer . . . either wrote, revived or translated many of them. All those to which no authors' names are affixed, it is natural to suppose are of this description.'[69]

Concluding this rambling catalogue of moralities, Dibden added his apologies: 'Perhaps it may be wrong to dwell so minutely on the subject of these representations. Many of which are miserable trash, and the best but fanciful and fantastic rhapsodies, calculated, one should think, more for drolls and puppet shows than to make up the delight of kings and courts.'[70]

As the didactic predilections of the neo-classical age became less and less fashionable, it was becoming less clear that the moralities were in any sense an improvement on the miracle plays, or anything else for that matter. One casual browser of the period described them this way:[71]

> compositions as *inartificial*, as crude and jejune, as can well be
> imagined .... If they do attempt to delineate character we
> must confess we think it a lamentable failure .... It may
> seem strange to us, that exhibitions of this kind, without plot,
> or character, and with no scenic illusion, should have
> attracted such attention and excited such interest amongst
> all ranks of society.

The author of these sentiments based his conclusions on five plays – *Everyman, Hickscorner, Lusty Juventus, New Custom*, and Lindsay's *Three Estates*. It is worth remembering that these were the only moralities available in modern editions. *Everyman* and *Hickscorner*, printed in the reign of Henry VIII, were thought to date from the same period; they were the oldest moralities known to exist. We should not underestimate the difficulty, under the circumstances, in reaching sound conclusions about the nature of the moralities.[72]

William Hone's *Ancient Mysteries Described*, published in 1823, is primarily a study of the Corpus Christi plays, from an aggressively anti-Catholic point of view. Hone sees the miracle plays as an abortive attempt to subvert the Wyclif Bible, as a weapon in the war of ideas finally won, thanks to Caxton's printing press, by the forces of enlightenment and Reformation. Even if its history is factious, Hone's book is commendably persistent in its attempt to set the early drama in a specific context, to see it as arising out of some practical need rather than merely rising and progressing with classical spontaneity. In this, and in many other instances, Hone is following up the hints and obliquities of Warton. Hone naturally emphasizes the controversial tendencies of the moralities (*Lusty Juventus* and *New Custom*), and follows Percy and subsequent critics in designating *Everyman* a pro-Catholic controversial piece of the Reformation period.[73]

But our particular interest in Hone's book here is that it contains word of a previously unknown play and an important manuscript. Hone calls the play 'The Castle of Good Perseverance' and describes it as a mixture of mystery and morality. He attempts to describe a drawing of the stage plan on the first page of the manuscript, from which he prints (and expurgates) some stage directions. It is understandable that Hone does not venture to explain what all this might mean. He had not seen the manuscript for himself, as he pointed out: 'To a bibliopolical [*sic*] friend I am indebted for notice of the Castle of Good Perseverance, which he saw in Dr. Macro's collection.'[74]

Cox Macro was an East Anglican antiquarian who collected manuscripts, including many formerly belonging to the abbey of Bury St Edmunds. When he died in 1767, his collection passed through various hands until it was sold at auction in 1820. Among the manuscripts purchased by Hudson Gurney at this sale was the now-famous Macro MS containing the texts of three fifteenth-century moralities.[75]

Two years after Hone's book appeared, Thomas Sharpe included in his elegant folio on the early drama at Coventry an engraved copy of the stage plan mentioned by Hone.[76] There was no discussion of the play but the plan was reproduced with acknowledgments to the new owner of the manuscript, Hudson Gurney. *The Castle of Perseverance* thus appears, unexpectedly, to challenge the firm conception of what the morality plays had been.

The discovery of the Macro MS came at an opportune time for a rising literary man named John Payne Collier, who was then engaged in research for the first truly comprehensive history of the pre-Shakespearean stage. Through the offices of Thomas Amyot, Collier received permission from Gurney to examine the manuscript.[77] He concluded that the three plays were of earlier date than any of the presently known moralities, but evidently of the same type. When his history was published, it contained no less than five chapters on the moralities (or as Collier preferred, 'moral plays'), and one of these chapters was devoted to the newly-discovered Macro plays. Collier printed plot summaries and extensive quotations from these three plays – *The Castle of Perseverance*, a second play full of elaborate stage effects which he named *Mind, Will, and Understanding* (now generally known as *Wisdom*), and a more earthy piece to which he gave the name *Mankind*.[78]

Along with the privilege of bringing these rare plays to public attention, Collier inherited the problem of accounting for their existence. Collier might well have been capable of this task; his infamy as a forger of records has obscured the fact that he was the foremost student of the early drama of his day. But Collier did not succeed in making sense of the Macro plays, and for a simple, all-too-familiar reason. He already *had* a theory of the development of the drama. And, whatever he might insist, it was far from original:[79]

I have . . . traced the connection between Miracle-Plays, consisting in the outset only of Scripture characters, and Moral Plays (or 'Moralities' as they have been of late years usually denominated), represented by allegorical personages; and I have shown how the first, almost imperceptibly, deviated into the last, by the gradual intermixture of allegory with sacred history, until Miracle-plays were finally superseded.

This view of the subject, which does not seem to have occurred to any who have gone before me, is succeeded by a similar investigation of the structure and design of the Moral-plays. I have endeavoured to point out the manner in which they, in turn, gave way to Tragedy and Comedy, by the introduction, from time to time, of characters in actual life . . . ultimately, as might be expected, the real was entirely substituted for the fictitious.

Collier restated this conviction at length in his introductory chapter on the moralities. Finding allegorical characters in the Corpus Christi plays, particularly the *Ludus Coventriae Parliament in Heaven*, he concluded that these characters changed the nature of the miracle plays:[89]

they interfered, to a certain degree, with the action and progress of the plot; scriptural characters . . . sank into comparative insignificance; and thus in process of time what was originally intended to be a poetical embellishment to a sacred drama, became a new species of theatrical exhibition . . . it consisted of mere allegory and abstraction, unenlivened by mental or personal idiosyncrasy . . . it must have been a very wearisome, and often unintelligible exhibition, ill calculated for a popular assembly.

Collier's nineteenth-century tastes thus began to collide with his theories. He felt bound to distinguish between miracle plays and moralities on the basis of characterization. But, abstraction being the opposite of characterization, in what sense did the moralities represent progress? In the sense, he reasoned, that they were failures:[81]

this kind of drama . . . could not exist long supported only by mere abstractions: accordingly, in the very earliest specimens . . . we find efforts made . . . to render them amusing . . . it was only, in fact, by abandoning the original plan, that this object could be accomplished. Thus deviations from the first design of miracle plays, by the employment of allegory, led to the performance of moral plays; and deviation from moral plays, by the relinquishment of abstraction for individual character, paved the way, by a natural and easy gradation, for tragedy and comedy, the representation of real life and manners.

Far from being a new theory, this is a culminating restatement of the ancient doctrine of the rise and progress of the modern stage. Collier, for all of his knowledge, had persuaded himself that the moralities were a transitional abortive species of miracle play trying to turn itself into real drama. That he insisted on this *in spite of* the Macro plays, and not because of them, is proved by the absurdity of the chronology. The moralities now stretch, by Collier's own reckoning, from deep in the fifteenth century to the onset of the seventeenth century.

In these circumstances Collier decidedly failed to make sense of this group of plays, of which he knew more than any man of his time. His chapter on the Macro plays is largely devoted to outlines and quotations, with few critical observations. He notes with some dismay the rather elaborate staging requirements of *The Castle of Perseverance* and *Wisdom* and the obscenity and satire of *Mankind*. He cites some points of resemblance between *The Castle of Perseverance* and the miracle plays, but he makes no real attempt to apply his inapplicable theories to these rare plays, which were not to be published in their entirety for nearly seventy-five years.[82]

In a second category, as 'Printed Moral Plays, relating to Mankind at large,' Collier placed most of the early Tudor plays, and gave the first detailed summaries of three which were virtually unknown at the time: Medwall's *Nature* (not edited until 1898), *Mundus et Infans* (which Collier himself had recently published in the third edition of Dodsley's *Old Plays*),[83] and *Youth* (which was to have no modern edition until 1849). We should note, to Collier's credit, that he perceived the essential kinship of these plays with *Everyman* and the Macro plays as allegories of what he called 'the contest between good and evil in the mind of Man.'[84]

Collier did not succeed, however, in making historical sense of the morality corpus. His conception of the development of the morality was at best stubborn and at worst in bad faith. He was convinced, as we noted, that the moralities were progressive only in so far as they failed, and demonstrated the need for realistic characterization. To emphasize this point he brought forward 'evidence' of a morality performance at the court of Henry VIII in 1514. Of the two plays presented on this occasion the first, a mythological trifle with elegant songs and dances, was a great success; the second was a morality 'wryten by mayster Midwell, but yt was so long yt was not lyked: yt was of the fyndyng of Troth, who was caryed away by ygnoraunce & ypocresy. The foolys part was the best, but the kyng departed befor the end to hys chambre.'[85]

Two trends would be evident from this account – first, that moralities were already, in 1514, considered long and tedious; second, that extraneous characters, such as fools, were being introduced in an effort to modernize an old-fashioned form. According to Collier the report came from a paper found folded up in the rolls of the Revels accounts; subsequent observers have been unable to find the paper, and have concluded that it never existed except in the inventive mind of the great literary forger, J. Payne Collier.

There remains the great bulk of the extant moralities, and Collier continued his survey, methodically touching play after play, and concluding with a chapter full of 'Moral Plays resembling Tragedy and Comedy.' When the whole corpus of the morality genre lay behind him, he turned back with relief to the reign of Henry VIII, to the time of Heywood's interludes and the rise of secular comedy. It was here that the moralities ought to have died; and where, lacking the evidence, Collier had contrived their epitaph.

3 In search of sources 1835–1914

Collier's survey of the early drama stood unchallenged until German scholarship happened upon the field in the last quarter of the nineteenth century, in pursuit of Shakespeare's origins. In the meantime, however, significant discoveries were made. Three important manuscripts of early moralities came to light, none of which fitted easily into Collier's scheme of categories and pattern of development. Ironically enough, two of these were discovered and published by Collier himself. The first of these manuscripts quite unexpectedly linked the moralities with the Elizabethan history play. It was apparently discovered among papers relating to the corporation of Ipswich and proved to be one of the lost plays of John Bale. Collier himself seems to have overseen the acquisition of the manuscript by the Duke of Devonshire; his edition of the play, under the title *Kynge Johan*, was published in 1838.

In his introduction Collier pointed out that the play was a work of religious controversy, supporting the Reformation. This controversy was, however, couched in terms of historical events in the reign of King John, and its cast list included both historical figures and abstractions. Without stopping to consider any deeper implications, Collier gave this as evidence of a transition toward the mature forms of Elizabethan drama by means of secularization.[86]

The other play which Collier brought to light was yet another controversial piece of the Reformation period, also in manuscript. It had been part of the collection of Cox Macro, and, like the 'Macro plays' themselves, it was acquired by Hudson Gurney in 1820. Collier had been unaware of this manuscript in 1831, but it soon came to his attention. The play, which carried the name

Respublica, was bound for his use in 1836.[87] *Respublica* had been
written in the first year of the reign of Mary Tudor; and, unlike
King John and the other previously discovered controversial
moralities, it satirized the Protestants and the Reformation. Like
King John, however, it proclaimed the necessity of strong monarchy.

It is crucial to the development (or, more properly, *lack* of
development) of modern definitions of the morality play that these
two plays should have been discovered after the fact of Collier's
History, in inhospitable times. *Respublica* was not even published
until thirty years after its discovery.[88] Any possibility that *Respublica*
and *King John* might throw new light on the nature of the morality
genre seems hardly to have been considered. In fact these two plays,
taken together with Lindsay's *Three Estates* and a few fragments and
accounts of lost plays, gave evidence of a crucial functional stage in
English dramatic history. For the time being, however, the importance of this new evidence was unrecognized. When interest
began to be focused on the early drama once again toward the end
of the century, the intention was not to comprehend a tradition but
to dissect for sources and establish categories. As it was, these
political plays were chiefly noted as further examples of the barren
controversial tendencies of the Tudor period, more of the contentious
drabness out of which emerged the glorious Elizabethan dawn.

A further potential complication to the accepted picture of the
early drama came with the discovery of the fragment of a morality
play in the Account Rolls of the Priory of the Holy Trinity, Dublin,
for the years 1337–46. This play centered on the figure of an arrogant
King, 'Rex Vivus,' who is vanquished by Death but achieves salvation. Published in 1891 (unaccountably titled by its editor *Pride of
Life*), it was quickly recognized as the earliest extant play of the
morality genus, dating from the late fourteenth or possibly the early
fifteenth century.[89] Again, the possibility that its discovery might
necessitate fundamental revisions in the prevailing concept of the
morality play seems hardly to have been considered. There were
sufficient problems with its chronology (a disturbingly early date)
and thematic relations (its similarity to *Everyman*). *The King of Life*
(to give it the name of its chief character) was quietly assimilated
into the list of 'allegorical' plays which now stretched over four
centuries of dramatic experience and two of critical misconception.

The period 1875–1914 was most productive of new editions,
including W. C. Hazlitt's revised and enlarged edition of Dodsley's
Old Plays, adding eight moralities, including the first modern
editions of two youth plays – *Nice Wanton* and *The Disobedient
Child.*[90] Less widely available, but of considerable importance was
a collection by Alois Brandl, with German parallel texts and commentary. In this unlikely form were found the first modern editions

of *Mankind*, *Nature*, and the newly-discovered Elizabethan MS play *Misogonus*, as well as texts of *The King of Life* (*Pride of Life*), *Respublica* and *Common Conditions*.[91] There followed the belated first edition of the Macro Plays (*Castle of Perseverance*, *Wisdom*, and *Mankind*) in 1904, and Ramsay's edition of *Magnificence* in 1908, both issued under the auspices of the Early English Text Society.[92]

In the period at hand critics continued to work in the time-warp of German source study. A. W. Ward followed the trail of personified characterization back to the neo-Terentian cloister dramas of the tenth-century nun Hrosvitha. For the motif of *Everyman* he supplied a remarkable pedigree, stretching back through the Dutch *Rederijker* stage, the Golden Legend and Vincent of Beauvais in the thirteenth century, to a parable in the eighth-century religious romance *Barlaam and Jehosaphat*, which was apparently drawn from Buddhist sources.[93] But the main attention of source critics of the morality was devoted to identifying and classifying motifs of allegory. The most generalized of these allegorical themes, the conflict of vices and virtues, was traced back to Roman literature. Here the German scholar Wilhelm Creizenach discovered the prototype of the morality play in the works of the fourth-century Christian poet Prudentius. It was in the epic poem *Psychomachia*, where personified vices and virtues battled within the soul of man, that he saw the origins of the morality form.[94]

In the same way Creizenach traced the debate of the four daughters of God from the climax of the *Castle of Perseverance* back through its appearance as a separate play in the *Ludus Coventriae* cycle to origins in a medieval allegory of the Psalms of David.[95] In the motifs of the Dance of Death other source critics found a common origin for the death themes of *Everyman* and *The King of Life* (*Pride of Life*).[96] The investigation of such sources was, of course potentially a productive line of research, particularly if it helped to establish a context for the works themselves. But the danger lay in confusing sources with components until the process degenerated into a mechanical system of categorization or a meaningless recital of ancestries.

R. L. Ramsay's prolix introduction to Skelton's *Magnificence*, (comprising two-thirds of the volume's 300-odd pages) illustrates the virtues and limitations of source criticism. Ramsay draws together the various strands of allegory which occur in the moralities to form a kind of proto-allegory, of which the particular plays are more or less partial exemplifications. He elaborates this method in evaluating the characters of the plays on the basis of relative abstractness, constructing a hierarchy of which *Hickscorner* is the summit and *The Castle of Perseverance* the bottom. He concludes that during the late fifteenth and early sixteenth centuries allegory, fortunately, was declining.[97]

We noted in Collier's *History* the increasing difficulty of portraying the morality as a transitional phase in the rise and progress of the English stage. The discovery of the Macro plays had pushed the historical context of the morality play well back into the fifteenth century, and the date of *The King of Life* now extended the origins back to the verge of the fourteenth century.[98] Further surprising discoveries were made. A reference in Wyclif's *De Officio Pastorali* (1378) indicated the existence of plays of the Lord's Prayer. Though the texts were lost, records of these Paternoster Plays turned up in the archives of York, Lincoln, and Beverley, indicating that the plays were probably proto-moralities dating from the fourteenth century.[99] In the other direction, the genre's persistence was extended into Caroline drama by Symonds' identification of Thomas Nabbes' *Microcosmus* (1637) as a well-preserved, if belated, morality.[100]

In the face of such evidence it was no longer possible to insist, with Collier, that the morality had developed out of the miracle plays and led inevitably into regular tragedy and comedy. The critical problem now was to account for the diversity and longevity of the moralities. The solution which the late Victorian and Edwardian critics achieved retained the notion of a rise and progress but one which took place within the morality genus itself. The rise was in fact a descent from airy abstractions to realistic representation; the progress was a diminution in scope – the complete history of all mankind giving way to partial and particular cases.

This process was depicted as one of secularization, through which religious drama of the Middle Ages made way for the secular, humanistic drama of Shakespeare. A. W. Pollard took the lead in promoting this conception, contrasting the early moralities 'that touch the whole of human nature' with the later plays, which are typically shorter and concerned with partial, limited aspects of life, such as youth or Reformation controversy.[101] E. K. Chambers' *The Mediaeval Stage* accurately reflected the current fashions of criticism in 1904. Here the term 'morality' was reserved for the earlier plays. Characteristically, they were lengthy (approaching *Castle of Perseverance*, *c.* 3500 lines), designed for elaborate outdoor staging, and comprehensive (or 'full-scope') in theme, depicting human life from the cradle to Judgment Day. Later smaller plays, such as *Hickscorner* and *Youth*, were called 'moral interludes,' small-scale indoor entertainments suitable for banquets and state functions.[102]

These divisions were not without their difficulties. Chambers felt obligated to define *Magnificence* and *Three Estates* as moralities (chiefly because of length), the other controversial plays as interludes, and *Nature* as somewhere in between. Writing four years later, C. M. Gayley calmly demolished these categories by pointing out only a few superficial contradictions. If the *Castle of Perseverance* was lengthy, *Mankind*, *Mundus et Infans*, and *Everyman* were short. *The King of Life* (*Pride of Life*) was not full-scope, nor indeed, was *Everyman*; but the 'moral interludes' *Longer Thou Livest* and *Nice Wanton* were so. *Three Estates*, a late 'morality,' was also the longest.[103]

Despite the glaring problems, the main outlines of this theory were adopted by such important historians of the drama as Schelling and Tucker-Brooke. Schelling preserved the term 'interlude' in Collier's sense to describe completely secular plays such as Heywood's farces;[104] but he divided the moralities into full-scope and limited-scope plays. He found only five full-scope plays (*Castle of Perseverance*, *Mundus et Infans*, *Nature*, *Mankind*, and Bale's *Three Laws*). The remaining plays he divided according to theme (e.g., religious – *Everyman*; controversial – *New Custom*, *Respublica*).[105]

Tucker-Brooke, on the other hand, restricted the term 'morality' to five early plays – *The King of Life* (*Pride of Life*), the three Macro plays, and *Everyman*. All the rest he described as 'interludes' of one sort or another – educational, political, for amusement only, and so forth. The rise and progress of the Elizabethan drama, he observed, had come with the cross-fertilization of the rude but vital native stock of interludes with the structural sophistications of regular tragedy and comedy. The picture was of a pure form (the morality) broken up and scattered in a multitude of parts and directions under the pressures of secularization.[106] Under the influence of source criticism the task of literary historians became one of reassembling the scattered fragments into a series of logical categories on the basis of motifs and thus distinguishing somehow between moralities and interludes. This task became as traditional and respectable as it was insoluble.

Such was the condition of the morality as it appeared in its first full-length study under the scrutiny of W. Roy Mackenzie. Mackenzie argued, plausibly, that no coherent definition of the moralities existed and that there was no way of distinguishing authentic moralities from derivative developments which had borrowed morality features. To solve this dilemma he examined all plays of the sixteenth century or earlier which had allegorical characters and didactic purposes. Those which also had what he called 'allegorical structure,' were moralities. 'Allegorical structure' was a kind of litmus test for secularization. If a drama was too obviously based on real life, it failed this test, was expunged from the list of moralities, and became merely a 'play.' Those which survived (and such generally accepted examples as *Nice Wanton* did not) were unchronologically sorted according to allegory:[107]

1 The Conflict of Virtues and Vices
  a for supremacy – *Hickscorner, New Custom, Three Laws, Three Ladies in London*
  b for possession of man
    i Spiritual – *Castle of Perseverance, Mankind, Nature,* . . .
    ii Intellectual – *Four Elements*
    iii Attributes – *Wisdom, Wit and Science,* . . . .

It is not clear what, outside of itself, such a set of categories indicated, but Mackenzie pursued his task indomitably for 270 pages.

In a study published quietly four years earlier there were more hopeful signs. E. N. S. Thompson's *The English Moral Plays*, made the first important strides in transcending the superficial rigidities of source studies. Thompson pointed out the specific relation of the morality drama to the medieval sermon tradition. Allegory could be seen less as the cause, more as the sermon-playwright's mode of expression. Thompson concluded that these allegories concerned 'three great crises' in human life – the moral struggle of good and evil based on the freedom of the will (the *Psychomachia*), the sureness of death (the Dance of Death), and the Christian fact of hope for the sinner through grace (the Parliament in Heaven). This work was unique in its time in considering the morality play as an end in itself.

This brilliant study, published in an obscure monograph,[108] was slow to make its impact; and in the dominant critical view the moralities remained allegorical potpourris of personifications, vaguely uplifting in sentiment, and fortunately transitional. It would have been difficult to deduce from the prevailing image of the morality that it had ever belonged to an authentic stage, much less to a human audience. But Thompson's study had opened the way to the roots of the morality tradition. And almost unnoticed in the limbo of literary critics, a morality play had come alive and had become a modern classic.

Chapter IX

Everyman in the Twentieth Century

1 The *Everyman* stage revival

The 1901 stage revival of *Everyman*, undertaken by William Poel and the Elizabethan Stage Society of London as an antiquarian experiment and a charitable benefit, was so successful that it soon took on the appearance of a public triumph. The critic of the *Morning Post* urged Poel to schedule more performances, observing: 'The programme had indeed many of the elements of a popular success. To use a phrase that one must immediately explain, there is money in it.'[1]

In 1902 the *Everyman* production was revived for a series of indoor, non-charity performances at St George's Hall, London. In June, as festivities began for the coronation of King Edward VII, the production moved to the Imperial Theatre, Westminster, 'for a few afternoon representations by request of a large section of the public who were unable to gain admission.' Despite the illness of King Edward and the postponement of the coronation, *Everyman* concluded a remarkable four weeks' run at the Imperial on 9 July 1902. It had indeed proved capable of 'attracting all London and becoming the "sensation" of a season,' as the critic of the *Athenaeum* had predicted.[2]

To what extent did the original play of *Everyman* become lost in the process? Prompt books of the Poel production over a five-year period (1901–6) indicate that the text of the play was increasingly cut in performance, and additional spectacle and music introduced. Certain passages of the play had been excised to begin with (e.g., Fellowship's offer of a woman to Everyman, and the allegations of Knowledge regarding the illegitimate children of sinful Priests), and these excisions increased in number and scope in later versions. The general effect was to remove the rough medieval edges of *Everyman*, and give it a more congenial pre-Raphaelite texture.[3]

From its commercial triumph in London, the Poel production of *Everyman* went on to gain international notoriety. After a lucrative tour of the provinces, the American impresario Charles Frohman decided to bring the company across the Atlantic. The production was now in the hands of Ben Greet, an obscure actor-manager who had joined the 1902 revival of the play. Poel, who had lost interest in the production, returned to his Elizabethan experiments, and did not accompany the troupe on its tour. He continued to receive royalties on the production (which he eventually sold outright to Greet) but of all Poel's experimental productions, it was his only commercial success. In later years Poel virtually repudiated the play. As a confirmed skeptic he found its religiosity indefensible.[4]

But *Everyman* had been launched on its commercial way, and it opened in New York on 13 October 1902. There were many difficulties. Frohman, unable to secure a theater, had booked the production into a concert hall. And when it became known that Almighty God was a character in the play, an ecclesiastical uproar broke out and the yellow journalists of turn-of-the-century New York launched a moral crusade against moralities. The producer found a hiding place on the stage for God, but the reviewers were not to be appeased. William Randolph Hearst's *New York American* warned:[5]

JEHOVAH SEEN IN THE OLD MORALITY PLAY 'EVERYMAN' –
MUCH THAT CHURCH PEOPLE WILL NOT COUNTENANCE –
In spite of the fact that much was done last night . . . to
oust some of the sacrilegious atmosphere that pervaded the
production in London . . . the appearance of the *Deity*! –
not in the center of the stage, as in London – but aloft, behind
a lattice, with blue electric light . . . .

The *New York Daily Tribune* pronounced *Everyman* 'a Dismal Experiment . . . trite didacticism and ponderous dulness,' and Pulitzer's *New York World* reported with alarm:[6]

BAREFOOT ACTORS IN THE AUDIENCE –
'Everyman' an uncanny affair, Draws a Small Audience. . . .
Doubtful reception from Churchmen . . . a thing of the
Dark Ages. The insatiate craving of theater goers for the
sensational, the morbid, and the unusual in stage representations
and the crafty ingenuity of managers for filling the voracious
demand . . . .

Whatever his motives, Charles Frohman at first lost money; audiences were small. But with the help of many perplexed and intriguing notices the play eventually became, as in London, the talk of the town.[7]

H*

Probably the strangest little drama ever played here . . . . The
entire human race is represented in one person . . . .
Morning Telegraph 15 October 1902.

whole bushels of 'quaints' dropped in the porch of the
Mendelssohn Hall last night when an awed, but drowsy
audience emerged into the twentieth century . . . . The
familiar first night faces had a hushed half-scared look . . . .
Evening World 15 October 1902.

the queerest of queer entertainments . . . a performance
altogether quaint transformed the upper Tenderloin into
early England . . . the most remarkable matter ever
presented on the stage . . . .
Press 14 October 1902.

Aside from the content of the play the reviewers were particularly
amazed to find the usual footlights and curtain missing. It was,
in fact, the first professional production in America to use a quasi-
Elizabethan stage.[8] After three weeks in the Mendelssohn Hall
Frohman booked *Everyman* into a succession of theaters and then
sent it on the road to Boston, Philadelphia, Chicago, and
Indianapolis on the first swing. The production returned to New
York and took to the road once more the following season, traveling
to Hartford, Pittsburgh, Toledo, and as far west as St Louis. By and
large *Everyman* seems to have been cordially received, with occasional local exceptions:

a small audience nearly froze at the Parsons theater last
evening for the sake of seeing the morality play 'Everyman.'
Hartford *Courant* 28 November 1903.

the theatergoer of today is so worldly wise. He knows his
Pinero and Tolstoy and Fitch so well that he is rather inclined
to demand the highest form of modern art . . . .
Toledo *Blade* 3 November 1903.

A revealing note in the program for the Odeon in St Louis
indicates that a further retreat by the Deity had become necessary:[9]

It has been found preferable during the performance of
Everyman in public halls and theaters to have the speech of
Adonai given off the stage, owing to its liability of interruption,
coming, as it does, at the commencement of the play.

As a manager, Ben Greet seems to have introduced additional elaborations – processions, Gregorian chants, symbolic action – to mollify the audiences and as the years progressed, more and more of the didactic material came to be cut out. Ben Greet's star, Edith Wynne Matthison, was pleased neither with Greet's 'improvements' nor with his quaint neo-medieval habit of omitting the names of the company (except his own) from the program, to follow the 'modest ancient custom of anonymity.'[10]

In this fashion Ben Greet turned *Everyman* into a personal enterprise. The production returned to New York in 1904, and again in 1907, for 'its seventh year in the company's repertory.'[11] Greet revived *Everyman* in England on numerous occasions in the years that followed; and in 1935, shortly before his death, Sir Phillip Ben Greet appeared as the Doctor in a production of *Everyman* at the Ambassadors Theatre, London. He had been knighted in 1929, thanks in good part to his career as a purveyor of theatrical antiquities to the theater-goers of two continents.[12]

2 Some responses to *Everyman*: Shaw, Yeats, and von Hofmannsthal

As the *Athenaeum* critic had pointed out, the significance of *Everyman* depended upon the point of view from which it was regarded. But in any case it was no longer the exclusive possession of specialists and antiquarians. Poel's production had made *Everyman* a contemporary fact, and the morality play a part of the twentieth century. As such it became susceptible to various twentieth-century interpretations, without regard for its medieval intentions or its historical functions in the rise and progress of the English stage. Whether the revivified *Everyman* was in fact a theatrical *tour de force*, a religious service, a drama of ideas, a poetic allegory, or a good commercial investment depended largely upon whether one was, say, George Bernard Shaw, W. B. Yeats, or Max Reinhardt – to name but three turn-of-the-century men of the theater who saw *Everyman*, and drew their own interesting conclusions.

Bernard Shaw's conception of the theater, from the beginning, was in terms of its didactic possibilities. Thus he saw Ibsen not so much as an apostle of Realism but as the wielder of an acute moral instrument, a means of social criticism.[13] It was in search of this kind of theater that he began to write plays of his own.

In the early years of his playwriting career, Shaw was gainfully immersed in the commercial theater as a professional dramatic critic. Implicitly and explicitly he called for a theater that could

take on the neglected role of the church as a locus for the conscience
and intelligence of the community, the place where social problems
and ultimate questions could be brought to the common attention.[14]

His critical approach to the theater of the 1890s was ruthless,
but habitually constructive. The sight of a bad melodrama provoked him not to a damnation of outworn conventions but to the
thought of what a good melodrama should be like:[15]

> the whole character of the piece must be allegorical, idealistic,
> full of generalizations and moral lessons; and it must represent
> conduct as producing swiftly and certainly on the individual
> the results which in actual life it only produces on the race
> in the course of many centuries.

Shaw was no longer writing a weekly column of dramatic
criticism when William Poel's production of *Everyman* reached the
stage. He therefore did not review the performance at the Charterhouse. But in publishing *Man and Superman* (1903) Shaw let it be
known that he had been present and had been impressed. His
preface contained a characteristically Shavian set of acknowledgments, giving the literary genealogies of the characters of *Man and
Superman*:[16]

> I should make formal acknowledgement to the authors whom I
> have pillaged in the following pages if I could recollect them
> all . . . . Ann was suggested to me by the fifteenth century
> Dutch morality called Everyman, which Mr William Poel
> has lately resuscitated so triumphantly. I trust he will work
> that vein further, and recognize that Elizabethan
> Renascence fustian is not more bearable after medieval
> poesy than Scribe after Ibsen. As I sat watching Everyman at
> the Charterhouse I said to myself Why not Everywoman?
> Ann was the result: every woman is not Ann; but Ann is
> Everywoman.
> That the author of Everyman was no mere artist, but an
> artist-philosopher, and that the artist-philosophers are the only
> sort of artist I take quite seriously, will be no news to you.

There is always a danger in taking Shaw literally when he begins
listing predecessors and influences. His prefaces are strewn with
illustrious and exotic pedigrees constructed for the sake of argument.
The general purpose of such ancestries is to demonstrate that he is,
after all, an imaginative genius in his own right. Thus Eric Bentley
concludes, in the present instance:[17]

As to sources proper, Shaw often gets an idea from an
earlier work which has no necessary relation to it. He sees
a performance of *Everyman* and thinks: Why not Everywoman?
The result is the character of Ann Whitefield in *Man and
Superman*!

But the connection is finally not so obscure; particularly if it is
borne in mind that the character of Everyman, in Poel's production, was played by a woman.

Poel's choice of a young woman for the role of Everyman was the
one feature of the production to be widely criticized by the reviewers.[18] Nevertheless it established a precedent, and a career for
the actress in question – Edith Wynne Matthison – who toured in
the part throughout Europe and America thereafter. She had
played the role nearly 300 times by April, 1903, according to an
interview published in the New York *Evening World*, under the title
'Enters Grave Nightly.'[19]

To Shaw, the sight of a young woman presenting universalized
humanity came at a convenient time. In 1901 he was in the process
of writing *Man and Superman*, in response to a friend's suggestion for a
Don Juan play. Whether this suggestion preceded the Charterhouse
performance is not certain. Two facts are clear: that Shaw began
work on *Man and Superman* in that same year that he saw the Poel
Everyman, and that *Man and Superman* was a new sort of play. As
Shaw described it later, his playwriting career thus far had only
produced:[20]

a series of comedies of manners in the classic fashion. . . .
But this, though it occupied me and established me
professionally, did not constitute me an iconographer of the
religion of my time, and thus fulfil my natural function as an
artist. . . .
Accordingly in 1901, I took the legend of Don Juan in its
Mozartian form and made it a dramatic parable of
Creative Evolution.

In *Man and Superman*, Ann Whitefield is the living demonstration
of the dynamic principle of Shaw's Creative Evolution. It is she,
representing the Bergsonian Life Force, who fulfills its purposes by
selecting the hero Tanner for the father of her children and by
pursuing him relentlessly into submission. She can be seen in the
light of the morality tradition as a splendidly realized embodiment of
an idea. But the debt of *Man and Superman* to *Everyman* transcends this
characterization. The heart of the play, as Shaw pointed out, is the
dialogue in the third act now generally known as *Don Juan in Hell*.

This episode begins with the arrival in Hell of the aged Doña Ana (Ann Whitefield) who had just died. The Commander (Ann's father) and Don Juan (Tanner) encounter her, and there ensues Shaw's magnificent debate on the merits of heaven and hell. This argument is based upon a principle of Shaw's afterworld that can easily be overlooked – the afterlife is a condition of free will. As a new arrival, Ana must choose between the constructive dullness of heaven and the irresponsible pleasures of hell. The Heaven-bored Commander and the Hell-weary Don Juan are changing sides, but though they and the Devil do much of the arguing, it is Ana's choice around which the whole argument convenes. Ana's choice of Heaven, like Everyman's, is a discovery of her own true nature, as she progressively casts off her pious Christian illusions that life is over once one is dead. Chesterton shrewdly observed that a Shaw play is nearly always 'the dialogue of a conversion.'[21] So it is with Ana. In the end she is reborn, accepting the link to the Life Force, which is her immortality.

Thus *Everyman*, transmogrified by the philosophical wit of Shaw and fitted out with the trappings of Goethe, Mozart, and the Creative Evolutionists, becomes *Man and Superman*, 'a dramatic parable of Creative Evolution.' The example of *Everyman* had arrived at a crucial moment, as Shaw later observed:[22]

> the worst convention of the theatre current at that time was
> that intellectual seriousness is out of place on the stage;
> that people go there to be soothed after the enormous
> intellectual strain of a day in the city: in short, that a
> playwright is a person whose business it is to make
> unwholesome confectionery out of cheap emotions. My
> answer to all this was to put all my intellectual goods in the
> shop window under the sign of *Man and Superman*.

At the time of the *Everyman* revival, W. B. Yeats was already deeply involved in the Irish National Theatre Society. In its later form, as the Abbey Theatre, this project was to spawn the lyrically realistic plays of Synge and O'Casey. But in its inception Yeats thought that he was creating a theater of fantasy. 'Our plays,' he wrote, 'will be for the most part remote, spiritual, and ideal.'[23] In emphasizing spirituality, Yeats was not promulgating conventional Christianity, but rather endeavoring to express a mystical Irish spirituality of his own. What he seems to have lacked throughout his career as a playwright was a form for the expression of these beliefs. It was here that he was influenced, briefly, by the renascent morality play.

It is quite probable that Yeats saw the Poel production of *Everyman* at St George's Hall either in March or May of 1902.[24] On 13 June, three days after *Everyman* had begun its successful stand at the Imperial Theatre, he wrote to Lady Gregory:[25]

I have almost finished a first draft of that little play I told you of, *The Fool and the Wise Man*. Gordon Craig is greatly delighted with the scenario which I read him, he wants to show the play to Irving but my belief in the commercial theatre liking such a thing is but slight.

As Yeats predicted, *The Fool and the Wise Man* was produced not by the commercial theater but by his own company. Retitled *The Hour Glass*, this play had its first performance the following year in Dublin. The printed version of *The Hour Glass* was subtitled 'A Morality,' and it was as 'a morality play' that Yeats wrote of it at the time.[26] The play concerns a wise man who has taught every sensible person (everyone, that is, but the local fool) to believe in nothing but the visible tangible realities of life. To this man comes the angel of God turning his hourglass and informing him that he has but one hour to live. He will be saved from damnation, however, if he can find one person who still believes. The wise man looks for such a person among his students, his wife and children, but he has taught them too well. They reject him in turn, and he dismisses them from the house until only the fool is left. In despair the wise man asks the fool and from him learns humility: 'I will speak to them. I understand it all now. One sinks in on God; we do not see the truth; God sees the truth in us . . . . But no, I will pray – yet I cannot pray. Pray Fool . . . . Your prayers are better than mine.'[27] He dies, wishing for a sign. The fool prays; and the students, who have been summoned to their lessons, arrive in time to see (or *think* they see) the soul of the wise man rise to heaven.

Besides sharing the premise of a situation – the sudden coming of death – *The Hour Glass* echoes *Everyman* in many informative ways. The setting is similarly indefinite in time and space, and the characterizations are formalized in the morality manner, conceived in terms of their relationship to the Wise Man. It is he, like Everyman, who defines the play and is its purpose. Though *The Hour Glass* became a familiar part of the repertory of the Irish National Theatre Society, and later of the Abbey Theatre, Yeats was never pleased with the play. He intended the ending to be ambiguous, and poetic – but it proved to be highly theatrical. It evidently had a direct impact upon its audience that Yeats could not recognize as his own. It was, as he would write later, 'only too effective – converting a musical hall singer, and sending him to Mass for six weeks.'[28]

In 1912 Yeats completely rewrote *The Hour Glass*, converting the prose to blank verse and the ending to an enigma. He explained the change this way:[29]

> I have for years struggled with something which is charming in the naive legend but a platitude on the stage. I did not discover till a year ago that if the wise man humbled himself to the fool, and received salvation as his reward . . . so much more powerful are *pictures* than words, no explanatory dialogue could set the matter right . . . . I was always ashamed when I saw any friend of my own in the theatre.

Yeats abandoned not merely the prose of the early version, but also its morality structure. Only the verse revision, which never carried the subtitle 'A Morality' and had no close resemblance thereto, found a place in the final *Collected Plays*.

Thus Yeats reclaimed himself, in the end, from the fleeting influence of *Everyman* and pursued his rather strict and lonely theatrical ideals, which were not really medieval at all except in a very distant pre-Raphaelite sense. The way for Yeats led out of the public arena to the private exquisiteness of Japanese Noh-drama. The morality play had been for Yeats but one in a series of distant forms which had failed to create the kind of mystical communion he was always seeking in principle and avoiding in fact.

It is sometimes alleged that a classic is an equivocation, necessarily all things to all people. In this case it is evident that the revived *Everyman* moved its imitators in a remarkable variety of directions. To West End managers, *Everyman* had demonstrated the lucrative possibilities of religious sentiment on the stage. To Shaw it suggested an incarnated Life Force; to Yeats, mysticism and simplicity. But the German Director Max Reinhardt also saw the play at the Charterhouse in 1901,[30] and drew his own extravagant conclusions. Returning home, he induced Hugo von Hofmannsthal to join him in creating a German version entitled *Jedermann*.[31] Reinhardt and Hofmannsthal de-emphasized the specific ritual of *Everyman* (its lesson in the necessary art of dying) and converted it into an epic parable of the materialism of modern man, subtitled 'The Play of the Rich Man's Death' (and performed in the cathedral square in Salzburg). *Jedermann*'s hero becomes a greedy materialist, exploiting the poor and reveling in a life of luxury. Death's arrival interrupts a symbolic Belshazzar's Feast of prosperity. The voices of death are heard from all sides, proclaiming the name of 'Jedermann.'[32] Every opportunity for grandiose spectacle is seized and expanded, and much new material is added. Everyman now has a mother, to whom he must bid farewell. He must struggle with Mammon and Mephistopheles before he is saved by last-minute repentance, with musicians and actors deployed atop buildings of the surrounding square.[33]

The Salzburg performances, in the late afternoon, were timed to coincide with the setting of the sun. The play ended with a crescendo of orchestra, chorus, organ and the pealing bells of the cathedral tower. Yet for all its trappings, *Jedermann* struck many as a diminution of the original idea. Harley Granville-Barker explained it this way: 'At no time did I want to go on my knees. And I could hardly keep from it when old Poel first did it – the real thing, not Hofmannsthal.'[34]

Jedermann nevertheless proved to be durable in its own right. Around its annual performances grew up the Salzburg festival. Reinhardt brought the production to America in 1927 and staged it in English at the Hollywood Bowl in 1935. The annual Salzburg production, suppressed by Hitler in 1937, was resumed in 1946 and has continued to the present day.

Though *Jedermann* is in many ways a late Romantic period piece, it familiarized the German-speaking world with the abstract concept of morality characterizations, and its influence was felt in the avant garde drama of its own day which we now call Expressionism. The faceless and even nameless human components of Kaiser's *Gas* plays and Toller's *Mass Man* or the Robots of Capek's *RUR* are indeed abstract. It is even likely that these abstractions of Expressionist drama are based in part on medieval example, as filtered through *Jedermann*. But the difference between Everyman – the epitome of fallible yet transcendentally destined man – and the heroes of Expressionist theater – lowest common denominators, unknown citizens, dehumanized void unpersons – is worth observing. It is something of the difference between the Middle Ages and 1984.

3 Moralities in performance

The success of *Everyman* on the stage set a precedent for stage revivals of other moralities. Nugent Monck, whose work spanned the gap between William Poel and T. S. Eliot, led the way in producing revivals of the medieval drama in England. After leaving Poel he founded the English Drama League in 1905. He staged the first modern production of the interlude of *Youth*, a production which had numerous performances in the years 1905–7, including a tour of provincial cities and a performance at Court before Queen

Alexandra. Monck in 1909 attempted to stage scenes from the *Ludus Coventriae* plays, but his unexpurgated production violated the Blasphemy laws, and was suppressed by the police. He moved on to Norfolk where he gave *Mundus et Infans* its first modern production.[35] During a stay in Dublin in 1911 he mounted production of both *Mundus et Infans* and *Youth* at the Abbey Theatre, and also founded an acting school.[36] Eventually Monck became director of the illustrious Maddermarket Theatre, Norwich, from which base he continued his career as a producer of many revivals, including a performance of *Everyman* at the first Canterbury Festival in 1929.[37]

Revivals of moralities at the Malvern Festival, under the direction of Barry Jackson, included the first modern production of *Hickscorner* in 1931. Among those who saw and enjoyed this rough-edged genre comedy was Bernard Shaw, who delighted in its satire and characteristically pronounced it superior to Elizabethan comedy.[38] In the 1934 Festival a production of *Youth* was given in repertory with Marlowe's *Dr Faustus* and Henri Gheon's *Marvellous History of St Bernard*.[39]

Two other moralities received their first modern productions in America, in the wake of the *Everyman* revival. The fifteenth-century play *Mankind* was performed in New York in December, 1910, by the American Dramatic Guild.[40] In the following March in New York, *Nice Wanton* was performed on a bill with the Chester *Noah's Flood*. The production was combined with a lecture by Brander Matthews of Columbia University and attracted considerable attention. *Nice Wanton* was performed by an all-male cast before a stage audience of parents and children, who 'hissed the villain . . . just as in a Theodore Kremer melodrama.'[41]

In 1903, flushed with success in *Everyman*, Ben Greet had informed the press that he intended to revive *The Castle of Perseverance*.[42] But he apparently had second thoughts (or perhaps read the play) and never carried through the ambitious production that would have been required. It was not until 1939 that this archetype of the moralities was finally staged, under university auspices, by the Oxford Experimental Theatre.[43] Further morality revivals have been undertaken by various academic groups in recent years, notably at the 1964 Bristol Shakespeare Festival (featuring a production of *Nice Wanton* and the first modern productions of Udall's *Respublica* and Bale's *King John*) and in the series of productions undertaken at the University of Toronto since 1965.[44]

Radio versions of a wide number of moralities were prepared by Raymond Raikes and John Barton for the BBC series, 'The First Stage,' in 1956–7. These superb productions, which brought the spirit and sound of the early drama to a wide modern audience, have since been issued as a series of recordings.[45] However, perhaps the most important morality revival since Poel's *Everyman* took place neither as an educational nor a religious event, but as a large-scale professional venture for the Edinburgh Festival. The project began with the decision of the Festival authorities to produce a play in Scots dialect for the 1948 Festival and to hire Tyrone Guthrie to direct the performance. From among the meager list of classic Scots plays, Guthrie selected Lindsay's *Three Estates*, which had not been produced since the sixteenth century. His reasoning was theatrical and experimental:[46]

> Gradually, as I toiled through the formidable text, it began
> to dawn that here was an opportunity to put into practice
> some of the theories which, through the years, I had been
> longing to test. Scene after scene seemed absolutely unplayable
> on a proscenium stage, almost meaningless in terms of
> 'dramatic illusion'; but seemed at the same time to offer
> fascinating possibilities.

After much searching for theaters, Guthrie determined to produce the *Three Estates* in the huge Assembly Hall of the Church of Scotland. Here he constructed a stage surrounded on three sides by audience. It was 'a tryout . . . a first sketch for the sort of Elizabethan stage I had long hoped, somehow and somewhere, to establish.'[47] The vast text of *Three Estates* was condensed into the size of an evening's performance, and under Guthrie's energetic direction the ancient play scored a remarkable and unexpected success with the critics and the public. The court of King Humanity came alive with crafty Scots vices, forlorn virtues, flags, pageantry, and hypocritical clerics. The *Three Estates*' success at the 1948 Festival was repeated in subsequent years.

Guthrie notes gleefully that his production restored the *Three Estates* to the position of a Scots classic and a required text for university students (to whom he presents his condolences). It is none the less true that his production, as an act of imagination, rescued another morality play from almost total obscurity. He proved once more that these plays were written to be played and that their characters, if conceived in terms of a performance, are not lifeless abstractions but plausible characters in a play.

The staging in the Assembly Hall was a revelation, for Guthrie at least:[48]

> it threw a new light for me on the whole meaning of
> theatrical performance.
>   One of the most pleasing effects of the performance was the
> physical relation of the audience to the stage . . . . Seated

around three sides, they focused upon the actors in the brightly lit acting area, but the background was of the dimly lit rows of people similarly focused on the actor. All the time, but unemphatically and by inference, each member of the audience was being ceaselessly reminded that he was not lost in an illusion, was not at the court of King Humanitie in sixteenth century Scotland, but was, in fact a member of a large audience, taking part, 'assisting' as the French very properly express it, in a performance, a participant in a ritual.

The stage and auditorium of the Assembly Hall formed the basis for the design of Guthrie's open stage theaters in America, the Festival Theater of Stratford, Ontario, and the Tyrone Guthrie Theater of Minneapolis, and numerous 'thrust' stages built in imitation of them throughout the United States and Britain. It is too early to assess the full impact of these new stages on the direction of twentieth-century theater. But at the source lies, of all things, a morality play. The *Three Estates* attacked the problem of the theater in our own day, beyond the illusions of realism.[49]

. . . a piece that depended little upon illusion and much upon making contact between actors and audience extremely intimate and flexible. Much of the play is addressed directly by the players to the audience. There is indeed, virtually no story; a series of ideas is forcibly canvassed 'at' the audience, whose cooperation is directly and explicitly sought . . . clearly the relation was a very intimate and sociable affair.

In other words, the text of *Three Estates* was built on an assumption – that the audience and actors could, under the right circumstances, achieve a sense of mutual participation in 'a series of ideas.' The morality play conjured up, without illusions, the possibility of ritual. To the mid-twentieth century this possibility had begun to seem the true end of the theater, as it had been the beginning.

4 Religious drama and T. S. Eliot

The revival of *Everyman* had a formative influence on the whole idea of modern religious drama. Shaw, Yeats, and von Hofmannsthal were not alone in being influenced by the success of a morality play. Other lesser talents responded with plays which borrowed outward devices and motifs. In *The Fool of the World* (produced in London, April, 1906) Arthur Symonds dramatized the coming of death in a manner reminiscent of Yeats' *Hour Glass*, using the morality forms to conjure up an exotic and vaguely symbolic *fin de siècle* setting.[50] Another play in this vein was *Life's Measure*, written by Nugent Monck. The play concerns Youth, beset by temptation and ultimately visited by Death. The coming of death in all these plays has a grim post-Victorian finality fundamentally different from the moment of climax which death represented in the medieval scheme of man's life. But the influence of *Everyman* is none the less palpable.[51]

Religion, or at least pietistic spectacle, had been a part of the London commercial theater since 1896 when *The Sign of the Cross* initiated the fashion of corrupt pagans, Christian martyrs and chariot races.[52] From Poel's *Everyman* came a realization that there were personal religious experiences dramatic enough to serve a melodramatic purpose. Charles Rann Kennedy, a member of the Poel production of *Everyman* and the husband of its star, Edith Wynne Matthison, put his years of touring experience in *Everyman* to profitable account in *The Servant in the House* (1907). This play, produced at the Adelphi Theatre in 1909, records the wonders wrought by a miraculous butler who enters the service of a minister and teaches him true Christianity. In the end, as the reformed clergyman sets to work to clear out the symbolically clogged drains of his church, the butler reveals himself as a long-lost brother. In Jerome K. Jerome's *The Passing of the Third Floor Back* (1908) another mysterious stranger appears this time in a boarding house, as the self-effacing new resident whose holiness converts his noxious fellow-boarders.[53] These two plays achieved a phenomenal success; they began the stage vogue of what Gerald Weales has called 'Sentimental Supernaturalism.'[54] The novelty consisted in introducing a supernatural character, indeed a Christ figure, into the context of everyday life (or that portion of it customarily represented in melodrama). These plays can be seen, in essence, as Edwardian travesties of the *Everyman* motif. The agent of reformation was not the strict fact of death, but the example of virtuous humility; the reform was not from ignorance to knowledge, but from moral callousness to cleanliness, kindness, and self-righteousness.

Something of the same spirit vitiated the effectiveness of Galsworthy's experiment in this genre, *The Little Man* (1915). Subtitled 'a farcical morality' this play records the charitable deeds of a nondescript railway passenger ostracized for his pains by his fellow travelers (who are nationalistic stereotypes) but revealed in the end to be a saint.[55] Before long the subject of death came habitually to be dramatized in terms of supernatural appearances. In Barrie's *A Well-Remembered Voice* (1918) and Sutton Vane's

Outward Bound (1923) the fact of death is systematically clothed in euphemisms masquerading as allegory. The dead speak to the living to assure them that there is nothing whatever to worry about. The lonely way of Everyman acquires the pomposity and camaraderie of an ocean voyage to a mysterious destination.

Plays like *Outward Bound* are pertinent to this study only in so far as they are frequently cited as 'modern morality plays.'[56] This label apparently designates plays with painfully obvious 'messages' in which the characters, while pretending to be real people are in fact symbolic. In such cases critics presumably do not mean that the play is a formal imitation of a morality play (in the sense of *Jedermann*) or even that it borrows devices and elements from early drama (in the sense of Yeats' *The Hour Glass*). Rather they allege that the play is naïvely and obviously symbolic, *like* a morality play (or better, their debased concept of one).

As an attempt to describe or justify slightly non-realistic drama by identifying it with a medieval precedent, the 'modern morality play' is perhaps a harmless critical conceit. As a simile it is brittle, but as an equation it is disastrous. It provokes the widely-received conclusion that the original moralities were at best medieval versions of *Outward Bound* or *The Passing of the Third Floor Back*, after-dinner exercises in middle-class complacency. Thus Graham Sutton can say 'Outward Bound is pure Morality; *mutatis mutandis* it is as medieval (and modern) as *Everyman*.'[57]

The term 'morality play,' loosely applied, has few present rivals as a critical factotum. In its primary or literary sense of 'a symbolic play with a moral' it has been used to describe everything from Dennis Hopper's *Easy Rider* to Mary Shelley's *Frankenstein*, as well as the plays of Harold Pinter, Tennessee Williams, e.e. cummings, Robert Bolt, Samuel Beckett, Eugene O'Neill, Archibald MacLeish, Edward Albee, Friedrich Durrenmatt, Somerset Maugham, and Rochelle Owen to name but a few. A paperback collection of one-act plays, a miscellaneous assortment of contemporary religious-poetic drama, has been issued under the subtitle 'modern morality plays.'[58] Northrop Frye has redefined the morality play – ancient and modern – in Jungian terms, its characterizations being allegedly projected aspects of the personality who participate in an 'archetypal masque, the prevailing form of most twentieth century highbrow drama.'[59] But the final denigration of terminology is best demonstrated in the cross-indexing of the main catalogue of the New York Public Library. There the classification 'modern morality play' serves as a repository for earnest pageants and the unwanted religious verse plays of trinonymous lady poets.[60]

In England one of the early amateur church drama groups did, indeed, adopt the name of the Morality Play Society. This group was formed in 1911 by Mabel Dearmer, authoress and contributor to the *Yellow Book*, for the purpose of producing a religious play which she had written. *The Soul of the World* is a verse rendering of the nativity and passion, set in the frame of a debate between Time and Eternity. [61] Mrs Dearmer followed with an Old Testament play, *The Dreamer*, for the society production in 1912. In subsequent years other poetic-religious plays were performed, including the verse version of Yeats' *The Hour Glass*. The genteel proceedings of the Morality Play Society were permanently disrupted by the outbreak of World War I in 1914. [62]

After the trauma of 1914–18, amateur religious drama resumed with a new seriousness in England in the postwar period, and occasional professionals, such as Laurence Housman and John Masefield, began to contribute plays to be performed under church auspices. It was a successful performance of Masefield's *Coming of Christ* at Canterbury Cathedral that led to the foundation of a Canterbury Festival of Music and Drama. The opening festival, in 1929, featured a performance of *Everyman* directed by Nugent Monck, of the original Poel production. [63]

Three years later the Canterbury Festival presented an abridged version of Tennyson's verse drama *Becket*. The appropriate locale suggested a tradition. Thus it was that when the organizers of the 1934 Festival asked T. S. Eliot to write a play for them, its subject was virtually predetermined.

In dramatizing the life of Canterbury's martyr Eliot was pursuing a new-found interest in the theater. Earlier in 1934 he had collaborated in a semi-expressionistic pageant play, *The Rock*, which stated the case for traditional Christianity and denounced the current fascist and communist attacks upon it. [64] In so far as dramatic techniques were concerned, Eliot was, as always, conscious of precedents: [65]

> The great vice of English drama from Kyd to Galsworthy
> has been that its aim of realism was unlimited. In one play,
> *Everyman*, and perhaps in that one play only, we have a
> drama within the limitations of art. . . . It is essential that a
> work of art should consciously or unconsciously draw a circle
> beyond which he [the playwright] does not trespass: on the one
> hand actual life is always the material, and on the other
> hand an abstraction from actual life is a necessary condition
> to the creation of the work of art.

Murder in the Cathedral, Eliot's festival piece, was not a 'modern morality play'; in outward form, with its chorus and sure inevitability of action it far more resembled Greek tragedy. Nevertheless it is clear, both from the play and from Eliot's own statements about it, that *Murder in the Cathedral* was strongly influenced by *Everyman*. As Eliot indicated, it was more a matter of suggestion than of imitation.[66]

In constructing the poetic dialogue of the play, Eliot felt the need to avoid pseudo-Shakespearean blank verse and also the flat contemporary sound of his own verse. The play needed some sense of the twelfth-century historical event, short of wallowing in archaisms:[67]

> I wanted to bring home to the audience the contemporary
> relevance of the situation. The style therefore had to be
> *neutral*, committed neither to the present nor to the past.
> As for the versification, I was only aware at this stage that the
> essential was to avoid any echo of Shakespeare. . . .
> Therefore what I kept in mind was the versification of
> *Everyman*, hoping that anything unusual in the sound of it
> would be on the whole, advantageous. An avoidance of too
> much iambic, some use of alliteration, and occasional
> unexpected rhyme, helped to distinguish the versification
> from that of the nineteenth century.

The neutral style of *Everyman*, which distinguished it from most of its contemporaries, served Eliot well in this respect. The versification proper of *Everyman* is notably irregular both in length of line and in meter. Its line is not regularly syllabic, much less iambic. Although not alliterative it is probably best described as a late development of the native accentual line.[68] Eliot's verse did not imitate this roughness, but smoothly 'kept in mind' *Everyman*. In other words Eliot, using a very faint stress line in principle, wrote a modern irregular line of his own.

Everyman, like all the moralities, is mainly in rhymed verse. As Eliot points out, rhyme in *Murder in the Cathedral* is both 'occasional' and 'unexpected.' In the early part of the play, rhyme is nonexistent. It only begins with the fading away of Becket's welcomers and the entrance of the First Tempter:[69]

> You see, my Lord, I do not wait upon ceremony:
> Here I have come, forgetting all acrimony,
> Hoping that your present gravity
> Will find excuse for my humble levity.

With the sudden intrusion of irregular stress couplets, a critic has observed, 'the action moves smoothly onto the plane of a medieval morality, the plane of abstractions, "the strife with shadows." '[70]

The First Tempter, a hedonistic courtier, comes to remind

Becket of his former worldly pleasures but fails to shake his determination. With his departure, the play resumes its unrhymed form. The Second Tempter, a political courtier who does not speak in rhyme, offers Becket his former power as Chancellor. He also fails, as does the Third Tempter, a bluff country baron offering alliance against the king.

The first three Tempters are useful to Eliot in providing quick exposition of the past (Becket's worldly background, friendship with the king, and power as Chancellor) and present situation (a brewing revolt by the barons). They are not really tempters but reminders; Eliot presents them in the guise of visitors to the newly-arrived Becket, merely editing away the naturalistic trappings. In this sense the Tempters resemble dream-figures, appearing and disappearing as if within Becket's mind, but they are natural (albeit anonymous) characters, familiar to Becket. Refuting their familiar arguments, he remains resolute. In the last twenty-five lines of Becket's scene with the Third Tempter, the play modulates into rhyme once more. The reason becomes evident with the entry of another Tempter:[71]

> THOMAS . . . But if I break, I must break myself alone.
>> (*Enter* FOURTH TEMPTER)
> TEMPTER Well done, Thomas, your will is hard to bend.
> And with me beside you, you shall not lack a friend.
> THOMAS Who are you? I expected
> Three visitors, not four.
> TEMPTER Do not be surprised to receive one more.
> Had I been expected, I had been here before.

The Fourth Tempter, representing Becket's aspiring pride in seeking martyrdom, lifts the play to its true subject.[72] In this scene, the heart of the play, occurs its only genuine dramatic conflict – the struggle of Becket to prepare his own soul for the ordeal of martyrdom. If he goes to his death proudly, with visions of his vindication on earth (as a canonized saint) and in heaven (dwelling in the presence of God), all is lost. The implications of the Fourth Tempter are those with which Becket himself has wrestled many times, and which he must subdue. He is nearly brought to despair, as the lamentations and fears of chorus, priests and tempters increase. It is only when he finds them pleading that he save himself, that he is impersonally freed from all doubts.[73]

> Now is my way clear, now is the meaning plain:
> Temptation shall not come in this kind again.
> The last temptation is the greatest treason:
> To do the right deed for the wrong reason.

In the medieval play it is Everyman's attributes, in abandoning him, who teach the lesson of *ars moriendi*. Here it is Becket, in abandoning his past, present, and even the hope of a future, who teaches himself how he must die. The remainder of the play is devoted to demonstrating, on a naturalistic level, that such a death did take place and might at any time.

Murder in the Cathedral has been criticized for failing to prove that Becket's martyrdom was indeed an act of humility.[74] Such a demonstration cannot, perhaps, be accomplished in terms of naturalistic representation. The scene with the Fourth Tempter reaches above external evidence to the substance of the matter. If Eliot had chosen to touch that level again in the play (a dangerous but intriguing possibility) he might have achieved, with Becket's death, the conceivability of martyrdom. As it was he had written an important and influential play.[75]

The detachment of the latter half of *Murder in the Cathedral* (and the style – much of it prose) is perhaps indicative of Eliot's unwillingness to write a modern *Everyman*. The high affirmation and medieval certainty of *Everyman* were not Eliot's theme or belief, despite his orthodox Christianity. The mystical experience of martyrdom, or even the understanding of a martyr's complex state of mind, was not for Everyman. The chorus of Canterbury women were, for all their knowledge, spectators.[76]

> Forgive us, O Lord, we acknowledge ourselves as a type
> of common man. . . .
> Who fear the blessing of God, the loneliness of the night of
> God, the surrender required, the deprivation inflicted. . . .
> Less than we fear the love of God. . . .
> Lord, have mercy upon us.
> Christ, have mercy upon us.
> Lord, have mercy upon us.
> Blessed Thomas, pray for us.

Murder in the Cathedral rises out of and high above the ordinary level of modern religious drama; it dominates the terrain in much the same way that Ely or Chartres or Wells dominate the cathedral towns in which they happen to be located. In accounting for the success of *Murder in the Cathedral* where so many others have failed, it is useful to note how clear the author is about the nature (and the dangers) of *Everyman* as a precedent. Perhaps only a poet of Eliot's skill and associated sensibility could manage to write a modern religious verse drama about a medieval crisis of faith.

Nevertheless, if it is true that *Murder in the Cathedral* is Eliot's best play, part of the explanation may lie in the social and political concern with which Eliot turned to the theater, and which motivated his early religious plays. We may note that Eliot's involvement with the drama was less a poetic experiment than an act of religious commitment. As Eric Bentley has judiciously noted, 'His best dramatic writing was done in the decade of propagandist theater – the thirties – and was by way of a counterblast at the Marxist.'[77]

5 Didactic theater and Bertolt Brecht

When revolution and talk of revolution is in the air, the devices of art come to seem a potential weapon in the political struggle. The 1930s were such a period, and the interaction of politics and theater is observable in the work of many playwrights of all commitments, whether newly-converted Christian conservatives like T. S. Eliot or convinced Marxists like Bertolt Brecht.

We have seen how useful the example of *Everyman* proved to Eliot in his construction of *Murder in the Cathedral*. For Brecht, Sean O'Casey, and other playwrights of the political left, the idea of the morality play exerted an equally strong, though very different influence. While they rejected its Christianity as naïve and obsolete, they found themselves drawn toward its radical conceptualization of human affairs, the determinism of its characterization, and its view of life as a process.

It is difficult to evaluate the extent of this influence. The conventions of morality drama reach playwrights of the 1930s directly (chiefly in revivals of *Everyman*) and also indirectly (through the medium of Expressionism).[78] Nevertheless if we consider the achievements and limitations of political drama in the period it seems obvious that it is significantly affected, for better and for worse, by the precedent of medieval didactic theater.

The unfortunate influences are epitomized by the popular figurative idea of a morality play as a bogus event in which alleged forces of good confront alleged forces of evil. In this guise, as a journalistic metaphor of opprobrium, the term 'morality play' is commonly employed in the public media. Thus the 1970 conspiracy trial of the 'Chicago Seven' could be described by an observer as 'a modern and satanic morality play which sets the stamp of legality on the execrable.'[79] The phrase suggests that what is worst about the propaganda drama of our century – its artificiality, deterministic simplifications and wooden unreality (whether in the courtroom or the theater) – is attributable to the pernicious imitation of a medieval art form.

Something of the element of truth in this hypothesis is to be seen

241

in the career of Sean O'Casey. In his early plays, *Juno and the Paycock* and *The Plough and the Stars*, O'Casey manages to blend successfully his evocations of Irish life with topical political themes. But his later work is, in the opinion of many critics, marred by overt didacticism.

O'Casey, increasingly under the influence of the Expressionists, subtitled *Within the Gates* (1933) 'A Morality in Four Acts.' The play is in part a political debate – (with type-character Hyde Park ideologists) – and in part a melodrama – the story of a young woman dying after a sinful life. Contending for her soul are a dreamer, who represents poetry, nature, and freedom, and a Bishop (in reality her long-lost father) who represents hypocrisy and conventional religion. Her death achieves a synthetic compromise, as the Bishop is converted to a kind of natural Christianity and hope is born for the tramping masses of the unemployed.[80] The young woman's choice is depicted as representing, and being crucial for, all humanity. Whether O'Casey was more than superficially influenced by the medieval tradition is not clear; we are only assured that he knew of (and disliked) *Everyman*.[81] But expositions of politics, always an important theme in O'Casey's work, became thoroughly dominant in propaganda plays such as *The Star Turns Red* (1940), and some critics have interpreted the didacticism of O'Casey's later plays in terms of medieval precedent: 'They are all in a general sense modern morality plays . . . about symbolic characters who . . . represent and project a larger theme.'[82]

A more significant critical statement might be that what is wrong with O'Casey's political plays is quite the opposite – they are not *sufficiently* like morality plays. Fundamentally *Within the Gates* and *The Star Turns Red* do not break with the theatrical tradition of realism and the social 'problem play.' Indeed the evil fascists of *The Star Turns Red* are far closer to the mustache-twisting villains of melodrama than to the dissembling and plausible tempters of the morality.

If we turn from the example of a playwright whose work is marred by didacticism to one who made an art of it, we find in Bertolt Brecht a playwright who thought long and seriously about the means and ends of didactic theater. In doing so he evolved a new theatrical style of presentation which embodies, for our own time, many of the ideas which originally constituted the morality play.

In the wake of his success with the *Threepenny Opera*, and in the shadow of depression and civil disorder in Weimar Germany, Brecht set about experimenting with a form of theater which would speak directly and influentially to the public. Rejecting realistic norms completely, Brecht put together what he called *Lehrstücke* or learning plays designed to teach performers and audiences alike to accept a collective political responsibility. His appeal was not to individual empathy, but rather to collective awareness; the *Lehrstücke* 'would not even try to arouse emotion by depicting the fate of individuals, but would teach social attitudes by showing the highly formalized actions of abstract social types.'[83]

From these experiments, including the radio play *The Flight of the Lindberghs*, emerged Brecht's idea of an 'epic' theater which would present the truth behind the appearances of everyday life. Instead of being swept up into the action of a play in willingly suspending disbelief, the audience was encouraged to observe objectively, to study, to make decisions, to recognize that 'the human being is the object of the inquiry . . . alterable and able to alter . . . man as a process.'[84] Brecht pursued the ideas of learning and epic theater in his plays of the Weimar era, including *The Mother, St Joan of the Stockyards,* and *Man is Man*. The characteristic style of performance, as he later recalled it, involved:[85]

the use of the film projection to help bring the social complex of the events taking place to the forefront; the use of music and of the chorus to supplement and vivify the action on the stage; the setting forth of actions so as to call for a critical approach, so that they would not be taken for granted by the spectator and would arouse him to think; it became obvious to him which were right actions and which were wrong ones . . . . With the learning-play, then, the stage begin to be didactic (a word of which I, as a man of many years of experience in the theatre am not afraid). The theatre becomes a place for philosophers, and for such philosophers as not only wish to explain the world but wish to change it.

In a series of plays written during his period of exile in Scandinavia and California, Brecht refined this idea of an epic theater. With his revolutionary ardor qualified by an ironic perception of the perversity of human nature in a world as yet 'unchanged,' Brecht wrote *Mother Courage, Galileo, The Good Woman of Setzuan, Arturo Ui,* and *The Caucasian Chalk Circle,* generally considered the most significant body of his work. In the introduction to the first American collection of Brecht's plays, Eric Bentley, his most influential critical advocate, emphasized the religious aspect of Brecht's theatrical didacticism:[86]

Place, like time, is abstract. This feature represents an inheritance from Expressionism. Brecht's work is continuous with that of the Expressionists to the extent that he tried to construct abstract models of his subject . . . . But Brecht sank his roots much deeper in human history than the

Expressionists did – and in the history of the abstract in drama.
Obsessed with religion – a subject he could not keep away from
for more than a few pages at a time – he often thought in
terms of traditional religious abstractions. He wrote a
Seven Deadly Sins and talked of writing a *Dance of Death* . . . .
His 'invention,' the *Lehrstück*, is a sort of Catholic morality
play revised by a Marxist reader of Luther's Bible.

Was Brecht indeed influenced by the morality play? If so, it was
not so much the letter of the genre (its plot and modes of characterization, for example) as by the spirit of it – the sense in which the
morality play is the archetype of the theater of ideas in our western
tradition of drama. Brecht was not interested in historical reconstruction or restorations, but rather in historical precedent. His
commitment to a political change in the world committed him in
turn to a renewal of the theater as a place of ideas in conflict, in
which the real object is to open the eyes of the audience to its true
situation, by showing it a working model of the facts, and the
human solution to them.

The paradox of human nature is at the heart of Brecht's best plays,
embodied in a series of memorable central figures. Galileo, the
all-too-human man of soaring vision, is compromised and ultimately
betrayed by his own flesh, though the reality he discovers transcends
and outlives this weakness. Mother Courage is a courageous and
venal figure of humanity at war, fighting and defeating its own
better nature. Shen-Te, the good woman of Setzuan, must hide her
innocence and charity behind the mask of an experienced exploiter
in order to do anyone any good. Arturo Ui, an everyday petty
criminal, is transformed by society's own logic into a terrifying
international gangster. Grusha, in the *Chalk Circle*, saves a baby and
undertakes a pilgrimage to justice, through adversity, self-sacrifice,
and revolution. All of these heroes are engaged in the old ceremony
of experience, viewed with wry Brechtian cynicism and hope.
Brecht's microcosmic and parabolic stage is wide enough for all
these twentieth-century everymen and their contemporary, prescriptive self-discoveries.

In citing the precedents for epic theater, Brecht showed his
awareness both of the perennial and the contingent criteria of a
theater of ideas:[87]

Stylistically speaking, there is nothing new about the epic
theatre. Its expository characters and its emphasis on
virtuosity bring it close to the old Asiatic theatre. Didactic
tendencies are to be found in the medieval mystery plays and

the classical Spanish theatre, and also in the theatre of the Jesuits.

These theatrical forms corresponded to particular trends of their own time, and vanished with them . . . . Up to now favourable circumstances for an epic and didactic theatre have only been found in a few places and for a short period of time.

Brecht's example, and those of his predecessors, remain to inform our own search for better meaning in the idea of theater, and the image of society. My aim in this study, as it evolved over a number of years, has been to define as carefully as possible a kind of didactic theater which existed in the Middle Ages, and from which many have usefully and subsequently borrowed for their own purposes. It occurs to me that the morality play is still of use to us, and may be so for as long as the human predicament remains unsolved, and the greater madness of our lives remains in need of a figurative exemplification. What Brecht wrote of the epic theater, in 1939, remains true:[88]

the effort must be continued. The problem holds for all art, and it is a vast one. The solution here aimed at is only *one* of the conceivable solutions to the problem which can be expressed so: How can the theatre be both instructive and entertaining? How can it be divorced from spiritual dope traffic and turned from a home of illusions to a home of experiences? How can the unfree, ignorant man of our century, with his thirst for freedom and his hunger for knowledge; how can the tortured and heroic, abused and ingenious, changeable and world-changing man of this great and ghastly century obtain his own theatre which will help him to master the world and himself?

Notes

Prologue   London, 1901

1 On the circumstances of the production, see Robert Speaight, *William Poel and the Elizabethan Revival*, Cambridge, Mass., 1954, p. 161. Sometimes thought of as a medieval tradition, and distantly based on a medieval text, the Oberammergau Passion Play is a seventeenth-century innovation, much revised and modernized thereafter. The modern script cannot in any sense be described as a medieval play.

2 *The Times*, London, 15 July 1901, p. 8.

3 London *Daily News*, 15 July 1901, p. 7.

4 *Pall Mall Gazette*, 15 July 1901, p. 31.

5 London *Morning Post*, 15 July 1901.

6 *Ibid.*

7 *Pall Mall Gazette*, 15 July 1901.

8 *St James's Gazette*, 15 July 1901, p. 6.

9 The Lord Chamberlain evaded ruling on the censorable portions of the script on the grounds that the play had been printed before the adoption of the Blasphemy Laws. See the proceedings of the Royal Commission on Censorship, 29 July 1909, pp. 15–17.

10 *Athenaeum*, 20 July 1901, p. 103.

11 *The Times*, London, 27 July 1901, p. 4; 8 August 1901, p. 9 and Speaight, *op. cit.*, p. 283. For further productions of *Everyman* and the influence of the morality play on modern theater, see Chapter IX below.

12 In the collections of Hawkins (1773) and Hazlitt's *Dodsley* (1874–6). Excerpts were printed in Pollard's *English Miracle Plays, Moralities and Interludes*, Oxford, 1890. In the same period three scholarly editions – in 1849, 1865, and 1892 – were primarily devoted to the tangled question of *Everyman*'s text and literary relations.

13 These approximate figures are based on the listings of Carl J. Stratman, *Bibliography of Medieval Drama*, Berkeley, 1954, pp. 241–8.

14 Gerald Weales, *Religion in Modern British Drama*, Philadelphia, 1961, pp. 96 ff.

Chapter I
The idea of a morality play

1 The critical re-evaluation of the cycle plays and their origins has been reinforced, and in some cases initiated, by stage revivals at York, Chester, and elsewhere. The influential critical studies include F.M. Salter, *Medieval Drama at Chester*, Toronto, 1955; Glynne Wickham, *Early English Stages*, Vol. I, London, 1959; Eleanor Prosser, *Drama and Religion in the English Mystery Plays*, Stanford, 1961; O. B. Hardison, *Christian Rite and Christian Drama*, Baltimore, 1965; V. A. Kolve, *The Play Called Corpus Christi*, Stanford, 1966.

2 The term 'morality' is French in origin. It is unknown in England at the time of the composition of the plays, and does not enter the language until early in the eighteenth century. The contemporary phrase used (not with any great frequency or consistency) to describe the genre is 'moral' or 'moral play,' as in the prologue to *Everyman* (ll. 2,3):

> . . . this matter . . .
> by fygure a Morall playe.

Scottish court records for 1503 state that 'a moralite was played' at the marriage festivities of James IV and Margaret Tudor; from the strong French influence at the Scottish court, this is most easily explained as a non-recurrent borrowing. The first use I have found of the critical term 'morality' is in an anonymous 1741 English translation of a French history of the theater, Luigi Riccoboni's *Réflections historiques et critiques sur les différents théâtres de l'Europe*, where 'morality' appears in a discussion of French medieval drama as a translation of '*moralité*.' English critics and antiquarians such as Charles Dodsley thereafter adopt the phrase and apply it to early English plays with abstract personages.

3 On the preaching tradition, see G. R. Owst, *Literature and Pulpit in Medieval England*, Cambridge, 1933. The confusion of the morality play with the *Psychomachia* of Prudentius is considered further in Chapter II.

4 *Magnificence*, ed. R. L. Ramsay, EETS, E.S. 91, London, 1904: 'Home to your paleys with Ioy and Ryalte' (l. 2562).

5 *The Castle of Perseverance*, ed. Mark Eccles in *The Macro Plays*, EETS, O.S. 262, Oxford, 1969.

6 Shakespeare, *As You Like It*, II, vii, 139–66. Citations from Shakespeare are to the *Complete Works*, ed. G. B. Harrison, New York, 1952.

7 See, for example, Ernst Cassirer, *An Essay on Man*, New Haven, 1944, pp. 92 ff.; and Claude Lévi-Strauss, *The Savage Mind*, London, 1966, Chapter VIII.

8 Suzanne Langer, *Philosophy in a New Key*, New York, 1948, p. 124.

9 J. G. Frazer's pioneering work on this subject is summarized and evaluated in *The New Golden Bough*, ed. T. H. Gaster, New York, 1959, pp. 283–4.

10 Joseph Campbell, *The Hero with a Thousand Faces*, New York, 1956, pp. 383–4.

11 On ritual and Greek tragedy see Jane Ellen Harrison *Themis*, Cambridge, 1912, particularly ch. ii, 'The Dithyramb, the *Dromenon*

and the Drama,' and Gilbert Murray's 'Excursus on the Ritual Forms Preserved in Greek Tragedy,' following ch. viii; see also A. W. Pickard-Cambridge, *Dithyramb, Tragedy, and Comedy*, Oxford, 1927. For a stimulating challenge to the theory of ritual origins see H. D. F. Kitto, 'Greek tragedy and Dionysus,' *Theatre Survey*, 1960.

12 Illustrated in Bamber Gascoigne, *World Theatre*, Boston, 1968, pp. 18–21.

13 Benjamin Hunningher, *The Origin of the Theater*, New York, 1961, pp. 99–103. Hunningher presents an interesting if somewhat exaggerated account of the ritual element in medieval drama.

14 R. J. E. Tiddy, *The Mummers' Play*, Oxford, 1923.

15 E. K. Chambers, *The English Folk-Play*, Oxford, 1933, pp. 6–9; 211 ff., 233; see also Margaret Dean-Smith, 'The life-cycle play or folk play: some conclusions following the examination of the Ordish Papers and other sources,' *Folklore*, LXIX, 1958, p. 244, and Alex Helm, 'The mummers' play,' *Theatre Notebook*, XVIII, 1963–4, pp. 54–8.

16 W. K. Smart, 'Mankind and the mummers' play,' *MLN*, XXXII, 1917, 21.

17 The beheading cure is a particularly strong element in folk plays of the sword-dance type. A further instance of the beheading motif in the moralities may be inferred in *The Cradle of Security*; in this lost play the seduced hero was fitted out with a swine's head, secured to the vices by wire chains. See R. Willis, *Mount Tabor*, London, 1639, pp. 110–14.

18 *Mankind*, line 458, in *The Macro Plays*, ed. Mark Eccles, EETS, O.S. 262, Oxford, 1969, p. 168.

19 The Norfolk fragments (fourteenth century) suggest a lost morality concluding with the request that the audience patronize a church ale, apparently sponsored in connection with the play. See Iris G. Calderhead, 'Morality fragments from Norfolk,' *MP*, XIV, 1961, pp. 1–9.

20 *Mankind*, line 461.

21 C. R. Baskervill, 'Dramatic aspects of medieval folk festivals in England,' *SP*, XVII, 1920, pp. 33–44; 56–60.

22 John Redford, *Wit and Science*, Malone Society Reprints, Oxford, 1951, ll. 145–242; 983–1001.

23 Arthur Brown, 'Folklore elements in the medieval drama,' *Folklore*, LXII, 1952, 65–78.

24 Epistola LXIV '*Ad Augustinium Anglorum Episcopum*,' *Patrologia Latina*, ed. J. P. Migne, LXXVII, p. 1191.

25 *The King of Life ('Pride of Life')*, ed. Norman Davis, *Non-Cycle Plays and Fragments*, EETS, S.T. 1, Oxford, 1970.

26 For various analogues in Frazer consult the sections, 'Death and resurrection' and 'Dying and reviving gods.' See note 9 above.

27 'If anything is in need of proof to Primitive Man it is not the fact of immortality but the fact of death,' Ernst Cassirer, *An Essay on Man*, p. 84.

28 T. H. Gaster, notes on 'Dying and reviving gods,' in *The New Golden Bough*, p. 392.

29 R. C. Mortimer, *The Origins of Private Penance*, Oxford, 1939, pp. 111 ff.

30 O. D. Watkins, *A History of Penance*, London, 1920, I, pp. 466–96.

31 John T. McNeill and Helena M. Gamer, *Medieval Handbooks of Penance*, New York, 1938, pp. 28 ff., including translations of many of the important early penitential books.

32 *Patrologia Latina,* CXCII, pp. 868 ff.

33 I.e., the pseudo-Augustinian *Liber de Vera et Falsa Poenitentia.* On this subject, see the useful, if polemical, account of H. C. Lea, *A History of Auricular Confession and Indulgences,* Philadelphia, 1896, I, pp. 205 ff.

34 Based on the words of Christ to Peter, 'And I will give to these the keys of the kingdom of heaven, and whatsoever thou shalt bind on earth, it shall be bound in heaven: and whatsoever thou shalt loose on earth it shall be loosed also in heaven,' Matthew xvi:19.

35 Canon xxi, '*omnis utriusque sexus fidelis, postquam ad annos discretionis pervenerit, omnia sua solus peccata saltem semel in anno fideliter confiteatur proprio sacerdoti. . . .*' The text is reprinted in full in O. D. Watkins, *A History of Penance,* II, pp. 733–4.

36 '*De Informatione Simplicium,*' in David Wilkins, *Concilia Magnae Britanniae et Hiberniae,* London, 1737, II, pp. 54–7.

37 *Instructions for Parish Priests,* ed. Edward Peacock, EETS, O.S. 31, London, 1868.

38 *Lay Folks Catechism* (Archbishop Thoresby's Instructions for the People), ed. T. F. Simmons, EETS, O.S. 118, London, 1901, pp. 65–6.

39 W. A. Pantin, *The English Church in the Fourteenth Century,* Cambridge, 1955, p. 192.

40 See Thomas of Ecclestone's *Tractatus de Adventu Fratrem Minorem in Angliam,* ed. A. G. Little, Manchester, 1951.

41 David Knowles, *The Religious Orders in England,* Cambridge, 1955, I, pp. 185–8.

42 A. G. Little, *Studies in English Franciscan History,* Manchester, 1917, p. 120.

43 *Canterbury Tales: The Clerk's Prologue,* ll. 12–13; citations from Chaucer are to *The Works of Geoffrey Chaucer,* ed. F. N. Robinson, 2nd ed., Boston, 1957.

44 See G. R. Owst, *Literature and Pulpit,* particularly chs iv–vi. For further insight into the Franciscans' predilection for realism, see Erich Auerbach, *Mimesis,* Princeton, 1953, pp. 169–70.

45 Owst, *Literature and Pulpit,* pp. 77–85; Morton W. Bloomfield, *The Seven Deadly Sins,* East Lansing, Mich., 1952, pp. 92–3.

46 Owst, *Literature and Pulpit,* pp. 527–33. See also Owst's earlier *Preaching in Medieval England,* Cambridge, 1926, pp. 341–4.

47 Wilhelm Seelmann, *Die Totentänze des Mittelalters,* Leipzig, 1892, p. 17.

48 Emile Mâle, *L'Art religieux de la fin du moyen âge en France,* 5th ed., Paris, 1949, pp. 361–2.

49 See James M. Clark, *The Dance of Death,* Glasgow, 1950, pp. 90–105.

50 The seven cardinal virtues are Fortitude, Prudence, Temperance, and Justice (adapted from Cicero) and the three Christian virtues of Faith, Hope and Charity. No standard list of *remedia* evolved; Chaucer's list differs from *Perseverance* in two cases, from Langland in only one. *Piers Plowman* (B Text), ed. W. W. Skeat, EETS, O.S. 38, London, 1869, v, 629–32.

51 Hugo of St Victor, '*Liber Secundus in Matthaeum . . .* Ch. II *De Oratione Domenica,* Ch. III *De Septem Peccatis Mortalibus,*' *Patrologia Latina,* ed. Migne, CLXXV, pp. 767–89.

52 For evidence of the substitution of the Paternoster for pagan charms, see

McNeill and Gamer, *Medieval Handbooks of Penance*, pp. 330 ff., and Robert J. Menner, *The Poetical Dialogues of Solomon and Saturn*, New York, 1941, pp. 39 ff. *The Lay Folks Mass Book*, ed. T. F. Simmons, EETS, O.S. 71, London, 1879, pp. 202, 216, gives instructions for the use of the Paternoster in the Mass.

53 Etienne Boyleaux, *Les Métiers et corporations de la ville de Paris*, Paris, 1879, pp. xxvii–xxix, 60–82.

54 *The English Works of Wyclif*, ed. F. D. Matthews, EETS, O.S. 74, London, 1880, pp. 429–30, and note pp. 530–31. *De Officio Pastorali* is dated 1378 by the editor (p. 405).

55 From the English translation in Lucy Toulmin-Smith, *English Guilds*, EETS, O.S. 40, London, 1870, p. 137. See also Karl Young, 'The records of the York play of the Pater Noster,' *Speculum*, VII, 1932, p. 541.

56 The compotus roll in which this evidence occurred is quoted by Lucy Toulmin-Smith, *The York Mystery Plays*, Oxford, 1885, p. xix. By 1932 the document had disappeared (see Karl Young, *loc. cit.*) and has not been recovered. The present author searched without success for this document, and for the lost Paternoster playbook, in the archiepiscopal archives of York in 1964.

57 This identification was first made by Wilhelm Creizenach, *Geschichte des neueren Dramas*, Halle, 1893, I, p. 463.

58 Beverley Minute Book, fol. 105, quoted by A. F. Leach, 'Some English plays and players 1220–1548,' in *An English Miscellany Presented to Dr. Furnivall*, Oxford, 1901, p. 221.

59 R. S. Loomis, 'Lincoln as a dramatic center,' in *Mélanges offerts à Gustave Cohen*, Paris, 1950, pp. 241–7.

60 Robert Davis, *York Records of the Fifteenth Century*, London, 1843, pp. 269–70. On the consistent suppression of the religious drama in Elizabethan times, particularly in the North, see Harold C. Gardiner, *Mysteries' End*, New Haven, 1946, and Wickham, *Early English Stages*, II, pt I, London, 1963, pp. 75–90.

61 *Registra Grindal*, fol. 166 (Visitation of 1571), quoted by John Strype, *The History of the Life and Acts of Edmund Grindal*, Oxford, 1821, p. 247.

62 On this subject see H. F. Westlake, *The Parish Guilds of Medieval England*, London, 1919, pp. 38–44.

63 See *The King of Life*, ll. 93–108; *The Castle of Perseverance*, ll. 2779 ff.; *Mankind*, ll. 547–73; *Youth* (ed. J. S. Farmer, in *Six Anonymous Plays*, London, 1906), p. 115. The Copland edition of *Youth* (1560) significantly alters 'beads' to 'books.' See the comparative edition of Willy Bang, *Materialen zur Kunde des alteren englischen Dramas*, XII, Louvain, 1905.

64 E. K. Chambers, *The Mediaeval Stage*, Oxford, 1903, II, pp. 154–5.

65 *Shakespeare and the Allegory of Evil*, New York, 1958, pp. 100, 108–9.

66 Hardin Craig, *English Religious Drama of the Middle Ages*, Oxford, 1955, pp. 337–41, and the chapter, 'Painted sermons and the Pater Noster plays,' in M. D. Anderson, *Drama and Imagery in English Medieval Churches*, Cambridge, 1963, pp. 60–71.

67 In a review of Gustave Cohen, *Mystères et moralités du manuscrit 617 de Chantilly*, Paris, 1920; *MLN*, XXXVII (1922), pp. 106–10.

68 In the Liège play the virtues are Humility, Charity, Patience, Perseverance (vs. 'Besyness' in *Perseverance*), Largesse, Abstinence, and Chastity.

69 *Moralité des Sept Péchés Mortels et des Sept Vertus*, MS. Chantilly 617, in
Gustave Cohen, *Nativités et moralités Liègoises du moyen âge*, Brussels, 1953.
The source of this play is Robert de l'Omme's thirteenth-century
Miroir de Vie et de Mort. See Gustave Cohen's *Étude d'histoire du théâtre en
France au moyen âge et à la Renaissance*, Paris, 1956, pp. 32–42.
70 *Piers Plowman* (B Text), ed. W. W. Skeat, EETS, O.S. 38, London,
1869, v, 8.
71 *Piers Plowman*, ed. Skeat, v, 510–12.
72 See ch. vii, 'The sacrament of penance,' in Gertrude Hort, *Piers Plowman
and Contemporary Religious Thought*, London, 1938, pp. 130–55.
73 *Piers Plowman*, ed. Skeat, v, 348–401; the above-mentioned documents
of the York guild of the Paternoster point out that 'those who continue
in their sin are unable to call God their father.'
74 *Canterbury Tales: The Parson's Tale*, ll. 1042–6, in *Works*, ed. Robinson,
2nd ed.
75 *Parson's Tale*, l. 1056.
76 *Piers Plowman*, ed. Skeat, v, pp. 286–9.

Chapter II
Medieval plays: the repentance drama
of early England

1 Dates are based on Alfred Harbage and Samuel Schoenbaum, *Annals of
English Drama 975–1700*, London, 1964. Quotations from the plays are
taken from the editions cited in this list.
2 See E. T. Schell, 'Youth and Hyckescorner: which came first?,' *PQ*, XLV,
1968, pp. 468–74.
3 See the remarks of Bishop Percy, quoted in Chapter VIII, below.
4 The *Psychomachia* is reprinted in the Loeb Classical Library Series.
H. J. Thomson, ed., *Prudentius*, Cambridge, Mass., 1949, I, pp. 273–343.
The identification of the morality play with the *Psychomachia* was first
made by Wilhelm Creizenach, *Geschichte des neuren Dramas*, Halle, 1893,
I, p. 463.
5 The virtues and vices of the *Psychomachia* are as follows:

Fides	*Veterum Cultura Deorum*
Pudicitia	*Libido*
Patientia	*Ira*
Mens Humilis	*Superbia*
Sobrietas	*Luxuria*
Ratio	*Avaritia*
Concordia	*Discordia*

See Adolf Katzenallenbogen, *Allegories of the Virtues and Vices in Medieval
Art*, London, 1939, and Morton Bloomfield, *The Seven Deadly Sins*, East
Lansing, Mich., 1952, pp. 64–5.
6 'The English moral play before 1500,' *Annuale Medievale*, IV, 1963,
pp. 9–12.
7 *Mankind*, ll. 876–9.

8 Bloomfield, *Seven Deadly Sins*, pp. 66–7.

9 The Digby *Mary Magdalene* play utilizes the structure and many of the conventions of the morality play. As Ramsay has pointed out, the morality element in the play occupies some 500 lines of the text. See R. L. Ramsay, introduction to Skelton's *Magnificence*, EETS, E.S. 98, London, 1908,p. clx, and the text of the play in *The Digby Plays*, ed. F. R. Furnivall, EETS, E.S. 70, London, 1896. The parable of the prodigal son is dramatized in the French *Courtois d'Arras* (thirteenth century), not to mention the neo-Terentian revivals of the sixteenth century, such as Gnaephus' *Acolastus*.

10 See the chapter, 'Gothic espousal and contempt,' in Willard Farnham, *The Medieval Heritage of Elizabethan Tragedy*, Berkeley, 1936, pp. 30–68.

11 On the Paternoster play see Chapter I, above.

12 The recently discovered Durham Prologue (fifteenth century) distinctly resembles *The King of Life* in this respect. The extant 36 lines are apparently from the prologue of a lost play, in which a rich and powerful knight falls into poverty, is tempted by offers of wealth from the Devil, but saved by the intercession of the Virgin Mary. See June Cooling, 'An unpublished Middle English prologue,' *RES*, n.s. x, 1959, pp. 172–3, reprinted in Norman Davis, *Non-Cycle Plays and Fragments*, EETS, S.T. 1, Oxford, 1970, pp. 118–19.

13 See Owst, *Literature and Pulpit*, pp. 533–6. The traditional seven ages are *Infantia, Pueritia, Adolescentia, Juventus, Virilitas, Senectus*, and *Decrepitas*.

14 'EVERYMAN Good Dedes, haue we clere our reckynynge? GOOD DEDES Ye, in dede, I haue it here.' (ll. 652–3).

15 An excellent study of *Everyman* is Lawrence V. Ryan, 'Doctrine and dramatic structure in Everyman,' *Speculum*, XXXII, 1957, pp. 722–35.

16 Sister Mary Philippa Coogan, *An Interpretation of the Moral Play 'Mankind,'* Washington, DC, 1947, p. 97.

17 The disguising in *Wisdom* encompasses ll. 685–776. The legal satire continues until l. 873, at the entrance of Wisdom. On the basis of these references, John J. Molloy has suggested that *Wisdom* is an Inns of Court play. *A Theological Interpretation of the Moral Play, Wisdom, Who Is Christ*, Washington, DC, 1952, pp. 191–2.

18 For this theory see Jacob Bennett, 'A linguistic study of *The Castle of Perseverance*,' unpublished PhD dissertation, Boston University, 1960, *DA*, XXI, 1961, p. 872.

19 On the Welsh *Soul and Body*, see Chapter VII, below.

20 For an analysis of the theology and structure of *Wisdom* see Molloy, *Theological Interpretation*. Molloy refutes earlier speculation that *Wisdom* was written for a monastic audience, and stresses the play's application to mankind in general (pp. 198 ff.).

21 The change of costume to denote repentance is a well-established morality convention (cf. *Wisdom*, ll. 1068 ff., etc.), which is probably borrowed from medieval customs of public penitence and endures on the stage well into Elizabethan times (thus Hal's appearance in armor in *Henry IV, Part I*). On this subject, see T. W. Craik, *The Tudor Interlude*, Leicester, 1962, pp. 73–92.

22 At l. 851 above occurs a previous parallel ('O Iesu, helpe! All hath forsaken me') with Christ's words on the cross. See Thomas F. Van

Loon, '*Everyman: a structural analysis,*' *PMLA,* LXXVIII, 1963, pp. 465–75.

23 *Mankind* is dated 1464–8 on the basis of coins mentioned in the text, by Donald C. Baker, 'The date of *Mankind,*' *PQ,* XLII, 1963, pp. 90–1. On the geography of the play see W. K. Smart, 'Some notes on *Mankind,*' *MP,* XIV, 1916, pp. 306–7.

24 A. W. Pollard, introduction to *The Macro Plays* ed. F. R. Furnivall, EETS, E.S. 91, Oxford, 1904, pp. xi–xii; Smart, *op. cit.,* p. 312.

25 *Mankind,* ll. 43, 227.

26 Coogan, *Interpretation,* p. 94.

27 On this subject see Gertrude Hort, *Piers Plowman and Contemporary Religious Thought,* London, 1938, pp. 138–41.

28 For a brilliant reconstruction of one such celebration, see Richard Southern, *The Medieval Theatre in the Round,* London, 1957.

Chapter III
Renaissance plays: Skelton, Medwall, and the morality of state

1 For the activities of this circle and a summary of Medwall's life, see A. W. Reed, *Early Tudor Drama,* London, 1926, pp. 101–4; also Pearl Hogrefe, *The Sir Thomas More Circle,* Urbana, Ill., 1959, pp. 259–60.

2 For a fuller account of Collier's fabrication, see Chapter VIII, below.

3 *Nature,* Tudor Facsimile Texts, London, 1908, sig. E2^v. In the absence of a dependable modern edition, all citations are to this facsimile.

4 Sensuality proposes a familiar compromise: he offers to take control of Man during his youth on the understanding that in old age Reason may have dominance. Reason naturally (and rationally) refuses to sanction this arrangement, yet must endure it according to the usual life-cycle structure in practice. W. Roy Mackenzie points out certain evident similarities between the early portion of *Nature* and Lydgate's mythological allegory, *Reason and Sensuality* ('A source of Medwall's *Nature,*' *PMLA,* XXIX, 1914, pp. 188–99).

5 *Shakespeare and the Nature of Man,* Cambridge, Mass., 1943, p. 57.

6 The domestication of the sins in *Nature* sets a precedent for similar scenes in *Magnificence* and *Respublica* and subsequent plays in the morality tradition.

7 R. L. Ramsay, introduction to Skelton's *Magnificence,* EETS, E.S. 98, London, 1908, p. clxi.

8 Sig. E3^v. Indications of an evening indoor performance include 'thys nyght to appere' (sig. A2^v), 'all thys nyght' (sig. F1^v), 'this fyre' (sig. F2^r).

9 Farnham curiously detects a prototragic 'sinister note' in the implication that a law of retribution operates in the world (*The Medieval Heritage of Elizabethan Tragedy,* pp. 200–1). Such warnings against trusting to the mercy of God are in fact traditional in the moralities.

10 *Four Elements,* Tudor Facsimile Texts, London, 1908. (On the relation of

Four Elements to *Nature,* see Reed, *Early Tudor Drama,* pp. 104–6.)
Rastell's use of contemporary scientific texts has been lavishly explored;
see Johnstone Parr, 'More sources of Rastell's *Interlude of the Four
Elements,*' *PMLA,* LX, 1945, pp. 48–58.

11 *Wit and Science,* Malone Society Collections, Oxford, 1951.

12 Ian Gordon, *John Skelton, Poet Laureate,* Melbourne, 1943, pp. 144 ff.
For dating of the play, see Ramsay, intro. to *Magnificence,* pp. xxi–xxv.
All text citations are to this edition. On 'Nigramancer' (fabricated by
Warton and ascribed to Skelton), see Chapter VIII, below.

13 For a balanced view on this subject, see David Bevington, *Tudor Drama
and Politics,* Cambridge, Mass., 1968, pp. 54–63.

14 R. Willis, *Mount Tabor,* London, 1639, pp. 110–14.

15 'I had not been here with you this nyght' (*Magnificence,* l. 356), and cf.
T. W. Craik, *The Tudor Interlude,* Leicester, 1962, p. 22 n.; Bevington,
From Mankind to Marlowe, pp. 52–3.

16 Ramsay, intro. to *Magnificence,* pp. cvi–cxxviii.

17 William Nelson, *John Skelton, Laureate,* New York, 1959, p. 138.

18 Gordon, *John Skelton, Poet Laureate,* p. 146.

19 A. R. Heiserman, *Skelton and Satire,* Chicago, 1961, pp. 73–83; William O.
Harris, *Skelton's Magnyfycence and the Cardinal Virtue Tradition,* Chapel
Hill, N.C., 1965, pp. 71 ff.

20 See Ramsay, intro. to *Magnificence,* p. lxxi.

21 Quoted in *ibid.,* p. xxxiii.

22 Heiserman, *Skelton and Satire,* pp. 120–3.

23 Ramsay, intro. to *Magnificence,* pp. c–cii.

24 Heiserman, *Skelton and Satire,* pp. 84–7.

25 Maurice Pollet, following Ramsay's division of the play into five stages
(Prosperity, Conspiracy, Delusion, Overthrow, and Restoration), hails
Skelton as a pioneer of regular five-act structure (*John Skelton, contribu-
tion à l'histoire de la pré-renaissance anglaise,* Paris, 1962, pp. 105 ff.).

26 Magnificence's purported ignorance of the proper form of prayer,
coupled here with an emphasis on submission to God's will, suggests an
allusion to the Paternoster (which the unrepentant sinner was thought
to be unable to pronounce).

27 Harris, *Skelton's Magnyfycence,* pp. 145–62, citing an excellent analogy
between Magnificence and the king figure Fortitude in the fragmentary
morality, *The Four Cardinal Virtues.* The text of this play may be found in
Malone Society Collections, IV, 1956, pp. 41–54.

28 See Heiserman, *Skelton and Satire,* p. 125.

29 Marlowe, *Tamburlaine the Great, Part One,* II.vii.27–9.

Chapter IV
Reformation plays: Lindsay, Bale, Udall,
and the political morality

1 Wickham, *Early English Stages,* I, London, 1959, p. 59. On pageantry
see also Robert Withington, *English Pageantry,* Cambridge, Mass., 1920.

2 Ricardus de Maydiston, *De Concordia inter Ricardus II et civitatem London*, ed. Thomas Wright, London, 1838, and cf. Wickham, *Early English Stages*, I, pp. 64–71.

3 Wickham, *Early English Stages*, I, pp. 75–8; *The Quenes Maisties Passage Through the City of London to Westminster*, ed. James M. Osborne, New Haven, 1960.

4 Wickham, *Early English Stages*, I, p. 63.

5 See Irving Ribner, *The English History Play in the Age of Shakespeare*, Princeton, 1957, pp. 33 ff., and 'Morality roots of the Tudor history play,' *Tulane Studies in English*, IV, New Orleans, 1954. For an account of the developing political drama, with attention to non-morality antecedents as well, see David Bevington, *Tudor Drama and Politics*, Cambridge, Mass., 1968.

6 Edward Hall, *Chronicle*, ed. Henry Ellis, London, 1809, p. 641. Alfred Harbage and Samuel Schoenbaum, *Annals of English Drama*, London, 1964, identify this entertainment as *Frendship, Prudence, and Might* by William Cornish and describe it as 'a political moral' (pp. 20–1). For a highly conjectural account of Cornish, see C. W. Williams, *Evolution of the English Drama*, Berlin, 1912.

7 Hall, *Chronicle*, p. 719.

8 *Ibid.*, p. 735.

9 E. K. Chambers, *The Mediaeval Stage*, Oxford, 1903, II, p. 220.

10 See the account of the Suffolk May Game of 1537 in Madeleine H. Dodds, 'Early political plays,' *The Library*, 3rd series, V, 1913, pp. 393–408. Mrs Dodds also connects the play of *Albion Knight* with the Pilgrimage of Grace.

11 Quoted by Gardiner, *Mysteries' End*, p. 49. On this subject see also Wickham, *Early English Stages*, II, part 1, London, 1963, pp. 60 ff.

12 These developments have parallels in Continental Protestant drama. It is Cranmer, in fact, to whom the polemical neo-Latin play *Pammachius* (updating the Antichrist legend) was dedicated by its German author Thomas Kirchmayer. Cromwell supported a number of anti-Catholic playwrights, notably John Bale. See Gardiner, *Mysteries' End*, pp. 50 ff.

13 Letter from Sir William Eure to Thomas Cromwell, Lord Privy Seal of England, dated Berwick Castle, 26 January 1540, quoted by Douglas Hamer, ed., *The Works of Sir David Lindsay*, Edinburgh, 1931, II, p. 2.

14 He was responsible for the pageantry welcoming the new Queen to Edinburgh in 1578. On the life of Lindsay, see *Works*, ed. Hamer, IV, ix–liv.

15 *Ibid.*, II, p. 5.

16 *Ibid.*, II, p. 6.

17 *Ibid.*, II, p. 2.

18 Gardiner, *Mysteries' End*, p. 53 n.

19 The summary of the 1540 performance enclosed with Eure's letter indicates a simple indoor production with scaffold, dais, and raised seat for the player king. The occasion of royal instruction was lacking at the 1552 performance in Cupar; the royal family was not in attendance. However, Queen Regent Marie was present at the 1554 performance in Edinburgh. See *Works*, ed. Hamer, IV, pp. 139 ff.

20 On the triumphant revival of the *Three Estates* at the Edinburgh

Festival in recent years, see Chapter IX, below.

21 *Works*, ed. Hamer, II, p. 10.

22 Bevington (*From Mankind to Marlowe*, pp. 70, 128) estimates that a cast of at least thirty actors would be required, and somewhat unjustly dismisses the 'panoramic and non-doubling structure' of *Three Estates* as 'antiquated display.'

23 Anna J. Mill, 'Representations of Lyndsay's *Satyre of the Thrie Estatis*,' *PMLA*, XLVII, 1932, pp. 636–51, and cf. *Works*, ed. Hamer, IV, pp. 153–5.

24 George Saintsbury, *A Short History of English Literature*, New York, 1924, pp. 176–7; Anna J. Mill, 'The influence of the Continental drama on Lyndsay's *Satyre of the Thrie Estatis*,' *MLR*, XXV, 1930, pp. 425–42.

25 *Works*, ed. Hamer, IV, pp. 157–60.

26 *Three Estates* ll. 71–7, ed. James Kinsley, London, 1954. All citations are to this edition.

27 *Ibid.*, ll. 224–7. Hamer (ed. *Works*, IV, pp. 172–3) notes that this is one of the earliest uses of the *tabula rasa* figure, which may have originated in the medieval *speculum principis* tradition.

28 On this scene as a liturgical parody see Edwin Shepard Miller, 'The christening in *The Three Estates*,' *MLN*, LX, 1945, pp. 42–4.

29 So-called in stage directions in both extant texts of the play. The fact that Flattery is also clearly a 'Fool' has caused some discomfort to those attempting precise definitions of such categories.

30 *Respublica*, ll. 17–18, ed. W. W. Greg, EETS, O.S. 226, London, 1952. All citations are to this edition. See Bevington, *Tudor Drama*, pp. 114–20.

31 *Respublica:* 'the partes and names of the plaiers.'

32 See Chambers, *Mediaeval Stage*, II, pp. 451–2, and Gardiner, *Mysteries' End*, p. 53, n. 30. The circumstantial attribution of *Respublica* to Udall, explored by Leicester Bradner, 'A test for Udall's authorship,' *MLN*, XLII, 1927, pp. 378–80, is confirmed by W. W. Greg in the introduction to his EETS edition, London, 1952, pp. viii–xviii. On *Roister Doister* as a Marian court play, see Bevington, *Tudor Drama*, p. 121.

33 These acts of 'reformation' are both economic and political in the sense that the episcopal hierarchy has been infiltrated and subordinated to the secular control ('a verse of latynne he cannot vnderstand,' l. 921) of Oppression.

34 Udall's play is pedantically divided into formal acts and scenes in the neo-classic manner. It is not really, however, an example of 'correct five-act structure' (Bevington, *From Mankind to Marlowe*, p. 28). It can be seen to observe tripartite morality structure, as follows:

Part One		
Innocence (conspiracy)	Act I – 438 lines	
	II – 120 lines	= 558 lines
Part Two		
Sin ('Reformation')	III – 410 lines	
	IV – 200 lines	= 610 lines
Part Three		
Repentance	V – 769 lines	

35 Cf. the concluding scene of *Perseverance* (ll. 3130 ff.) for the other appearance of the four daughters of God in English morality drama.

36 See Craik, *The Tudor Interlude*, pp. 91–2.

37 Cf. the shriving of Avarice in *Piers Plowman*, Passus V. See Chapter I, above.

38 The spelling 'John' is employed by Bevington in *Tudor Drama*. Experience in staging a modern revival of the play (at the Bristol Shakespeare Festival, 1964) led me to adopt the same opinion; the audience seeing and hearing the name 'Johan' (as in Strauss) initially imagined that the play was taking place in Ruritania. Because there is ample manuscript authority for the spelling 'John' (see Barry B. Adams, ed., *King Johan*, San Marino, Calif., 1969, ll. 9, 588, 759, 908, etc.), it is hereby recommended to future critics, editors, and directors of Bale's eminently stageworthy play.

39 For speculations on Bale's Paternoster play see Chapter I, above and W. T. Davies, 'A bibliography of John Bale,' *Proc. Oxford Bibliographical Society*, v, Oxford, 1940, p. 210.

40 Honor McCusker, *John Bale Dramatist and Antiquarian*, Bryn Mawr, Pa, 1942, pp. 6–11.

41 John S. Farmer, ed., *The Dramatic Writings of John Bale*, London, 1907, pp. 1–82. The first edition of this play bears the colophon 'compyled by Johan Bale Anno M,D. XXXVIII, and lately inprented per Nicolaum Bamburgensem.' The play may have been written as early as 1538; but the final stanzas in praise of the reforms of the late King Henry, the young King Edward, and the Lord Protector prove that this edition dates from 1547. It was probably prepared during Bale's first period in exile.

42 Reported in Gardiner, *Mysteries' End*, pp. 52–3 and nn. 27, 29.

43 Bale presented some of his plays in outdoor performances in Ireland. The reference in Gardiner's *Mysteries' End*, p. 52, n. 25, to a performance of *King John* in Kilkenny is erroneous, however. The play presented was Bale's *John the Baptist*.

44 The unique MS of *King John* is a composite revised version. For a summary of the difficult textual problems, see the introduction of Barry B. Adams, ed., *King Johan*, San Marino, Calif., 1969. Citations are to this edition.

45 The practice of representing vice characters as popish priests became widespread in subsequent plays. See Ranier Pineas, 'The English morality play as a weapon of religious controversy,' *Studies in English Literature*, II, 1962, pp. 169–70.

46 On Bale's use of historical sources see Herbert Barke, *Bales 'Kynge Johan' und sein Verhältnis zur zeitgenössischen Geschichtsschreibung*, Würzburg, 1937.

47 Bale, in his attack on confession, seems unaware that he is using a dramatic form originally devised in support of the sacrament of penance.

48 On the parodies of ritual and sacrament see Edwin S. Miller, 'The Roman rite in Bale's *King Johan*,' *PMLA*, LXIV, 1949, pp. 802–22. The antipenitential character of the play is most pronounced; Miller notes eight derogatory representations of confession and the power of the keys. Of these, the concept of confession as a vast intelligence network (l.

273) is particularly noteworthy, as is the ironic reference to Reformation in the present passage.

49 S. F. Johnson, 'The tragic hero in early Elizabethan drama' in *Studies in English Renaissance Drama in Memory of Karl Holzknecht*, ed. Josephine Bennett, London, 1959, pp. 163 ff.

50 Bale may well have been the first English playwright to use the term 'act' to describe the subdivisions of his plays. See Jesse W. Harris, *John Bale: A Study in the Minor Literature of The Renaissance*, Urbana, Ill., 1940, p. 63.

51 References to suppression of the Anabaptists give proof of a final revision of the text sometime between 1560 and Bale's death in 1563, possibly for a royal performance in Ipswich in 1561, as Collier claimed. See J. H. P. Pafford's introduction to *King Johan*, Oxford, 1931, pp. xiv–xix.

52 Verity here is a masculine quality ('Sir, my bretheren and I, woulde gladly knowe your name,' l. 2233) rather than a daughter of God, as in *Respublica*.

Chapter V
Early Elizabethan plays in the morality tradition

1 Figures based on Alfred Harbage and Samuel Schoenbaum, *Annals of English Drama*, London, 1964. Only complete plays are listed; fragments, lost plays, neo-Latin plays and quasi-dramatic events (e.g., royal entertainments) have been excluded. Since many of the tragedies listed here were never intended for staging, the predominance of the morality tradition on the stage was perhaps even greater than the statistics indicate.

2 Edgar T. Schell and J. D. Shuchter, eds, *English Morality Plays and Moral Interludes*, New York, 1969, p. 309; Alan Dessen, *Jonson's Moral Comedy*, Northwestern, 1971.

3 Ed. J. S. Farmer, London, 1905.

4 Ed. J. M. Manly, *Specimens of the Pre-Shakespearean Drama*, New York, 1897, Vol. I, p. 457.

5 *Shakespeare's Dramatic Heritage*, London, 1969, p. 38. Wickham's account of sixteenth-century dramatic revivals at Bristol in 1964 includes descriptions of performances of *Fulgens and Lucrece*, *Everyman*, *Respublica*, Bale's *King John*, *Gammer Gurton's Needle*, and *Ralph Roister Doister*.

6 Ed. John S. Farmer, *The Dramatic Writings of Ulpian Fulwell*, London, 1906, p. 2.

7 Louis B. Wright, 'Social aspects of some belated moralities,' *Anglia*, LIV, 1930, pp. 107–48.

8 Ed. John S. Farmer, *Anonymous Plays: Third Series*, London, 1906, p. 226.

9 Ed. J. Payne Collier, *Illustrations of Early English Popular Literature*, Vol. II, London, 1864.

10 *From Mankind to Marlowe*, Cambridge, Mass., 1962, particularly Chapters II–V.

11 *All for Money*, ll. 612–16, eds Schell and Shuchter, *English Morality Plays and Moral Interludes*.

12 *Wealth and Health* (1554) is written to some extent within the political morality tradition. Its sentiments are pro-Catholic, and the figure of authority known as Good Remedy may possibly represent Cardinal Pole. See T. W. Craik, 'The political interpretation of two Tudor interludes,' *RES*, N.S. IV, 1953, pp. 98–108.

13 Proclamation of 16 May 1559, in E. K. Chambers, *The Elizabethan Stage*, Oxford, 1923, IV, p. 263.

14 See Wickham, *Early English Stages*, II, part 1, London, 1963, pp. 55–90; Gardiner, *Mysteries' End*, pp. 65–93.

15 *The Life and Death of Jack Straw*, ed. J. S. Farmer, London, 1911; *Woodstock, a Moral History*, ed. A. P. Rossiter, London, 1946. On these plays see Rossiter's excellent introduction and Irvin Ribner, *The English History Play in the Age of Shakespeare*, pp. 74–9, 136–45.

16 *Gorboduc*, II, i, 140–43, 152–5, ed. J. M. Manly, *Specimens of the Pre-Shakespearean Drama*, New York, 1897, Vol. II.

17 F. P. Wilson, *The English Drama 1485–1585*, Oxford, 1969, pp. 133–5.

18 *Gorboduc*, V, ii, 276–9, ed. J. M. Manly.

19 *Henry IV, Part One*, II, iv, 368–9.

20 *Cambises*, pp. 1058–9, ed. J. M. Manly, *Specimens*, Vol. II.

21 See Willard Farnham, *The Medieval Heritage of Elizabethan Tragedy*, Berkeley, 1936; this pioneering work is still the best survey of its kind. On the morality play in the development of homiletic tragedy, see H. H. Adams, *English Domestic or Homiletic Tragedy*, New York, 1943.

22 It is sometimes inaccurately claimed that *Enough is as Good as a Feast* has twin central figures, one damned and one saved, in the manner of the French dualistic moralities. The focus is in fact quite clearly on Worldly Man; Heavenly Man functions in the traditional role of agent of repentance.

23 W. Wager, *Enough is as Good as a Feast*, ll. 934–8, ed. R. Mark Benbow, Lincoln, Nebraska, 1967.

24 W. Wager, *The Longer Thou Livest* and *Enough is as Good as a Feast*, ed. R. Mark Benbow, Lincoln, Nebraska, 1967; *Trial of Treasure*, ed. John S. Farmer, *Anonymous Plays, Third Series*, London, 1906; see also David Bevington, *From Mankind to Marlowe*, pp. 152–5 and 163–5.

25 *Shakespeare and the Allegory of Evil*, Chapter VIII.

26 *Horestes*, ed. Alois Brandl, *Quellen des Weltlichen Dramas in England vor Shakespeare*, Strasburg, 1898.

27 Lewis Wager, *Mary Magdalene*, ed. F. I. Carpenter, Chicago, 1904.

28 *Patient and Meek Grissell*, eds W. W. Greg and R. B. McKerrow, Malone Society Reprints, London, 1909; *Godly Queen Hester*, ed. John S. Farmer, London, 1906; *Virtuous and Godly Susanna*, eds B. Ifor Evans and W. W. Greg, Malone Society Reprints, London, 1937.

29 *Shakespeare and the Allegory of Evil*, pp. 262–78.

30 *Appius and Virginia*, ed. John S. Farmer, *Five Anonymous Plays*, London, 1908, p. 40.

31 An early example of the incompatibility may be seen in the curious case of *Calisto and Melibea*, 1527(?). This anonymous play, printed by John Rastell, is mainly a close adaptation from the Spanish romantic novel

La Celestina, featuring a chaste heroine, a pining Petrarchan hero, and conniving servants and bawds. The playwright, in attempting to supply an ending of repentance and salvation to this comedy to replace the original love tragedy, succeeds only in destroying the entire dramatic procedure.

32 *The Conflict of Conscience,* ll. 1756–9, eds. Schell and Shuchter, *English Morality Plays and Moral Interludes.*

33 *Conflict of Conscience,* ll. 2077–8 (first issue of the play), eds Schell and Shuchter, pp. 547–8.

34 *Conflict of Conscience,* 'Act six, scene last' from the second issue of the play, in Schell and Shuchter, p. 549.

35 *From Mankind to Marlowe,* p. 247.

Chapter VI
Marlowe, Shakespeare, Jonson:
the apotheosis of the morality play

1 David Bevington, *From Mankind to Marlowe,* Cambridge, Mass., 1962, p. 251.

2 *Dr Faustus,* II, ii, 106–7, ed. Irving Ribner, *The Complete Plays of Christopher Marlowe,* New York, 1963. Citations are to this edition.

3 On the dagger as a traditional stage emblem of despair see T. W. Craik, *The Tudor Interlude,* pp. 52, 65.

4 There is interesting precedent for such a counter-repentance in the fifteenth-century play *Mankind,* where the hero awakens from a diabolically-induced dream and assures the three vices that he has repented of repenting.

> I drempt Mercy was hange, þis was my vysyon,
> Ande þat to yow thre I xulde haue recors and remocyon.
> Now I prey you hertyly of yowr goode wyll,
> I crye yow mercy of all þat I dyde amysse.
> (*Mankind,* ll. 655–8; ed. Eccles, *The Macro Plays.*)

5 ' "The form of Faustus' fortunes, good or bad," ' *Tulane Drama Review,* VIII, no. 4, 1964, p. 92.

6 *Richard II,* V, v, 38–41. On *Richard II* and the morality tradition see E. M. W. Tillyard, *Shakespeare's History Plays,* New York, 1947, p. 262, and Irving Ribner, *The English History Play,* pp. 156–67.

7 The remark of the Archbishop of Canterbury (*Henry V,* I, i, 67) seems to me indicative of Shakespeare's concern that a mythic and medieval event (the reformation of Prince Hal) be dramatized in a credible manner for a 'modern' (i.e. Elizabethan) audience that would question the divine melodrama of a saints, play life of Henry V. 'Miracles are ceased' means miracle plays, as well as the age of miracles.

8 J. Dover Wilson, *The Fortunes of Falstaff,* Cambridge, 1943. The performance of *Youth* occurred at the Malvern Festival (p. 18); though Dover Wilson cites no date, there are records of a performance of the

play at Malvern in 1934. (See Chapter IX.) Wilson cites as an additional source brief published references to a possible morality interpretation of *Henry IV* in Arthur Quiller-Couch, *Shakespeare's Workmanship*, London, 1918. On Falstaff and the deadly sins tradition see John W. Shirley, 'Falstaff an Elizabethan glutton,' *PQ*, VII, 1938, pp. 271–87.

9 *The Fortunes of Falstaff*, pp. 20, 14.

10 *The Brut, or the Chronicles of England* (c. 1479), Lambeth MS. 84, quoted by A. R. Humphreys, introduction to the Arden Edition, *The First Part of Henry IV*, Cambridge, Mass., 1960, p. xxix.

11 *The Famous Victories of Henry V*, ed. J. Q. Adams, *Chief Pre-Shakespearean Dramas*, Cambridge, Mass., 1924.

12 The dumb show's last action (the poisoner's wooing of the queen) would be a completely indecorous and implausible conclusion for an Elizabethan play, but a very traditional act ending for a revenge tragedy in progress. See, for example, the ironically happy ending of the first act of *The Spanish Tragedy*, which displeases the vengeful ghost of Don Andrea:

> Come we for this from depths of underground
> To see him feast that gave me my death's wound?
> These pleasant sights are sorrow to my soul:
> Nothing but league, and love, and banqueting?

13 See Bertram Joseph, *Conscience and The King*, London, 1953, pp. 108–10

14 There are no stage directions in the early texts to indicate where Hamlet draws the sword, prior to stabbing Polonius. In some productions he enters the closet with drawn sword; in others he only draws at the sound of Polonius' voice. Is it possible he draws the sword in speaking the line 'Go, go, you question with a wicked tongue'? This would motivate the otherwise curious response of Gertrude 'Why, how now, Hamlet!' (III, iv, 12).

15 *The Castle of Perseverance*, ll. 1377–82, ed. Eccles, *The Macro Plays*.

16 *Wisdom*, ll. 901–2, ed. Eccles, *The Macro Plays*.

17 The phrase is that of Patrick Crutwell, 'The morality of Hamlet – "sweet prince" or "arrant knave"',' *Stratford on Avon Studies 5*, New York, 1964, p. 122.

18 *Everyman*, ll. 22–4, 45–9, 63, ed. A. C. Cawley.

19 Helpful studies on the connection of *Volpone* and the morality tradition include Ian Donaldson, '*Volpone*: quick and dead,' *Essays in Criticism*, XXI, 1971, pp. 121–34; Alan C. Dessen, '*Volpone* and the late morality tradition,' *MLQ*, XXV, 1964; John S. Weld, 'Christian comedy: *Volpone*,' *SP*, LI, 1954, 172–93. Mr Donaldson's conclusions, which largely are negative, have been of particular assistance to me in formulating the present essay. Mr Dessen's *Jonson's Moral Comedy*, Northwestern, 1971, includes a revised essay on *Volpone* and the later moralities in its comprehensive study of Jonson's debt to the morality tradition.

20 *Volpone*, I, iv, pp. 142–51. Citations are to the Yale edition, ed. Alvin B. Kernan, New Haven, 1962.

21 Dessen, '*Volpone* and the late morality tradition,' p. 388.

22 Dessen is right in stating that this scene is 'closer to the morality tradition in spirit and technique than any other part of the play' (*Jonson's Moral*

Comedy, p. 88) but wrong, I believe, in imagining that a Jacobean audience would not have found it amusing. The incongruity between Volpone's realistic threat and Bonario's theatrical intervention seems deliberate (and inspired) on Jonson's part.

23 Epistle dedicatory to *Volpone,* l. 115.

24 See David C. McPherson, '*Volpone* improv'd,' a forthcoming article.

25 See the discussion of Dr Faustus' counter-repentance in this chapter, and the reference to a similar incident in *Mankind.*

26 *Respublica,* ll. 1957–64, ed. W. W. Greg.

27 *Everyman,* ll. 897–901, ed. A. C. Cawley.

28 '*King Lear* . . . does appear to disclose a mode of imagination not so very far removed from the mode with which, we must remember, Shakespeare was perfectly familiar in morality plays. . . .' A. C. Bradley, *Shakespearean Tragedy,* London, 1904, p. 265.

29 *Gesta Romanorum,* ed. S. J. H. Heritage, EETS, E.S. 33, London, 1879, p. 53. The *Gesta* are fifteenth-century translations of an Anglo-Latin anthology of legends about kings and emperors, with Christian moral interpretation. Of seventy-seven such stories, the king figure is moralized eleven times as 'Every man,' 'Eche Christian Man' or some comparable variant of the Mankind figure.

30 *Mundus et Infans,* ll. 267–70, ed. J. M. Manly, *Specimens of the Pre-Shakespearean Drama,* Vol. I.

31 In the account of Geoffrey of Monmouth (ed. Sebastian Evans, London, 1904) the love trial occupies approximately 40 percent of the story; more than half of Holinshed's version concerns the trial, and in the source play *King Leir,* all of Acts I and II. The same scene occupies about 9 percent of Shakespeare's 3330-line play. On the opening scene see William Frost, 'Shakespeare's rituals and the opening of *King Lear,*' *Hudson Review,* x, Winter, 1957–8, pp. 577–85.

32 *Shakespeare and the Allegory of Evil,* pp. 413–14.

33 See T. W. Craik, *The Tudor Interlude,* p. 95.

34 See J. F. Danby, *Shakespeare's Doctrine of Nature,* London, 1949, and William R. Elton, *King Lear and the Gods,* San Marino, California, 1966, pp. 9–33.

35 *Wisdom,* ll. 965–9, ed. Eccles, *The Macro Plays.*

36 On the conventional rope and dagger as symbols of despair, see Craik, *The Tudor Interlude,* pp. 52, 65.

37 A. C. Bradley, *Shakespearean Tragedy,* p. 285.

38 G. Wilson Knight, *The Wheel of Fire,* London, 1930, pp. 178, 195.

39 O. J. Campbell, 'The salvation of Lear,' *ELH,* xv, 1948, p. 94.

40 Willard Farnham, *The Medieval Heritage of Elizabethan Tragedy,* pp. 451–2. For some challenges to this tradition of Christian optimism see Robert Ornstein, *The Moral Vision of Jacobean Tragedy,* Madison, Wisc., 1960; Jan Kott, *Shakespeare Our Contemporary,* Garden City, New York, 1964; William Elton, *op. cit.*; Maynard Mack, *King Lear in Our Time,* Berkeley, 1965; and John Lawlor, *The Tragic Sense in Shakespeare,* London, 1969.

41 An irony pointed out by G. B. Harrison, *Shakespeare: Complete Works,* New York, 1962, p. 1139.

42 *Everyman,* ll. 45–7, 63, ed. A. C. Cawley. The resemblance is noted by

F. K. Salter, 'Lear and the morality tradition,' *N & Q*, N.S. I, 1954, pp. 109–10.

43 See for example *Everyman*, l. 638, ed. A. C. Cawley; *Hickscorner*, l. 874, ed. J. M. Manly; *Youth*, l. 757, ed. J. S. Farmer.

Chapter VII
European plays: the morality tradition
from the Middle Ages to Calderón

1 Anna Jean Mill, *Medieval Plays in Scotland*, Edinburgh, 1927, p. 320, n. 1.

2 For a discussion of Lindsay's play, see Chapter IV, above.

3 *Non-Cycle Plays and Fragments*, ed. Norman Davis, EETS, S.T. 1, Oxford, 1970, p. xcix.

4 *The Soul and the Body*, ll. 145–9, in Gwenan Jones, *A Study of Three Welsh Religious Plays*, [Aberystwyth?], 1939, p. 251. Jones refers in passing to an additional Welsh morality, the manuscript play 'Debate between the Gentleman and the Priest.'

5 See Theodoor Weevers, *Poetry of the Netherlands in its European Context*, London, 1960, pp. 55–7.

6 Henry de Vocht, '*Everyman*: a comparative study of texts and sources,' *Materialien zur Kunde des Altern Englischen Dramas*, Vol. xx, Louvain, 1947; E. R. Tigg, 'Is *Elckerlijc* prior to *Everyman*?,' *JEGP*, xxxviii, 1939, pp. 568–96.

7 *Everyman*, ed. A. C. Cawley, Manchester, 1961, pp. x–xiii, xxxiv. On Eliot and *Everyman*, see Chapter IX, below.

8 Weevers, *Poetry of the Netherlands*, pp. 102–4.

9 Charles de Tolnay, *The Drawings of Peter Breughel the Elder*, London, 1952, p. 75.

10 Weevers, *Poetry of the Netherlands*, pp. 102–7. For further investigation of the Dutch morality tradition, see J. A. Worp, *Geschiedenis Van Het Drama En Van Het Tooneel in Nederland*, Groningen, 1904, Vol. 1, pp. 110–27.

11 *The Play of Antichrist*, ed. and trans. John Wright, Toronto, 1967. See also the facinating *Ordo Virtutum* (c.1146), ed. Bruce W. Hozeski, *Annuale Medievale* xiii, 1972, pp. 45–69.

12 M. O'C. Walshe, *Medieval German Literature*, Cambridge, Mass., 1962, p. 300. The story perhaps may shed some light on Hamlet's motives in presenting the Murder of Gonzago before a murderer. See Chapter VI, above.

13 Heinz Kindermann, *Theatergeschichte Europas*, Salzburg, 1959, 1, pp. 442–3.

14 The prodigal son theme becomes entwined with the morality tradition in England in its later stages. See F. P. Wilson, *The English Drama 1485–1585*, Oxford, 1969, pp. 96–101, and the forthcoming study of Richard Helgerson exploring the links of the morality tradition to Elizabethan narrative fiction.

15 '*Come le sette peccata mortali si conducono a contrizione*,' in Vincenzo de

Bartholomaeis, *Laude Dramatiche e Rappresentazioni Sacre*, Florence, 1943, Vol. I, pp. 366–7. For other examples of the conversion of the sins in medieval drama and literature see Chapter I, above.

16 Alfredo Cioni, *Bibliografia delle Sacre Rappresentazioni*, Florence, 1961, p. 60; Mario Apollonio, *Storia del Teatro Italiano*, Florence, 1953, Vol. I, pp. 158–60, 313–14.

17 Described, but not reprinted, in Vincenzo de Bartholomaeis, *Laude Dramatiche*, Vol. III, pp. 189–90. On the Italian folk tradition of the '*Testamento*,' or satirical public revelation of sins during Carnival, see Paolo Toschi, *Le Origini del Teatro Italiano*, Turin, 1955. Creizenach mentions in the context of the moralities an Italian dramatic version of the dispute between Lent and Carnival, a motif which is also extant in early Swedish and Spanish versions. See *Geschichte des neuren Dramas*, Vol. I, pp. 459–60.

18 In Luigi Banfi, ed., *Sacre Rappresentazioni del Quattrocento*, Turin, 1968, pp. 111–51. Belcari's and Avaldo's play is an interesting example of the coherence of Judgment and morality motifs; it confirms some of the observations made by David J. Leigh, 'The Doomsday mystery play: an eschatological morality,' *MP*, LXVIII, 1970, pp. 211–23. There is no reason to accept Leigh's speculation that the morality derived from the Judgment play (there being no chronological basis for such a derivation), but the parallels are nevertheless extremely enlightening.

19 Francesco de Sanctis, *History of Italian Literature*, trans. Joan Redfern, New York, 1931, p. 111.

20 *Ibid.*, p. 110. *The Commedia Spirituale dell'Anima* is extant in twelve editions, 1575–1620.

21 See *John Milton: Complete Poems and Major Prose*, ed. Merritt Y. Hughes, New York, 1957, pp. 174–5, 250.

22 '*Etiam sub forma moralitatum.*' See Grace Frank, *The French Medieval Drama*, Oxford, 1954, p. 247.

23 For example, in Gustave Cohen, *Le Théâtre en France au moyen âge*, Paris, 1938, 2 vols, the religious and secular moralities are treated as a group in the second volume, *Le Théâtre profane*, rather than the first, *Le Théâtre religieux*.

24 L. Petit de Julleville, *Répertoire du théâtre comique en France au moyen-âge*, Paris, 1886, pp. 31–103; *La Comédie et les moeurs en France au moyen-âge*, Paris, 1886, pp. 44–51.

25 John S. Weld, 'Repertory of medieval French allegorical plays,' *Research Opportunities in Renaissance Drama*, XII, 1969, pp. 107–32.

26 Gustave Cohen, *Nativités et moralités Liègeoises du moyen âge*, Brussels, 1953; *Étude d'histoire du théâtre en France au moyen âge et à la Renaissance*, Paris, 1956, pp. 32–42.

27 From the archives of the *hôtel-de-ville de Tours*, reprinted in Petit de Julleville, *Répertoire du théâtre comique*, p. 324.

28 Petit de Julleville, *Répertoire du théâtre comique*, pp. 41–3, and *La Comédie en France*, pp. 88–91.

29 *Mundus, Caro, Daemonia* is reprinted in Edouard Fournier, *Le Théâtre français avant la Renaissance*, Paris, 1872, pp. 199–209.

30 In Fournier, *Le Théâtre français*, pp. 216–71.

31 There have been few specific explorations of literary relationships

between the two dramas, though it seems likely that Lindsay's *Satire of the Three Estates* has a French lineage in some degree. See J. M. Smith, *French Background of Middle Scots Literature*, Edinburgh, 1939, pp. 125–30.

32 *Danza General en que entran todos los Estados de Gente* in Fernando Lázaro Carreter, *Teatro Medieval*, Madrid, 1965, pp. 226–48. See also L. F de Moratin, *Orígenes del Teatro Español*, Paris, 1838, p. 57.

33 J. P. Wickersham Crawford, 'The Catalan *Mascarón* and an episode in Jacob Van Maerlant's *Merlija*,' *PMLA*, xxvi, 1911, pp. 31–50. For an attempt to account for the 'late' development of the morality in Spain, marred by some chronological and generic misconceptions, see Alexander A. Parker, 'Notes on the religious drama in medieval Spain and the origins of the *Auto Sacramental*,' *MLR*, xxx, 1935, pp. 170–82.

34 Gil Vicente, *Auto da Moralidade*, ed. I. S. Revah, Lisbon, 1959. This is a unique instance of the use of the generic term 'morality' in the title of a Spanish or Portuguese play, though the qualifier '*moral*' is common – '*auto moral*,' '*farsa moral*,' etc. The term '*auto*' or '*aucto*' means 'act,' or more precisely, 'play.'

35 *Lyrics of Gil Vicente*, trans. Aubrey F. G. Bell, Oxford, 1914, pp. 10–11.

36 *Gil Vicente: Obras Completas,* ed. Marques Braga, Lisbon, 1951, ii, pp. 39–169. Also see Jack Horace Parker, *Gil Vicente*, New York, 1967, pp. 54–7.

37 *Gil Vicente: Obras Completas,* ed. Braga, ii, pp. 1–37.

38 The play is reprinted in *Autos, Comedias y Farsas de la Biblioteca Nacional*, Madrid, 1962, Vol. i, pp. 81–144. López de Yanguas was a cleric and schoolmaster in the province of Soria, according to J. P. W. Crawford.

39 J. P. Wickersham Crawford, *Spanish Drama Before Lope de Vega*, Philadelphia, 1937, p. 60; *Autos, Comedias y Farsas*, Vol. i, pp. 9–31. The text of Aparicio's play includes eight woodcuts – possibly costume designs for the actors in the play – bearing the names of characters.

40 On the *auto sacramental*, see the excellent and witty introduction by R. G. Barnes, in his *Three Spanish Sacramental Plays*, San Francisco, 1969; also Bruce W. Wardropper, *Introducción al Teatro Religioso del Siglo de Oro*, Madrid, 1954, pp. 19–29 *et passim*.

41 Wardropper, *Introducción*, p. 192.

42 Diego Sánchez de Badajoz, *Recopilación en Metro* [facsimile of the 1554 edition], Madrid, 1929, p. lxvi. See also J. López Prudencio, *Diego Sánchez de Badajoz*, Madrid, 1915.

43 Diego Sánchez, *Recopilación*, p. xliiii.

44 *Ibid.*, p. cxxxvii.

45 *Ibid.*, pp. cxlvi–cxlvii. The translation is mine.

46 Crawford, *Spanish Drama*, pp. 148–50.

47 N. D. Shergold, *A History of the Spanish Stage*, Oxford, 1967, pp. 89–97.

48 *Colección de autos, farsas, y coloquios del siglo XVI*, ed. L. Rouanet, Barcelona and Madrid, 1901, 4 vols. The latter play is reprinted in *Autos Sacramentales*, ed. Eduardo Gonzales Pedroso, Madrid, 1930, pp. 62–6, 41–6.

49 *Four Autos Sacramentales of 1590*, ed. Vera Helen Buck, University of Iowa Studies in Spanish Language and Literature, No. 7, Iowa City, Iowa, 1937, pp. 62–98.

50 H. A. Rennert, *The Life of Lope de Vega*, New York, 1904.

51 *Lope de Vega: Obras Escogidas,* ed. Federico Carlos Sainz de Robles, Madrid, 1955, Vol. III, p. 13. Translation by Robert P. Brandts.

52 *El Gran Teatro del Mundo* in Ángel Valbuena Prat, ed., *Calderón de la Barca: Autos Sacramentales,* I, Madrid, 1967.

53 *El Gran Teatro del Mundo,* ll. 1409–26. My translation.

54 Alexander A. Parker, *The Allegorical Drama of Calderón,* Oxford, 1943, pp. 150–2.

55 *El Gran Teatro del Mundo* is the last, and in many ways the greatest, of the morality plays written in the direct line of medieval tradition. The *auto sacramental* lingers on, declining in prestige and quality until 1765, when, under pressure from neo-classic critics, the playing of *autos* was prohibited by ministerial decree. Calderón's *autos* survive to be rediscovered by German Romantic critics, praised by Shelley, and paid perhaps the ultimate compliment of imitation by Pirandello, who may have borrowed the idea of *El Gran Teatro del Mundo* for his *Six Characters in Search of an Author.* There is evidence that the morality tradition, imported to the new world by the Spaniards, has been assimilated into Mexican folk dance and drama. See Frances Toor's description of a 'dance of the three powers,' involving Christ, an angel, the World, the Flesh, the Devil, the Body and the Soul, and other familiar figures. 'Fiesta de la Sta. Vera Cruz en Taxco,' *Mexican Folkways,* VI, 1930, pp. 84–99.

Chapter VIII
Rediscovering the evidence: 1660–1914

1 William Webbe, *A Discourse of English Poetrie,* 1586, in Joseph Haslewood, ed., *Ancient Critical Essays,* London, 1815, II, pp. 39–40.

2 Richard Flecknoe, *Love's Kingdom,* London, 1664, sig. G4ᵛ.

3 Thomas Rymer, *A Short View of Tragedy: its original excellency and corruption,* 1693, ed. Curt A. Zimansky, *The Critical Works of Thomas Rymer,* New Haven, Conn., 1956, p. 112.

4 Rymer, pp. 129–30. Cf. John Stow, *A Survey of London,* ed. W. J. Thomas, London, 1876, pp. 7, 337.

5 Rymer, pp. 144–5.

6 James Wright, *Historia Histrionica: An Historical Account of the English Stage,* London, 1699, pp. 15, 18–20.

7 *Ibid.,* pp. 20–25. Wright's emphasis on pageants, echoed by Warton, was eventually to be adopted by such modern scholars as George Kernodle and Glynne Wickham.

8 *Ibid.,* p. 27.

9 Charles Gildon,'Essay on the art, rise and progress of the stage in Greece, Rome and England,' in the *Works of Mr. William Shakespeare,* ed. Nicholas Rowe, London, 1710, VII. lxvi. Gildon's essay was subsequently incorporated into Pope's *Shakespeare,* 1725.

10 Gildon, 'Essay,' pp. xli–xlii. Cf. Dryden's echo of Bossu: ' 'Tis the moral that directs the whole action of the play to one centre; and that action

or fable is the example built upon the moral, which confirms the truth of it to our experience' – Preface to *Troilus and Cressida*, London, 1679.

11 *The Works of Shakespeare in Seven Volumes*, ed. Lewis Theobald, London, 1733, IV, p. 446 n.

12 Samuel Harsenet, *A Declaration of Egregious Popish Imposture*, London, 1603, p. 32.

13 See Chapter III, above, for the fabricated account of Skelton's 'lost' play *Nigramancer* by Warton. For current views of stage devils, see A. P. Rossiter, *English Drama from Early Times to the Elizabethans*, London, 1950, pp. 91–2, and Bernard Spivack, *Shakespeare and the Allegory of Evil.*

14 Theobald, IV, p. 447 n.

15 *Biographie Universelle*, Paris, n.d., XXXV, pp. 567–8; *Nouvelle Biographie generale*, Paris, 1863, XLII, pp. 150–1.

16 L. Riccoboni, *An Historical and Critical Account of the Theatres in Europe*, London, 1741, p. 123. For 'morality' as a type of drama, the *OED* gives (def. 4b) 'app. adopted in the 18th c. from French literary historians; the F. *moralite* had this sense in the 16th c. but in English we find only *moral* and *moral play*.' Its use in Riccoboni antedates the first citation by more than thirty years. On the other hand, 'moralite' is used to describe an entertainment at the marriage of James IV of Scotland and Margaret Tudor; see John Leland, *De Rebus Britannicis Collectanea*, London, 1770, III, p. 300, and Chapter VII, above.

17 Riccoboni, p. 162.

18 *The Life and Exploits of . . . Don Quixote*, trans. Charles Jarvis, London, 1742, I, sig. b*4ʳ. The 'supplement' is printed on four unpaginated leaves inserted between xxiv and xxv, sigs. b*1–4.

19 *Ibid.*, sig. b*4ᵛ.

20 *Ibid.*

21 The lists are those of Rogers and Ley (1656), Archer (1656), and Kirkman (1661 and 1671). They are reprinted, together with complete bibliographical information in W. W. Greg, *A List of English Plays Written Before 1643 and Printed Before 1700*, London, 1900, and 'Notes on dramatic bibliographers,' *Malone Society Collections*, Vol. I, parts 4 and 5, London, 1911, pp. 324–40. Plays appear on all lists, with the following exceptions: Kirkman only – *Wit and Science*; Archer and Kirkman only – *Nice Wanton, Three Ladies*, and *Youth*. Figures cited are based on Harbage and Schoenbaum, *Annals of English Drama*.

22 Gerard Langbaine, *An Account of the English Dramatic Poets*, Oxford, 1691, p. 535.

23 *A Select Collection of Old English Plays*, ed. Robert Dodsley, London, 1744–5. This, the first of four editions, consisted of ten volumes issued 1744–5 and two additional volumes issued 1745.

24 *Ibid.*, I, p. xiii.

25 *Ibid.*, I, p. xv.

26 *Ibid.*, I, p. 2.

27 *Ibid.*, I, p. 2.

28 John Stevens, *Additions to Dodsworth's and Dugdale's Monasticon Anglicanorum*, London, 1722, I, pp. 139–53.

29 Dodsley, 1744, I, p. 41. Thomas Nabbes' 'moral masque' *Microcosmus*, 1637, also appears in the collection, but the late date and superficial

'regularity' of the play obscure its genuine connection with the morality tradition, not recognized by the critics until the close of the nineteenth century.

30 *Catalogus Bibliothecae Harleianae*, London, 1743–5, 5 vols. *Three Estates* is assigned catalogue number 5993.

31 The scheme of doubling parts, typical of plays designed for small itinerant companies of actors, seems to Dodsley 'contrived so that four people might act it; this was frequently done for the convenience of such as were disposed to divert or improve themselves, by representing these kinds of entertainments in their own houses.' *Old Plays*, I, p. 41.

32 *The Works of Shakespeare in Eight Volumes*, ed. William Warburton, London, 1747, v, p. 265.

33 This essay appears, unpaginated, on four leaves following page 338 of Volume v. Warburton's emendation has been rejected and ridiculed by subsequent editors.

34 William Rufus Chetwood, *The British Theatre*, London, 1752, p. v. See note 31, above. The same essay is incorporated without credit into S. Bladon, *A Theatrical Dictionary*, London, 1782.

35 Thomas Wilkes, *A General View of the Stage*, London, 1759, p. 204.

36 Dodsley, 1744, I, p. 2.

37 Robert Dodsley, *A Select Collection of Old English Plays*, 2nd ed., ed. Isaac Reed, London, 1780, I, pp. xiii–xiv.

38 S. H. Harlowe, 'Letters from Dr. Percy to T. Astle,' *N & Q*, 4th ser., III, 1869, p. 53.

39 *Ibid.*, p. 54.

40 Thomas Percy, *Reliques of Ancient English Poetry*, Dublin, 1766, I, pp. 101–28.

41 It is not certain when Percy began work on this piece, but he completed his 'slight essay' in 1764 and sent drafts to at least three other scholars for comment before he published it, i.e., to Farmer, Evans, and Hailes. See *The Correspondence of Thomas Percy and Richard Farmer*, ed. Cleanth Brooks, Baton Rouge, 1946, p. 170; *The Correspondence of Thomas Percy and David Dalrymple, Lord Hailes*, ed. A. F. Falconer, Baton Rouge, 1954, p. 72.

42 Percy, I, p. 103.

43 *Ibid.*, I, p. 104.

44 *Ibid.*, I, p. 104.

45 *Ibid.*, I, p. 105.

46 See *Everyman*, ed. A. C. Cawley; Glynne Wickham, *Early English Stages*, I, London, 1959, pp. 158–9.

47 Percy, I, pp. 105–6.

48 *Ibid.*, I, p. 113. For the Jarvis essay and Warburton's use of it, see above, pp. 198, 202. Percy criticized this essay in a letter to Evan Evans dated 20 March 1764: 'As he derives all his information from the French critics and his instances from the French stage; you will conclude that he is *often* wide of the mark and generally superficial.' *The Correspondence of Thomas Percy and Evan Evans*, ed. Aneirin Lewis, Baton Rouge, 1957, p. 72.

49 A vast error. Stage directions are commonplace in the texts of medieval plays. *Everyman*, with virtually none, is exceptional.

50 Percy, I, pp. 109–10. The masque, derived from the elaboration of the earlier disguising, has no linear connection with the morality tradition. Its allegorical personages are usually mythological deities.
51 *Ibid.*, II, p. 120.
52 Letter to Thomas Warton, 10 April 1771, in *The Letters of David Garrick*, eds D. M. Little and G. M. Kahrl, Cambridge, Mass., 1963, p. 732.
53 Thomas Hawkins, *The Origin of the English Drama*, London, 1773, I, p. I.
54 *Ibid.*, I, pp. vii–viii.
55 *Ibid.*, I, p. viii.
56 *Ibid.*, I, pp. 27, 69, 113; cited by the *OED* as the earliest use of the term in this sense. See note 16, above.
57 Thomas Warton, *History of English Poetry*, London, 1778, II, p. 365.
58 *Ibid.*, I, p. 242. Cf. Percy, *Reliques*, I, p. 103 quoted above.
59 Warton, II, p. 378; III, p. 170; II, p. 238; II, p. 296. Warton calls *Three Laws* 'a satirical play' rather than a morality. *Nature* he describes, from its title page, as an 'interlude.' For *Three Estates* he cites not merely the 1602 printed edition but the interludes in the Bannatyne MS. He is not aware that these represent two versions of the same work.
60 These remarks are printed among emendations and additions in an appendix to volume II of the 1778 edition, sigs. K4^v–LI^v. For the mistaken theory that this summary was compiled by Warton, but left unpublished until the 1824 revision by Richard Price, see *Magnificence*, ed. R. L. Ramsay, EETS, E.S. 98, London, 1908, p. xviii.
61 The account is in Volume II, pp. 360–3, buttressed with imposing but irrelevant footnotes. For a close consideration of this matter, strongly indicating that 'Nigramancer' is fictitious, see H. E. D. Blackiston, 'Thomas Warton and Machyn's diary,' *EHR*, XI, 1896, pp. 282–300; *Magnificence*, ed. Ramsay, p. xix; Joseph Ritson, *Bibliographia Poetica*, London, 1802, p. 106.
62 Warton, II, p. 366.
63 Edmund Malone, 'Historical account of the rise and progress of the English stage,' in *The Plays of Shakespeare*, London, 1790, II, p. 136.
64 Malone, II, p. 136n. The plays are *Magnificence, Impatient Poverty, Mary Magdalene, Trial of Treasure, Nice Wanton, The Disobedient Child, The Marriage of Wit and Science, Youth, The Longer Thou Livest, Wealth and Health, All for Money, Conflict of Conscience, Three Ladies of London, Three Lords and Ladies of London, Tom Tyler and His Wife*. This list could have been derived from the early play lists; all appear on them, including *Impatient Poverty*, which seems to have been lost until 1906. But how Malone determined that these plays were moralities is not clear.
65 Malone, II, p. 137.
66 Charles Dibden, *A Complete History of the Stage*, London, 1800, II, p. 221.
67 For the lists which Bale the antiquarian compiled of the works of Bale the playwright, see W. T. Davies, 'A Bibliography of John Bale,' *Proc. Oxford Bibliographical Society*, V, Oxford, 1940, pp. 231 ff. Besides *Three Laws*, Dibden names as moralities *Papist Treacheries, Becket,* and *Against Adulterers*, all of which are lost. Bale's only other known morality, *King John*, had not yet been recovered; and Dibden guessed incorrectly that it was not a morality.

68 Tarleton is the supposed author of the Elizabethan episodic play *The Seven Deadly Sins*, of which only the stage 'plot' is extant. This outline, suggesting a stage manager's cue sheet, is reproduced in W. W. Greg, *Dramatic Documents from the Elizabethan Playhouses*, Oxford, 1931.

69 Dibden, II, p. 330.

70 *Ibid.*, II, p. 332.

71 'Mysteries, moralities, and other early dramas,' *Retrospective Review*, I, 1820, pp. 332–5. This anonymous article seems to be the first concerning the moralities to appear in a periodical.

72 Other works of this period which touch on the moralities in conventional terms include Joseph Strutt, *The Sports and Pastimes of the People of England*, London, 1801, III, p. 113; and Thomas Gilliland, *The Dramatic Mirror*, London, 1808, I, p. 20.

73 William Hone, *Ancient Mysteries Described*, London, 1823, p. 228.

74 *Ibid.*, p. x.

75 Alfred W. Pollard, introduction to *The Macro Plays*, EETS, E.S. 91, London, 1904, p. ix.

76 Thomas Sharpe, *A Dissertion on the Pageants, or Dramatic Mysteries Anciently Performed at Coventry*, Coventry, 1825, plate 2, p. 23.

77 J. Payne Collier, *The History of English Dramatic Poetry*, London, 1831, p. xiv.

78 *Ibid.*, II, pp. 279–97. The 1820 sale catalogue lists 'three ancient masques. The Masque of Wisdom, The Masque of Mercy. – The Masque of the Castle of pseverance' – A. W. Pollard, intro. to *The Macro Plays*, p. xxviii n.

79 Collier, I, pp. x–xi.

80 *Ibid.*, II, p. 271.

81 *Ibid.*, II, p. 272.

82 *The Macro Plays*, eds F. J. Furnivall and A. W. Pollard, EETS, E.S. 91, London, 1904.

83 Robert Dodsley, *A Select Collection of Old English Plays*, 3rd ed., London, 1825–7.

84 This group also includes *Hickscorner*.

85 Collier, I, p. 69.

86 *Kynge Johan*, ed. J. Payne Collier, London 1838, pp. x–lx. The play is mentioned in Bale's lists of his own plays. See note 67 above. On the MS see *King Johan*, ed. John H. P. Pafford, Malone Society Reprints, Oxford, 1931, pp. v–xxix.

87 *Respublica*, ed. W. W. Greg, EETS, O.S. 226, London, 1952, p. viii.

88 In the first volume of Collier's *Illustrations of Old English Literature*, London, 1866.

89 *Account Roll of the Priory of the Holy Trinity*, ed. James Mills, Dublin, 1337–46, Dublin, 1891. The central figure is called *Rex Vivus* in speech assignments, and 'The King of Life' in the text itself.

90 W. Carew Hazlitt, *A Select Collection of Old English Plays originally published by Robert Dodsley*, 4th ed., 15 Vols, London, 1874–6. The other new plays are *Everyman*, *Hickscorner*, *Lusty Juventus*, *Wit and Science*, *Youth*, and *Liberality and Prodigality*. On earlier editions see notes 23, 37, and 83 above.

91 Alois Brandl, *Quellen des Weltlichen Dramas in England vor Shakespeare*, Strasburg, 1898.
92 *The Macro Plays*, eds F. J. Furnivall and A. W. Pollard; *Magnificence*, ed. R. L. Ramsay.
93 A. W. Ward, *A History of English Dramatic Literature*, London, 1875, I, pp. 119–21.
94 Wilhelm Creizenach, *Geschichte des neueren Dramas*, Halle, 1893, I, p. 463.
95 'Mercy and truth are met together: Justice and Peace have kissed,' *Psalms* 85:10.
96 Brandl, pp. xiv–xix, following W. Seelmann, *Die Totentanz des Mittelalters*, Leipzig, 1872.
97 Ramsay, intro. to *Magnificence*. See in particular, the subsections 'Plot,' pp. cxlvii–clxxii, and 'Characterization,' pp. cxciv–cxcvi.
98 Brandl, pp. xii–xiii.
99 *The English Works of Wyclif*, ed. F. D. Matthews, EETS, O.S. 74, London, 1880, p. 429, and note pp. 530–31. The ordinances of the York Guild of the Lord's Prayer, relative to these plays, were first published in Toulmin-Smith, *English Guilds*, EETS, O.S. 40, London, 1870, pp. 137–40. See Chapter I, above.
100 John Addington Symonds, *Shakespeare's Predecessors in the English Drama*, London, 1884, pp. 139–40.
101 A. W. Pollard, *English Miracle Plays, Moralities and Interludes*, Oxford, 1890, pp. li–lii. This misleading anthology of excerpts has been through eight editions and is still in print.
102 E. K. Chambers, *The Mediaeval Stage*, Oxford, 1903, II, 149–76 (Chapter XXIII 'Moralities, Puppet Plays, and Pageants').
103 Charles Mills Gayley, *Plays of Our Forefathers*, New York, 1907, pp. 279 ff. But his own set of categories is even worse.
104 Until well into the sixteenth century 'interlude' was the common term for drama of all kinds. In late Elizabethan times it acquired the special sense of an old-fashioned doggerel play. It is this special Elizabethan sense which Chambers and his contemporaries re-introduce into the armory of criticism, where it remains to this day (cf. T. W. Craik, *The Tudor Interlude*, Leicester, 1962) together with the original catch-all meaning *and* the Collier term, not to mention the theory occasionally advanced that the interlude was a scene of comic relief thrust in to leaven out the sober theme of a didactic play. A melancholy study could be made of the functional history of such terms as 'mystery,' 'miracle,' 'morality' and 'interlude.'
105 Felix S. Schelling, *Elizabethan Drama*, Boston, 1908, I, pp. 54–72.
106 C. F. Tucker-Brooke, *Tudor Drama*, Boston, 1911, pp. 47 ff.
107 W. Roy Mackenzie, *The English Moralities from the Point of View of Allegory*, Boston, 1914.
108 E. N. S. Thompson, 'The English moral plays,' *Transactions of the Connecticut Academy of Arts and Sciences*, xiv, no. 5, New Haven, 1910.

Chapter IX
Everyman in the Twentieth Century

1 London *Morning Post,* 15 July 1901. On the original Poel Production, see 'Prologue: London, 1901,' above.
2 *Athenaeum,* 20 July 1901, p. 103.
3 On the early commercial performances see *The Times,* London, 19 March 1902, p. 7. The five early prompt books of the Poel *Everyman* which I have examined are a part of the Enthoven Collection, Victoria and Albert Museum, London.
4 See Robert Speaight, *William Poel and the Elizabethan Revival,* Cambridge, Mass., 1954, pp. 162–6.
5 Alan Dale, *New York American,* 15 October 1902.
6 14 October 1902.
7 I. F. Marcosson and Daniel Frohman, *Charles Frohman,* New York, 1916, p. 226.
8 Wendell Cole, 'Elizabethan stages and open-air performances in America a half century ago,' *Quarterly Journal of Speech,* XLVII, 1961, pp. 41–50.
9 For the week beginning Monday, 30 November 1903; Theater Collection, New York Public Library.
10 From a letter of Edith Wynne Matthison, written 12 November 1903; in the Locke Robinson Collection, vol. 340, p. 105, Theater Collection, New York Public Library.
11 Program for the Garden Theater, New York, for the week beginning 25 March 1907. See Ben Greet's edition of the play *Everyman*: 'Being a Moralle Playe of the XV Centurie, Now done with a Forworde and Mater of helpe. By Ben Greet,' Boston, 1903.
12 *Dictionary of National Biography 1931–1940.*
13 See Archibald Henderson, *George Bernard Shaw,* New York, 1956, pp. 407–8.
14 For an example of Shaw's equation of church and theater, see *Our Theatre in the Nineties,* I, pp. 263–4.
15 In *ibid.,* I, p. 93.
16 Bernard Shaw, *Man and Superman, A Comedy and a Philosophy,* London, 1931, pp. xxvii–xxviii.
17 Eric Bentley, *Bernard Shaw,* Norfolk, Conn., 1957, p. 132.
18 *The Times,* London, 15 July 1901; *Pall Mall Gazette,* 15 July 1901; London *Morning Post,* 15 July 1901, etc.
19 *New York World,* 9 April 1903.
20 Bernard Shaw, preface to *Back to Methuselah,* New York, 1921, pp. xcviii–xcix.
21 G. K. Chesterton, *George Bernard Shaw,* London, 1909, p. 121.
22 Preface to *Back to Methuselah,* p.c.
23 'The theatre,' (1899) in *Ideas of Good and Evil,* London, 1914, p. 180.
24 Direct proof is lacking though critics are virtually unanimous in recognizing the influence of *Everyman* on *The Hour Glass.* The chronology of Yeats' letters indicates that he was in Ireland at the time of the Charterhouse performances in 1901, and the date of the first draft of *The*

Hour Glass is almost coincident with the opening of *Everyman*'s commercial run at the Imperial Theatre in June, 1902. This production also visited Dublin in 1902, as Yeats later recalled ('Samhain: 1904,' in *Explorations*, London, 1962, p. 79).

25 *The Letters of W. B. Yeats*, ed. Allen Wade, London, 1954, p. 375.

26 In a letter to Sydney Cockerell, 18 March 1903, *Letters*, ed. Wade, p. 397. See Una Ellis-Fermor, *The Irish Dramatic Movement*, London, 1954, p. 215.

27 *The Hour Glass* (original prose version), in *North American Review*, CLXXVII, 1903, pp. 445–56. The prose version in *Plays in Prose and Verse*, New York, 1924 reflects Yeats' revisions in the intervening years.

28 W. B. Yeats, *Plays in Prose and Verse*, New York, 1924, p. 430.

29 W. B. Yeats, *Responsibilities*, New York, 1916, p. 188.

30 Robert Speaight, *William Poel and the Elizabethan Revival*, p. 165.

31 Brian Coghlan, *Hofmannsthal's Festival Dramas*, Cambridge, 1964, p. 21 n., quotes sources claiming that the idea for the production was initially Hofmannsthal's, on hearing of *Everyman* from another German, Clemens Frankenstein, who had seen the production in London. The adaptation is also influenced by Hans Sachs' *Hekastus*, as Martin Stevens has recently pointed out (at the Medieval Drama Seminar, MLA, 1970.)

32 This moment is amusingly parodied in the final scene of Max Frisch's *Biedermann and the Firebugs* subtitled 'A learning-play without a lesson,' 1958.

33 Randolph Goodman, *Drama on Stage*, New York, 1961, p. 74. This textbook anthology contains several articles by participants in the Reinhardt *Jedermann* which, while irrelevant to the text of *Everyman* which they are supposed to explain, describe *Jedermann* most graphically.

34 From a letter of 1936 to Harcourt Williams, in C. B. Purdom, *Harley Granville-Barker*, Cambridge, Mass., 1956, p. 246. See also a similar comparison by W. Bridges-Adams, *The Irresistible Theatre*, London, 1957, I, p. 75.

35 Joseph Wayne Barley, *The Morality Motive in Contemporary English Drama*, Mexico, Mo., 1912, pp. 116–17.

36 Lady Gregory, *Our Irish Theatre*, New York, 1913, pp. 264–5.

37 On Monck's career see June Ottawa, 'Nugent Monck of Norwich,' *Christian Drama*, II, 1953, and Gerald Weales, *Religion in Modern British Drama*, Berkeley, 1954.

38 'Dramatic antiquities at Malvern' in the *Malvern Festival Book*, 1933; reprinted in E. J. West, *Shaw on Theatre*, New York, 1958.

39 Neo-medieval revivals in France have been reflected in the work of Gheon, André Obey and Paul Claudel, among other (mainly Catholic) playwrights.

40 Barley, *The Medieval Motive in Contemporary English Drama*, p. 117. A program from the production, preserved in the Theater Collection of the New York Public Library, lists its cast of characters, including a Mr [Sidney?] Greenstreet as Nought. Typed in on the program is the following: 'Hackett Theatre 6 Dec. 1910.' No press accounts have been found and the performance must have been private. The freewheeling obscenity of *Mankind* may have been at issue.

41 *New York Herald,* 28 March 1911.
42 As interviewed by Charles M. Gregy in the *Pittsburg Gazette,* 4 October 1903.
43 The production was favorably reviewed in *The Times,* London, 8 July 1939, on the occasion of its performance on the steps of St George's Chapel, Windsor. See the note by Neville Coghill in *The Castle of Perseverance, A Free Adaptation from the Macro Play,* ed. Iwa Langentels, London, 1948.
44 For details of the Bristol performances, see *New Theatre,* v, 1964, pp. 11–19; Bamber Gascoigne's review in the *Observer,* 10 May 1964; and Glynne Wickham, *Shakespeare's Dramatic Heritage,* London, 1969, pp. 30–9 and Plate II.
45 Spoken Word Recordings, 99705–99722, 18 vols, 38 sides. Reissued by Dover Publications, New York, 1970.
46 Tyrone Guthrie, *A Life in the Theatre,* New York, 1959, p. 306.
47 *Ibid.,* p. 309.
48 *Ibid.,* p. 311.
49 Tyrone Guthrie, 'On three productions,' in *The Year's Work in the Theatre 1948–1949,* London, 1949, pp. 30–3.
50 Arthur Symonds, *Poems: Volume Two,* London, 1924, pp. 3–25, 163–70.
51 See Weales, *Religion in Modern British Drama,* p. 96.
52 Shaw's devastating review of this production appears in *Our Theatre in the Nineties,* II, pp. 13–14.
53 Jerome K. Jerome, *The Passing of the Third Floor Back,* New York, 1925.
54 Weales, *Religion in Modern British Drama,* p. 38.
55 In *The Works of John Galsworthy,* Manaton ed., New York, 1928, XXI.
56 A point of view pursued in detail by Sister St Regina Marie Heffernan, 'The re-emergence of the morality play' (unpublished MA thesis), Fordham University, 1948, p. 74.
57 *Some Contemporary Dramatists,* New York, 1924, p. 184.
58 *Religious Drama 3,* ed. Marvin Halverson, New York, 1959.
59 Noithrop Frye, *Anatomy of Criticism,* Princeton, 1957, p. 290.
60 There are upwards of fifty entries from England and America alone.
61 Posthumously published in Mabel Dearmer, *Three Plays,* London, 1916.
62 Weales, *Religion in Modern English Drama,* pp. 100–3.
63 Barley, *The Morality Motive in Contemporary English Drama,* pp. 116–17.
64 'Men have left God not for other gods, they say, but for no god; and this has never happened before that men both deny and worship gods, professing first Reason, and then Money, and Power, and what they call Life, or Race, or Dialectic.' (*The Rock,* London, 1934, p. 51.)
65 T. S. Eliot, 'Four Elizabethan dramatists,' in *Elizabethan Essays,* London, 1934, pp. 10–11.
66 'We have to make use of suggestions from more remote drama, too remote for there to be any danger of imitation, such as *Everyman* and the late medieval morality and mystery plays, and the Greek dramatists.' (T. S. Eliot, 'The need for poetic drama,' *Listener,* XVI, 1936, pp. 994–5.)
67 T. S. Eliot, *Poetry and Drama,* Cambridge, Mass., 1951, pp. 28–9.
68 *Everyman,* ed. A. C. Cawley, pp. xxvii–xxviii.
69 T. S. Eliot, *Murder in the Cathedral,* New York, 1936, p. 23.
70 David E. Jones, *The Plays of T. S. Eliot,* Toronto, 1960, p. 59.

71 *Murder in the Cathedral*, p. 35. Cf. *Everyman*, ll. 212–40.
72 'I did not want to write a chronicle of twelfth century politics, nor did I want to tamper unscrupulously with the meager records as Tennyson did . . . I wanted to concentrate on death and martyrdom' (*Poetry and Drama*, p. 29).
73 *Murder in the Cathedral*, p. 44.
74 'An actor who has often played the role of Becket put the matter succinctly: "I know I am being murdered on stage, but not once have I really felt dead!" ' – George Steiner, *The Death of Tragedy*, New York, 1961, p. 341.
75 On the wide influence of *Murder in the Cathedral* on modern religious drama, see Weales, *op. cit.*, p. 193 n.
76 *Murder in the Cathedral*, pp. 85–6.
77 Eric Bentley, *The Dramatic Event*, New York, 1954, p. 197.
78 Evidence for the influence of medieval drama on Expressionism is explored by George Stephen Troller, 'Expressionism and the medieval play' (unpublished MA thesis), Columbia University, 1949. Troller establishes a useful set of similarities, and a hypothetical line of influence, in which von Hofmannsthal's *Jedermann* partakes.
79 By the sociologist John Seeley, in a speech introducing William Kunstler (defense lawyer for the accused) at a rally in Isla Vista, California. In a civil disturbance subsequent to Kunstler's speech a bank was set on fire and burned to the ground by demonstrators – an act which itself in turn was described in the press as a 'medieval morality play.' See *El Gaucho*, University of California, Santa Barbara, 26 February 1970 and 29 July 1970.
80 Sean O'Casey, *Collected Plays*, London, 1950, ii, pp. 112–231.
81 See Robert Hogan, *The Experiments of Sean O'Casey*, New York, 1960, p. 12.
82 David Krause, *Sean O'Casey*, New York, 1960, p. 132.
83 Martin Esslin, *Brecht: The Man and his Work*, New York, 1961, p. 44.
84 Bertolt Brecht, 'The modern theatre is the epic theatre,' in *Brecht on Theatre*, ed. John Willett, New York, 1964, p. 37.
85 Brecht, 'The German drama: pre-Hitler,' in *Brecht on Theatre*, ed. Willett, pp. 79–80.
86 Eric Bentley, introduction to *Seven Plays by Bertolt Brecht*, New York, 1961, p. xi.
87 Brecht, 'Theatre for pleasure or theatre for instruction,' in *Brecht on Theatre*, ed. Willett, pp. 75–6.
88 Brecht, 'On experimental theatre,' in *Brecht on Theatre*, ed. Willett, p. 135.

Index